Love and the Idea of Europe

Remapping Cultural History

General Editor: Jo Labanyi, New York University

Published in association with the Institute of Germanic & Romance Studies, School of Advanced Study, University of London

The theoretical paradigms dominant in much of cultural history published in English tend to be derived from northern European or North American models. This series will propose alternative mappings by focusing partly or wholly on those parts of the world that speak, or have spoken, French, Italian, Spanish or Portuguese. Both monographs and collective volumes will be published. Preference will be given to volumes that cross national boundaries, that explore areas of culture that have previously received little attention, or that make a significant contribution to rethinking the ways in which cultural history is theorised and narrated.

Love and the Idea of Europe

Luisa Passerini

Translated by
Juliet Haydock with Allan Cameron

Berghahn Books
New York • Oxford

First published in 2009 by
Berghahn Books
www.berghahnbooks.com

©2009 Luisa Passerini
Originally published as *Storie d'amore
e d'Europa* by l'ancora del mediterraneo, Naples.
© l'ancora del mediterraneo

Library of Congress Cataloging-in-Publication Data
Passerini, Luisa.
[Storie d'amore e d'Europa. English]
Love and the idea of Europe / Luisa Passerini ; translated by Juliet
Haydock with Allan Cameron.
  p. cm. -- (Remapping cultural history ; v. 9)
Originally published under title: Storie d'amore e d'Europa.
Includes bibliographical references and index.
ISBN 978-1-84545-522-4 (alk. paper)
1. Love--Europe--History. 2. Love--Europe--Public opinion. 3. Courtly
love--Europe. 4. Friendship--Europe. 5. Love in literature. 6. National
characteristics, European 7. Europeans--Attitudes. 8. Europeans--Social life
and customs. 9. Public opinion--Europe. I. Title.

GT2630.P3713 2009
306.7094--dc22
                                    2008047739

British Library Cataloguing in Publication Data
A catalogue record for this book is available from the British Library
Printed in the United States on acid-free paper.

ISBN: 978-1-84545-522-4 (hardback)

Contents

List of Illustrations

Acknowledgements

It would not have been possible to produce this book or complete the ten years of research that went into it without the support of the Kulturwissenschaftliches Institut (KWI) in Essen, which awarded me the 2002–2004 Land Nordrhein-Westfalen Research Prize. I particularly wish to thank the Institute's president, Jörn Rüsen, and its vice-president, Norbert Jegelka. The book owes much to Gesine Worms and Brigitte Brockhaus of the KWI library for their valuable help with my biographical research. The research group was made up of Liliana Ellena, Alexander Geppert, Jo Labanyi, Ruth Mas, Almira Ousmanova and Alison Sinclair. I am particularly grateful to project consultants Lutz Niethammer and Hartmut Kaelble, while I wish to thank project guest members Sally Alexander, Caroline Arni, Dipesh Chakrabarty, Marci Shore and Svetlana Slapsak for their comments.

I began researching this book in 1993 at the Wissenschaftskolleg in Berlin, and continued my work at the European University Institute throughout the years 1994 to 2002. Throughout this period I was fortunate enough to benefit from the help and friendship of Marina Nordera, to whom I give my affectionate thanks. Her active assistance made it possible to compare the three editions of *L'Amour et l'Occident*; I intend to file the three texts with our original annotations with an appropriate institution.

I owe much to the staff at the following libraries: the library of the European University Insitute in Florence, Genoa University Library, the Bibliothèque Nationale de France, the Fondation Nationale des Sciences Politiques, the Bibliothèque Sainte-Geneviève and the Bibliothèque de la Sorbonne of Paris. I am grateful to Silvia Alessandri of the Biblioteca Nazionale Centrale of Florence and to Marisa Scioratto of the Biblioteca Nazionale Universitaria of Turin, as well as to the staff of the State Archives of Genoa, Milan and Turin.

During the course of my research, I received valuable assistance from Karen Diehl, Elizabeth Fordham, Roberta Fossati, Julia

Guimier, Sharon Bar Kochva and Giovanna Tinunin. Stefania De Franco revised the bibliography. Graziella Bonansea, Enrica Capussotti, Alberto Cavaglion, Liliana Ellena, Marcella Filippa, Giuseppe Lauricella and Roberta Mazzanti commented on certain sections. For Chapter 1, I would like to thank Ernesto Treccani, Lydia de Grada and Maddalena Muzio Treccani, and Gianni and Marilena Puecher for the conversations I had with them in Milan. I also thank everyone I contacted during my research into Giorgio Quartara in Genoa: la Archiepiscopal Curia, Paola D'Arcangelo, Paola de Ferraris and Giuliano Galletta, Giuliana Lanata, and the company *Dynamic*. I was able to call on the valuable advice of Marco Novarino and Fulvio Conti for information on Freemasonry. I also thank the following for documentation: the Unione Femminile Nazionale of Milan, in particular the president, Maria Teresa Sillano, and the researcher Cristina Ghidini; the Istituto Mantovano di Storia Contemporanea; Alberto Simonetta for the Ada and Beatrice Sacchi archive; Marijke Peters of the Archive of the International Association of Women; Katiana Orluc for consulting the Coudenhove-Kalergi archive in Moscow; David Dougan of the Fawcett Library of London; Pietro Bigatti, president of the Società per la Cremazione in Milan.

For the chapter on Leo Ferrero, I am very grateful to Bosa Ferrero Raditsa and Delfina Dolza; the research was conducted mainly at the Fondazione Primo Conti in Fiesole, of which I thank the archive staff; thanks also to the Centro Studi Piero Gobetti of Turin, where part of the material on Leo Ferrero is kept.

For Chapter 3, I engaged in a useful correspondence with Philippe Joutard and Alain Paire, for which I give thanks. For Chapter 4, I am deeply grateful to Simonne Vion Sinclair, who agreed to answer my questions, and to Martine de Rougemont, who read and commented on the chapter; to Bruno Ackermann for his advice and to the director of the Bibliothèque Publique et Universitaire of Neuchâtel, Maryse Schmidt-Surdez, for her courtesy and skill in helping me consult the Rougemont Foundation – and to Luigi Santucci for granting me an interview. Sergio Rostagno was indispensable for helping me to understand the thoughts of Karl Barth and their resonance with the beliefs of Denis de Rougemont. I also thank Mariella Tagliero, director of the Biblioteca di Torre Pellice.

For Chapter 5, I would like to thank Carlo and Lucia Toso and Giorgia Ferro for helping me to consult the Lodovico Rocca archive;

Maestro Andrea Lanza, Rosy Moffa, Santina Mobiglia and Marina Pantano of the Teatro Regio di Torino; Pietro Crivellaro and Anna Peyron, director and librarian of the Centro Studi del Teatro Stabile di Torino, respectively; Isabella Rozenbaum of the Musée d'Art et Histoire du Judaïsme of Paris; the staff of the library at the Alliance Israélite in Paris and of the Biblioteca della Comunità Ebraica of Turin; the staff of the Library-archive of the Teatro Regio di Torino and Sigrid Sohn for her translations from the Yiddish. I am deeply grateful for the responses I received to my requests for information from experts on Jewish history, namely Jean Baumgarten, Jonathan Boyarin, Monica Miniati and Gabriella Safran. I also thank Michele Calandri and Adriana Muncinelli of the Istituto per la Storia della Resistenza in Cuneo, Annalisa Capristo and Giorgio Fabre, and Professor Avrom Udovitch of Princeton University.

For Chapter 6, my warmest thanks go to Giorgina Arian Levi, whose friendship has been a constant inspiration. I am also grateful to the Archivio Diaristico Nazionale of Pieve Santo Stefano and to Loretta Veri in particular; to Stefania Pini of the Vincenzo Chiarugi Library of the Vincenzo Chiarugi psychiatric hospital in San Salvi (OPSS) of Florence, which houses the Heinz Arian Foundation; to Sabine Hank of the Centrum Judaicum of Berlin; to Michele Sarfatti of the Centro di Documentazione Ebraica Contemporanea of Milan and to Renata Yedid Levi of the Fondazione Istituto Piemontese Antonio Gramsci of Turin. My conversations with Alberto Cavaglion were an essential source for Chapters 5 and 6.

Lastly, I would also like to express my heartfelt gratitude to Corrado Agnes who was beside me and encouraged the long gestation of this book.

Forms of Love and Limits of Europeanness

Intentions and Assumptions

Over the past fifteen years, in an attempt to explore the relationships between political forms of identity and cultural attitudes in the sphere of the emotions, I have found myself pursuing the theme of the relationship between European identity and conjugal love in its courtly and romantic forms. Such love typically reveals an often perverse dialectic between desire and the impossibility of fusion between the lovers, even if the love is fully reciprocated. In the beginning I was intent, above all, on criticising the Eurocentrism implicit in the conceit – dating from the closing decades of the eighteenth century – that Europeans had invented a certain type of loving relationship, mainly heterosexual and exclusive to Western civilisation, defined by its contrast and supposed superiority to the cultures of other continents. Though I have not abandoned this angle, which is valuable because it considers sexism and racism as part of the same critique, I have also begun to pursue other interests more explicitly: the first being the relationship between the individual and the collective, and the second being the limits of Europeanness.

In the first case, love constitutes a unifying force that works in a similar way whether it is keeping a couple together or laying the foundation stones of a cohesive society. Various cultural traditions assume a direct link between both forms of love, in particular both Protestant and Catholic versions of Christian love, despite the considerable differences between the two forms (Passerini 1999). This direct link also lies at the basis of all analyses of the crisis in

European civilisation – a central theme in cultural debates between the two wars – which consider this crisis to be rooted in the relationship between man and woman, seen as the bedrock of civilisation. This view was shared by those who set out to subvert the order of society through a radical revival triggered by *amour fou* or the 'community of lovers' that André Breton and Georges Bataille envisaged during that period.

The link between public and private is conceived to be not only extremely close but also direct and conditioning. Certain aspects of European cultures, nevertheless, provide us with opportunities to argue for a less direct relationship, requiring two independent foundations instead of one alone and accepting a certain amount of discontinuity between the public sphere and the private sphere, despite all the bridges that may and must be laid down between the two. On the contrary, I cherish the idea of discontinuity, because it seems to me to encourage a view of the male–female relationship that does away with the dual trap of complementarity (whereby man and woman are dovetailed into a fixed joint from which they cannot escape) on the one hand, and a rigid and unalterable dichotomy between the sexual genders on the other. This view is supported by the line of thought, exemplified by Maurice Blanchot and Roland Barthes, whereby the 'neuter' acts as a sort of starting point from which the duality may be changed and shifted. This view may break the deterministic relationship between a private order based on the heterosexual couple and a public order guaranteed by a love that holds a community together. Incidentally, this same determinism – but in the opposite direction, namely, from the public to the private instead of the other way round – also crops up in the classic approach of the Third International, according to which a change in the socio-political system would automatically determine a change in private relationships and emotions.

Significant support for the argument of discontinuity is offered in this book by the play *Dybbuk*, written between 1912 and 1919 by the Belarus ethnologist and revolutionary Shlomo Ansky. The play, based on an oral Hasidic tradition, met with great success in the period between the two wars, even in Western Europe, as a result of a production by the Habima company of Moscow. The *Dybbuk* introduces the view that two foundations are present, that of the conjugal relationship implemented by the community through shared religious worship, and that of the loving relationship that draws directly on a supernatural divine and demonic order. The hindered love that led to the death of the young lover is reaffirmed by the dead lover entering the woman's body in the form of a dybbuk. At this point, an androgynous figure is introduced, which mixes male and female in the body of a woman. Although the religious and social order of the community is respected (the dybbuk obeys the rabbi when he orders it to abandon the body of the beloved), the new being is located on another level by the independent decision taken by the young woman, released from the dybbuk, to choose death in order to be rejoined with her lover. Love which meets strong opposition, even when it results in death, speaks of freedom because it questions the unambiguous relationship between social cohesion and private love and alludes to the need for a dual foundation for both spheres.

On a methodological level, the decision to build up the book with case studies – of individuals and texts – was determined by the centrality of the relationship between public and private, which runs as a theme through the entire work, with specific reference to the 1930s. This period is marked not only by the political coercion of private individuals in countries with totalitarian regimes such as Italy, but also by the acute awareness of the link between private emotions and public affairs in debates on marriage, sex and divorce conducted in democratic countries such as France. In the book's structure, my insistence on the private sphere, as evidenced by my choice of microhistories, is intended to safeguard the relative autonomy of the private. Private histories may never be reduced to mere examples of great processes, since they always have a way of breaking out and to some extent contradicting them. My methodological approach rules out any comparison on a national scale, rather favouring the tracing of exchanges and resonances between case studies in different countries.

Access to some archives of private correspondence has allowed me to explore the relationship between public and private. In the case of Leo Ferrero, the documents revealed the concomitance of his intellectual and sentimental development, in the friendships with his male contemporaries and his tireless quest for a happy loving relationship. These emotional investments parallel Ferrero's intellectual exploration of European love. In the case of Rougemont, it is possible to document the emotional roots of the success of *L'Amour et l'Occident* through its reception not only by the press and critics but also by individuals, from unknown readers to well-known personalities such as Jakob Humm, Etienne Gilson and Théo Spoerri, all of whom were deeply moved by reading the work. In the case of Giorgina Levi and Heinz Arian, it was possible to highlight, on the basis of their correspondence, the link between a loving relationship and shifts in identity between the two poles of being Jewish and being European. As I had found in a previous study of love letters between a German man and a British woman (ibid.: Ch. 7), the different sense of national belonging fosters a discourse of European perspective, even in private correspondence.

My second interest, concerning the limits of Europeanness, emerged as a necessary antidote to the conceptual effort of opening up the sense of European belonging and making it multicultural. If we renounce any essentialism, for example by criticising the allocation of values such as democracy and equality exclusively to Europeanness, we cannot merely claim such values for humanity and oppose Eurocentrism. In this case Europeanness would run the risk of claiming itself to be all-inclusive, with a paternalistic or falsely universalistic slant. Our critique must, therefore, be accompanied by a recognition of the limits of that which may be called European in different historical periods. Though my intention is certainly not to repudiate the critique of Eurocentrism, which I have pursued on both conceptual and imaginative levels (Passerini 2004: 21–33; Passerini 2007a, Part 2), it is crucial to detail the new potential forms of Europeanness so that it may conceive of itself as limited. This limit may be understood in at least two ways. In the first place, we need to acknowledge on a historical level that Europeanness has always had its limits, which have assumed from time to time specific characteristics determined by space and time. One limit to forms of Europeanness may be found by postulating key historical discontinuities, refusing to accept a single root and a linear course, whether from antiquity, the Middle Ages or the modern age, to the concept of Europe and Europeanness.[1]

As far as cultural policy is concerned, a second limit may be applied explicitly to the way Europeans feel a sense of belonging, promoting a non-inclusive Europeanness that renounces claims of imposed universalism, while maintaining its concern for humanity as a whole. A critique of ideologies is not enough to achieve this step. If we mercilessly deconstruct Europeanness without saving anything, instead of looking for its limits we are left 'without any bread to eat', as Dipesh Chakrabarty pointed out to me. This requires us to set limits to our critique of Eurocentricism, introducing a note of *pietas* to our treatment of the past. While Eurocentricism was an intrinsic limit to all forms of European belonging, at the same time even those forms could contain elements of intercultural solidarity. Love itself in certain cases set a limit on Europeanness, forcing it to accept the other in all its specificity.

The protagonists of this book, who are in various ways Eurocentric, touch the limits of their Europeanness when they acknowledge the other and refrain from assimilating it. The common strand that joins the case studies I have chosen is that all of them – human beings and texts – encounter others, internal and external, European and non-European, in their quest for Europe. The encounters set a limit to their being European, but also provide an opportunity to feel empathy and solidarity. It is not up to us as historians to say how individuals should have behaved in the past, although we are free to discuss their choices. On the contrary, it is up to us to recognise that under those conditions some individuals helped to redefine themselves and their own Europeanness in their dialogue with others. Thus Quartara, on meeting Africans when he went ashore in West Africa during his return from Latin America, on the one hand treats the males only in the aesthetic terms of their physical beauty, yet on the other hand is concerned for the very young African mothers and how they will manage to cope with their difficult conditions. When Leo Ferrero espies in the old *india* woman in whose house he is lodging in Mexico a closeness to the divine that allows him to criticise an aspect of his own religious culture, he finds a new sense of religiousness that drives him towards Asia. The editors of and contributors to *Cahiers du Sud* turn to Islam through the Mediterranean, setting out to re-establish a fundamental relationship between European culture and Arab culture based on the love typical of ancient Provence. Denis de Rougemont constructs his great book against the backdrop of an imagined East, so his work is not free of orientalism, but his attempt moves in the direction of taking the naturalness out of loving passion and restoring it firmly to a cultural construct. The resulting historicisation helps to lay the foundations of a European identity that is no longer essential and eternal, but the result of many influences. Moreover, the reception of *Dybbuk* in France and Italy is a coming to terms between Jewish and non-Jewish Europeans, and between this collective and the Jews of Central Eastern Europe, in which the limits of reciprocal identity are simultaneously expanded and redefined. Lastly, when Giorgina Levi states that Europeans do not have the sense of space that is sometimes present in Latin America, she is not claiming to absorb everything, but instead suggesting that a limiting effect is at work in her acknowledgement of what a European is not.

If one premise of this work and its methodological choices is to take issue with the presumed continuity of cultural processes in time, another corresponding premise is that of the deterritorialisation of the continent. Current migration patterns are having the twofold effect of deterritorialising Europe and of delineating a possible Europe that still does not fully exist. The space within which the migratory routes are plotted is already European, but is still affected by former hierarchies between the centre and the periphery, between East and West and between North and South – and by value judgements that establish different levels of Europeanness.[2] Deterritorialisation, or the act of not acknowledging oneself to be connected to a single territory, may be an individual and collective experience, but it may also be a cultural operation, such as that of disassociating Europe from its traditional boundaries and taking into consideration its relationships with other continents. Being European 'amongst other things', in the words of Derrida (Derrida 1992), may be the preserve not only of individuals but also of countries and cultures. While it is no longer of any interest to debate whether Turkey or Morocco belong solely to Asia or Europe, it is very important to work in two directions on this score as well: on the one hand keeping open an idea of Europe where countries that are not considered geographically part of the continent are in some sense considered 'European'. On the other hand, we cannot claim that countries such as Russia and its culture are exclusively European, as though they *also* have other claims on their provenance. The recognition that other countries and cultures may *also* be European helps safeguard against the possibility of a new European cultural imperialism.

The need is, therefore, to ensure that Europe is not blocked by frontiers established by mistrust of the insufficiently 'European', but at the same time to understand what Europe has been: to give historical form to places that past investments in identity have made 'European', just as others may be made European in the future. Whereas in *Europe in Love* I focused on Great Britain, an area considered 'peripheral' to both Europe and love, in this book I have shifted my attention to areas that are 'central' in both respects, namely French-speaking Switzerland, southern France and Italy, as well as to the relationships between the west and the central eastern part of the continent. Paying attention to specific places when delineating a European territory is crucial: for this reason each chapter opens with a passage in italics that evokes one of the places where the love stories in the book take place or are imagined. In the first part: Genoa and the area around Florence; in the second: Marseilles and the Gotthard; in the third: the theatres of Paris and the Bolivian landscape, all places loved by the protagonists and for this reason given extra meaning that sheds light on the European space. Apart from this, the characters in the first part are active in Paris, move towards the Americas and dream of Africa or Asia. The passages in the second part are based on networks that traverse many European countries, from France and Switzerland to Germany and Great Britain, and are directed towards the Mediterranean, North Africa and the Middle East. The third part deals with Central Eastern Europe and northern Italy, and extends to Latin America. In this way the book builds up a picture of the European horizon in the world between the two wars, criss-crossed by pathways dictated by cultural goals, political purposes and emotional reasons, and open in many directions.

The three parts of the book correspond to ideas that stand as conceptual pillars of my study and weave together various intentions and goals. The first part is centred on individual stories: it combines the biographies of two men, illustrating specific characters and collective attitudes, and introduces the various theories they developed to interpret the relationship between the discourse on Europe and the discourse on love. This part starts in Italy, but both protagonists find a sympathetic ear in France. The second part shifts to texts produced in France: the *Cahiers du Sud* and *L'Amour et l'Occident* by Denis de Rougemont, both considered from the viewpoints of their development and reception. These texts bring out themes of the relationship between Europe and the Mediterranean and between European culture and Christianity, as opposed to Eastern religions. The third part introduces the theme of the relationship between Europe and its 'internal other': Jewishness, an obligatory choice for Europe in the 1930s, whereas nowadays the same topic would require other subjects. As Talal Asad and Thierry Hentsch have noted, nowadays in the West Arabs and Muslims have to some extent replaced the Jews both as an undesirable element in our societies and as a symbol of the insidious power of money.

Connections and Contrasts

Part I of this book examines what could be defined as the two archetypal ways of configuring the link between Europe and love. Quartara, a marquis and lawyer, formulates the link in terms borrowed from nineteenth-century materialism, offering an interpretation that adopts Bachofen's ideas on original matriarchy, and foreseeing sexual liberation as a correlate of social revolution. Quartara opens the book for the very reason that he represents a link with the nineteenth century, both positively through the international pacificism and feminism in which he was engaged, and also negatively, in his arguments against Marxism and communism. His view of Europe is strongly political: he draws inspiration from Masonic ideas and bases his writings on a firm belief in the monarchy – an idea of a united Europe for which no further tangible hope exists after the defeat of Aristide Briand's Memorandum at the Society of Nations in 1930. His was an isolated voice in the Italian cultural world and was to become even more isolated as fascism took hold. His political ambiguity of the 1930s would lead to a dramatic and enigmatic outcome at the beginning of the 1940s.

Leo Ferrero, on the other hand, was from the very outset part of a strong cultural, social and intellectual tradition due to his family and education. His concept of women and love, nevertheless, gradually moves away from the positivism of Lombroso and Guglielmo Ferrero and eventually, as a result of his religious conversion, embraces a form of spiritualism that anticipates that of Rougemont. He, therefore, connects 'Europe' and 'love' in a non-confessional form of Christianity that allows him to make intercultural comparisons with other world religions and cultures, in his quest for syncretism between East and West. Leo Ferrero's concept of Europe is culturalist. He no longer sees it as a 'young Europe', modern, industrial and democratic like the Europe of his father, but as a Europe of the heart and of religiousness. Although he harks back to traditions that join European culture with the continent's political problems, such as the tradition of Mazzini and the civil-democratic approach of Piero Gobetti and his followers, Ferrero differs from them in applying a 'culturalist' filter to the political implications of ideas on Europe. This filter is in certain respects a way of giving in to the constrictions of fascism, but in other respects provides us with elements we may use to compare the fascist idea of Europe and Europeanness. In the latter sense, it heralds an idea of Europe that has emerged in recent decades, which uses a concept of cultural identity to criticise the construction of a political, economic and bureaucratic idea of a European union.

Quartara and Ferrero are joined by their ideas and by certain anthropological and existential attitudes, despite the differences between their systems of thought. In both cases, their way of seeing the link between Europe and love is influenced by their ideas about women; both are upholders of women's emancipation in their different ways. In Quartara this tendency is guided by the tenets of Italian and international suffragists and emancipatory feminism. Ferrero's position, on the other hand, is linked to his relationship with his mother, Gina Lombroso, which leads him to condemn the subordination of women, albeit in an ambivalent manner. Both men managed to deal with the stereotypes of virility that they shared, but sometimes fell victim to, particularly Ferrero. Their biographies show similarities and differences. Central to both characters is an unresolved relationship with their mothers, which may have been the underlying reason why they found it difficult to form happy loving relationships and enter into marriage. In the case of Ferrero, there is a parallel between the special relationship with his mother and his relationship with a young peer group, which contributes to form his identity, given that he emphatically avows his membership of a specific 'young' generation at the end of the 1920s and at the beginning of the 1930s. The ages of Quartara and Ferrero were separated by a twenty-year gap as they were born in 1883 and 1903 respectively. This is the reason why the theme of the male generation, so marked in Ferrero, is not present in Quartara. The pair also represent different ways of considering the association between a sexual and a loving relationship. Quartara believes that they overlap and mingle and his view involves striking contradictions, such as his campaign against prostitution at the same time as he was taking part in it. For Ferrero, who was a stranger to this practice and painted it in all its squalor, love is never conceived as free of sexuality. He rejects the idea of sex as sin and attaches no blame to it, in line with his education based on a secular form of Jewishness. The tension between these two figures is a step towards a pluralisation of the category of maleness, to which my research intends to contribute.

The arguments they raised and in particular the way they linked Europe and love were destined to be at odds with the prevailing Italian environment. The two themes were pursued separately, in a climate of bitter diatribe against any line of thought that denied Mussolinian cultural autarchy and the foundation of a 'new' Europe. Even Drieu la Rochelle was acidly rebuked by the review *Antieuropa* – which proclaimed itself 'the heresy of modern Europe' (Gravelli 1929: 2–11)[3] – for having defined Maurras as 'the inventor' of fascism (ibid.: 28–29; editorial note). Interestingly enough, the only reference to the arguments discussed in this book to be found in *Antieuropa* take the form of a 'European' love dialogue between Don Juan and Petrarch's Laura, written by the Spanish author Giménez Caballero (Giménez Caballero 1935: 567–99).[4] The dialogue presents the two fictitious characters as European models of love, the anarchic male hero the opposite of the courtly lover, defined as effeminate, and the inaccessible lady who refuses to submit. The solution to the conflict between the two, which is leading the West to sterility, is to force both to marry and discover love through the sacrifice imposed by having children. This dialogue finds a counterpart in the series of unhappy encounters between Italian men and women from other countries, painted by Corrado Alvaro as places of absolute non-communication and frustration.[5] Still more drastic are the images of a loving relationship between an Italian woman and an African man that the 1934 novel *Sambadù Amore Negro* presents as regressive compared to European civilisation (Ellena 2004: 225–72).

By contrast, Part II of the book takes us to francophone areas, where we find ourselves in the nerve centres of European culture at that time. The areas in question were remote from Paris, because the cultural and emotional roots of the two case studies considered lie in the southern part of the country, in Marseilles and Provence, for *Cahiers du Sud*, and in French Switzerland for Denis de Rougemont. The continuities with the first section should not be underestimated. In all these studies, love in all its various historical and cultural forms represents a unifying force between public and private: in Quartara between European federalism and free love, in Ferrero between civilisation and passion, in Joë Bousquet and Simone Weil between culture and *eros*. Also of particular interest are the intellectual cross-references between Leo Ferrero and Rougemont, acknowledged by the latter in *L'Amour et l'Occident*. While Ferrero was intent on questioning the connection between love and the Christian religion through his desire to secularise European faith and establish syncretism between Eastern and Western beliefs, Denis de Rougemont set out to restore the link between love and Christianity through a process of redefining both and applying psychology to literature. Both were interested in bringing sacred love and profane love back under the same aegis.

Cahiers du Sud and Rougemont are brought together not only by the awareness that leads them to combine the two themes of Europe and love,[6] but also by the political importance they attached to such a combination in the task of refounding a free Europe. The same combination existed in completely different forms during the 1930s, for example in the writings of Pierre Drieu la Rochelle, who combined an interest in a Europe capable of rediscovering a unity 'against nations' with an obsession for 'foreign' Jewish or American women, in a view that saw only Europeans as truly capable of loving. For him, the relationship between love and Europe was situated within the framework of the 'immense healthy revolution' promoted by fascism: the regeneration 'in the blood' of European unity and European patriotism against the invasion of the Russian hordes, in the tradition of the Holy Roman–Germanic empire and in accordance with an order watched over by 'the Christ of the cathedrals, the great white, virile God'.[7] Drieu has the merit of not concealing the 'white' nature of his Europe within the framework of the Hitlerian *'nouvelle Europe'* anticipated by several French intellectuals in the 1930s (Bruneteau 2003: Part 1, 353n.).

The connection between Europe and love is an implicit presupposition of European culture, which can have very different political and cultural aims. Opposite intentions to Drieu were evident in *Cahiers du Sud* and Denis de Rougemont, as they took up ranks against Nazi fascism. Central to their writings considered here is the conviction that Provençal culture lies at the origins of European consciousness: for *Cahiers*, in the hope of reopening an age of European renaissance; for Rougemont, with a pessimism shot through with bitterness over the fate of the continent. Both *Cahiers* and Rougemont converge in diagnosing the fatal crisis in the European spirit, but are hostile, albeit in different ways, towards the type of moral clerical commitment to Europe dreamed of by Julien Benda. Rougemont believed that European culture could be refounded through a crucial return to religion, mediated by the thoughts of Kierkegaard and Barth and deeply rooted in the individual. As far as the editors of *Cahiers*, namely Jean Ballard, Joë Bousquet, Gabriel Audisio and René Nelli, are concerned, Europe's salvation lies in a cultural commitment, that is, a prioritisation of language and poetry, an idea shared by Simone Weil. This proposal involves the reintroduction of values considered typical of Mediterranean culture: tolerance, respect for the human person, intellectual curiosity, and a certain style of living and loving. This vision is entirely secular and for this reason distant from the Rougemontian view, but both cases envisage a form of Europe based on types of belonging that are not necessarily national, but in fact often regional.

Such values may be revived in a meeting of civilisations that hinges on the reforging of bonds between Europe and Islam, in a concept of Mediterranean unity that is set against Mussolini's ideas of a Latin race and 'mare nostrum'. This Mediterranean alters the very idea of Europe, opening it up to Africa and Asia through a cultural movement that is particularly relevant today. On the one hand, it exemplifies the deterritorialisation mentioned earlier, while on the other hand it alludes to a multifaceted and open Europe that is no longer the centre of the world, but a place of reciprocal communication and listening between cultures, reviving and updating an ancient trade tradition (Passerini 2002: 70–71; Chambers 2005: 423–33). This discussion of the Mediterranean restores a utopian charge to the debate on Europe. *Cahiers* reveals an awareness of Europeanness as an alternative to bellicose and belligerent nationalism, and recognises – with Valéry or with Nizan – the limits of Europe and its smallness as a peninsula or offshoot of the great mass of Asia. *Cahiers* does not set Europe (despite treating it as part of the West) against the East, and its criticism of the United States is gentler and more self-mocking than that of authors such as Georges Duhamel or Robert Aron and Arnaud Dandieu, who expressed strong forms of cultural anti-Americanism.

Rougemont's book *L'Amour et l'Occident* (referred to hereafter as *AO*) was destined to become a best-seller and strike a chord both with academics and the more general public. The network of relationships that grew up around the book is an illustration of the common sentiments that it expressed, in the sense of acknowledging oneself to be European and capable of love, with all the contradictions typical of the age. *AO*, Rougemont's life work, represents a distillation of the public and private concerns of its author, who subjects the crisis in marriage and the crisis in Europe to the same impassioned scrutiny. Rougemont draws parallels between the private *eros* and the unbridled passion of Hitlerian totalitarianism, and between *agape*, capable of fidelity in marriage through a pact between the individual and God, and European democratic federalism, in which he was actively involved after the Second World War, when he also became an eco-warrior. *AO* is a multifaceted work that combines different intellectual movements in an original way: the philosophical and political, drawn from the personalism the author shared with other contemporaries; the theological, from Kierkegaard and Barth; the historical and political, arising out of his direct observation of Nazism; and the anthropological, from his contact with the Collège de Sociologie. A textual comparison between the three editions of 1939, 1956 and

1972 has revealed his incessant changes to the work and the crucial psychological slant he added to the second version. By stressing an approach that sets the first five books of *AO* within an openly psychological context, Rougemont anticipates one of the most original interpretations of courtly love, namely, a view inspired by psychoanalysis in general and Lacanian psychoanalysis in particular.

AO sets out to establish a connection between the public and private, between the political and the personal, striking a bold and fascinating balance. Tristan and Europe are figures of nostalgia for life choices that are no longer open to the author himself, who wishes to leave behind the figure of Don Juan. In the absence of documentation and serious research, Rougemont's biographical details leave us with unresolved enigmas surrounding the contradictions between his life and thought. *AO* imposed its own rules on its author, namely, fidelity to the bitter end, against divorce, deemed typical of the US lifestyle in which European civilisation could also founder. Despite this, Rougemont himself chose divorce in the end to make his second marriage possible.

Denis de Rougemont's work met with criticism from many sides, from historians such as Irving Singer, who studied ideas of love and considered the book to be superficial and historically unfounded (Singer 1984, 1987), to young academics who noted the absence of references to a new role of women or sexuality, since the work upholds the idea of formal respect for the other without actually mentioning a change in the role of women, even in the early 1970s edition (Cirulli 2002–3). Recent interpretations of the poetry of the troubadours have discharged Rougemont's interpretation. Despite these criticisms and irrespective of whether we agree with them, *AO* remains a 'long haul book' to use Starobinsky's term, able to take into account contemporary views of consciousness, literature, customs, political tensions, and the links between them. The work still lives a life of its own, having been translated and read throughout the world. The translators themselves were bowled over by it, as was the case with the Dutch translator P. Hymans, who claimed that the book had changed his life and not just his intimate life. The same was true of the Italian translator Luigi Santucci, who went so far as to purloin *AO* from the library of Princess Caracciolo, who housed him in Switzerland during the Resistance, and carry it around in his knapsack throughout his partisan period. We may read this small anecdote as a confirmation of *AO*'s resonance with that 'Tempo d'Europa'[8] characterised by the Resistance movement's struggle against Nazism and fascism.

In addition to the intentional connections, some unexpected links emerged from my studies, which corroborated the appropriateness of the choices I made. A network of friends and cultural networks emerge, linking people who often did not know each other with invisible threads: Quartara and Leo Ferrero both contributed to *Il Lavoro* of Genoa when this newspaper, edited by the socialist Giuseppe Canepa, represented one of the few relatively free voices in fascist Italy. The editors of *Cahiers* and Rougemont shared the same cultural readings and circles. The former were strongly linked to Paul Valéry, who was to constitute an important cultural and social reference for Leo Ferrero. Ferrero's texts were reviewed by *Cahiers du Sud* and read by Denis de Rougemont, who was also in touch with Guglielmo Ferrero and Gina Lombroso in Geneva. Karl Barth and Charlotte von Kirschbaum, so important in the formulation of Rougemont's religious beliefs, fought in a group inspired by Freies Deutschland, the same movement in which Heinz Arian was active in Latin America. Moreover, the *Dybbuk* was performed at the Teatro di Torino founded by Riccardo Gualino, who was central to a network of intellectuals who shared the same ideas on Europe – ideas which aroused opposition despite their vagueness. These ideas originated in the circles influenced by Gobetti and *Solaria* and frequented by Leo Ferrero; Paola Lombroso Carrara, Leo's aunt, visited Palestine in 1932 on a trip organised by the Zionists with whom Giorgina Levi was in contact. The cultural networks are, nevertheless, open and inclusive. While the networks shared by most of the protagonists who appear in the book display the common characteristic of resistance and opposition to fascism, the overall picture also includes characters who acquiesced to fascism, such as Ludovico Rocca, composer of the opera *Il Dibuk* in 1934.

The two protagonists of Part I both demonstrate that the link between Europe and love is formulated within a male sexist framework and this is borne out by the works studied in Part II, which give priority to the male subject. *Cahiers du Sud* speaks of love within the conceptual framework of a 'contemporary male consciousness' that they are, nevertheless, aware is in crisis, as is the increasingly 'male' figure of the female. To get around this dual crisis of gender, René Nelli puts forward the idea of a passionate love founded on a spiritual, almost comradely communion, a friendship between both sexes – which in certain aspects resembles *amour fou* – but is able to return to ancient forms of sensuality such as the *assag* of Provençal and Eastern origin. This form of friendship is hardly reconcilable with the view of 'Woman' as the quintessential foreigner, who presides over the relationship between life and death, between waking and sleeping. Few real women stand out against this male-dominated background: the one woman to stand out is Simone Weil, whose exceptional articles on the Languedoc civilisation represented an act of spiritual resistance.

The female counterpart to the male subject of whom Rougemont speaks is not a woman guardian of love and death, but a true companion, seen as a person in the fullest sense. He, nevertheless, fails to acknowledge her complete subjectivity. From the perspective of *agape*, passionate love remains a sublime form of love-dominion, which yet again enslaves women by connecting love-fidelity to God. These concepts, as in those of Quartara and Leo Ferrero before, are responsible for a typical European male myth, which may be defined as the Pygmalion complex: the obsession with forming a woman in one's own image and semblance. This complex also crops up in the letters of Heinz Arian, for whom – as for the other protagonists – it amounts to a longing implicit in the European culture and spirit. The Pygmalion myth seems to embody a cliché of *Homo europaeus* in matters of love, in the sense that such men require total devotion even on an intellectual level and aim to win back, at least in the cultural arena, a mastery that has been lost in other areas.

Identity and Otherness

Far from taking an essentialistic and privileged view of the connection between being Jewish and being European, Part III argues for the possibility of an open way of experiencing that connection, in opposition to fascist and Nazi ideas of a Europe 'expurgated' of the Jews. This possibility is still highly significant for us today, in our efforts to help formulate new forms of Europeanness, as opposed to versions of a cultural Fortress Europe, even though the forms and subjects of exclusions have changed. For this reason we are still inspired by those who, like Giorgina Levi and Heinz Arian, lived a double identification, as Jews and Europeans, in the 1930s and 1940s. This is particularly significant in the period of 'persecution of the lives of Jews', using the term coined by Michele Sarfatti (Sarfatti 2000). However, the question of Jewish identity is posed very differently today than in the 1930s. The decimation of European communities due to the Shoah and migration, the existence of the state of Israel and the growing numerical and political weight of US Jewish communities on the international scene have changed the global relevance of European Judaism. Not only does the state of Israel pursue a cultural policy that relegates its European past to a role of secondary importance (Cohen 2004: 107–20), but some Jews from Eastern Europe also consider being Jewish incompatible with being European (Pinto 2004). The 'reconciliation' between Judaism and Europe that Simone Veil spoke of so optimistically just twenty or so years ago now appears a very difficult task, although no less necessary.[9] However, the possibility of creating a third pillar of Jewish identity – a European one, with strong links to the memory of the Shoah, but innovative in respect to the past – has been mooted (Michman 2004: 123–35).

In the 1930s, the European dimension of Judaism involved the recomposition of the Jewish community in the continent. Western European Jews, including the French and Italian Jews, had experienced a relatively swift cultural and legal emancipation with an accelerated process of social integration. The Jews of Eastern Europe formed a spiritual nation that had preserved its many languages and cultures, including Hasidism. The cases studied in Part III mirror each of these two realities, without claiming to represent them exhaustively, due to the multiplicity and wealth of Jewish cultures in the various areas of Europe. Furthermore, the Hasidic culture and the left-wing humanist Judaism depicted in Chapters 5 and 6 respectively deal with minorities compared to the Jewish people as a whole. The two examples reflect the coming and going of people and cultural processes between the East and West of the continent. The interpretation of the *Dybbuk* as belonging to European culture reminds us that Europe and Europeanness are hybrid forms par excellence and that the parallels drawn between the legendary wandering Jew and Nietzsche's Shadow are not unfounded.

Both cases studied in Part III illustrate movements between Eastern and Western Europe which took place literally (Ansky's exile, the peregrinations of Heinz Arian) and metaphorically (Ansky's tendency to enlightenment and his return to the Jewish tradition; the act of opening up to another's culture in the case of Giorgina Levi and Heinz Arian). The following double movement may be considered a promise of a form of Europeanness to come: on one hand, a critical revisitation of a *Lebenswelt* such as that of the shtetl; on the other hand, a critique by tradition and the community against the system of individual rights arising out of the Enlightenment. The binary nature of this movement means that neither of the two critiques is completely right and that only the tension between both processes – one of secularisation and individualisation, and the other involving a transformation of one's faith without total loss of faith – maintains some of the promises of freedom, justice and happiness offered by both. The two-way movement must be incessant if we are not to lose the moment of truth contained in each of the two worlds.

A similar tension is also present in the cases discussed in Part III. Both illustrate the connection between Europe and love and at the same time are illuminated by it. In the case of the *Dybbuk*, a work of fiction, love acts as a liberating force against repressive dogmas and the domination of the old and the rich – who are, however, rightly concerned with the fate of the community and no strangers to love and pain. The character of Leah is central to this dual aspect, and she herself is binary, female and male, living and dead. This is an illustration of the contradictions in the way women are represented in Jewish tradition and particularly in the Kabbalah, but perhaps also an indirect allusion, through the theme of the androgynous, to the new aspirations of Jewish women in the first half of the twentieth century. These aspirations are embodied in the historical experience of Giorgina Levi, who was a leading light of female emancipation in the intellectual, social and political field. We are struck by her strength in committing to and enduring her risk-filled union with Heinz Arian, and her ability to turn her image of herself as a European woman in relation to the Bolivians into a Europeanness open to others and to an acknowledgement of her own limits. All this assumes particular significance nowadays, when the presence of migrants forces Europeans to take other cultures into account in reformulating their own sense of belonging. The female figures in the first two parts of the book stand out as indispensable supports to the men in the case studies, yet remain peripheral despite their strength and importance – from Vittoria Gavazzi Quartara, Gina Lombroso Ferrero and some female friends and lovers of Leo, to Charlotte von Kirschbaum and Simonne Vion de Rougemont. Part III, however, finally sets women centre stage, both in fiction, in the case of Leah in the *Dybbuk*, and in historical reality, through the figure of Giorgina Levi. They allow us to break away from the blinkered view that the subject of any European discourse on love must be exclusively male and Christian.

Changes in identity induced by the bond of love demonstrate how love makes it possible to put oneself in someone else's place and illustrate the osmosis between identity and otherness. For Giorgina, such changes meant extending her sense of Italianness to a European identity, fed by cultural references, some of which – such as Stefan Zweig, who was simultaneously a Jew and a 'great European' – embraced Central Europe, Arian's place of origin. The heritage of political opposition that came to her from her family added a further international and cosmopolitan dimension to her Europeanness. For Heinz Arian, Giorgina represented a place of identification, which in 1938 he compared to a beloved country, known only to him, a form of identification by which the other became himself. For both of them, 'mother Europe' or the 'European motherland' became a reality not only due to the persecutions but also to their reciprocal understanding of one another. In the 1930s, Europe was still of central relevance to them as their pole of identification; they were hardly affected by the idea of a Zionist homeland, a role allocated to Palestine first and foremost. Though both were aware of the appeal of Zionist arguments, the impact was lessened by their leaning towards Marxism.

We cannot let the happy end to the last love story make us forget the tremendous risk that Heinz and Giorgina had taken. The theme of separation emerges dramatically in Part III, as the link between love and death in the case of the *Dybbuk*, while in the second case study the whole of Europe appears as a killing field. It is, however, very different if the link between love and death arises as the object of a polemic, even if this is turned against oneself – and this applies to both Ferrero and Rougemont – or as a longing that is indulged for self-gratification. No one in this book fully represents the second attitude, though it could apply to Drieu la Rochelle, if we were to dig deeply enough into his reasoning.

The link between love and death does not appear in Part I, which underscores the intellectual links between dissertations on Europe and on love. It is particularly absent in Quartara, for whom love is an affirmation of vital and free sexuality. We find hints in Leo Ferrero, who knew the anguish of the demand for infinite love, when he highlights the unhealthy link between the decadence of Western civilisation and love – passion. In *Cahiers du Sud*, love is connected with non-tragic death, resembling sleep, as well as to the abandonment of the male within the female, as in Joë Bousquet, for whom love is a cosmic force that alleviates pain and relates it to transcendence. In the case of Weil, death is in the background, in the massacre of the Albigensian civilisation, where the fusion between civilisation and love had reached one of its greatest heights. Rougemont unravels the knot between love and death: there is a love that is indissolubly joined to death, a love whose aim is fusion and which threatens to eradicate individuality. The love associated with life respects distances and differences: between God and human beings, between woman and man, between public and private. Rougemont believed death to be disease and the extreme outcome of love–fusion, a paroxysmal exaltation of religious origin, as in deviant mysticism or Nazism. Within this framework the confusion between public and private corresponds to the fusion that sees death as the only outcome of a loving relationship.

The *Dybbuk* also shows us the risk of fusion, although it exalts death as freedom from an oppressive community and emancipation from an insuperable divide between male and female. We are in the realm of a painful utopia, which separates the public and private spheres by establishing a relationship between the latter and transcendence. The sixth case study takes us back to historical experience: Giorgina Levi and Heinz Arian are forced to combine public and private more than they would have wished in order to escape Europe and death. Their experience of exile was to contribute to this union, but in general both retain their individuality within their relationship, despite the forms of osmosis described above.

The actuality of the link between Europe and love operates on different levels. An awareness of this link may be useful to keep alive an idea of a Europe vaster than the European Union. Nowadays we cannot pretend not to be in Europe and neither can we claim to reject our heritage. We can no longer share the type of Europeanism that existed in the past, Eurocentric and male-centred; we must find new forms of Europeanness that allow the full respect of differences. This means we cannot avoid passing through a critique of Europe's cultural legacy, within which the attitude to love is a central element. While it is important to break away from Eurocentricism in order to establish relationships with other peoples and cultures that contain an element of loving emotion, it is essential to recognise the limits not only of Europeanness but also love itself in its historical forms. This thought runs through the letters written by Jews imprisoned in concentration camps in France between 1941 and 1944, who were often deported and killed in Auschwitz (Sabbagh 2002). Many of these letters, some exchanged between married and engaged couples, are full of love, but they do not succeed in expressing that love, except in their obsessive need to alleviate their physical misery with their despatches and in their pitiful reassurances that they were surviving quite well. A few salutations such as 'adorée', 'mon tout', 'mon amour', punctuate the letters, paltry scraps of loving words suffocated by the atrocity of events. Even love can succumb to extreme violence, but sometimes it is able to project a message of union – not of fusion – beyond the violence, which allows people to endure the current oppression and look forward to other realities both in public and in private.

Notes

1. For a criticism of the term 'Europe', considered as 'a stable, unchanging referent', see J. Boyarin, 'From Derrida to Fichte? The New Europe, the Same Europe, and the Place of the Jews', in Boyarin (1996: 109–39).
2. On the process of European deterritorialisation due to migrations, see Passerini et al. (2007b).
3. This journal was against democracy, communism, Malthusianism – in short, all 'decrepit parliamentarian and internationalist European civilisation'.
4. See also J. Labanyi, '(Un)requited Conquests: Love and Empire in the Work of Ernesto Giménez Caballero and Salvador de Madariaga', forthcoming.
5. I am thinking of stories such as 'Il Mare' (in which 'the resentments between men and women of different race' are discussed at length) or 'Stranieri', in which a relationship between a young Italian and a German widow does not improve the opposition between both cultures but exacerbates it. See Alvaro (1994: 45, 247). Or stories about unions that came about during the migrations to America, such as 'La Donna di Boston', and 'Il Marito', which express the lack of communication between cultures within couples (ibid.: 198–204, 205–10).
6. An awareness that is similar in certain respects also crops up in other essayists of the period, who do not, however, discuss the same themes. Gaston Riou, for example, suggests a link between the West, Provençal love and Christianity, central to *La Naissance de l'Amour* (1927), and defines 'white civilisation as not only a technique but a mystique', that of the human person, in *Europe, ma Patrie* (1928: 289), but does not develop the connection between private love and the public sphere. Other important writings on love, such as that of Emmanuel Berl, above all *Le Bourgeois et l'Amour* (1931) and *Recherches sur la Nature de l'Amour* (1932), leave the theme of Europe in the background, even though the first is a rough caricature of the sentimental conformism typical of Western, but above all European, middleclasses, incapable of considering women as people or of taking love seriously.
7. I refer not only to some of the main works of Drieu la Rochelle, such as *L'Europe contre les Patries* (1931) and *Gilles* (1939), but also to minor and partly unpublished works. The quotations are taken from Drieu la Rochelle (1939: 672–75, 687).
8. I have taken this expression from M. Giovana's book *Tempo d'Europa* (1952), which considers the Resistance a European phenomenon since it was triggered by the general crisis in the continent and inspired by principles that exceeded national boundaries.
9. See Veil (1984) and Pinto (2004) respectively.

PART I

MALE PORTRAITS

Chapter 1

'Free Love and Fraternity between the Federated Peoples of Europe':

Giorgio Quartara, Supporter of European Integration and Feminism

The Lovers' Dialogue

To get to the villa called Castellaccio, a large building with black and white stripes in the Genoese style, you walk uphill in the Righi district of Genoa towards the line of fortifications through what remains of a park that once covered most of the hill (Ernesto Treccani recalls it as a 'vast garden with the sea below'). The stripes on the façade on Via Mura delle Chiappe, which is decorated with marble friezes, are faded and one of the Quartara family mottoes, 'Nemini iniustum', can be read above the tower, now bristling with aerials. Bas-reliefs are set in the wall on the other side of the house, one of which depicts a Bacchic scene of satyrs and nymphs. Parts of the port can be seen between the pinasters and other evergreen vegetation. There are signs of decay: an old tennis court and a fountain that no longer produces any water. After many generations in one branch of the Quartara family, the whole property was taken over by the Church in 1957, and a seminary for the archbishopric was built on the lower part of the park and the villa rented out to private individuals, who will allow you to visit the two great halls that run into each other at different levels. Perhaps one was for the orchestra and the other for guests at soirées of music and dance. The interiors retain their charm and elegance, in spite of having been divided up by apartments and partition walls. One window has a beautiful view of the sea, and another looks onto the line of fortifications around Genoa.

Giorgio Quartara used this setting, with its view of the city he loved, for an excursion by the two lovers who are the principal characters in his dialogue *Gli Stati Uniti d'Europa e del Mondo* (*The United States of Europe and the World*), which was published by Bocca at the beginning of 1930. The young lovers, Ada and Leo, are depicted walking in various parts of the city and its surrounding area engaged in seven dialogues that discuss the problems whose resolution is a prerequisite for the creation of a European federation. In the first dialogue, which is on war, the two climb 'the walls of the high fortress Sperone at the top of the fortifications that surround Genoa' and they admire the city from above (Quartara 1930: 1).

However, the two could not fail to note the contrast between the social organisation and the 'spectacular movement of the ships' in the port of Genoa. Ada exclaims: 'So much mechanical progress and yet such a poor and miserable life for the people. We are like those savage kings that go naked wearing a top hat' (ibid.: 2). Faced with this scene that combines natural beauty and technological progress in a contradictory manner, the two lovers (who are also aware of the child they are expecting) represent the most advanced form of European consciousness. This presents the book's twin purpose of depicting the ideal form of love between two people and making a contribution to the improvement of the continental and world order.

Perhaps because of this unusual combination, *Gli Stati Uniti d'Europa e del Mondo* sold very well in the early months of 1930, and Quartara reported to his French friend Pierre Mille that the book was about to be sold out, when two unexpected events occurred. On 15 May 1930, the police commissioner for the province of Milan received a telegram from Bocchini, the head of the Central Police Department, ordering all copies to be seized, and two days later he replied that the matter had been dealt with.[1] Although confiscation of the book was justified in the regime's opinion because of its underlying message, it came as a surprise to the author, who only a few months earlier had been summoned by the prefect of Milan to receive a personal declaration of support from Mussolini,[2] with reference to a memorandum examining the New Criminal Code, which Quartara sent to the Ministry of Justice on his own initiative and in which he carried out a critical analysis of the proposal. Giorgio Quartara was not a supporter of fascism.

According to his nephew, the artist Ernesto Treccani, the family still remembers him as an oppositionist, although in his own particular way (ET 1 [*Interview*]). From the beginning he had been a member of the Radical Party, which was founded in Rome in 1904, and regularly contributed to the Genoese daily newspaper *Il Lavoro*, which was edited by the socialist Giuseppe Canepa. His strongest political sentiments were anticlericalism and loyalty to the monarchy. He came from a noble family, and between 1924 and 1926 he obtained recognition of his title of marquis and his coat of arms through decrees signed by Mussolini and King Victor Emmanuel III (*I Quartara – Nobili – Magnifici – Marchesi*: 1931; *Libro d'Oro della Nobiltà Italiana*: 1977–80). Quartara's attitude to fascism was, however, ambivalent and subject to vacillations and inconsistencies.

After his book had been seized by the authorities the Vatican violently attacked it in two front-page leaders published in *L'Osservatore Romano* on 25 May and 1 June 1930. The articles had no difficulty in ridiculing the 'two living together in a free union' who discuss international arbitration while enjoying 'panoramic and gastronomic delights'. However, *L'Osservatore Romano* considered the text to be 'the product of a well thought-out hatred of religion that expresses itself through pseudo-scientific invective' ('Angoli bui', 'Una ipotesi' [1930]). Although fiercely anticlerical, Quartara had friends who were priests and greatly respected others. Always inclined to mock, he justified keeping such company by telling his family (which was devoutly Catholic on his mother's side) that 'priests know how to eat well' (ET 2 [*Interview*]).

While *L'Osservatore Romano* was attacking Quartara, the affair was being reported in France in the pages of *Le Quotidien*, a newspaper founded to defend and improve republican institutions.[3] The writer and journalist Pierre Mille wrote two articles explaining the European dimension to the Quartara question precisely at the time that Aristide Briand was submitting his Memorandum for a European Federation to the League of Nations, and Mussolini made speeches in Leghorn and Florence exalting armaments and war. Mille asserted that freedom of thought and of the press had been abolished in Italy, and that the fascist government wanted to persuade Italians that militarism was the only possible policy, given the need to defend themselves from supposed French aggression. He also informed the reader that Quartara had shown him his fascist membership card during a trip to Paris in early 1930 following his meeting with the prefect (Mille 1930a: 1; 1930b: 1). In the preface to the French edition, *Les Etats Unis d'Europe et du Monde*, which he dated 1931, Quartara expressed his hope for the 'complete success of Briand's splendid Memorandum' (Quartara [*Translation*] 1931: ix).

Quartara's dialogue contained many elements that could have upset the fascist authorities, and they were not restricted to those that affected good relations with the Vatican: the appeal 'to the mother of the Unknown Warrior', at the beginning and the end of the book, used one of the principal rhetorical resources that the regime employed to build its secular religion based on the war dead; the arguments in favour of free trade and a European federation clashed with the regime's nationalist policies; and the eulogy of free love could not be well received by a regime intent upon demographic growth centred on the family. This is not to mention the statements with the following tenor: 'impudent rabble-rousers inflamed the crowds with loutish idiocies' (Quartara 1930: 3), or that Quartara cited the defunct German empire and the United States of America as examples of strong and wise governments.

The narrative form enhanced the book's scandalous nature. It translated into a particularly vivid format the ideas the author had put forward two years earlier in a learned work entitled *Le Leggi del Libero Amore* (*The Laws of Free Love*), which had already provoked a mixture of hostility to its ideas and admiration for Quartara's extensive research. This admiration was even shared by those who did not agree with him, such as Teresa Labriola who, writing in *La Donna Italiana*, defined his work as 'an interesting but unacceptable volume which is both erudite and full of ideas' (Labriola 1930: 331–36).

His dialogue can be seen as central both to his work as a whole and to a cultural and political dispute. The literary genre is that of the political philosophical dialogue, but the protagonists are untypical of this genre and the settings contrast with the abstract nature of the ideas, which occasionally cause the reader to smile. Of the two lovers, the man is a primary schoolteacher and the woman a typist for a legal firm. She is a highly symbolic figure: she shares her name with Ada Sacchi Simonetta, the active feminist and chairwoman of the Italian section of the International Alliance of Women for Suffrage and Equal Citizenship. Ada in the dialogue comes from Pieve di Teco, where the Quartara family originated. She is a self-ironic representation of the author, given that she carries a copy of another of Quartara's books under her arm, *Dalla Guerra Mondiale alla Civiltà Internazionale* (*From World War to*

International Civilisation), which she has just finished reading. Quartara has Leo say that, 'having given [the book] a cursory glance, it appears the most effective of soporifics' (Quartara 1930: 32). Moreover, Ada works for a woman lawyer and can use her vast collection of books, which undoubtedly reflects the Marquis Quartara's own collection (sadly this has been almost completely lost along with his documents and papers). Indeed, Ada represents the author, albeit a feminine version, and his attempt to take on a feminine role in relation to matters of the heart and mind. This figure suggests Quartara's complex relationship with the feminine, which emerges both in his ideas and on the existential level.

Leo is a typical Lombard schoolteacher, who represents common sense. He is a good person with a strong sense of religion, but he is also prejudiced. Indeed, he refused to marry Ada at the beginning of their relationship because she had been raped by her employer. He now regrets his refusal and would like to marry her, particularly as they are going to have a child together, but she reproaches him for his previous refusal. In the end she only accepts for the good of their child. Leo is deeply in love with Ada and often adopts her ideas, but is not willing to yield on the existence of God, in whom he continues to believe. Ada respects his faith and declares herself agnostic, assuring Leo that she places her faith solely in him, their child, their country, the European and World confederation, and humanity and its continuous progress.

The dialogue is set amongst local places of significance for the daily lives of the Genoese, irrespective of their class background, which were also those dear to the author. The two lovers share a small bedroom and kitchen on the top floor of a house set in an area very close to Villa Quartara. They therefore live in a high position, and from the even higher position of their small terraced roof they are able to see the port and the great ships that 'connect us to the fantastic city of New York, the peoples' mirage' (ibid.: 29).[4] The two lovers are well placed to observe the world from the heights of their youth and intelligence. Their dialogues always take place on a Sunday, their only day off, which they devote to strenuous walks. On the third Sunday (the day of the dialogue on the various types of possible confederation between states), the 'terrible Genoese wind, the cousin of Trieste's "bora"', begins to blow and the two lovers have to hide in a grotto. The setting is a tempest, and yet, Quartara comments, 'the brute forces of the inclement weather proved less irresponsible than the peoples of Europe' (ibid.: 92). Comparisons between humanity and nature are a recurring theme in Quartara's writings. Even on the ship that would take him from Trieste to South America, he feels that the dolphins, swallows and seagulls wish to tell men that they are better organised, 'particularly when it comes to procreation' (Quartara 1939: 8).

Fortunately the following Sunday is springlike and warm although it is the middle of winter. The couple discuss free trade along 'the very long and steep pathway through the woods to the Sanctuary of Madonna della Guardia', where many thousands of people headed on their days off, to 'find excellent refreshment in the large taverns hidden away in that vast building erected for the faith' (Quartara 1930: 93). In one of these taverns, Ada and Leo eat and drink a carafe of the white wine used by Genoese priests in the elevation of the host. Understandably, these details did not please the leader writers of *L'Osservatore Romano*, but above all they were upset by the setting for the last dialogue, which unsurprisingly deals with the question of secularism. It takes place in bed after a bath in what the leader writer described as 'a bestial encounter'. Quartara used a very different tone:

> They were both statuesquely beautiful. The marble firmness of their forms and their flashing and penetrating eyes demonstrated the purity and temperance of their ecstasy. Healthy minds in healthy bodies.

> The two perfect lovers clung to each other breathlessly on the bed like giant snakes, like ivy round an oak. For an hour their hearts and touches quivered divinely and innocently in the orgasm of love until they relaxed. Afterwards Ada and Leo lay still in each other's arms for some time, and serenely prepared themselves for the resumption of their conversation. (ibid.: 161)

The depiction of their embrace did not only respond to Quartara's ideals of healthy sexuality, but also to his voyeuristic disposition.

The distinctive feature of this dialogue on the United States of Europe is the emphasis it puts on gender. At the beginning and the end of the work, the author addresses an appeal to the mother of the Unknown Warrior, expressly based on gender: '[Y]ou, woman and sole responsible person … run and gather together your sisters … Let every feminine society, every woman and every invalid unite with you'. It is a feminism directed towards the social, but very far from all forms of socialism. Ada, whom Quartara depicted as a feminist through and through, declares that if she had drawn up the Treaty of Versailles, she would have called 'mothers, widows and disabled servicemen', as well as industrialists, in order to hear their opinions. However, she does not mention workers, which indicates that she is distancing herself from socialism. Ada's criticisms of politicians are not based on class injustice, but on their natures which are those of 'macho, political wheeler-dealers' (ibid.: 6). Ada bases her pacifism on her own identity as a woman: 'As one that is soon to be the mother of your child, I have never been able to understand war', but she immediately adds, 'and from what I have read, many men have also failed to understand it' (ibid.: 10).

Ada summarises Quartara's ideas in every field of his thought. When she eloquently explains to Leo why 'mutual virginity was not possible for either of us', she is not simply telling her own life story, but is also restating some of the questions put forward in *Le Leggi del Libero Amore* and other previous writings: sexual violence, the law's iniquitous treatment of women, parity of desire between men and women. Here they appear in a personalised and dramatised form, and demonstrate the author's twin identification with the heroine and her 'female lawyer'. Thus when Ada retells the latter's account of her journey through North America, it is as though Giorgio Quartara is personally recounting his memories of a similar experience (ibid.: 75).

The dialogue's most interesting feature is the way it closely associates the question of gender to the proposal for a European federation. Ada reviews the stages through which philosophy has passed since the eighteenth century to bring us this idea, and she dwells on 'Kant's melancholy conclusions', both because she does not agree with his preference for a republic over a monarchy, and because she argues that perpetual peace can only be achieved on the basis of a universal state. She also convinces Leo of the advantages of free trade and demonstrates that a European federation would meet the needs of economic and social progress: while the abolition of customs frontiers will slowly amalgamate the peoples in industry and trade, free love and national pensions will guarantee their welfare. Free love, understood as a voluntary union of a loving and sexual nature which must be acknowledged in law, will also improve the physical constitution of the European peoples.[5] The private sphere, and more precisely the intimate sphere of affections that form the basis of a family, are thus the basis for the renewal of public life. In turn, economy of the libido and the material existence are transformed and safeguarded by law reform and the federation of nation-states.

The whole dialogue is highly symbolic: Leo's 'common sense' is contrasted with Ada's superior 'good sense', while their love symbolises the truth and the unborn baby represents progress. The conclusion expresses the danger faced by truth and progress in the contemporary world: a few months after having legitimised their union in a civil wedding, the two lovers fall victim to mindless violence. Leo is fatally wounded by a pistol shot while unsuspectingly passing a gang war. Ada, left on her own, is attacked by 'a brutish and lecherous old man', and the serious injuries suffered cause her to give birth prematurely. They both lie dying in the wards of a public hospital and the premature baby is handed over to 'hired hands'. According to the dialogue's symbolism, good sense and common sense are also in mortal danger: truth is shattered and human progress is in doubt. Nor is there any certainty that physicians can be found to save them. The dialogue ends with this uncertainty and a plea for the life of Ada, Leo and their son to the Unknown Warrior's mother, the 'only real doctor'.

The dialogue on the United States of Europe was translated in France and Spain, but in Italy it was strangled at birth. This was the fate of many of Quartara's books. The majority of his works, or to be precise all those works that came out after 1927, were published by Bocca, the publishing house with secularist sympathies and positivist ideas (Decleva 1997: 225–98 and Ragone 1999). Several books affected by censorship appeared in a list of works provided by the publisher in 1945 at the beginning of *Del Risorgimento Legislativo*. Apart from *Gli Stati Uniti d'Europa e del Mondo*, which was seized in 1930, *Le Leggi del Libero Amore* (1928) was subject to a ban on display and reviewing. *La Riforma del Codice Civile* (1938) was seized.[6] This work, which was a collection of articles published over the previous two years in *Il Lavoro*, dealt with family questions. *L'Italia Tradita* (1941) was seized, and to replace it the author published *La Futura Pace*. Quartara quite reasonably complained about this continuous persecution:

> [M]y books, which have been seized, banned from reviews, and excluded from publishers' catalogues, window displays and stalls, [were] all fascist delights, because I have discovered that the prefectures of this kingdom have two lists of prohibited books, one drawn up by the government and one by the Church authorities. I am to be found in the latter. I was able to see this with my own eyes at the Prefecture of Genoa. (Quartara 1945: 45)

The worst thing was the absence of reviews and the almost total silence in relation to his major works, which caused difficulty in communication and his increasing sense of isolation. *Le Leggi del Libero Amore* was very briefly referred to in the *Rivista di Diritto Processuale Civile* (1928: 383), in an affected and rather antagonistic piece. The few reviews that appeared in the late 1930s for minor works such as *Un Viaggio nel Sud-America* did not do him justice. They accused him of pessimism and being outdated, and disliked what they considered his negative perception of everything European and his belief that everything in North America and northern Europe was perfect.[7] Even the readers attacked Quartara's books: an unknown reader wrote in pencil on the copy of *Le Leggi del Libero Amore* held by the Biblioteca Nazionale Centrale in Florence, 'unscrupulous feminist / should be in the dock!' The only copy of *L'Italia Tradita* in the same library remained uncut until 2000. Moreover, examination of the archives has not borne any fruit,[8] and information about Quartara's private life is even more difficult to obtain.

The 'Perfect Gentleman'

Giorgio Quartara was born in 1883 at Carate Lario, the home of his mother, Vittoria Gavazzi, who came from a well-known Lombard family of silk manufacturers. His father's family came from Liguria, and the first Quartara in the family tree notarised in 1928 is Alemanno, who owned a *palazzo* in Genoa. Giorgio Quartara's ancestors included captains of warships, magistrates of the Republic of Genoa, lawyers, canons and mayors. The Quartara family divided at the end of the eighteenth century, and Giorgio came from the branch descended from Giuseppe Antonio, who was governor of Mexico and California during the last years of Spanish dominion in America. This line included Giorgio's father, Ernesto Barnaba (1852–1917), director general of the Ministry of the Navy. The latter's marriage (1882) to Vittoria Gavazzi (1860–1936) produced Giorgio and Giulia (1889), who married Giovanni Treccani degli Alfieri, the founder of the Istituto dell'Enciclopedia Italiana (Institute of the Italian Encyclopedia).[9]

His noble birth was a matter of some importance to Giorgio Quartara. He took a great deal of trouble to have it legally recognised and made it part of his political and social convictions. He deplored the decree issued by the Heraldic Commission in 1926 that restricted the inheritance of noble titles to the male line, 'an unjust decree and one contrary to the most elementary principles of law' (Quartara 1928: 598). Quartara founded his existential and political identity on his title of marquis; indeed his works are full not only of his perception of constitutional monarchy as an ideal form of government, but also his admiration and affection for the royal houses of Europe. His membership of an aristocratic family guaranteed a degree of political protection and financial security which gave him freedom to study and to travel, along with an important network of acquaintances. Some aristocratic exponents of European unity, such as Count Sforza or Count Coudenhove-Kalergi, inherited an ideal of Europe that was more dynastic than national, and looked back to a medieval and early modern European identity founded on kinship and shared values. A further network was made up of aristocrats working in diplomatic services who fulfilled an important role in the establishment of European Freemasonry (Beaurepaire 2002: 44 ff.).

The family of Giorgio Quartara's mother, the Gavazzis, also boasted a complex dynastic background, in their case of an entrepreneurial nature as they were heavily involved in banking. They came from Canzo, close to Lecco, and could trace their family tree back to the late fifteenth century. The relevant branch of the family was started by Pietro, who encouraged his sons to set up a textile mill in Desio. His granddaughter Vittoria became the mother of Giorgio and Giulia. The Gavazzis were a Catholic, conservative and slightly authoritarian family, but not without a certain openness on social questions.[10]

Giorgio Quartara lived either in the Castellaccio in Genoa or his mother's home in Milan. His family also owned a house in Rome called Palazzo Fiano, where they presumably lived while Giorgio's father worked for the Ministry of the Navy. Receptions were held every Tuesday at Palazzo Fiano, and they were attended by leading politicians such as Salandra (with his wife), Crispi (with his wife and daughter), Bettolo (with his family), Rattazzi the Younger, and composers such as Mascagni and Cilea (the Quartara family had their own seats at the Costanzi Theatre where Mascagni presented his works). Apart from these associations, Quartara recalled that Vittorio Emanuele Orlando 'used to welcome him with paternal warmth' at his detached house (Quartara 1945: 19). He was, therefore, part of the political and intellectual elite of prefascist Italy. Giorgio studied law at the Sapienza University in Rome, but he never practised in the legal profession. He speculated on the stock exchange and exploited the wealth in Gavazzi shares he inherited from his mother's side.

He was in Genoa mainly during the summer months. The Castellaccio was enormous and there was room for each family nucleus or single individual, as in his case, to have a separate apartment, although they came together for meals. Giorgio Quartara linked the villa and its annexe with another wing, and put up marble copies of Greek statues around the grounds, most of which were nudes, to express his veneration of the young and beautiful body. The oral tradition amongst the current tenants of the Castellaccio is that the Church buried them in the embankment next to the house. Quartara himself was prophetically incensed about the censorship of statues and particularly the clerical party's desire to place 'a kind of fish between the legs' of the bronze water nymphs on the fountain outside Rome's main railway station (Quartara 1928: 16).

His passion for the naked body, particularly the female one, was both aesthetic and erotic. He had his own box at the theatre in Milan that put on operetta (his favourite work was *Al Cavallino Bianco*), and the family remembers his attraction to ballerinas, with whom he would mix after the show. He was a well-known womaniser and disagreed with marriage. His nephew Giulio Treccani, who was a child at the time, recalls that he was considered to have some interest in 'pornography', because he had such works as a clandestine edition of Bataille's *Histoire de l'Œil* (which was published in Paris in 1928). It was really more typical of a voyeurism spiced up with 'sophisticated tastes' (ET 2). Comedy was one of his passions: in Genoa he was a great admirer of Gilberto Govi's plays in dialect, and the few remaining books of his vast library include several volumes from a series of classical funny books published by Formiggini in the 1930s.[11] The little information we have suggests a likeable and impetuous person who was certainly opinionated, sometimes provocatively so, but also generous and entertaining.

Quartara was 'massive and imposing', and as a young man he had been 'a swordsman in a class of his own', wrote the Genoa-based newspaper *Il Lavoro* on his death. For decades the paper had given space to 'his wise comments', and added that he had been a 'perfect gentleman' who 'combined vast legal knowledge, unswerving loyalty to the monarchy and a Voltairian spirit', who had treated the great problems of humanity and his beloved Genoa as his own.[12] We can recognise this portrait from the mind behind *Gli Stati Uniti d'Europa e del Mondo*: the mixture of the old and the new that typified his language and ideas.

There is a clear link between his combative literary style and his own character, which is remembered as irascible and quite different from that of his sister, who was pious and meek. According to his nephew Ernesto Treccani, he had the air of 'a revolutionary, but not in the communist sense, a revolutionary loner profoundly attached to aristocratic values' or, in other words, monarchist and antifascist ideals. He was capable of important insights, but was often a strange man, and, being nonconformist and intractable, he could not adapt to the fascist world. Even though he was authoritarian and did not open up to his family, his relations with them were good and full of affection. When he died, his nephew Ernesto wrote to his mother recalling his uncle as 'a man who was dear to us' and 'a man of great worth' who had to be 'looked on with respect' (ETL [*Interview*]).

We find that the family's image of him was partly contradicted by some of Giorgio Quartara's behaviour during the 1930s and 1940s. On the whole, he was a man of conflicting natures who wished to enjoy life, love and good food, had many friends, but ultimately was very much on his own. He must have been very close to his mother, who lived until 1936, and this relationship was probably the most important emotional tie in his life. He never married and there are no traces of his sentimental attachments, even though his writings mention his desire for a single great love and reject the definition of womaniser attributed to him by the family: 'It has always been my dream and aspiration to love only one woman in my life, a woman to whom I would be attracted both physically and morally, and I have never taken advantage – as most men do – of the anarchic freedom granted to men in matters of pleasure' (Quartara 1911: 140).

Equally he took offence at the accusations that were probably made against him in the academic world because of the themes he discussed, and he insisted that his aims were 'anything but libertine and revolutionary' (ibid.: Preface). There can be no doubt that he was very attracted to women and, in spite of his feminism, shared the typical attitudes of the Latin male. He recounted that during his journey to Latin America he met a professor of medicine from New York, and they entertained themselves by discussing 'the classification of the beautiful women on board' (Quartara 1939: 20).

He travelled a great deal and went to Latin America on several occasions, where his works were successful, as can be seen from the review that appeared in 1917 in *Nosotros*, a magazine with socialist sympathies founded in Buenos Aires by intellectuals of Italian origin. The reviewer agreed with the idea of a European federation, but considered that of a confederation between the United States of Europe, Asia and America to be utopian (Albasio 1917: 536–38).

Quartara's works were ignored, seized and banned during his life, but even after his death they continued to be veiled in silence. This was in spite of the moving clause that ends his will, 'I urge my heirs to promote my books'.[13] They were the thing he held most dear. His great library was dispersed and everything concerning his studies was lost. Quartara died in 1951 and the Castellaccio was sold to the Archbishopric in 1957. Ernesto Treccani recalls that the heirs were entitled to choose what they wanted from the large family house, and out of loyalty to his convictions of the time, which condemned private property, he only took a Fiat 1500 and renounced his noble title and his second surname, 'degli Alfieri'. A trunk that was lost with Giorgio Quartara's papers contained letters that revealed a secret love story with an unmarried friend of his mother no longer in her youth, with whom he went to India. These letters were read by his nephews and nieces without anyone knowing, and according to a great-nephew the trunk also contained Masonic works (ET 1; ET 2). Only one photograph of Giorgio Quartara has survived and not a single private letter. The one remaining image shows a tall man who was young for his age and looked at his mother with an expression of affection and satisfaction (Fig. 1). We are therefore obliged to fall back on the information that can be gleaned from his reading and writing.

A few clues are provided by the small remaining number of books that belonged to him.[14] Apart from the Michelin Guides from the period around 1900 'on offer to car drivers', the collection includes some family books from the nineteenth century acquired before Giorgio's birth, such as Homer, Dante, Petrarch, Metastasio, Eugène Sue, Malthus, and a collection of ancient and modern poets published in Milan in 1836.

Figure 1 The Marquis Giorgio Quartara with his mother, Vittoria Gavazzi (courtesy of Maestro Ernesto Treccani)

The books published from 1900 onwards, such as Lamarck and Darwin (the latter in French translation), could have belonged to him and demonstrate his interest in natural sciences and biological evolution. The complete plays of Molière, published in Paris in 1932, contain notes written in pencil that appear to express the sentiments of a reader like Quartara, such as those on atheism and the hypocrisy that hides under the cloak of religion in *Don Juan ou le Festin de Pierre*. Even though these texts were only a tiny part of the original library, they provide us with interesting insights into his character and confirm his love of laughter and verbal transgressions, his anticlericalism and his interest in science, all based on a wide-ranging classical education that came from both his mother's and his father's families.

However, our knowledge of Quartara is almost entirely founded on his published works, which when read carefully with reference to his private life do tell us many things, although they also remain silent on much else. There are signs of a close friendship or possibly a love affair with his sister's friend, Lia Gianelli, who later became famous as the maternal aunt of the partisan Giancarlo Puecher. Between the wars, she was a member of the Milanese upper middle class, 'very religious, but not overly so; hers was an intelligent religiosity'. She was a very close friend of his sister, Giulia, who was also very religious. In spite of this difference, Lia Gianelli frequented Giorgio, who was four years older, and they even undertook a trip to Latin America together (although his book on that particular journey makes no mention of his travelling companion). They shared an enthusiasm for travelling. Miss Gianelli was a member of the Milanese branch of the Italian Maritime League, which organised luxury cruises, and she went on many of these, which took her as far as India and Ceylon. They also both believed passionately in the monarchy. They respected each other's different religious views, except on a few rare occasions. The Puecher family tell of an incident that occurred when they arrived in Rio de Janeiro and saw the enormous statue of Christ. Giorgio Quartara is supposed to have exclaimed, 'There he is, the puppet!' and Lia reprimanded him severely, saying that he should feel ashamed of such a quip (P1 [*Interview*]).

Quartara was surrounded on his mother's side by profoundly religious, although not dogmatic, people. An interesting episode is mentioned in *Dalla Guerra Mondiale alla Civiltà Internazionale*, the book published in 1917 that he had Ada carry under her arm. In it he refers to his 'greatly missed cousin', Luigi Gavazzi,[15] who had written a study on the advantages of a customs union for the peoples of the Allied Powers of the First World War. In 1904, Luigi had married Andreina Costa, the daughter of the Russian socialist Anna Kuliscioff, exiled in Italy, which, in the words of his mother-in-law, caused 'an uproar in the newspapers'. In spite of the difference in wealth and ideas, his parents did not oppose the marriage. The newspapers argued that the choice of a religious marriage had to be seen as a triumph of the famously religious Gavazzi family over the other party, but Anna Kuliscioff considered this interpretation to be ridiculous (Turati and Kuliscioff 1977: 162, 169, 174). It can be inferred from all this that at least one branch of Quartara's family on his mother's side was open-minded, in spite of their wealth and political conservatism. It also seems likely that Quartara liked the idea of a great love that united two young people of such different ideological pedigrees.

Giorgio Quartara died suddenly on 2 December 1951 at the Galliera Hospital in Genoa. The death certificate states that he was 'unmarried and well-to-do'.[16] In spite of the convictions he had held throughout his life, a mass was said for him at the request of the other branch of the Quartara family, which was traditionally Catholic.[17] In his will, which was written by himself in Milan on 11 July 1951 on paper showing his coat of arms, the Marquis Quartara, lawyer by training, asked to be cremated: 'any of the subjects who oppose this shall be disinherited'. He left 200,000 lira, as well as the funeral expenses to be paid to the Cremation Society of Milan, of which he was a member.[18] He did not forget to nominate in his will the caretakers of the villa in Genoa, who must have been looking after him in his solitude for some time.

Federal Fraternity

The book under Ada's arm, *Dalla Guerra Mondiale alla Civiltà Internazionale*, was dedicated to 'the Allies' war dead, disabled servicemen and their loved ones' and contained a preface by Vittorio Scialoja. It was Quartara's first work to put forward the idea of a European federation, and it was not without significance that the preface was written by the person who probably converted him to the European ideal.[19] Scialoja's commitment combined international politics and plans for legislation on natural parent–child relationship and the abolition of a husband's authority over his wife. He, therefore, shared the same twin interests as

Quartara, and he may have contributed to them. It was Quartara's essay on the 1865 Article 57 of the Civil Code (Quartara 1910: 73–88) that caused Vittorio Scialoja to invite Quartara to work together at the offices of his legal firm. The essay concerned the uncertainty of paternity, 'the core argument for the laws of free love'. It fiercely criticised the conditions of women in patriarchal society (ibid.: 11), and explained the history of the law that prevented women from remarrying after the dissolution or annulment of a marriage.

Scialoja's duties as the Italian representative at the League of Nations from 1921 to 1932 concerned arms reduction and the peaceful arbitration and settlement of international disputes. At the tenth plenary session of the League of Nations, held on 16 September 1930, he expressed the Italian views on the Memorandum Briand submitted in May on the question of a European federal union. Quartara interpreted this speech over-optimistically in terms of a pan-European agenda (Quartara 1933: 3). Although Scialoja acknowledged the merits of having submitted the project, he followed the fascist government line of coming up with endless obstacles to its realisation, which in reality postponed it *sine die*. His speech rejected the European principle and stressed that the problems posed by Briand could be resolved only by the governments concerned and not by the League of Nations. This confirms Scialoja's ambiguous position once he started to distort his liberalism in order to maintain his support for Mussolini, a position that ultimately led him to right-wing conservatism dominated by nationalism (*Enciclopedia dell'Antifascismo e della Resistenza* 1987: 448).

However, Scialoja was not the only influence leading towards Quartara's support for European federalism; the First World War was another powerful factor pushing him in that direction. We do not know if he personally took part in the war, but in the introduction to *Dalla Guerra Mondiale alla Civiltà Internazionale*, he declares that the war convinced him of the need for states to come together in large federations governed by sophisticated systems of arbitration, while in the longer term they would merge into larger political structures until eventually there would be one political structure for the whole world. However, arbitration is not enough; steps also have to be taken towards a confederation of European states (Quartara 1917). One chapter is devoted to the 'historical crime of the Germans', that of having provoked a European and world war. Quartara does not shy from calling them such extreme and virulent names as 'bestial violators of Belgium' and 'a murderous and thieving people' (ibid.: 27, 29). The text contains a review of plans for peace and European unity, including the great exponents of a European confederation going back to the eighteenth century, as well as an analysis of the various systems of federation. Quartara recommends for the European union a type of federal state in which states renounce most of their autonomy and submit themselves to the central government. They would have to relinquish all rights to representation, particularly in international relations, but could retain complete administrative autonomy.

Quartara was thinking about the alliance in the First World War built around France and Britain and including Russia and Italy. Unification had to take place gradually and had been inspired by wholly liberal values. One important step was a customs union, and on this point he quotes his cousin Luigi Gavazzi's 'invaluable study' published in the fortnightly socialist magazine *Critica Sociale* (Gavazzi 1917: 106–8).[20] Gavazzi's article, published during a period in which peace seemed close, expresses his hope for a customs union embracing the peoples of the allied countries 'with their vast colonies', which would amount to a grouping that would cover most of the globe. There had been talk of this customs union since the 1870s, but it was only in the 1920s that the idea really took off. In 1924, an international committee was set up to promote it by French, German and Hungarian economists, who had an important role in the debate on the United States of Europe.[21] Quartara, who was a member of Union Douanière, had also published an article in *Critica Sociale* in 1915, in which he argued that a European confederation could bring an end to the war through arbitration (Quartara 1915: 359–61). It was only later that he started to attack socialism fiercely.

Dalla Guerra Mondiale alla Civiltà Internazionale contains a precise declaration of the author's political faith, which was that of a founding member of the Radical Party. Quartara was persuaded that all parties would agree on a European programme, whether Catholic, socialist, liberal, centrist, republican or radical (Quartara 1917: 88). The Radical Party, founded in 1904, has been called 'an army of generals without soldiers, deputies or candidates' (Orsina 1998: 10). It was a third force in an intermediate position between socialism and liberalism, which lacked electoral support and membership, but was strategically positioned. Like most of his party, Quartara held to a positivistic faith in progress and in the possibility of applying the experimental method used in science to political phenomena. In his works he occasionally spoke of 'we positivists' to underscore the impartiality and objectivity of his approach (Quartara 1919). He belonged to a minority of radical free marketeers who based their principles on Anglo-Saxon liberalism. One of these, Maffeo Pantaleoni, whom Quartara referred to as his mentor (Quartara 1949), placed the individual and his liberty of action at the very centre of his own social philosophy, and he rejected collectivism and the primacy of the state or political objectives over the individual, which were widely held views in the party at the time. Ultimately he probably appreciated the fact that the Radical Party believed in the sovereignty of the people without adopting an exclusively republican position.

The collection of Quartara's articles published in one of his early books (*I Diritti della Donna e della Prole*) was originally published in *La Vita*, the newspaper founded in 1905 through the efforts of the Radical Party (Orsina 1998: 190). It was co-directed for a period by the suffragette Olga Ossani Lodi, and was alone amongst the male-dominated press in opening its pages to the debate on female emancipation (Buttafuoco 1988).

The Radical Party was well known for its close relationship with Freemasons, based on shared cultural and ideological beliefs, similar aims and strategies, and the fact that many people were members of both. From the early nineteenth century, most Freemasons had been supporters of democracy and argued for the formation of anticlerical alliances ranging from left-wing liberals to socialists (Mola 1999). In fact the Italian Freemasons included members of several parties: monarchists, radicals, republicans, and reformist and revolutionary socialists, as well as members not affiliated to any party. Vittorio Scialoja, whom Quartara always referred to in tones of gratitude and reverence, was probably a 'sleeping' or inactive member of the Freemasons (ibid.; see also Vannoni 1979: 276n.). Quartara also respected and trusted Giuseppe Canepa,[22] whom he described as his 'generous and kindly editor and mentor' (Quartara 1945: 15). Quartara wrote over a long period for *Il Lavoro*, the daily organ of working-class organisations, and Canepa had been its editor since its foundation in 1903.[23] The paper claimed to be independent of the Socialist Party and under fascism it maintained a relatively nonconformist stance. During the Socialist Party's internal conflicts before the First World War, Canepa enlisted the support of the Freemasons to fight off competition from the candidate of the right (Manzotti 1965: 58).

There were, therefore, many connections between Quartara and the Freemasons: the constant company of people like Canepa and Scialoja; his repeated mention of others such as V.E. Orlando, Giovanni Bettolo, Vincenzo Morello, Antonio Salandra and Sydney Sonnino;[24] membership of the Radical Party; contacts with the French daily newspaper *Le Quotidien*; anticlericalism; and the wish to be cremated. He mentioned jurists and politicians like Carlo Schanzer (who was sent by Italy on several occasions to the League of Nations), Epicarmo Corbino and Rattazzi the Younger. They all belonged to the prefascist political class which had a liberal background and was willing to compromise itself considerably with the fascist regime in order to maintain important positions at national and international level.

Even the reference to the 'world' in the title *Gli Stati Uniti d'Europa e del Mondo* could be seen as Masonic, as could another of his titles, *Per l'Umanità*, which was published in 1919 and dedicated to his father who died in 1917. The very term 'federal fraternity' takes up the Masonic theme of 'brotherhood', a key word for Mazzini and Garibaldi. It had a predominantly political meaning within the Freemasonry (Mola 1983: 153–72), and conformed perfectly with the meaning Quartara attributed to 'fraternity' between European peoples.

In spite of these clues, I have not discovered any documentary proof that Giorgio Quartara was a member of the Freemasons.[25] The only mention of the Freemasons in his works appears in *La Donna e Dio* (*Woman and God*), which attacks the fascist regime's clericalism and in particular the law against Masonry of 1925 (Quartara 1944: 239–40). However, there is clear evidence of closeness to the Masons in terms of ideas. The fundamental tenets of the Grand Lodge of Italy were a commitment to democracy, a belief in science and progress, anticlericalism somewhere between atheism and rationalism, the rejection of class struggle and attention to social questions (Novarino 2003: 21), and they are clearly to be found in Quartara's thought. Italian Freemasonry did not always follow this credo. For example, the Grand Lodge of Italy continued to believe in a supreme being, in spite of its anticlericalism (Esposito 1987). This suggests that Quartara was more influenced by Francophile Freemasonry, which was more open to atheism and feminism than the strictly Italian version.

The most significant agreement between Freemasonry and the ideas that appear in Quartara's writings concerned Europeanism and Europeanness. The importance of the European dimension in the history of Freemasonry has been established, as has the converse significance of Freemasonry in the creation of a Europe that acts as a space for the circulation of ideas and persons (Cazzaniga 1999; Beaurepaire 2002). Nineteenth-century Freemasonry believed in the idea of the United States of Europe, often with an anti-Christian slant. Adriano Lemmi, who was the Italian Grand Master from 1885 to 1896, constantly used the adjective 'inevitable' in relation to the future European federation. Masons saw such a federation as a first step towards a universal federation or United States of the World (the same expression used by Quartara) that would remove all the barriers between peoples and create 'the reunited human family' (Esposito 1979: 304). Masonic Europeanism took up Mazzini's ideals and message that the continent should become an ideal and physical space defined as 'humanity' (Comba 1983: 141–51) and representing a way to reconcile humanitarian universalism with nationalism.

This Europeanism also developed on a practical level and promoted an institution for international arbitration to resolve conflicts between nations, to which Quartara attributed much importance. The Freemasons can take the credit for helping to introduce a spirit of non-aggression in international relations and associating pacifism with free-market economics. They consequently were interested in putting forward proposals at an international level for supranational legal structures. Between 1902 and 1936 many Freemasons received the Nobel Peace Prize. International institutions promoted by Freemasonry from many countries and not only Italy included the International Court at The Hague and even the League of Nations. The founder of Paneuropa, Count Richard Coudenhove-Kalergi, was initiated in Vienna in 1922, in the liberal and pacifist lodge 'Humanitas'. The foreign ministers Aristide Briand and Gustav Stresemann, both exponents of a rapprochement between France and Germany, and supporters of the League of Nations, shared the Nobel Peace Prize in 1926. The former was close to the Freemasons and the second was a Freemason (Combes 1986).

In September 1929, Briand put his proposals for a European Union to the League of Nations. It was to be a union that stretched to the Baltic States and reached to borders of the USSR. The proposals were well received, but he had no success with his Memorandum of 17 May 1930 calling for a European conference of all European governments in the League of Nations in order to create a federation with a common market. Stresemann's death in

1929 and Briand's in 1932 finally killed off the project. As we have already seen in Scialoja's speech, Italy did not support the Memorandum.

Pacifism was another area of agreement between Quartara's professed ideas and the Freemasons, which combined cosmopolitanism, humanitarianism and pacifism. Their fundamental beliefs had always included brotherhood and tolerance, the essential elements for creating peace (Novarino 1996: 23–32). In the second half of the nineteenth century, the pacifist movement developed in a Europe dominated by the balance of powers, and it created a new civic conscience in relation to the international community in general and the European community in particular (Grossi 1994). The slogan of a United States of Europe was associated with various movements, including the feminist one. During the period between the wars, international peace conferences often brought together feminist associations such as the International Women Suffrage Alliance, pacifist associations, some religious associations and the International Masonic Association (Ferrer Benimeli and de Paz Sanchez 1991: 150–51). This was precisely the period in which new forms of pacifism were developed, such as the feminist and dissident radical ones, although they were not always in agreement with each other (Ingram 1993: 31–32).

Quartara shared the moderate pacifism of the Masons, which stopped short of the fundamental and absolute pacifism of American and British origin, often based on an ethical and religious interpretation, and favoured a qualified and democratic pacifism that did not reject war per se and acknowledged its legitimacy in self-defence or when rights or justice are threatened (Conti 2003a: 231–40). This is precisely the position adopted by Scialoja in the preface to Quartara's book. Indeed, Freemasonry not only supported the struggle of peoples for independence and rights, such as those fought by the Cubans and Cretans during the nineteenth century, but in Italy even defended the country's expansionist plans into the Adriatic and the Balkans after 1917. Besides, many middle-class pacifists, like Teodoro Moneta and Guglielmo Ferrero, supported Italian involvement in the First World War (Moneta, who won the Nobel Peace Prize in 1907, even supported the war in Libya) (Oliva 1993).[26] Given this heterogeneous nature of the pacifist movement, which brought together very different political currents, the pacifist debate became bound up with the debate on anticolonialism, but the two positions did not always coincide. Indeed, colonialism was considered a means for avoiding war, because it reduced the demographic pressure in Europe (Spironelli 1998: 169–70). We find similar positions in Quartara's works.

Lastly, the emancipation of women was taken up by the Freemasons, although they were strongly against mixed lodges and limited themselves to supporting the material and moral emancipation of women. This was particularly true in Italy, while France became the exception since Maria Deraismes and George Martin established a mixed lodge in Paris as early as 1893 (Vigni and Vigni 1997). In Italy, the exclusion of women from public life started to be challenged in the second half of the nineteenth century, because it excluded them from the new secular elite and left them under the influence of the Church. The Masonic membership produced proposals for a more equitable position for women in society, but they did not go so far as complete equality. One of the areas where they failed to do so concerned public office. Women had to be guided towards their 'moral' emancipation through a complete education free from prejudice (Vigni 1990: 187–96). One question about which Freemasons were particularly concerned was prostitution. Here again Quartara was in agreement, but his closeness to the scientific and materialist tradition meant that he could not share views to be found in relations between Masons and women, which included the theme of spiritual regeneration and mysticism (Scaraffia and Isastia 2002).

Quartara's ambivalent attitude towards fascism was in part connected to his closeness to Freemasonry. There is a complex history of relations between the Masons and fascism in Italy. At the beginning, Masons strongly supported fascism, which they much preferred to socialism and the liberal policies of Prime Minister Giolitti. Many fascists were members of Masonic lodges, while many Masons took part in the March on Rome and became members of the Fascist Party. Good relations continued during the very early period of the regime, in spite of differences over the attitude to the Church. However, relations broke down at the beginning of 1923, when Mussolini, now secure in government, would no longer tolerate the presence of other centres of power. In the face of fascist threats, the Freemasons adopted a defensive and subservient attitude, and restricted themselves to pronouncements on their patriotism. However, when Giacomo Matteotti was murdered in 1924, their response was to condemn it. During this period, fascist gangs destroyed Masonic premises and private homes in many parts of the country. In 1925, all associations, including Freemasonry, became illegal. The Masons themselves decided to dissolve their organisation with a decree from the Grand Master Domizio Torrigiani, condemned to five years of forced residence in a remote place in 1927.[27]

The Masonic origins of the idea of Europe contained in Quartara's works explains the mixture of practical and utopian elements in his Europeanism. In order to put his ideas in context, it is important to remember their similarity with those of Paneuropa, whose founder, Coudenhove-Kalergi, knew of Quartara's book *Gli Stati Uniti d'Europa e del Mondo*. In 1932 Quartara received an invitation to take part in the Third Congress of Paneuropa, which was held in Basel in September of that year. His reply on 9 September 1932 was to accept the invitation with pleasure and to compliment the count for his 'worthy and admirable' efforts.[28]

According to the account that appeared in *Paneuropa*, the official organ of the association, the Basel Congress was opened on Saturday 1 October 1932 by the Basler Liedertafel Choir, which sang Beethoven's 'Die Ehre Gottes in der Natur'. This was followed by a welcome from the leader of the cantonal government and greetings from representatives of the twenty-three countries taking part, each in his or her own language 'in an atmosphere of true European solidarity'. Marquis Giorgio Quartara brought greetings from Italy and gave a speech on 'The Organisation of European Peace through a Federation' (Quartara 1932). Other speakers included Coudenhove-Kalergi, Leo S. Amery (previously the British minister for the colonies), and Selma Lagerlöf. Patrons included Ortega y Gasset and Germaine Malaterre-Sellier, the vice-president of the International Women Suffrage Alliance.[29]

Quartara's speech in Basel supported Briand's programme, but introduced an important difference: it no longer made economic union the priority for achieving a European federation. It had to be admitted that the efforts of the Union Douanière Européenne, 'of which', Quartara said, 'we have the honour of being an enthusiastic member', had only managed to obtain warm words of agreement from European governments. He proposed an opposing route that started from political interests by setting up three supranational ministries in Geneva: for war, foreign affairs and joint finances. A European popular referendum would achieve a favourable vote on this issue, because it would be supported by mothers and soldiers. Quartara referred to 'Switzerland, this admirable country that is hosting us now, and a perfect example of the utility of a federation of three great European nationalities'. He did not fail to put forward Italy's territorial claims, but he did it without aggression or chauvinism, 'Italy believes that some of its regions are still under foreign domination'. He felt that this question could only be resolved within a European union (Quartara 1932: 117n.).

In his memoirs, Coudenhove-Kalergi attributes to Quartara a more official role in the Basel Congress than he could actually have had. In his opinion, Mussolini, who had ignored the first two congresses of the pan-European movement, held in Vienna in 1926 and Berlin in 1930, in 1932 gave permission for an Italian delegate, namely Marquis Quartara, to take part in the third congress (Coudenhove-Kalergi 1943). While it is true that Quartara was not prevented from going to Basel, it could not be claimed that he represented Italy. He insisted on the importance of the Briand Memorandum and its central position in any European programme, whereas the fascist regime had discouraged its implementation. Perhaps Coudenhove-Kalergi's opinion was based on a third letter from Quartara sent in 1936, in which the latter thanked him for his invitation to the congress in the autumn of the following year, but declared that he could come 'without saying or writing anything, because I no longer have permission'.[30] In fact, Asvero Gravelli had represented Italy at the Vienna Congress of 1935.

In his relations with Paneuropa, Mussolini adopted his typically opportunistic attitude, veering between various positions according to what appeared to be in his interests at any one particular moment. This is demonstrated by Count Coudenhove-Kalergi's own account of relations with the Italian dictator. Mussolini encouraged and subsidised the magazine *Antieuropa* directed by Asvero Gravelli, which combined fascist ideals and pan-European ideas, and the count wrote, 'Gravelli attacked us in every issue and promoted the idea of a European union under Mussolini's moral guidance'. He concluded that in practice this had the opposite effect of preaching pan-European ideas to fascist Italy. According to Coudenhove-Kalergi, Mussolini had tended towards a broader European policy since concluding the Lateran Pacts with the Catholic Church. His promotion of a four-sided alliance between Italy, France, Germany and Great Britain could be interpreted as a pan-European initiative, and therefore Coudenhove-Kalergi hoped to encourage the Italian dictator along the path of this new strategy. While he had worked for reconciliation between Germany and France between 1924 and 1932, the count radically changed his position after Hitler came to power and opted for a Franco-Italian alliance with the inclusion of Austria, Czechoslovakia, Poland, the Balkans and Belgium.[31]

Mussolini allowed Coudenhove-Kalergi to express his views freely, and pretended to be in agreement or at least uncertain and willing to be persuaded. They had at least three discussions between 1933 and 1936, during which the count explained his new strategy: a powerful 'Latin Europe' founded on a Franco-Italian axis that would resist Hitler's hegemonic ambitions in Europe. In a conversation between them that took place in May 1936, Mussolini used all his charm and powers of persuasion. He treated his visitor 'as an old friend' and asked him to contact Léon Blum, who was preparing to form a Popular Front government and, therefore, could never have cooperated with fascist Italy. However, when the count returned in July to Mussolini's government residence, Palazzo Venezia, to report on his impossible mission, he found that the dictator was now unreservedly allied to Germany (Coudenhove-Kalergi 1943: 176).

On some points, Quartara was entirely in agreement with Coudenhove-Kalergi. One of these was the idea of an alliance between Italy and France, which other European nations would then join. Another point of agreement was a Europeanism characterised by 'benevolent' colonialism, an attitude common in the Italian Radical Party. It claimed to be a humanitarian concept of colonialism, as distinct from imperialism, and it aimed to civilise the less evolved peoples without the use of violence. One of the principal items in Paneuropa's programme was that the founding nations of the European federation should bring their colonies with them to share the advantages of exploiting a Eurafrica that would have united civilised white races with primitive black ones, thus resolving the national divisions between Europeans (Ellena 2004: 241–72).

Finally, a crucial aspect of Quartara's Europeanism was its anticommunist function of containing the Soviet Union. As the years went by, his polemic against socialism and communism became increasingly virulent. He believed that a system of thoroughgoing laissez-faire economics was the only way to resolve the problems of poverty, 'the wasting disease' of capitalism, along with a state with social responsibilities capable of guaranteeing the 'right to life'. He reasserted these positions in *Per l'Umanità*, in which he reviewed a wide range of welfare systems in various countries inside and outside Europe. He reproached socialists for favouring the interests of male privileged workers over women and less privileged men. In other works, he attacked 'the fabulously rich Marx and his faithful lieutenant, Engels'. His criticisms were occasionally worthy of note, when he observed, for example, that *The Manifesto of the Communist Party* contains principles that are

shared by liberal and radical parties, but there is not a single word
on the old, the disabled, mothers or those who have been struck by
calamities, nor is there anything about free love. His harshest words
are reserved for Lenin, the 'red dictator' (Quartara 1934: 62, 70),
whose rise to power was due to Kerensky. Quartara felt that the
latter should have retained tsarism in the form of a constitutional
monarchy. His ideal was a British-style constitutional monarchy
that implemented 'radical' social reform (Quartara 1919: 343) which
could meet socialism head on: 'Every council must have its home for
old people, disabled people, mothers and their children who do not
have their own home or the home of relations or friends, even when
the state pays them a pension. State pensions must be introduced for
old age, disability, maternity and childhood.'

The European federation was supposed to be the guarantor of
this reform, an idea that was shared at the time by other supporters
of European unification in other countries, such as Margaret Storm
Jameson in England (Passerini 1999: 239–47). One key element in
the radical reform envisaged by Quartara concerned marriage and
the family: only the future federation would be able to offer the
total renewal of sexual relations.

Family Law and Matriarchy

Quartara's main proposal concerning free love was the radical
transformation of family law, which constituted his primary
intellectual interest and remained so throughout his life. His first
book, *I Diritti della Donna e della Prole*, published in 1911, put
forward his basic positions on matrimony and love, to which he was
to return many times later in his life. He supported equal rights for
legitimate and illegitimate children, the repeal of marital authority,
female suffrage, the right of women to practise all professions and
stand for all public offices, and divorce following the example of the
procedure introduced by the French Revolution in 1792 (which
included the wish of a single spouse as a cause for divorce), as well
as the example of ancient Rome. He fiercely disagreed with state
regulation of prostitution.

Quartara perceived these reforms for the immediate future within
a historical context that presupposed the existence of an original
matriarchy. He recalled that during his university days in Rome,
'professors and course books took matriarchy to be an established
fact' (Quartara 1911: 132), and invited 'Italian women' to translate

the 'truly immortal' Swiss thinker Johann Jacob Bachofen in response to Westermarck, who rejected the idea of an original matriarchy. Quartara knew the principal texts that gave rise to the late-eighteenth-century debate on the origins of the family, primitive communism and kinship systems, including the theories of original matriarchy. Quartara based his arguments on Bachofen's *Mutterrecht* (1861), John McLennan's *Primitive Marriage* (1865) and Lewis Morgan's *Ancient Society* (1877). Friedrich Engels used the same texts for *The Origin of the Family, Private Property and the State*, although Quartara does not mention it, probably out of his loathing for communism.

Basing himself on the Enlightenment works of such writers as Voltaire, Montesquieu and Diderot, Quartara emphasised the benefits of sexual freedom as against European customs and laws, which not only violated civil rights but also crushed 'the most sublime impulses of the heart', as Quartara wrote with particular reference to the conditions of illegitimate children and unmarried mothers. In his opinion, Christianity was the original cause of their pariah status: it was 'a product of history that differed greatly from Christ's gentle philosophy and religion' (Quartara 1911: 45), and it had arrogated family legislation and subjugated the whole of Europe to its narrow precepts.

In place of ecclesiastical regulations, Quartara proposed a system based on love, which 'is as universal as suffering' (Quartara 1930: vi). By love he meant a heterosexual union that always involved a physical relationship. His approach had important legal consequences. On the basis of the assertion that 'only a union without love is immoral' (Quartara 1911: 78), any sexual relationship that leads to procreation has to be considered on a par with marriage and the man has to fulfil his responsibilities. At the same time, there can be no recognition of the crime of adultery, as this conflicts with personal freedom. Love presupposes the free will of both partners, a faculty wholly denied to women and in particular young women who, unlike men, are forced to enter marriage in a state of virginity. Quartara adopted a very firm stance on this point and argued that all marriages contracted in Italy by virgin women could, without exception, be annulled by them on the basis of Article 105 of the Civil Code, 'a marriage may be contested by one of the spouses, where that spouse did not give consent freely' (ibid.: 86).

The reforms Quartara was most interested in and competent to speak on were of a legal nature. He believed the 'legal subjugation of women' to be at the root of many evils, including prostitution, which in Italy was governed by laws introduced by Crispi and his successors. Compared with Cavour's law of 1860, the law of 1888 was in fact a partial move towards abolitionism, but its efficacy was soon undermined by bureaucratic measures introduced by those who preferred it to be regulated. It was as late as 1958 before Italy got an abolitionist law comparable with the English one of the 1880s or the American one of 1910 (Gibson 1986: 65 ff.). The fascist statutes of 1923, 1931 and 1940 also aimed to regulate prostitution. Quartara proposed severe penalties against anyone running brothels or attracting business to them (Quartara 1911: 109), and more generally he wanted to abolish all clauses in the Civil Code that denied the principle of equality, such as the need for a husband's authorisation which he defined as 'illogical and unjust' (ibid.: 114). It was partially abolished in 1919.

Quartara would return to these themes and develop them further in later works, but some personal obsessions had already appeared, such as matriarchy and marriages between young women and old men. He projected his own aspirations onto the supposed original matriarchy, and defined 'the gynaecocratic epoch [as] the poetry of history'. He unconditionally approved what he believed to be a matriarchal rule: the chastity of young men. This fantastic vision satisfied his aesthetic passion for 'statuesque' bodies. In no other era, he argued, was there greater consideration for beauty of the body and respect for its inviolability. It was a vision of matriarchy spiced up with nostalgic fantasies of a sacred embrace in which 'an extraordinarily beautiful woman, who represented the divinity, directed the sacred functions of propitiating love for all, and with a most beautiful man demonstrated on a raised piece of ground all the allures of love, including their complete fulfilments' (ibid.: 134).

These visions prefigured a future capable of founding a matriarchy, which would reappear in accordance with Vico's cyclical laws of ebb and flow (*corsi e ricorsi*), along with civil and political equality between the sexes, without which it would be impossible to restore perfectly that golden age:

[A]ll couples shall be equally young, equally beautiful and equally in love; life shall be transformed for the entire nation and become for everyone noble, pure, attractive and truly human; the law shall tear happiness away from the stage, from poetry and the novel to distribute it amongst the crowd. Civil and political equality! That shall be the motto. (ibid.: 143)

In the Genoese newspaper *Il Lavoro*, Quartara found a platform from which to express these ideas, occasionally in unsigned articles that can reasonably be attributed to him.[32] However, he really developed them in his main work, *Le Leggi del Libero Amore* (1928), which is more than 600 pages long and dedicated 'To women'. This work was a tremendous effort to systemise and document his beliefs, and contains a vast bibliography, detailed information on legislation and several tables with statistics on many countries around the world.[33]

His comparative study of different legislation awarded the laurels to England. Although he acknowledged some admirable aspects of the Soviet legislation (such as absolute equality of women in relation to their husbands and children, and parity between all children), Quartara argued that the Soviet legal system was defective because it did not take into account the work women carried out in the domestic sphere. As a fervent monarchist, he reproached the Bolsheviks for having overthrown the tsars who, in his opinion, 'had bequeathed a magnificent feminist inheritance on the vile revolution' (i.e., the separation of assets within marriage and divorce). He proposed that communism should renounce its boastfulness, break up its vast Russian territories, and offer them to women as their absolute property on which to establish matriarchy (Quartara 1928: 405).

The work's ambitions go beyond legal proposals. It constituted a comprehensive survey on the female condition, structured in parts devoted to women's 'sufferings': the suffering of wives, lovers, prostitutes, spinsters and nuns, as well as 'a history of women's martyrdom in newspaper reports'. Quartara was highly sensitive to the daily violence inflicted on women and reported in the crime sections of daily newspapers. He argued compassionately that all female conditions contain an element of suffering, 'everywhere women in tears' (ibid.: 3).

He engaged in a sustained polemic against the 'antichristian aberrations of canon law', which included celibacy for priests, a sign of serious decay. He reminded readers that Jesus never proclaimed the inferiority of women in any of his parables; indeed, everything he said asserted the social equality of everyone who loves God (ibid.: 570), and declared that 'if God exists, those swindlers who pass themselves off as canonists will have a nasty surprise when they wake up in the next life!' (ibid.: 574). However, the Catholics were not the only targets of Quartara's attacks; there were also the socialists and the followers of Cesare Lombroso.

Among the latter he included not only Lombroso himself but also Lambert Quetelet and Angelo Messedaglia.[34] He considered them all to be 'frivolous exponents of a false and offensive theory that put female prostitution on a par with male criminality!' (Quartara 1928: 155–56). He countered their arguments with statistics on prostitution and criminality in many countries which demonstrate 'the colossal superiority of women', given that four out of five criminals in Italy and abroad were men and less than one out of five were women (ibid.: 173). The statistics demonstrate not only the 'massacre of women', but also the 'shameful acquittals', and the fact that when it came to violent crimes against the person, such as rape and abductions, infinitely more were committed against women. On the other hand, the typically female crimes of abortion and infanticide 'would disappear with changes to the male laws that force mothers to carry out such despicable outrages against the inviolable fruit of their wombs. Only then should they be punished' (ibid.: 183).

Quartara firmly argued that prostitution is not criminal because when women prostitute themselves they deal in their own bodies and do not damage anyone else. As with many questions that were close to his heart, Quartara introduced his own experiences into the discussion on prostitution. He vividly described his visit at the age of twenty-one to a brothel in Via Frattina in Rome, where he had been attracted 'having seen a young woman's fresh and attractive face'. It was the girl's first day in that life, but she refused to escape as he advised, although from then on she showed him gratitude and trusted him. He would see her 'at very long intervals' over the next two years and was able to witness her progressive decline. She had lost her beauty through this life: 'flabbiness, cheeks burnt by make-up, glassy and expressionless eyes, a coldness in her elation, the sensuality offered grown perverted and virtually unfeeling, and a false smile' (ibid.), Quartara declared in an almost clinical tone, but not without compassion.

On the question of prostitution, he also quoted with approval from the works of Giuseppe Tammeo and Guillaume-Schack,[35] which showed that on this point he was familiar with the latest international ideas. Quartara was in fact in agreement with the abolitionist movement, which had its roots in the Enlightenment and could be defined as pan-European, as it was active in many European countries in the campaign against what it defined as modern slavery induced by state-regulated brothels (Gibson 1986: 39 ff.). He attacked the socialists because they argued that prostitution was an institution so ingrained in bourgeois reality that it could not be abolished without the destruction of the related economic system. He was angered by Nordau,[36] because he criticised 'the charlatans who propose the emancipation of women': 'We feminist free marketeers are supposed to be charlatans. But who is really the charlatan? The feminist or the socialist?' (Quartara 1928: 41–42).

He was kinder to Bebel who, 'as a good and honest socialist, does not show signs of much education', but has 'such a feminist heart that he has gained the gratitude of us feminists' (ibid.: 28). This was a notable concession, given that August Bebel, the author of *Die Frau und der Sozialismus* (*Women and Socialism*), was the co-founder of the German Social Democratic Party. However, Quartara warns women against everyone: 'Women, expect salvation from your own forces, and not from black, grey, red or many-coloured charlatans. Trust no one but yourselves. Be simply feminists!' (Quartara 1928: 43). He therefore distanced himself from those exponents of free love who set the proposal in the context of a socialist or anarchist critique of bourgeois society. The Masonic anarchist Charles-Albert produced a work along these lines in Paris in 1898, which was translated into Italian in 1921 with a preface by Leda Rafanelli.[37]

The section on the suffering of 'spinsters' devoted a great deal of space to the right of women to enter all professions. The bibliography is again particularly significant and reveals a network of ideas, books and people in Europe at the time. As well as to Bebel and John Stuart Mill, whose *Subjection of Women* had been translated into Italian by Anna Maria Mozzoni, a feminist, suffragette and follower of Mazzini, he referred to the works of Jeanne Chauvin, Leroy-Beaulieu and Ostrogorski, all representative of the emancipationist culture at the turn of the century.[38] The reference to Ostrogorski, even though known only through translation, demonstrates that the Europe of these reforming and innovative writers also extended to the East.[39]

On the basis of these texts and an analysis of the Italian situation, Quartara fiercely attacked the exclusion of women from some teaching posts introduced in 1927 by the fascist regime. He forcefully declared that the exclusion of women from the diplomatic service went against justice, logic and utility, given that female diplomacy would bring harmony to international politics.

In this work, the author also used his knowledge and rhetorical skills to demand female suffrage and to argue against those who accused the suffragettes of engaging in a struggle that did not interest women. Even in the European states in which women already had the vote, it was too recent an event to allow 'its benefits [to bear] fruit', but European suffragettes were not to give up the struggle for their own civil rights and those of their children, and for perpetual peace (Quartara 1928: 600).

Le Leggi del Libero Amore concludes with a letter to the 'kind [woman] reader' that appealed to her to overcome political difference and create 'a common programme of emancipation':

> Organise yourselves: all of you join some women's association, link up the various associations and make them economically powerful. Money counts more than sentiment. If every woman, whether affluent or working for her living, were to pay her own feminist party one lira every month, you would gather every month enough millions to uphold through the press and your party the entirely sacred demands for yourselves and your children against the injustice of men.
>
> Act, struggle and prevail!
>
> Life must shine with civilisation ... the mythical golden age shall reappear on earth. (Ibid.: 636)

The manner in which *Le Leggi del Libero Amore* was received, after publication in 1928, must have disappointed the author. During the following summer, he met Aldo Moor of *Corriere della Sera*, who informed Quartara that he had read his book with great interest. He had then written a review full of praise, which was, however, rejected by the newspaper's editor on advice from the prefect. The book had in fact been included in the lists of literary works prohibited by the Catholic Church, which were not made public until 20 January 1945 (Quartara 1910: 57).

Political opportunism certainly provided the regime with reasons for not welcoming the book, even though it contained many proposals that Quartara was to put forward in his Memorandum of 1930, which met with Mussolini's approval. Those reasons included the book's fierce anticlericalism during a period in which the state and the Church were moving closer together, and his criticisms of the policy on women and the professions, and the fact that Mussolini did not wish to concede female suffrage. By no means the least important reason was the divergence from contemporary morality and the advocacy of laissez-faire in sexual relations.

In *Le Leggi del Libero Amore*, Quartara did not lose the opportunity to express graphically his horror at marriages between beautiful young women and old men. I have defined this aspect as voyeuristic, and it could be called pornographic in the broader or figurative sense of the term. It is important to note the close relationship between Quartara's public declarations and their roots in his own private life, the machismo of his defence of women, and the relative 'candour' of his voyeurism. It is already clear that the public and the private cannot be divided in this author's works, both from the way he treated the protagonists of the Genoese dialogue and from the various digressions in his non-fictional writing, such as his personal experiences of prostitution, which he did not hesitate to narrate.

At the beginning of *Le Leggi del Libero Amore*, Quartara used beach life as a source of important observations. He invited the reader to sit on a rock, as he perhaps liked to do, and observe 'older, ugly, sickly, scrawny, vulgar, unfaithful or depraved husbands', who are partnered with 'magnificent young wives of twenty or twenty-five years'. He was particularly distressed by 'an unhappy goddess' surrounded by a 'pretentious and jealous' husband, a mother-in-law who stood guard during his brief absences, and 'three gangling and surly sons' (Quartara 1928: 7) who bore witness to the woman's 'unhappy faithfulness'. At the moment of leaving with her repulsive family, the woman exchanged a glance with Quartara, whose attention she must have noticed. Her glance was a 'flashing blade', and he immediately asked himself whether the woman perceived, 'by way of contrast with the obscene revelation of the first night of her marriage, a sudden carnal vision of a sacred ideal love?' (ibid.: 7).

Drawn by this description, Quartara did not conceal his passion for dance shows that exalt the naked body. He recalled the Folies Bergères in Paris 'with naked or almost naked men and women', particularly a famous scene of Adam and Eve driven from the Earthly Paradise. He admired French liberty, but disapproved of any scene that suggested sadomasochism, and pointed out that even in Italy 'such obscenities are permitted in various famous brothels, where there are special leather whips for sadists available to customers and rubber dildos for women' (ibid.: 17).

For Quartara nudity and spectacle recall the original sacredness of the naked body and the sexual act, but he was also personally attracted to their pleasures. I defined his voyeurism as candid because it is openly confessed, but at the same time he defends himself against what he considers to be perversions. There remains the gaze, one principal component of machismo and masculinity in Mediterranean culture: the stare that cannot avoid assessing, comparing and cataloguing women's bodies and constitutes an eroticism that borders on the pornographic and, even when shared by women, puts greater value on the man as the dominant sex (Poulain 2000: 51–77). The insistence of the gaze, whether open or secret, and the detail of the descriptions were key elements of classical libertinism, with the associations of subtle seduction but also physical and moral violence. For this reason, Quartara feels the need to defend himself against the possible accusation of having strayed into sadism. It is not without significance that he owned the first edition of Bataille's *Histoire de l'Œil*, but what interests us here are his admiration for women as women and his defence of them as feminists.

'We Feminists and Free Traders'

Starting from his own positions on the history of civilisation and family law, Quartara came to adopt feminism as a personal commitment. There was an undeniable similarity between many of his arguments and the battles of some Italian feminists. Suffice it to recall that since 1872 Anna Maria Mozzoni had been campaigning against state-controlled prostitution and that all the feminist associations with their different political orientations shared the aims of female suffrage, legal equality, the establishment of paternal duties, equal pay and the rejection of state-regulated prostitution (Buttafuoco 1992: 21–45).[40]

At the end of the 1920s, Quartara was in contact with Ada and Beatrice Sacchi, and they found themselves in agreement on a great many ideas. He may have met Ada Sacchi in Genoa, where she graduated in literature and philosophy (Camatti 1994: 203–18), and Beatrice Sacchi in Rome, but apart from personal acquaintance, they may have known each other through their writing, given that Beatrice too was a contributor to *La Vita*, the publication close to the Radical Party. Ada was the name of the protagonist of *Gli Stati Uniti d'Europa e del Mondo*, which was published in 1930. The biographies of the two sisters show the wealth of ideas in Italian feminism, its involvement with welfarism and the promotion of women in the professions, and its integration of the national and international feminist networks with which Quartara was associated.

Ada and Beatrice came from a family that had been heavily committed to the patriotic movement during the Risorgimento (Farina 1995; Taricone 1995; *I Sacchi di Mantova* 1997). Ada, born in 1874, married Quintavalle Simonetta in 1899 and had three children. After a few years as a schoolteacher, she became the director of the municipal library and museum of her native city. She opened the library to as many people as possible, and also founded small libraries, one for the working class and others for soldiers. She was untiring in her organisational work in many fields:[41] 'I leave myself no time for leisure or amusement. I am very rarely to be seen out for a stroll, at the theatre, in a café, or in any other way passing my time without working', she wrote in a letter in 1917. However, because of the discrimination against her sex, her salary was lower than that of the vice-director at the same municipal library.

In Mantua, 'Mrs Sacchi Simonetta's aversion to fascism was well known', as the Legazione dei Fasci Femminili (the fascist women's organisation) wrote to the councillor responsible for education (Camatti 1994: 216). Consequently, she lost her post as library director in 1925, but remained active as the chairwoman of FISEDD (the Italian Federation for Women's Suffrage and Civil and Political Rights), the Italian section of one of the largest international feminist movements, the International Women Suffrage Alliance (IWSA), which even today is to be found in eighty countries around the world, but no longer in Italy. In 1935, she was replaced by a leading figure in the fascist women's organisation, who moved the IWSA offices to those of the fascist organisation, and very soon the IWSA effectively ceased to exist. Ada died in Brazil during the Second World War.

Beatrice, who was four years younger than Ada, became known for having put herself forward as a socialist candidate in the Budrio electoral list between 1904 and 1906, which was only possible because Italian constitutional law did not explicitly ban women from standing for political office, although it did ban them from voting for it. Her gesture encouraged other Italian women to attempt the same thing, but after several hearings their petitions were rejected by the courts. Beatrice, or Bice as she was known, graduated in mathematics, but was also interested in botany. She supported Italy's intervention in the First World War, and was a contributor to *Avanti!* and *La Vita*. Together with Ada, she took part in the organisation of the 9th Congress of the IWSA, which was held in Rome in 1923, and was active in its Italian section. She married Alberto Ducceschi and had no children; she died in 1931 (Taricone 1995).[42]

Ada was the chairwoman of FISEDD for seven years. The American Declaration of Independence was one of the founding principles of the IWSA, which was established in 1902 by a decision of the National American Suffrage Association. The IWSA offered bourgeois suffragettes an international resource that countered the influence of socialism. It competed with and emulated the Second

International, but the two organisations did influence each other. After the First World War, the IWSA's programme included universal suffrage, abolition of slavery, the right of married women to their own nationality and property, parental rights, pensions for widows, rights for illegitimate children, the demand for the same moral criteria to be applied to both men and women, and the suppression of trafficking for the prostitution market.[43] As we have seen, Quartara agreed on all these points.

Ada was one of the twelve Italian delegates at the 9th Congress of the IWSA, which was held in Rome in 1923 (*Ninth IWSA Congress Report* 1923; the list of Italian delegates is on pp. 13–14). It was the congress at which Mussolini appeared in order to make one of his theatrical performances. He entered with a large following of fascist officials and blackshirts, and he shook hands with all members of the international executive committee (Schreiber and Mathieson 1955). In his speech to welcome two thousand women from forty nations, Mussolini promised in rather vague terms that he would guarantee some political rights to widows and mothers of the war dead, a promise that turned out to be entirely hollow.[44] At the 11th Congress of the IWSA, which was held in Berlin in 1929, Ada announced that the Italian federation had been re-established after a hiatus, with eight branches in the same number of cities (*Ninth IWSA Congress Report* 1929: 417–19).[45]

In many ways, Quartara was very close to the positions of the IWSA and FISEDD, particularly when it came to the attempt to create an alternative to socialism, although on some matters his ideas were more radical, as in the case of divorce. He worked with Beatrice Sacchi on the initiatives to modify the reform of family law. During the so-called sixty-year period of no reform that went from the Civil Code of 1865 up to the First World War, several proposals for reform on single issues were put forward, particularly on divorce and the status of married women, but they generally failed to achieve a result. The significant legislative reform was in 1919, when marital authority was abolished and women were admitted to the professions and most public offices. During the interwar years there was a process of reform of the Civil Code that led up to its codification in 1942 (Ungari 2002). During the preliminary sessions of the commissions that prepared the reform, Quartara repeatedly put forward his arguments in articles and the 1930 Memorandum sent to the Minister of Justice (see 'Memoriale' in *Conference Reports*).

In this memorandum, which so caught Mussolini's interest that he sent its author a message through the prefect of Milan, Quartara wrote his observations on the project for a new criminal code in relation to women and children.[46] Particularly interesting are the parts on seduction, which he felt should be liable to criminal proceedings if the woman is younger than twenty-one years, and on abduction and rape, in relation to which he adopted a drastic position, 'the man should be condemned to death, because raping a woman is like murdering her'. On abortion, Quartara considers it 'right to permit abortion for women possessed by drunken, sick or criminal husbands, and always for raped women'. Quartara went so far as to talk of a 'legal massacre of women' and attacked the Italian Civil Code that 'contained the shameful distinction between a husband's adultery and a wife's, a distinction that is as humiliating as the lack of divorce'.

There was no shortage of the ritual references to Mussolini, who had opened new horizons in law, and homage was paid to 'his Excellency the Duce's unfailing and intuitively exact will, which is justly concerned about safeguarding families and births'. Even the references to Rome's great heritage could be interpreted in this context as a flirtation with the regime. The document concludes by asking 'pardon of your Excellency for its excessive liveliness in many places', which is justified on the basis of its not being 'truly personal, but simply objective'.

The recommendations in the memorandum written by Bice Sacchi and Valeria Benetti Brunelli, and sent by Ada to the IWSA in early 1930, were very similar to Quartara's.[47] The importance attributed to legal reforms by this wing of the feminist movement could be explained by the limitations imposed by fascism on feminist activity. Whereas it has been a crucial theme for Quartara for some time, not all Italian feminists shared this position; for example Teresa Labriola disagreed with a strategy centred upon the legal battle for the emancipation of women, which was the central plank of *Le Leggi del Libero Amore* (Taricone 1994).

Women's reactions to this book were both for and against. An early and very favourable review by Camilla Bisi appeared in *Il Lavoro*; she believed that the book was 'inspired by a highest moral standard, challenges conformism', and expressed 'an almost stupefied sense of joy' on encountering 'this friendly voice of an intelligent man' (Bisi 1930: 3). Other reactions were very critical, however, and demonstrated the internal differences within Italian feminism. Teresa Labriola fiercely attacked both Quartara and

Beatrice Sacchi. Labriola had been a dedicated feminist (Taricone 1994), who had also held socialist beliefs and been a member of the IWSA (*Third IWSA Congress Report* 1920: 91–93), but ended up adopting a feminism acceptable to the regime. In her article 'Problemi Morali del Femminismo', published by the monthly magazine *La Donna Italiana* in 1930, she accused Beatrice (whom she defined as 'my good friend') and other women writers of 'repeating parrot fashion – if you'll forgive me the term! – the assertions of men who support rakish behaviour and reject marriage' (Labriola 1930: 333). To be accused of being manipulated by libertine men was a serious matter, but the criticism against American feminists was even more serious: '[O]n the other side of the ocean there are dolls proclaiming their right to sexual experience' (ibid.) – which was certainly not true of the IWSA, always a rather puritan organisation. Labriola countered the American 'dolls' and the 'libertarian women of Europe' with 'a spiritual and ethical concept of life', one that had a clearly fascist imprint: 'Because I bring our principles, our fascist principles to the fore, I believe that there can be no right to free maternity (what kind of liberty is that!) … we fascists hold up the torch of spirituality … we Italians have shut ourselves up in the sacred fortress of our serene virtue' (ibid.: 334–35).

Quartara was undoubtedly one of the 'libertine men', but was only mentioned in a note acknowledging the erudition of his book *Le Leggi del Libero Amore*. However, the polemic was clearly directed against him, along with the accusation of wanting 'to destroy the institution of marriage' (ibid.: 332n.) and encourage free relationships for young women. Labriola totally rejected the idea that every union between a man and a woman was the equivalent of marriage.

Other feminist criticisms came from a very different point of view. In September 1930, *The International Woman Suffrage News, Jus Suffragii*, the official journal of the International Women Suffrage Alliance, printed a review of the French translation of Quartara's work, which had been published in Paris by Alcan the previous year. The review, written by TR,[48] praised its extensive research into injustice against women but severely criticised some of the author's assertions, particularly the hope that women would become as 'free as the air and men would be tied down with chains of iron'. The feminist reviewer protested, 'our commitment is to free our sex and not to chain down the other!', and she detected a serious error in Quartara's thought: he was obliged to invoke the chains because he wanted to give women equal moral freedom, while keeping them financially dependent on men. She accused Quartara of asking not for equality but preferential treatment, which could only alienate the sympathies of the man in the street for the feminist cause, whereas 'we cannot expect fathers and husbands to pay for our love affairs'. The review concluded that the author was 'an eager but somewhat misguided advocate in the cause of woman'.[49]

The writer of this review put more emphasis on the importance of economic freedom than sexual freedom. Indeed, she feared propaganda in favour of the latter, and preferred an economic argument that did not run the risk of producing puritan reactions, which were common amongst the Anglo-American leadership of the IWSA. Since the late nineteenth century the suffrage movement in the United States had decided to adapt to current moral convictions, and it ended up involving itself in Victorian morality and rejecting any sexual matter that was not considered conformist. Even political conflicts inside the movement were obstinately avoided because they were considered 'unladylike' (DuBois 1998: 246).

We can imagine the consternation of Quartara and his feminist friends on reading this review, and we can suppose that they discussed how to react. In October, the newspaper published Beatrice Sacchi's reply on this question. She proclaimed that marriage had to be a woman's principal profession, because it was an idea that had deep roots amongst Italian men and women. However, in Italy everyone had to have work, because wages and salaries were low and the man's earnings were not sufficient to maintain a family. The idea of making men financially responsible for natural wives encountered less hostility amongst Italian men than the idea of acknowledging a woman's right to engage in all types of work and receive the same remuneration. However, the majority of women wanted to have children and repeated pregnancies reduced the ability to work outside the home, which was not the case with fatherhood.

Sacchi pointed out that 'Italian feminists generally pursue the ideal not of abstract equality between the sexes, but of genuine justice', and she declared herself fundamentally in agreement with 'Mr Quartara'. It was right to fight for divorce and equal rights for wives and unmarried mothers. The IWSA did not want to take up the question of divorce, so as to remain rigorously apolitical, and had no intention of confronting religious prejudices for fear of upsetting its many Catholic members. On the question of sexual freedom, Sacchi stressed that Quartara's ideas included chastity for both sexes up to the ages of twenty-one or twenty-five years. She concluded with criticisms of the IWSA's policies, which in her opinion had to examine the question of the family with a broader and more practical approach than it had used in the past (*IWN* 1930b).

The positions expressed by Beatrice Sacchi display flexibility in adapting to the specific Italian situation. They also presented considerable differences from the political line put forward by the leadership of the Alliance. The debate over Quartara's book constituted a chapter in the recurrent disputes within the Alliance between feminists from neo-Latin countries and feminists from northern Europe and the United States. The leadership was in the hands of American, British, German and Swedish women. This was so much the case that Germaine Malaterre-Sellier, who was sensitive to the north–south rift in Europe because she was interested in the Mediterranean dimension to feminism,[50] observed in 1938 that the head office of the IWSA was dominated by a Nordic spirit and Latin and Eastern women felt a sense of isolation. The languages used in conferences and meetings were by preference English, French and German (Rupp 1997).

The differences within the IWSA were also between the women whose countries had already made significant steps towards female suffrage or had achieved it, and women whose countries, like Italy and France, had not. The IWSA was founded as a more political and openly feminist grouping than the International Council of Women, according to the intentions of the Americans Elizabeth Cady Stanton and Susan B. Anthony. These intentions, however, were only partially implemented: the IWSA adopted progressive positions on such questions as unmarried mothers, but it avoided many controversial matters and in the end was criticised for becoming a fossilised organisation. One of the internal tensions that was never mentioned in public was the domination of Christian women in the organisation, in spite of the presence of many Hindu, Buddhist, Confucian, Muslim and Jewish members. In 1939, there was conflict in the executive committee over the Palestinian question between an Egyptian and a Jew that demonstrated the difficulty of holding together the various ideological and religious positions. In general, the IWSA in Europe was characterised by forms of Eurocentrism that conflicted with its universalist ideals (ibid.: 25, 55, 60, 228).

Italy was represented on the IWSA's ruling bodies in 1920, 1923 and 1926. Giorgio Quartara, the senator Angelo Salmoiraghi and the vice-chairman of the Peace Society (Società per la Pace), Pietro Sacchi, were the only men among the fifty-one members of the Committee for Female Suffrage (Comitato Pro Suffragio Femminile) in Milan in 1930.[51] In 1931, Quartara even represented Italy at the International Peace Conference in Belgrade, organised by feminist associations around the world,[52] and spoke on behalf of the chairwoman of the Italian federation, which caused a bit of a stir. In two letters written to Ada Sacchi immediately after his return from Belgrade, Quartara reported, 'I was put through various torments because I was there as a delegate not of the female sex'.[53] This event reminds us of the rules of partial separatism implemented by feminist associations. For example, the Unione Femminile had three men amongst its founders, but it never allowed any men on the board except in a technical capacity (Buttafuoco 1988). Ada Sacchi must have been alarmed by Quartara's letter, because three days later he had to write to reassure her, 'Most worthy lady, I beg you not to take my words too literally'.[54] He wrote that Miss Manus, Mrs Ashby and 'the most kind Miss Morgan' were 'exquisitely well-mannered' towards him. These were the highest office holders in the international association, who belonged to the 'younger' generation and were, therefore, more or less Quartara's contemporaries.[55] The 'mothers' were the founders, such as Catt, an American born in 1859. She was considered a 'mother' by single women like Manus and by the association as a whole. Quartara was right to feel flattered by the attentions of these leading figures. He therefore begged Ada not to mention the incident: '[I]t would be a ridiculous piece of gossip. We need to win the argument by acting in a superior fashion'.

Ada evidently agreed. However, she wanted to make known in her progress report for FISEDD that at the Peace Conference held by the IWSA in Belgrade, FISEDD had had:

> [T]he good fortune to have as its delegate its distinguished member the lawyer Marquis Giorgio Quartara, author of invaluable works on the subject and, therefore, much more competent than any other member. The brilliant speech full of specialist knowledge that he gave there was greatly applauded and his involvement much appreciated. Thus FISEDD obtained specific expressions of praise and gratitude from the Alliance for its wise and very apt decision.

It is interesting that Ada Sacchi attributed specialist knowledge to Quartara's report to justify the choice of this delegate, in line with the position adopted by the Unione Femminile. Loyal to her belief in the political utility of men in the association even in the future, Ada added: '[I]mpartial and generous men will be of assistance to us. Some of their ranks are thankfully already with us, like us and regular members of the Federation. We salute them with thanks and we must try to increase the number of these precious elements' (Federazione Italiana per il Suffragio e i Diritti Civili e Politici delle Donne (FISEDD) 1932–33: 10).

The leaflet still ended with the slogan 'Recruit more women as members!', but the following year the report ended with a new wording, 'Recruit more women and men as members'. This policy was shared by suffragettes of other countries; for example, Bertrand Russell was a candidate for one of the British suffrage societies. From the late 1920s, the 'new' feminism or 'humanism' included political collaboration with men, which reversed the previous tendency to exclude such alliances. There continued to be a minority tendency within the IWSA, however, that preferred complete separatism and accused 'humanism' of suffocating feminism. It therefore refused to cooperate with men within pacifist initiatives and believed the main task to be equality between the sexes (Whittick 1979: 99).

On the whole, Quartara must have found his experience at the feminist conference in Belgrade to be a positive one, as he made two speeches to the Marseilles conference two years later (18–23 March 1933). This time, his position was less anomalous as he was accompanied by Ada Sacchi, who spoke enthusiastically of the Marseilles conference in her FISEDD report for 1932–33, and expressed her 'surprise, in spite of her frequent attendance' at international conferences, at seeing such a mass of women not only different in their political opinions and religious convictions but also in their language and race. They came from as far as Japan and the two Americas, but 'nevertheless found themselves perfectly at one when it came to the emancipation of women' (FISEDD 1932–33: 4–7).

Quartara's two speeches at Marseilles took up his usual themes and both referred to *Le Leggi del Libero Amore* (Quartara 1933a, 1933b). He ended his second speech with the formula that has been used for the title of this chapter, '[L]ove must again triumph between the sexes, just as federal fraternity must triumph in treaties between European peoples'. The tone of Quartara's feminist pronouncements was often essentialist, as when he based his invitation to the 'powerful feminist organisations of all countries' to save humanity from the immense disasters of periodic warfare on 'their maternal, balanced and diplomatic instinct'. This tone was also widespread amongst women at the time, both collectively and individually: the IWSA officially argued that all wars are the work of men, and only women could conclude a lasting peace owing to their innate sense of equity (Rupp 1997: 84–85). The essentialist positions provided a terrain on which very different tendencies could meet. In part, they were the basis for the links between Europeanism, pacifism, socialism and feminism, which since the mid-eighteenth century had become associated with each other through individuals and their ideas. These movements shared a belief in human progress and in the possibility of improving international coexistence and the legacy of European democratic culture that had remained faithful to the conquests of the French Revolution (Pieroni Bortolotti 1985).

However, positions based on women's pacific essence and natural predisposition to look after others also had something in common with fascism, at least in tactical terms. This left room for manoeuvre under the Italian dictatorship, but it forced Italian feminism into very ambivalent situations, at least until 1935 when the regime finally clamped down on the women's organisations. Even Bice Sacchi in her letter in defence of Quartara to *Jus Suffragii* had to include an acknowledgement to 'our premier' who, following protests from various women's organisations, had forced a minister to reinstate women whom he had previously banned from his office. In his second letter to Ada, Quartara very significantly observed that the German petition for peace had collected 17,000 signatures, while the one he had received from Ada only had 5,000: '[O]ur feminist organisation cannot compete with theirs unless all fascist women and related fascist women's organisations are numbered amongst the feminists. This would be of great benefit. Then our petition for peace would be larger than all the other nations.'

Besides, the IWSA's strategy forced the Italian affiliated organisations to enter into relations with the fascist government. Even Valeria Benetti Brunelli, whose book on women in modern civilisation made a detailed survey of international feminism, only mentioned fascist and Catholic women's organisations when examining the Italian situation between 1900 and 1931 (Benetti Brunelli 1933).[56] Non-fascist Italian feminism struggled valiantly to maintain its own space under the fascist regime, but from 1935 there was no longer any Italian representation in international feminist associations.[57]

Giorgio Quartara's story has provided us with a snapshot of a part of European feminism during the 1930s, with its inter-European tensions, its derivative relationship with the United States and its Eurocentrism, placing Italian feminism in an international context and demonstrating the extent to which Quartara himself was the product of a personal and intellectual feminist network. If we were to stop our story here, we would have the impression of a man who combined a materialist perception of Europe and love with a feminist and federalist commitment. Unfortunately Giorgio Quartara's destiny took an unexpected turn after the mid-1930s, and one that was far from positive.

Betrayals and Final Follies

Two of Quartara's books, *L'Italia Tradita*, published in 1941, and *La Futura Pace* in 1942, appear to be a betrayal of his previously held ideas. The first book was printed for the first time in 1933, but a sequestration followed, and it was republished in 1936 in Paris with the title *L'Italie Déçue*,[58] and also sold in Central and South America. In 1941, Quartara decided to republish it even though the international situation had radically changed. He claimed to have left the text unchanged, but in reality he made it harsher and increased its support for Italian expansionism. *Italia Tradita* dealt with the matters that were dear to him: the idea of the United States of Europe over the centuries, the accusation that Germany had triggered the First World War and violated neutral Belgium, and the absolute rejection of Hitler's claim that other states were responsible for the conflict and its economic consequences (Quartara 1941: 223).

The book's central argument was one Quartara shared with Coudenhove-Kalergi: an Italian–French alliance capable of 'joining up with Spain, which is also Latin, and reigning undisturbed in the Mediterranean' (ibid.: 364). This plan had clear imperialist ambitions, because Italy was supposed to obtain Nice and Corsica through the European–Mediterranean confederation, and also share the advantages of the French colonies. The imperialist perspective had Quartara praising Mussolini for having annexed the Dodecanese, reconquered Libya and established the Empire in eastern Africa. It even induced him to propose that Albania, Yugoslavia and Greece be 'federated to Italy' (ibid.: 361).[59]

In his opinion, this type of imperialism was the means to avoid war between European nations, which was largely due to demographic pressures on an old continent (ibid.: 131–32). However, it was no longer a matter only of leaving the sovereignty of the colonies to single powers, as he had written in his previous works; it was now a question of giving Italy its share of the colonial booty. The policy of annexations had to be extended to continental Europe by reuniting the Swiss canton of Ticino with its Italian motherland, 'ceding a small part of Austrian Tyrol to pay Switzerland off, in the event of an Anschluss between Germany and Austria' (ibid.: 361).[60]

From 1933 he developed further his positions on the imperial aspects of the European federation. Whereas Quartara had previously held that equal rights had to be granted to all Europeans in the colonies, his position now switched from Eurocentric to openly racist. In 1934, he claimed that the need for 'a solid barrier between white people and yellow people' meant that Russia had to be saved from Bolshevism. In 1939 he condemned European colonialism and its cruelties in Latin America – partly because it provided another chance to attack the Catholic Church – and spoke of 'indigenous Americans destroyed by Europeans who came armed with a sword in the right hand and a crucifix in the left' (Quartara 1939: 15). Quartara favoured a kind of benevolent colonialism that admired the supposed remnants of matriarchal institutions in Africa and the physical beauty of Africans. On his return from South America, which he cut short because of the outbreak of the Second World War, the ship he was travelling on stopped at the port of Dakar where 'the most beautiful, tall, slender and statuesque negro men and women [were] wandering around', and were 'most courteous, kind, intelligent and honest, but very sensitive if treated as inferiors, in which case they become furious' (ibid.: 155). He felt a degree of human solidarity towards them and wished to understand them; he was moved by the 'little mothers who were still girls' and wondered 'at what age did the suffering and worries of servitude commence for them'. He concluded: '[A]nd yet the Senegalese do not deserve such poverty! They want to work. They are capable. In the fifteenth century they formed the most important sub-Saharan empire in African history' (ibid.: 156–57).

On top of these ideas Quartara then came up with a surprising gesture of which the family had no suspicions and indeed retained no memory. The copy of *L'Italia Tradita* conserved in the Library of Congress in Washington has a handwritten dedication from the author, 'To the Führer of the titanic war for peace in Europe with the deferential admiration of an Italian, the most devoted Giorgio

Quartara 28.2.1941.XIX'. Comparison with Quartara's will shows that it is definitely his hand.[61] Quartara's political shift is confirmed by the book published the following year, in 1942. *La Futura Pace* is very similar to the previous book. Some chapters were simply lifted from *L'Italia Tradita*, but were now slanted in an entirely different direction; whereas in the one, responsibility for the First World War was attributed to Germany, the exact opposite was argued in the other (Quartara 1942: 13). The same argument and even the same words were used to assert the opposite of his previous theories: not only did Britain become the principal enemy, but the very idea of peace was abandoned and he admitted that war had proved inherent to humanity on every continent and in every era. He even withdrew his long-held views of Masonic origin and claimed that there had been a 'failure of arbitration' of the League of Nations, now considered 'an historical corpse' (ibid.: 293), and of the Paneuropean Union. While all these associations had achieved nothing, 'the arms of the Axis and its allies [would] achieve the miracle' (ibid.: 361) of implementing the Briand plan not with the old name of the 'United States of Europe' but with that of the 'New Europe', the 'great and true flag of international progress first raised by Mussolini and then by Hitler' (ibid.: 462). The alliance that would achieve European unity would, therefore, be the alliance between Italy, Germany and Japan.[62]

We do not know the reasons for such a radical and paradoxical change of heart by Quartara: they could have included opportunism, fear for himself or his family in relation to a deteriorating national and international situation, a personal disintegration due to his political isolation and the desire to be with the majority, the conviction that Germany alone could save Europe 'from the terrible threat of Stalin' (ibid.: 469), or a longing for the recognition that had always eluded him. It is certainly true that his solitude and the increasing gap between his expectations and his reality had exasperated his sense of hostility towards the world, while the eccentricity of some of his thoughts, which now appears interesting (e.g., his reassessment of pagan Europe), had degenerated into paradox and provocation. He may have been promised an official role in the regime: in *Del Risorgimento Legislativo*, which was published in 1945, he revealed that in the 1930s he had received the offer of a candidature for the Senate, but he refused it just as he had already 'refused a better offer' (Quartara 1945: 24). We do not know whether these offers were actually made or how he reacted. The fact is that after the war he asserted that 'he had never faltered in his beliefs' since he had first joined the Radical Party, and he fiercely attacked the 'fascist abuses of power, violence, impositions and illegal acts' (ibid.: 17, 20–21, 33). In *Del Risorgimento Legislativo*, Quartara appears to have been attempting to present his credentials as a long-standing liberal, because he referred to a great many old politicians with the implication that he was part of the ruling class of liberal origins that had adapted to fascism but claimed to have never become truly fascist.

Quartara 'betrayed' himself more than anyone else. The same could not be said of the fascist membership card he showed Pierre Mille in 1930. While not wanting to diminish the significance of that act, given that many refused and paid a high price for it, we cannot fail to note that many did become members often to keep their place of work, and then later became active antifascists. Quartara did not have such a need, as he was not engaged in any profession, but perhaps, as Mille suggested, he applied for membership following the favourable message from Mussolini concerning his Memorandum to the Minister of Justice, in the hope of who knows what advancement. To us the most serious and disturbing thing is the espousal of the extreme right's idea of Europe in place of his liberal and federalist convictions. The Nazi slogan of the New Europe, the most sinister of Europeanist ideas, could not be isolated from the idea of Nazi-fascist domination of the entire continent. Everything that had been most dear to Quartara in the past would have been utterly destroyed by this eventuality, including his vision of love.

Anticlericalism, in the absence of every political fixed point, was the one remaining theme to which Quartara was committed, since he lacked the ability or the opportunity to ally himself to some antifascist grouping. Once his involvement with feminism and intellectual research had come to an end, partly because of the lack of success of his books in Italy, he published more books that merely reworked and repeated his old ideas, but only after having subjected them to a political U-turn. These changes amounted to a mixture of naivety and arrogance. He became increasingly obsessed with anticlerical invective, although he did continue to write articles for *Il Sole* on technical aspects of social welfare. In 1934, the Parisian publisher Sans Pareil brought out one of his books. It was then published again by Alcan the following year and in Italy (in a revised form) in 1944. *La Femme et Dieu*, in its original title *La Donna e Dio*, was a bitter and truculent compendium of his anticlerical views. It argued that the Bible's ethical and social teachings were considerably inferior to the Koran's, particularly in relation to the family and women. It was dedicated 'To the victims of the Holy Inquisition, illegitimate birth and the indissolubility of marriage, all demands of Catholic policy'. He went on to propose the transformation of St Peter's into the World Temple of Venus. The altar 'where only the Pope can celebrate the sacrifice of mass and devour Jesus Christ' under Bernini's baldachin could be used for installing a nuptial bed where 'naked Venus and Apollo represent the embrace of Redemption in their splendour on purple drapes and among women who are singing and dancing naked' (ibid.: 232). Once his voyeurism was no longer channelled into his commitment to ideals and perhaps no longer sustained by the pleasure of life as in the past, it was projected outside the cabaret theatres and directed towards the temples of the hated priests. It thus merited the definition of 'coarse and morbid' attributed to it by historians of religion (Vasteenberghe 1936: 126).

From the late 1930s when he started to drift off in this manner, Quartara appears to have become obsessed with himself and his books' lack of success. This self-obsession led him to quote his own works ceaselessly and to use bombastic metaphors and a bellicose tone: 'I unmasked the English leaders in 1940 on the front page of *Il Lavoro*' (Quartara 1941: 322n.), with 'my crushingly precise argumentation' (Quartara 1949: 235). The inconsistencies, the smugness and the swagger do not conceal his sense of failure and isolation. It must have been a bitter experience for such a man, one who had fought in his own individual manner for Europe, peace and the emancipation of women, to find himself reduced to insisting that he had achieved something important and decisive.

In 1949, Quartara's last book, *Viva il Papa? O Viva il Re?* (if we discount the reprint of his essay on Article 57), displayed a further shift to the right and the adoption of a savage and fanatical tone. Quartara, who had been a supporter of Badoglio, fiercely attacked the governments that replaced fascism, and called them 'the new scabby party politics'. He insulted President Einaudi and Prime Minister De Gasperi, calling the former, who had been a distinguished economist, 'the worst of scientists' and the latter 'empty-headed' and 'father of a nun' (ibid.: 11–12). He accused the Catholic-communist 'twosome' of having caused Hitler's rise and the Second World War. One chapter was devoted to partisans and the Committees of National Liberation set up at the end of the war. Of the former he had time only for those who immediately went underground and were 'often heroes' (ibid.: 87), and of the latter only for those in good faith who did not sully themselves 'with blood and gold'. Of the partisans he wrote, 'Poor, enthusiastic and chosen youths ... they deserve the reverent admiration of all Italians'. Perhaps he was thinking of Giancarlo Puecher, the nephew of his old friend Lia Gianelli, who had been his travelling companion in the 1930s. Giancarlo Puecher was executed on 21 December 1943 following the sentence of a special tribunal in Erba of the fascist state in northern Italy, the Italian Social Republic.[63]

Two fixed points remained in spite of Quartara's ideological drift: anticlericalism and the hope that the House of Savoy would return to the Italian throne. The ideas that had illuminated his life in the early 1930s were now sterile and faded, submerged by depoliticisation and intellectual decay.

Quartara's existential and intellectual adventure only found redemption after his death. His desire to be cremated, as made explicit in his will, was carried out by the Cremation Society of Milan, of which he was a member. It was the first Cremation Society in Italy and served as a model for many others (Conti 1998). Its pioneering stance since 1877 had attracted many members of the upper and educated classes, including many women.

The practice of cremation, which appeared in the French Revolution, disappeared with the Restoration and returned to a limited degree during the nineteenth century, was spread in Italy by the Freemasons. Later it was adopted by other oppositionist cultures such as socialism and anarchism (De Luna 1998). During the years that followed Italian unification, the cremation movement discovered fertile ground in the positivist climate that had been created and its new preoccupations with medical hygiene. The Catholic Church conducted a fierce campaign against cremation, and in 1886 went so far as to excommunicate all cremationists, but Prime Minister Crispi legalised the practice in 1888 (Della Peruta 1998). Under the fascist regime, cremation represented one of the distinguishing marks of a kind of existential antifascism shared by Jews, socialists, communists, Waldensians, members of the Action Party, atheists and secularists (Filippa 1990).

The link between cremation and Freemasonry was part of the historical foundation of a secular morality inspired by progress, scientific experimentalism, rationalism and the secularisation of Judeo-Christian eschatology. The initiation rite and the funeral are key events for a Freemason. The first is the death of profane life leading to rebirth in the initiated life, and the second is perceived as a natural metamorphosis in which fire is both principle and symbol, and allows the individual body to burn and fuse with everything else (Isastia 1998b: 192). Quartara, with his irreverent and highly critical nature, probably did not share this mystical symbolism. However, by choosing cremation he reasserted his secular convictions, dignified his anticlericalism and demonstrated his ties with the movement of freethinkers, which included the Freemasons. While waiting for scientific progress to 'tame' death, as he had written in *La Donna e Dio*, his attitude to individual extinction appears to have been philosophic: 'The eternal indestructibility of matter and energy makes consciousness live forever, but not individuality. Just as our ego is born, so it must die' (Quartara 1944: 225).

After his cremation, his ashes were placed in the family chapel at the Milan cemetery.

Notes

1. Milan State Archive, *Gabinetto di Prefettura, I Versamento* (Political Papers from 1900 until the end of the Second World War): box file 423, cat. 18 Censorship and Sequestrations, contains Bocchini's telegram to the police commissioner on 15 May 1930 in which he ordered the sequestration of the book *Gli Stati Uniti d'Europa e del Mondo*. On 17 May 1930, the police commissioner replied that he had carried out the sequestration.
2. Ibid.: box file 361, cat. Heraldry, Giorgio Quartara's documents: 1926–1931, contains not only the notification of Marquis Quartara's receipt of the heraldic diploma on 8 March 1926, but also Mussolini's handwritten message: 10/2/30 (8th year of Fascist Era) at 15.45 in the Milan Prefecture, no. 4198. The following note was added in another handwriting: '10.2.930 The lawyer Giorgio Quartara came to the office to receive this communication – The Prefect'.
3. Founded in 1923, the newspaper was published until 1936. It was on the margins of the area between radicalism and socialism, and in the 1920s it reached a circulation of more than 200,000 copies. Herriot, Blum and Painlevé, who promoted the *Cartel des Gauches*, all wrote for it. Its readership included clerical workers in the civil service, teachers and workers in various sectors. Many Freemasons also read it.
4. In Quartara there is no trace of the anti-Americanism which was diffused in Italy at the time; see Nacci (1989).
5. However, there is no evidence that Quartara was interested in eugenics.
6. In 2000, the card for this book in the library's card index (Biblioteca Nazionale Centrale in Florence) still displayed the note 'not allowed to be read'.
7. See, for example, Ferrario 1939.
8. There is no record of the seizure of Quartara's books in the State Archives of Genoa and Turin or in the public records of the Prefecture. The only

references to him concern the two telegrams sent by Giorgio Quartara to Mussolini, of which the Ministry of the Interior was notified (Registration Reference 425 of 1930). There is no file on him in the Central Political Records of the Central Archive of Rome. The archive of the publisher Bocca, which was taken over by Feltrinelli in the 1950s, appears to have vanished. Moreover, Quartara does not appear to have ever been registered in the Professional Rolls of the Order of Lawyers and Magistrates of Milan and his name cannot be found amongst the members of the Cremation Society of Milan.

9. Ernesto Treccani, an artist and an antifascist, was one of their children.
10. See entry for 'Gavazzi' in Romano (1999); Gavazzi (2003).
11. This series included Rabelais, Trilussa, Renard, Hugo and Del Buono. Angelo Fortunato Formiggini, the radical socialist and Masonic publisher famous for his nonconformist spirit, committed suicide the day after the introduction of the race laws by throwing himself from the Ghirlandina Tower in Modena on 29 November 1938; see Filippa (2001: 82–83).
12. See the obituary in *Il Secolo XIX*, 5 December 1951.
13. Holograph will of Giorgio Quartara, dated Milan, 11 July 1951, can be consulted at the Notarial Archive of Milan.
14. They were first taken to a family house in Tuscany and then to the Milan home of Ernesto's daughter, Maddalena Muzio Treccani.
15. He was one of Egidio's sons, Egidio being the uncle of Giorgio Quartara's mother, Vittoria Gavazzi.
16. Extract held at the Genoa Civil State Archive.
17. Whereas the announcement of his death placed by his sister Giulia and his relations only mentioned the funeral in Milan (*Il Secolo XIX*, 4 December 1951), the next day an announcement appeared in the same newspaper of a mass to be said for the Marquis Giorgio Quartara, placed by Marquess Marianna Quartara, Emanuele Quartara and family.
18. Will referred to in note 15.
19. Vittorio Scialoja (1856–1933) was professor of Roman Law at Rome University, and held many positions of public office: Minister of Justice in 1909–10, Foreign Minister in 1919–20, Minister of State from 1927; Italian delegate to the peace conference of 1919–20 and the League of Nations from 1921 to 1932.
20. This essay was published under the pseudonym of Lambda-Gamma, which stands for the author's initials. An editorial note stated that the author 'is not active in our ranks, and is part of one of the countries largest textile companies', but cultivates 'wise and open-minded studies in his relative leisured existence'. The magazine did not come out in favour of Gavazzi's proposal, because it challenged both the idea of the Alliance and that of Mitteleuropa, 'which in reality are part of the same concept'.
21. The first congress of the Union Douanière Européenne was held in Paris in 1930, and expressed the hope for 'a rationally and scientifically organised Europe'. Its proposals included a European postal union, the suspension of passports, and a study into European agriculture. See Pegg (1983: 61, 146).
22. Giuseppe Canepa (1865–1948), socialist from Liguria. Initially he opposed the fascist movement, and the offices of *Il Lavoro* were destroyed in 1922. He

took part in the Aventine Secession, and in 1927 was one of the members of parliament whose term of office was cut short by the regime. The newspaper offices and his home were ransacked. After this, Canepa opted for compromise and aligned himself with those who accepted class collaboration and the corporative state; see De Clementi (1975).

23. Significant articles on the European question included: 'Inghilterra e Unione Europea', *Il Lavoro*, 24 March 1934, 1; a review of Sir Arthur Salter's *The United States of Europe*, London: George Allen and Unwin, 1933; and 'Italia e Francia', *Il Lavoro*, 5 April 1934, 1.

24. All mentioned in Mola (1999).

25. His name does not appear in the register of membership.

26. On pacifism in Italy, see also Rota (1952: 1963–2018).

27. The Grand Lodge of Italy was reconvened in exile in France and contributed to the development of the antifascist movement; see Conti (2003b: 287–320).

28. The letter on headed paper for the 'Legal Firm of Giorgio Quartara' is held with two others at the Moscow Special Archive, 554/4/175 (now also in the Historical Archives of the European Union at the European University of Florence, 'Pan/Europa sources' Collection, PAN/EU/10-554/4/175). In a later letter of 16 September, Quartara chose as the place for his intervention the First Political Commission, First Question, Organisation for Peace in Europe, which he thought 'the most complete for achieving Pan-Europe, i.e., the United States of Europe' (Moscow Special Archive, 554/4/168 and Historical Archives of the European Union, ASUE PAN/EU/04-554/4/168).

29. 'Europa-Kongress 1932', *Paneuropa*, 8, 8/9, October–November 1932, 223–31 and 266.

30. Letter sent on 5 August 1936 from Castellaccio, Moscow Special Archive, 554/4/257 and Historical Archives of the European Union ASUE PAN/EU/18-554/4/257.

31. Coudenhove-Kalergi believed that with the support of Great Britain and perhaps Russia, this alliance could evolve into a European federation, and block Hitler's plans. He had in fact changed his attitude to Britain during the 1930s: whereas he had excluded it from the Paneuropa project of 1923 (as well as Russia), with the advent of Nazism he repeatedly travelled to London and set up a pan-European committee there, which was made up of Leo Amery, Arthur Salter, Harold Nicolson and Gilbert Murray; see Passerini (1999: 270).

32. For example on 24 October 1928 on family law with reference to Scialoja's proposals. The newspaper also published articles by other authors on the same question; see Cirenei (1934: 5).

33. The principle that is presented at the beginning of the book is a clarification of an idea that had been previously aired: 'made every embrace a legal fact that generates all the rights and all the duties, irrespective of any formalities'. The legislative proposals on family law suppress the inequality between man and wife: no marital or parental authority; the mother's name is passed on to daughters or to children of both sexes; no sexual freedom is granted to the husband and prohibited to the wife; divorce is allowed; and national pensions are established for abandoned and destitute women and children.

34. The former (1796–1874) was a Belgian mathematician and statistician, and wrote *Physique Sociale* in 1869. The latter was professor of statistics at Rome University and author of works on crime statistics.

35. Giuseppe Tammeo (1851–98) was a lawyer and professor of statistics. He wrote studies on population and emigration, one of which was *La Prostituzione: Saggio di Statistica Morale* (1890). Gertrud Guillaume-Schack (1845–1903) was a founding member of Josephine Butler's abolitionist movement and organised working women.

36. Max Nordau (1849–1923) was a doctor and writer active in the Zionist movement up till Herzl's death.

37. He argued that only by violently overthrowing bourgeois society could an end be put to prostitution and women's social inferiority, thus achieving real autonomy of sexual experience from material conditioning (Charles-Albert, *L'Amore Libero*, Preface by L. Rafanelli, Milan: Casa Editrice Sociale, 1921). Charles-Albert was the pseudonym of Charles Daudet (1869–1957), an anarchist, socialist and Freemason; his book *L'Amour Libre* sold in huge numbers in France and abroad. Leda Rafanelli, an anarchic militant and writer, was active in the trade union and feminist movements, and was an antimilitarist, anticlerical and anticolonialist. Having believed in Mussolini when he was a socialist, she broke with him as a fascist in a drastic manner.

38. Jeanne Chauvin (1862–1926) was one of the first women to study law in France and to practise the profession of lawyer. Paul Leroy-Beaulieu (1843–1916), author of *Le Travail des Femmes au Dix-neuvième Siècle* (1873), was a French economist, journalist and professor of public finances and political economy. He rejected Ricardo's and Malthus's pessimistic conclusions, and Quartara took up this polemic against Malthus, whom he accused of being unscientific, because he was unable to see that free love allows for the self-regulation of population and the physical improvement of the species.

39. Moisey Jakovlevitch Ostrogorsky (1854–1919), born in Byelorussia, worked for the Ministry of Justice, but had to leave the country because of the tsarist reaction. One of his books, *La Femme au Point de Vue du Droit Publique* (1892), was translated into English, German and Polish.

40. However, the struggle for female suffrage was not without conflicts between Italian feminists: for example between the suffragette and supporter of Mazzini, Anna Maria Mozzoni, and the socialist Anna Kuliscioff, who had initially expressed some reservations on female suffrage, but from 1906 defended the women's vote and fiercely attacked Turati and campaigned in the Comitato Pro Suffragio; see Pieroni Bortolotti (1963).

41. She supported Italy's intervention in the war and was awarded the gold medal for her assistance to the war effort during the First World War. She founded the Mantuan sections of various feminist organisations, such as CNDI, Fildis and 'Per la Donna' (which had the task of looking after minors, removing illiteracy through secular schools and promoting legislation on divorce and suffrage). The Consiglio Nazionale delle Donne Italiane was established at the beginning of the twentieth century as a federation of welfare and philanthropic associations under the aegis of the International Council of

Women; see Taricone (1996). Fildis, which still exists, was founded in 1920 and was acknowledged in 1922 as a section of the International Federation of University Women, to fight for women's equal rights in the universities; see Taricone (1992). The fascist government forced it to dissolve in 1935.

42. An obituary for Dr Beatrice Sacchi was published in *Jus Suffragii*: see *International Women's News (IWN)* (1931). The magazine can be consulted at the Fawcett Library in London.

43. The information on the IWSA is based on the international conference reports in the IAW Archive. (See *Primary Sources and Archives*.)

44. The law of 1925 gave Italian women the right to vote in local elections, albeit with many restrictions concerning property, education and age. However, the law never came into force, because local elections were abolished in 1926 by the laws introducing *podestà* or Crown-appointed governors of towns. See De Leo and Taricone (1992).

45. Reports by previous leaderships, such as Margherita Ancona's report to the Geneva Conference of 1920, were overly optimistic and considered highly nationalistic by the international leadership (see *Eighth IWSA Congress Report* 1920: 172–77). In her report, Ada listed many attempts and failures, which had, however, served to increase the association's profile; see *IWN* (1928: 8).

46. The document consists of forty-five typewritten pages and is divided up into sixteen parts.

47. See *IWN* (1930a). The recommendations included the rejection of state regulation of prostitution, increase in the penalties to brothel owners for procurement, reduction in the excessive disparity in the treatment of men and women in cases of adultery, the decriminalisation of abortion resulting from rape, the complete removal of marital authority, and the demand that women be allowed to work in the police and magistrature. Valeria Benetti Brunelli, a pedagogist, was an active member of the Italian section of the Alliance and published many books and articles on pedagogy and political thought in the fifteenth century; see Gastaldi (1936).

48. It was not possible to discover the identity behind these initials, in spite of much assistance from Marijke Peters of the IAW Archive.

49. The review, entitled 'An Italian Feminist. *Les Lois du Libre Amour*, by G. Quartara', was published in *IWN* (1930b).

50. Germaine Malaterre-Sellier, who was born in Paris and graduated from the Ecole du Louvre, was a progressive Catholic who during the First World War served as a nurse in the Red Cross. From 1920 she was active in the women's movement and the pacifist movement, supporting moderate pacifism. She was vice-president of the Alliance (and president of the French section) and vice-president of the Women's Union of the League of Nations.

51. A list of 'members who paid their fee for 1929' to the Comitato Pro Suffragio Femminile is held by the Unione Femminile Nazionale in Milan. There were forty-nine, to whom Quartara and a female member were added in 1930.

52. The Belgrade Conference opened on 17 May 1931. Many European nations were represented, including Great Britain, Germany, Poland, Bulgaria, Rumania, Hungary, Sweden, Holland, Ukraine and a few South American

countries such as Brazil and Uruguay. France was represented by Germaine Malaterre-Sellier and Italy by Giorgio Quartara; see *IWN* (1931b and 1931c). At the end of the conference, they passed a declaration on disarmament demanding a sharp reduction in all armaments by member-states of the League of Nations. The declaration was published in *IWN* (1931d).

53. Letter by Quartara to Ada Sacchi from Milan of 23 May 1931, held by the Unione Femminile Nazionale in Milan.

54. Quartara's letter to Ada Sacchi of 26 May 1931, Unione Femminile Nazionale, Milan.

55. Margery Corbett Ashby, president of the IWSA from 1923 to 1946, was born in England in 1882. She was elected at the Rome Conference after Carrie Chapman Catt, and was described by her contemporaries as 'young and gracious'; see R. Deutsch (1929: 27). She was an excellent speaker, a capable organiser and gifted manager. She was also known for diplomacy and her prudent and conventional elegance; see Whittick (1979: 39). Rosa Manus, who was a Dutch Jew, also belonged to the younger generation, having been born in 1881; she was a Board member of the IWSA and very active in the European organisation and the pacifist campaigns launched by Lord Cecil; she died in Ravensbrück in 1943. The American Ruth Morgan chaired the Peace Committee created in 1926 at the IWSA Conference in Paris, which then organised the Belgrade Conference to prepare an international conference on disarmament, and launched a collection of signatures to the petition on disarmament.

56. A very favourable review of this book was published in *IWN* (1933b).

57. *IWN Jus Suffragii* regularly contained reports on the status of women under Italian fascism, dealing with such subjects as the denial of women's electoral rights (*IWN* 1929). It noted 'the [Italian] government's increasingly anti-feminist stance' (IWN 1933a: 34–35).

58. A brief report on the French edition appeared in *Revue des Etudes Historiques* (1937: 195), which considered the book 'not without interest' but did not share its confidence that there would be a United States of Europe.

59. Clarification added after the French edition of 1936.

60. Clarification added after French edition.

61. The book is part of the Third Reich Collection of the Library of Congress, which combines two collections, one made up of books, albums and printed matter taken from the Reich Chancellery in Berlin, which an American soldier sent to Washington at the end of the Second World War, and the other made up of privately owned books belonging to Hitler, Goering and Himmler, which another American soldier saved and also sent to the Library of Congress. The copy of Quartara's can be found in the Rare Book and Special Collections Division, which contains books that belonged to Adolf Hitler personally. The copy of *L'Italia Tradita* at the Library of Congress with the handwritten dedication to the Führer carries the mark D523.Q35.

62. *La Futura Pace* must be considered in the context of all Quartara's works, with which it has a relationship of both consistency and contradiction. It cannot be taken out of the historical context of its author and period, as Rodogno has done (2003).

63. The young man could have fled, but chose not to in order to avoid reprisals against his father. His Christian behaviour was exemplary right up to the end when he embraced one of the six men who would shoot him, and forgave them all. Later partisan units were formed under the name 'Puecher', including a detachment of the 52nd Garibaldi Brigade. Lia Gianelli (1887–1967) must have been a strong and determined woman, judging by her behaviour during the war and the Resistance. She looked after the family after her brother-in-law's arrest and made every effort to save both nephew and brother-in-law. The latter died in Mauthausen; see De Antonellis (1984).

Chapter 2

'Love Becomes Entangled with Civilisation'

Leo Ferrero, a Young European

The road between Florence and Chianti runs through hills covered in cypress trees. Where it rises from Grassina towards Greve after a long dry summer, the slopes reveal patches of white and ochre earth. Along a straight stretch of road, a garden wall has a small green door that leads to a house called Ulivello between vases of lemon bushes.

In the house, an entrance hall with dark furniture is separated by a wrought-iron gate from the stairs to the floor above. A chandelier, also made of iron, adds to the interwar feel of the place. A room is furnished as a sitting room, with a small sofa, an armchair and a coffee table. It was here in the early 1920s that Claude Dauphin dreamed of meeting Leo, seated on a wicker chair, and stopping on the threshold to savour the reunion with his friend. During the war the house was occupied first by the Germans and then by the British. However, something of the past still remains – of a past when the house was alive with guests from different European countries, the young friends of Leo and Nina Ferrero.

The large library is on the left as you enter the hall, and contains the books of Guglielmo Ferrero, Gina Lombroso and Leo Ferrero, as well as many papers, manuscripts and photographs. The stairs go up to the beautiful rooms on the upper floor. The central well-lit room looks over the garden and has a fireplace and decorations on the walls. It, too, is full of books and papers. Leo's bedroom looks out of the back with a panorama of the low and rounded hills so typical of the area around Siena. Another bit of garden can be seen just under the window. Here, Bosa Raditsa explains, an apricot tree used to grow and her mother, Nina Ferrero, told her that you could pick the fruit by leaning out of the window.

The European Heritage

Leo Ferrero grew up in a family environment that was European in outlook and in the company it kept. It conformed to that 'immense republic of cultivated spirits' that Voltaire in the final decades of the eighteenth century hoped to see develop in a Europe of science and progress, a continent of enlightenment and modernity. For Leo Ferrero, the link between the Enlightenment and Europeanness was not only one of direct derivation from one to the other (one of his essential terms was in fact 'the republic of letters' which originated with Voltaire), but was also based on the redefinition of the two terms by Piero Gobetti and his circle during the 1920s.[1] In Leo's family tradition,[2] Europe represented a community with which they identified and also a court of appeal for intellectuals who were persecuted or not acknowledged in their native country. His maternal grandfather, Cesare Lombroso, to whom academics were often hostile in Italy, was very well known abroad, particularly in Europe. He and his wife, Nina De Benedetti, kept open house in Turin on Sunday afternoons, and their guests were mainly from Europe, but many also came from Latin America and Africa (Dolza 1990: 53).[3] Lombroso's openness to European thought and his love of European company may have been connected to his Jewish cultural background, which in his case was secular and in his wife's religious.

   In Turin at the end of the nineteenth century, the links with European culture were particularly intense in the scientific and humanistic fields. Turin was a European city because of the community of scholarship and the forms of Europeanism it hosted.[4] The terms 'Europeanism' and 'European' were frequently used in progressive circles in Turin during the 1920s, often in a general sense to indicate a broad intellectual mindset and antiprovincialism. The term 'pre-Europeanism' was used by Edoardo Persico to signify 'the new culture [that] promises to become European'. This culture, which remained a minority phenomenon, had its roots in the spiritual crisis that followed the First World War. It pointed the way towards the creation of a 'modern European' (Persico 1927). Throughout the interwar period, many intellectuals in Turin appealed to a Europeanism that expressed the often rather vague aspiration for a broader and more lively culture, and for an ethical cultural commitment that opposed nationalism and fascism. This approach can also be found in Leo Ferrero, who maintained relations with Turin and wrote for *Il Baretti* when he was living in Florence. However, Leo, who soon became 'rootless', did not relate local identity to national and European identities, as was generally the rule with many intellectuals from Turin.

Leo's family moved to Florence in 1916, a few years after the death of Cesare Lombroso.[5] Leo's parents, too, moved in a European and cosmopolitan intellectual world, and in Florence they kept alive the Lombroso custom of open house on Sunday afternoon. They were visited on different occasions by people of international stature, such as the director of the French Institute, Julien Luchaire, the director of the British Institute, Arthur Spender (the poet Stephen Spender's uncle), Gaetano Salvemini, the Rosselli family and innumerable foreign intellectuals passing through Florence. When the Ferreros moved to Switzerland, their home in Geneva became a focal point for antifascist émigrés, and their guests included Don Sturzo, Rougemont, Madariaga, Count Sforza and Count Coudenhove-Kalergi.[6] Guglielmo Ferrero was aware of the European nature of his own education (Raditsa 1939: 80). 'Ferrero was, above all, a European', wrote Bogdan Raditsa, who became his son-in-law, and affirmed that Guglielmo Ferrero's enthusiasm for a new Europe included the 'Europeanisation of the Slavic populations of the Balkan peninsula' (Raditsa 1996: 89).[7] Florence, too, had its European heritage: suffice it to recall the tradition of Mazzini which was kept alive by Gaetano Salvemini and the Rosselli family. It also had a leading role in Italian Judaism, and was 'one of the centres where Judaism was being rediscovered, studied and affirmed', and a link between Europeanness and Judaism of an 'exquisitely literary' nature would develop (Pellegrini 1982: 1023; 1037n. *passim*). Leo Ferrero would become part of this literary experience through his involvement in *Solaria*.

Gina Lombroso had her first son study English, French and music (with carefully chosen private teachers), so the boy already knew foreign languages when he entered school. Leo would continue to deepen his understanding of the two languages to the point of perfect fluency in French.[8] His sister Nina also learned languages, but did not complete a formal education, a decision that reflects the way the Lombroso–Ferrero family perceived the female condition and women's intellectual abilities (Dolza 1990: 218n.).[9] The Ferreros travelled widely in Europe and the Americas, and they took Leo with them from when he was very small. Between the ages of three and five, he accompanied them on trips to Argentina, Uruguay, Brazil, England and France (Ferrero 1984). These journeys were of crucial importance in the formation of Leo's sense of European belonging. In 1919, at the age of sixteen, he had his first one-month stay in Paris (Bosetti 1993: 73–81),[10] and in 1922 he accompanied his father on a European lecture tour to Munich, Berlin, Stockholm and Copenhagen.

His travels around Europe played an essential part in defining Leo's intellectual activity, partly because he was ostracised by fascist-dominated cultural circles to the point that his father advised him to use a pseudonym, although he refused. He lived in Paris in 1926 and returned there in January 1928, and then moved to London for three months. On 10 April, he passed through Paris again, and then went on to Rome, Naples, Sorrento, Milan and Genoa (for his work with the newspaper *Il Lavoro*) (Ferrero 1999: 110).[11] At the end of April Leo was again in Paris, where he took up residence in October and would remain until 1932, while continuing to travel. In 1931, he was in what he called 'Balkania' (namely, Yugoslavia, Greece, Turkey and Rumania), and he often returned to the Tuscan countryside. Because of the continuous and intrusive surveillance by the fascist regime, the Ferrero family was obliged, in April 1927, to move to Ulivello, their country home near Florence. In September 1932, Leo left for the United States, where he received a Rockefeller scholarship to attend the seminar taught by Edward Sapir at Yale. During a journey that was supposed to bring him back to Europe through Asia, he died in a car accident in New Mexico in August 1933. Because of Leo's early death, his figure has remained fixed in his friend Aldo Garosci's judgement as 'a very promising delicate writer' (Garosci 1953: 255).

Apart from his membership of the community of cultured Europeans, Leo also inherited from his family a set of ideas that constituted veritable historical and cultural interpretations of European civilisation. One of these theories concerned the connection between Europe and love, which had been a central tenet of Guglielmo Ferrero's work *L'Europa Giovane*. His concept of this connection was based on another part of his family's cultural tradition: their views on women and the relationship between the sexes.

'The Normal Woman'

Leo Ferrero's family taught him a rigid perception of a woman's role, albeit one mitigated in practice, though not in theory, by his mother and his aunt, Paola Lombroso Carrara, both of whom pursued professional careers in an intellectual field. The traditional family view of women was based on a book jointly written by his father and grandfather (the former being the latter's student) and edited by his mother, *La Donna Delinquente, la Prostituta e la Donna Normale*, first published in 1893.

Even though Lombroso was at pains to point out in the preface that 'not one line of this work justifies the great tyranny that continues to victimize women' (Lombroso and G. Ferrero 2004: 37) the entire book argues the intellectual and even emotional inferiority of women. Women are considered men whose development has been stunted, similar to a child, and with clear atavistic and residual signs of primitiveness and animal natures (Frigessi 2003: 134–35). Even 'normal women' are considered as inherently deviant (Lombroso and G. Ferrero 2004: 29). The principle of women's 'lesser sensitivity' is primarily established on the basis of the natural sciences, but also of non-scientific sources such as popular proverbs, the Bible and the Koran, various literary works, and comparisons with primitive populations. Women are also supposed to have less sensitivity when it comes to love, and are inferior when it comes to experiencing its intensity. A woman's love is only a secondary aspect of maternity. The intellectual inferiority is accompanied by less moral sensitivity in women, whose capacity for compassion is simply a product of their maternal sentiment. This feature demonstrates the authors' misogyny even more than the imputation of intellectual inferiority: in this cultural context, moral deficiency justifies the removal of legal status for women in the public sphere.

The writers concluded that the principal mark of inferior intelligence among women compared with men was the deficiency of creative power, as shown by the lack of women of genius,[12] but they did not doubt that a greater participation by women in society's collective life would increase their intelligence, as had occurred in England and North America, particularly in literary and artistic journalism. Their book's logical conclusion is a clear division between the roles of each sex: women should be responsible for procreation and mothering, as well as intellectual solicitude in assisting men in their creations.

The paradigm proposed by Lombroso replaced the monosexual and hierarchical interpretation by which women were a less perfect version of men, with the bisexual concept that the two sexes are unalterable and give rise to society's bipolar structure (see Milletti 1994: 50–122). An advantage of the bisexual concept is that women can assert their unique qualities which were not admissible in the previous model. Moreover, they achieve more consideration than in the patriarchal family because of the importance attributed to maternity (Babini, Minuz and Tagliavini 1989: Introduction). The opinions of scientists did not differ greatly from the widely held stereotypes, but provided these with a greater degree of credibility. These positions were aimed at a specific target: the new breed of intellectual women and women who supported themselves through their intellectual labours (as was often the case with daughters and wives of the same scientists).[13] The insistence on demonstrating the inferiority of women in biological terms coincided with the new demands by women to have equality in the fields of work and politics (Frigessi 2003: 132). Nearly all the writers admitted that precisely these demands were responsible for driving them to exorcise the elements of the demands for women's equality with potential to subvert order in the family, particularly those elements concerning active and autonomous sexuality (Minuz 1989: 114, 142, 154).

Guglielmo Ferrero translated these positions into the language of social theory in his first really successful work, *L'Europa Giovane*.[14] In the central part of the book, which was devoted to 'Love in Latin and Germanic Civilisations', Ferrero explained the psychological difference between the so-called Latin races and the Germanic races by means of their different attitudes to sexual love, respectively the material and the moral possession of the beloved (G. Ferrero 1946: 124). Ferrero's position on women was contradictory in that it mixed respect for some of the gains in female emancipation with fundamental misogyny, which becomes particularly clear in his analysis of what he defined as 'the third sex'. This term defined the 'ageing spinsters of England', the women who were competing with men not without success. For Ferrero, women who do not become wives and mothers are incomplete women with 'deformed and crippled' personalities (G. Ferrero 1946: 318), and constitute a neutral sex that is very successful in the struggle for life, like the infertile worker bees. Because they are forced into 'masculine mimicry' by enforced spinsterhood, they are intelligent, courageous and superior to men in their activities, but their anomalous emotionality is transmitted to the entire society in which they live.

Gaetano Mosca's friendship with Guglielmo Lombroso did not stop him from writing a long review of *Europa Giovane*, in which he challenged the generalisations attributed to different races and nations, but, above all, he doubted the concept of love as the foundation for the social superiority of Germanic peoples.[15] Mosca, who disagreed with Ferrero's 'overly severe verdict on the gentle sex' and his concept of anti-Semitism (Mosca 1897),[16] was averse to every kind of materialistic or naturalistic determinism (Frigessi 2003: 365).

Twenty years later, in the self-critical introduction to a collection of his essays published in 1918 under the title *La Vecchia Europa e la Nuova*, Ferrero acknowledged that the war had forced him to change many of the ideas expressed in his book of 1897. However, all the changes concerned only one question: he no longer believed that the 'youthfulness of Europe' based on industrial power could be used to measure the progress of peoples, and was now convinced (partly adopting his wife's arguments against mechanisation and industrialism) that the 'old Europe', which was loyal to Athens and Rome, was right in judging the symptoms of decadence to be the increase in needs and the means to satisfy them, which industry compelled everyone to perceive as progress. There is not a single line in Ferrero's introduction that suggests he had changed his ideas on women and gender relations, with the exception of his comment that 'the only institution to emerge from the war as inalienable [was] the universal suffrage of men and women' (G. Ferrero 1918: 35).

Leo Ferrero had to face up to this set of convictions, a legacy that was something of a burden. His mother's ideas were no less problematic as an inheritance, given that they sprang from her experience as daughter and wife of intellectuals who pursued those convictions. Positivists were potentially open to revising traditional ideas on gender roles because of their claims to scientific credentials, even though they largely accepted those traditional ideas (Dolza 1990: Introduction). Both Lombroso's daughters, Gina and Paola, became professional intellectuals, which established a new model of behaviour compared with the previous generation of women. On the other hand, they suffered the conflicting pressures of the restrictive outlook that kept women in a subservient intellectual role.

Their subordinate position was confirmed when they moved from their role as daughters of intellectuals (Gina in particular did a great deal of work for her father)[17] to their role as wives of intellectuals who belonged to their father's circle of assistants. The situation was dramatic in Gina's case, as she married on the condition that she could continue to live and work with her father. Moreover, Gugliemo dangled before her the prospect of being able to collaborate with him on an equal basis that would bring to an end what he defined as her father's 'intellectual exploitation'. 'I had never thought of being able to write on my own' (Dolza 1990: 151), Gina would observe later. The collaboration between Guglielmo and Gina Ferrero never took place, because he concentrated on his own works. Gina produced numerous books and articles on anthropology, criminology and sociology, as well as works on the women's question, travel writing, short stories and works on family members.[18]

In her writings, Gina Lombroso expressed a hopeless pessimism for the 'tragic situation of women'.[19] For her, female altruism is a 'social instinct', a necessity for the species on which the social function of women is based, while the individual instinct is egoistic. Therefore, women find themselves in the tragic position of being unable to reconcile their passions with their interests (G. Lombroso 1921), their passions being represented by love and their interests by feminism. Gina acknowledged that the work of feminists 'has not been unhelpful' (ibid.: 229), but she believed they were wrong to demand the same rights, duties and education, as men and women are different physically, intellectually and morally. She introduced the idea of the 'superior woman' who is above average in her heart and her intelligence, and consciously *altercentric* (the term *alterocentrico*, which was invented by Gina Ferrero, is the opposite of 'egocentric' and means 'centred on the other'). She spoke of 'great women' who first bred silkworms, leavened bread or inspired kings and ministers (G. Lombroso 1926: 105), but she insisted that 'when it comes to science and culture, we are nothing more than subsidiary beings' (ibid.: 107). The superior women are not intellectual women, as the 'modernist women' claim, but rather are 'better women' in whom love is stronger than ambition (ibid.: 110). They are not enemies of other women, but they instinctively prefer authoritarian and selfish men who demand sacrifices from them (G. Lombroso 1921: 195).

Gina Lombroso even went so far as to claim that intelligence was an affliction for women (Dolza 1990: 222). She used the concept of a 'superior woman' to attribute a moral mission to women, and thus reversed the severe judgement of her father and husband, who argued that women were morally inferior. However, for the 'woman of superior mind and heart' the world is a place of exile in which the only remaining communal space is the family, a perception that belonged to the secular tradition of Jewish women of the liberal bourgeoisie in the north of Italy (Beer 1982: 156 *passim*). Gina opposed laws protecting women at work on the basis of her antiprotectionist convictions. She was even against female suffrage, which in her opinion did not respond to a genuine need for women (Dolza 1990: 83–85). In *Le Tragedie del Progresso* (*The Tragedies of Progress*) she argued with conviction against mechanisation and industrialisation, which threatened the family and traditions linked to the land. The polemic against feminism was also taken up by other women of great talents, such as Amelia Pincherle Rosselli, who was also a member of the intellectual and progressive Jewish bourgeoisie. In 1922, Amelia wrote to Gina mentioning 'the *hysterical nature* of feminism, a vacuous exercise in emancipation that does not correspond to any need, and a spurious independence' (Calloni and Cedroni 1997: 153).[20]

Gina Lombroso admitted the terrible cost and distress for the acceptance of what she considered her mission. Leo could hardly remain indifferent to all this, given his close relationship with his mother.

Gender and Generational Relations

In Leo's life and works we encounter attempts to go beyond the stereotypes of the time, his family's positions on the inferiority of women and on relations between the sexes,[21] although these attempts did not always meet with success. In his family tradition, women were intellectual intermediaries between the generations of men. Gina Lombroso's diary on the first twenty years of Leo's life (*Lo Sboccio di una Vita*) was mainly compiled for Cesare Lombroso, 'who wished to collect a series of notes of this kind' (G. Lombroso 1935: xii). Gina's book on her father was dedicated to twelve-year-old Leo, while the Italian edition of Leo's two plays, *La Chioma di Berenice* and *Le Campagne senza Madonna*, carries a dedication to his grandfather and mother (1924). Gina's work on Leo's papers after 1933 was similar to the work she had carried out in reordering her father's papers after his death. It was a labour of remembrance that manifested the extent of her devotion as well as her desire to control.

Her influence on Leo was immense and expressed itself in various ways. Leo often took up Gina Lombroso's themes of anti-mechanisation and anti-industrialism, explicitly quoting her as he did in *Paris Dernier Modèle de l'Occident* (L. Ferrero 1932: 40) or implicitly referring to her as he did in his American writings on the peasantry. Although he was surprised by Gina's 'extravagant admiration' for the United States, where 'industrialism has permeated everything' (L. Ferrero 1999: 319, 313), Leo came close to sharing his mother's ideas on the differences between European peasants and American farmers, who because of their specialisation are simply the product of the industrialisation of agriculture (L. Ferrero 1939a: 37).

Gina's influence on her son was not restricted to the world of ideas, however. It was even more important when it came to his approach to life, without a clear distinction between its intellectual and emotional aspects. While she was writing *The Soul of Woman*, Gina read extracts from the book to her fourteen-year-old son, and she recorded that 'he said I read well but always with the same whiny voice. He read to show me how you should read' (G. Lombroso 1935: 234). Simone Téry, who had an intimate relationship with Leo, wrote to Gina when Leo died, 'when he spoke of you, he came to life, forgot everything else and was happy at last' (ibid.: 338). Gina also instilled in Leo an entirely secular Jewish culture, and that secular nature is demonstrated *ex negativo* by the absence of a thematic approach to that culture in Leo's writings, even though he continually expressed his admiration for Jewish writers.

Gina Lombroso's diary of her son's life records a kind of folie à deux, with a process of identification that produced in Leo a vein of femininity of which he was aware. In a kind of osmosis with his mother, Leo developed a passion from the age of four for Gina's 'beautiful clothes' and he asked her to try them on in front of him (ibid.: 89). This indicates not only a precocious theatrical bent, but also a complex configuration of the male/female polarity. When Leo was nine, Gina wrote: 'I tell him about the initial ideas that occur to me on the differences between men and women. He understands them and comments on them in a marvellous way. He already has a magnificent intuition of the female mind' (ibid.: 178). Again, in October 1921, Gina observed that Leo 'conserves a truly feminine sensitivity' (ibid.: 296). 'Leo's almost feminine sweetness' was mentioned in an obituary.[22] In his unfinished novel, *Espoirs*, Leo described Bernardino, a character with autobiographic features, as a young man in whom 'women would immediately sense a need for tenderness and very feminine affection' (L. Ferrero 1935: 30).[23] It was certainly through his mother that Leo came to realise the inequality in gender relations, which he portrayed as the supreme injustice in his plays. Perhaps Leo's ability to create meaningful female characters in his plays was also due to this, as he acknowledged, 'I am better at doing women' (L. Ferrero 1999: 76).

Leo was, therefore, not only indebted to Gina for his intellectual development. In his poem 'Alla Mamma', which he wrote at Ulivello in August 1922, he recognised that his whole being derived from his mother, and he promised that he would continue to be inspired by her (L. Ferrero 1937: 44). However, the complete understanding between the pair did not stretch to Leo's love affairs, which inevitably modified their alliance. In *Espoirs*, there is a conversation between Bernardino and his mother, who senses his suffering over an unrequited love. He reacts to her solicitude with gratitude but also with guardedness and withdraws into himself (L. Ferrero 1935: 92). This reflects a real conversation that took place in 1922 (G. Lomdroso 1935: 308), in which Gina told her son that he still needed to reach a decisive 'turning point' in order to be truly grown up, 'that of love', and Leo replied: 'But how do you know that I haven't reached that turning point? I have already reached it.' Gina rejected this, as in that case Leo would not have been so obsessed with glory, and Leo protested that in reality he aspired to excellence and not to glory. But the idea of glory that Leo attributes to Bernardino in *Espoirs* is 'a theatre full of women who were all in love with him' (L. Ferrero 1935: 170).

The two dialogues, one imaginary and the other real, do not solely depict a young man's desire for autonomy and a mother's desire to take part in his affairs of the heart. There is a more complex inner tension that drove Leo to recreate his relationship with his mother in his relationships with other women, but on a conflictual basis. The poetry of his youth testifies to an eagerness to see 'desire placate itself in grave maternal tenderness', in the eyes of a woman who is 'both mother and lover' (L. Ferrero 1937: 84). In 'Amore di Donna', the carnal side of this desire also finds expression:

O my love,
when I looked on, relaxing in your tendered lap
the earth upturned and your sweet
eyes bent over my tortured face.
…
In that universal love I lost myself,
where you are both mother and lover. (Viareggio, April 1923)

The other important relationship that affected Leo's view of relations between the sexes was the one with his sister, to whom he was bound by deep affection while being acutely aware of the inequality of their positions within the family. He was the first-born and a boy, and always at the centre, while Nina appeared to be in a marginal position, at least when it came to intellectual matters. This inequality comes up in his fictional work. His novel *Espoirs* does not hide the cruelties of family life, which included Carlotta's (Nina's) suffering because her brother attracted all the attention to himself and often 'stole' her female friends. However, Gina wrote that the relationship between the two was one of mutual protectiveness, because they were successful in different aspects of life. Nina was capable of organising her own social life as well as one for Leo since they were aged fourteen and eight, respectively (G. Lomdroso 1935: 227).

Leo's attitude to women is depicted in many passages of his writing as towards the undifferentiated other: as late as 1932 he wrote from Paris to Marion Mitchell Stancioff: '[W]omen represent unity in the world. Everywhere they resemble each other, whereas men are different from each other'. Love relations with women were to be the area in which he suffered most, but also the one in which he developed original ideas in terms of both his personal and his intellectual life: in his own words, 'love is tragic but it also produces sumptuous fruits' (L. Ferrero 1939b: 166). As long as his mother remained the principal female figure in his life, the self-definition of his own masculinity became risky and male bonding became loaded with ambiguous connotations for and against his mother. In Mussolini's Italy, the ideology required people to exalt the leader, his real mother (Rosa Maltoni) and the symbolic mother (Italy); this was counterbalanced by the bonds between the men who were supposed to defend her from other men of opposite political ideas (Passerini 1991: 87 ff.).

In Leo's case, the relationships obviously did not follow this pattern, given that his was a progressive bourgeois family of Jewish descent. On the other hand, relations between mothers and sons in the Rosselli family were also very intense, but they could still reconcile themselves with the happy marriages of Nello and Carlo and good relations between their wives and their mother, Amelia Pincherle Rosselli (in their case they lacked a father figure). The corresponding relationships in the Ferrero family were possibly made more problematic by Leo's exceptional sensitivity and the disagreements between Gina and Guglielmo. But another difference concerned concepts of subjectivity: Leo was interested in the boundaries between the public and the private, and between Europe and love. This specific area of introspective research may have related to Leo's unspoken Jewishness: because traditional Italian Judaism distinguished between public and private morality (Pellegrini 1982: 1021), the attempt to overcome or modify this distinction may have caused a psychological and intellectual block.

Leo was acutely aware that the family wanted him to continue his father's and his grandfather's work. He had a problem with male identification and with asserting himself as a man, and not just as a son and a grandson. We find traces of this process in his writing and

Leo's perception of his own manhood, which are significant both for the age and the sex of the person who 'acknowledged' his manhood:

> Today while walking along a path, a voice from inside a farmhouse asked who was there, and a little child who saw me shouted, 'a man'. This was the first generic and tangible confirmation of my situation in relation to others. I have grown up without, as I had imagined, any well-defined chasm between my child self and my adult self. I put myself in the place of that little child and thought of myself as I was at his age looking at me with the eyes I had then. I was stunned at the idea that I could be for him that improbable, powerful and different thing that 'a man' had once been for me.

Themes that were to recur later can already be detected in this passage taken from Leo's Notebooks.[24] Those themes are generations, shared sexual identity, the shift from one age to another, and the circular relationship between identification with the other and the foundation of one's own identity.

Leo became aware of the bonds of experience and destiny that he shared with other men of his age, particularly the Rosselli brothers: '[O]ur generation no longer has a trade, customs, set traditions or milieu. Of Carlo, Nello and myself, none has a precise profession. We will be obliged to change it a thousand times' (quoted in JM 1938). Leo was a great friend of Nello, who wrote an emotional and perceptive obituary on Leo in *Nuova Rivista Storica* (N. Rosselli 1933: 546–54). Jean Luchaire, Alessandro Pavolini, Primo Conti and Alberto Carocci were all Leo's age,[25] and Leo shared their insistence, so typical of the time, on the question of generations and how their own was a tragic and disenchanted one. In a review (L. Ferrero 1927c), Leo wrote that Baty's theatre 'is the tragedy of the stupidly wise young generations who no longer have even the power to dream'. The diplomat Carlo Sforza, who was a supporter of European unity and wrote the preface to a collection of Leo's writings published in 1939, emphasised that the author 'belonged entirely' to his generation and shared with it the values that drove him to reject a pleasant career as a boy born with a silver spoon in his mouth (L. Ferrero 1939c).

How was this generation defined? The current definition, valid particularly for France, is the 'postwar generation' (Wohl 1980), which consisted of young men born around 1900 who avoided the First World War and were unsettled by their sudden change in circumstance after the war. They were sceptical about ideologies and ambivalent towards those who had fought the war. The Jean Luchaire affair dramatically symbolises the features of that generation.[26] His book *Une Génération Réaliste*, which was published in 1929, almost constituted a manifesto for the 'new generation' and justified the decision to 'associate only with other young people'. From the moment Luchaire started his activities, there were signs of ambivalence in identifying this generation, and this was accompanied by a sort of 'latent racism' that claimed the superiority of an ill-defined Latinity (Cabella 1985: 104).

Whereas Jean Luchaire founded a political association of under-thirties, another of Leo's friends, the Croat Bogdan Raditsa, expressed similar positions in terms of human affections. In a letter from Rome written in 1927, he wrote: 'I always find it an enormous pleasure and a great consolation to know a man who feels all the things I feel almost with the same sensitivity. It is a continual torment to live solely with old people who now find it very difficult to feel all our desires and passions.'[27]

Networks of peer groups based on gender and age were formed within the generation. Aldo Garosci has provided us with the image of a group of young Italian intellectuals who walked down the boulevard Saint-Michel in the autumn of 1932 to dine at 'Rouget'. The group included himself, Carlo Levi, Giansiro Ferrata[28] and a 'bespectacled young man dressed in a coat made of goat fur' typical of Parisian taxi drivers, as he described Leo (Garosci 1984: 5) (Levi painted some superb portraits of Leo during the same period – see Fig. 2).

Leo wrote about relations between young men in different ways according to the genre in which he expressed himself: poetry, correspondence and fiction. In his poem 'A Claude',[29] written at Ulivello in 1922, Leo evoked friendship and mutual support amongst men, in which identification and idealisation become intertwined, '[I]n your friendly gaze /... I was reflected back as though you were / another better and wiser me'. The poem spoke of the secrets about women shared amongst men, particularly by Leo who was caught up in his unhappy love affairs, and of the new understandings achieved through friendly debate. Once again, women were the passive idealised intermediaries of male alliances. The literary dimension, in which this attitude was rooted at least since the *dolce stil novo* poetry of the early fourteenth century, was of key importance in that Leo was conscious of the almost maternal role played by 'paper' in the development of his emotions. In *Espoirs*, he wrote of Bernardino, '[P]aper had taken the place of the ideal woman who should have understood everything, admired him without any reservations and brought his solitude to an end' (L. Ferrero 1935: 171).

Leo expressed a less idealised male solidarity in his everyday existence, as can be seen in his letters to male friends. Correspondence with people of his own age takes up a large part of his archive. His correspondence with Claude Dauphin started in 1918, and recorded Claude's attempts to set up a magazine for young people (which never came to fruition), his failure in school, and the hope of persuading his parents of his theatrical vocation. It reflects the social background of the young men to whom and of whom he wrote, all of them under the age of twenty. They included Jean

Figure 2 Carlo Levi, *Portrait of Leo Ferrero*, 1933 (courtesy of Fondazione Carlo Levi, Rome)

Luchaire, who since 1920 had been happily married, in spite of his adventures, with a woman 'who was a mixture of mother, friend, lover and daughter' (letter from Jean to Leo dated 20 August 1920). All this demonstrates a lively exchange between the young men, in which the main obsession is being loved and the extension of each individual's love affairs to a network of male solidarity.

In 1922, the correspondence with Claude intensified, when Leo reported on his sentimental attachments, such as the 'equally desperate and pointless love' for a Hélène[30] – *la dame* – a very theatrical story ('c'est du Shaw!') with a married woman who read him Sapphic poetry in English through rose-perfume-laden breath.[31] There is a literary flavour to these reports, as well as self-irony. In the account of another meeting with *la dame*, the bell rings after five minutes of passion and Leo is unceremoniously thrown out. Leo considered the episode to be Stendhalien.

The roles switched around in the correspondence between Leo and Claude. Whereas the former gave sound advice to the latter on how to manage his artistic vocation, it was Claude who took on the role of sage when it came to affairs of the heart. He pointed out that Leo did not love *la dame*, while only love could justify courting a married woman, and gave his judgement 'you failed in your duties as a Don Giovanni during the vibrant scene in her sitting room'.[32] Leo must have known that his letters had a wider audience than Claude alone, recognising his talent for overdramatising.

Leo did not limit himself to telling Claude the secrets of his love life; he informed him of how he was establishing contacts with the world of literature and the theatre, he discussed the advent of fascism in Italy and kept him up to date on the book he was writing with his father, *La Palingenesi di Roma*. His letters recorded the worsening political situation in Italy and the rampant and brutal antisocialism (13 October and November 1922). On 2 November, shortly after the March on Rome, he exploded into a violent tirade, 'c'est à vomir, mon cher Claude, c'est épouvantable. Nous sommes foutus!' ('It is enough to make you sick, my dear Claude; it is appalling. We're screwed!'). He watched the destruction and persecution of Salvemini and the Rosselli family perpetrated by the fascists and he asked himself, 'When will it be our home?' Leo reacted to these events on a moral basis that did not translate into political positions: 'je suis du parti de l'indignation' ('I belong to the indignation party'), he wrote in the same letter in a tone that was a foretaste of his *Diario di un Privilegiato*, a work that was put together posthumously using his Notebooks (Introduction by d'Orsi for L. Ferrero 1993: vii–xxxi; Ciferri 1993: 115–30).

The correspondence between Leo and Claude continued over the following years, even though it became less important than when they were between fifteen and twenty-one years old – the transition between adolescence and youth which is crucial in the formation of sexual identity through reciprocal recognition between peers. The habit of sharing secrets remained even once the need to have an alliance to face the world and women became less pressing, but by 1928 the tone was more relaxed and the narration more summary.

The male alliance in relation to women takes on very different tones in the correspondence. His relationship with Claude was profound on both sides, although one has the impression that Claude was more committed to the friendship than Leo.[33] Claude acknowledged Leo's greater intelligence, called himself 'a not very brilliant guest' at Ulivello, and felt confused 'about the idea of mixing with you lot who are so much better at everything'.[34] During military service, Claude found his correspondence with Leo represented the ideal and formed a marked contrast to the coarse reality and hard work of army life.[35] The two shared Claude's flat on Rue Lhomond, and when Leo was left on his own, Claude jokingly told him not to wear his new clothes.[36] In 1926, Claude declared that he would have given up twenty lovers for an hour chatting with Leo while smoking a pipe together, and he regretted that at their most recent meeting the presence of Leo's lover–friend, Yone, had made it difficult to talk openly.[37] In an undated letter (probably of 1924), Leo claimed to reciprocate his friend's attachment: 'You have many feminine characteristics in your delicate soul, young Claude. To be serious, *j'aime bien tes féminilités*. You also say overly kind things about me. I am as attached to you as you say you are to me'.

A different example of male correspondence (this time in response to Leo's letters on friendship) can be found in a letter written by Nello Rosselli from internment on Ustica in August 1927. He spoke with sensitivity and reserve of an 'entirely new adventure' with Maria Todesco, whom he married (Calloni and Cedroni 1997: 95). In a letter from another of Leo's great friends, Bogdan Raditsa, more carnal details emerge, typical of the attitudes amongst young European men at the time. These letters also reveal the extent of the network of young Europeans who moved about for professional reasons or out of cultural interests. Bogdan was born in Split and worked as the press attaché at the Légation Royale de Yougoslavie in Athens. He and Leo had established a kind of youthful alliance against the 'freemasonry of stupidity' (undated letter from Leo to Bogdan), an alliance made up of the 'wretches who refuse to take part' when faced with the stupid and ignorant people now woefully powerful in all countries. The relationship between Leo and Bogdan, who later married Nina, was rich and complex, and involved debates on every subject from philosophy to economics. Their correspondence was full of references to political and cultural themes, such as Leo's concern over the impending *finis Europae* in the event of another war.[38] It also contained the typical complicity of men who discuss women and love, and it occasionally echoed the essays and articles that Leo was writing on England. He wrote in 1928 from London to Bogdan in Paris 'all on his own and without a proper knowledge of French': 'You could console yourself with the Parisian women, because the women in England are awful. I have never before encountered such ignorance of the basic elements of love.'

In March 1929, Leo, now in Paris, advised his friend to read Zweig's *Vingt-quatre Heures de la Vie d'une Femme*; Bogdan read it and found it 'marvellous'.[39] The two young men's interest in Zweig's book demonstrates their shared convictions and cultural milieu. Zweig, a 'great European', a symbol of European intellectual life and a pacifist, wrote this tale – much admired by Gorky – of two passions that mirror each other, in a guesthouse on the French Riviera with German, Danish, English, Italian, Austrian and Polish protagonists. In each of the twin stories, an irreproachable woman's life is radically changed by a sudden passion. Apart from the admiration for Zweig's literary skills, Leo and his friends shared the narrator's position, 'I found it more honest that a woman should freely and passionately follow her instinct than that she should deceive her husband while in his arms with her eyes shut'.[40] The two young men recognised within the metaphor of love at first sight the sudden appearance of the radically new and the subversion of the repressive sexual order that made them suffer.

The correspondence with Bogdan registered the highs and lows of Leo's love life. In 1929 (with no clear dates), within multiple relationships, where dramatically low moments alternated with highs: '[W]ork, work … I am in love with two women – I am hot – I am tired, but full of energy – I am very much in despair – I take heart. I need peace. In ten days I have broken things off with a lady three times and then got back together again.' Bogdan reciprocated, in a much more light-hearted manner, and started on the confidential male exchanges about women's bodies and the 'possibility of getting somewhere' (i.e., managing in some way to have a sexual relationship). In a long letter from Athens in August 1929, he wrote:

> [Here] women are beautiful, but not collectively. The first impression is that women are ugly or at best beautiful up close. Then when you enter the world and society, you discover that women are beautiful, very beautiful. Of course, they are conservative. They do not allow you to approach them in the street. *È à peu près comme à Florence.* You have to have very good introductions, and then you can get somewhere, but they do defend their virginity.[41]

He shared the obsession with women's breasts common among young southern European men:[42] whereas women hid their breasts in Paris, Rome, Zagabria and Split, as contemporary fashion required women to flatten them, 'here they are the most conspicuous decoration that is put on display so that the whole world can look at them'. These arguments were the basis for a homoerotic relationship, as though talking of love for women was a way of talking of love between them: 'You're so lazy! I have written to you several times all over the place. You have forgotten me so easily!', Bogdan complained.[43]

Leo Ferrero portrayed male alliances more crudely in his fiction, and demonstrated the ways they could turn into something more negative, as he had experienced during military service.[44] In *Espoirs*, there is a significant passage about an archetypal group of males (soldiers) confronted by Bernardino's mother, who was obliged to ask permission from them to pass by in search of her son during the clashes in Florence caused by student support for Italy's entry into the First World War. Leo lucidly describes the soldiers' 'male concepts', in a crescendo in which the lieutenant puts on a show of gallantry to let the woman enter the area sealed off to the public. He looks at her as she moves away and comments 'jolie', but then 'fearing that he might be seen as overly sentimental and insufficiently military, he adds with a coarse laugh, *Belle croupe!*' (Ferrero 1935: 157).[45] Equally, the young men of Leo's social class who are doing military service with Bernardino are portrayed in a manner that demonstrates their moral baseness in relation to women.[46]

Using irony and self-irony, Leo expresses both the distance and the closeness between him and the young men portrayed. By varying the genres, he selects for each occasion from a range of relationships between the sexes, showing the multiplicity of forms that a male alliance may take on in different historical circumstances. The tension between artistic representation and experience renders explicit the anxiety that Leo felt over male alliances that have a potential for turning against women. It was primarily in his plays that he attacked the injustice in gender relations.

Mises en Scène

Leo's playwriting was for the most part unpublished at the time of his death, but is of considerable significance in the context of this study. One reason for this is that the prominence of the theatre in Leo's work related to 'his multiple psychological tendencies'.[47] This takes up meaning within a history of subjectivity. Long before psychoanalysis, the theatre evoked anxieties and inner conflicts and attempted their catharsis, while providing a sphere in which the public and the private overlap.[48] Indeed, the theatre alerts us to the subjective nature of Leo Ferrero's inspiration. Nello Rosselli wrote, 'Giovanni in *Campagne* and Catullo in *Chioma* were undoubtedly Leo' (Rosselli 1933: 548). According to Rosselli this inspiration not only concerned his plays but all his other works as well, and their unity consists of his pursuit of the relationship between the subjective and the objective: Leo was in his opinion a 'sensitive man listening to his inner voice' (ibid.: 549) and his interest was in a history of man viewed not from a historical point of view but rather from a moral and spiritual one.

Leo Ferrero started to write very young: his first plays were completed in 1915, when he was twelve years old. Between 1919 and 1923, Leo produced short stories and three plays of a poetic–mythological nature. These early plays dealt with the question of amorous relationships and relationships within peer groups, which were to appear again in Leo's later plays that were more concerned with social reality.[49] In 1923, the theme of intergender relations was also developed in *La Chioma di Berenice*. In this work, Lesbia is *une femme supérieure*, as he wrote to his friend Claude Dauphin (Kornfeld 1993: 336–37), using the term coined by his mother Gina, by which he meant a woman out of the ordinary, free from shame and rank, and thus able to conduct a free life.[50] The theme of the intragender group reappears. The three foolish male lovers act as foils to the three women who comfort Catullo before his death, while the male group ends up worse off, given its silly nature.[51] All the characters are determined by their biological traits, in accordance with the dictates of the Lombroso family philosophy.

In *Campagne senza Madonna* (1924), Leo started to adopt the theme of gender relations in its social context.[52] The play's three characters are archetypal: mother, son and wife find themselves in a countryside suffering from an epidemic of aphtha. The son, who has a passion for playing music and sculpting, cannot realise his dream of moving to the city because of his wife's opposition. She wishes to continue living off the fields as her family had always done in the past. The two women, who represent the way people can be tied to the land, prefer harsh and authoritarian men, a clear reference to Gina Lombroso's ideas. For the play's young male protagonist 'God does not exist' (L. Ferrero *CBCSM*: 99), whereas the two women put their trust in the Madonna. Once again it is the man who gives into the women, or rather to the feminine. There is something of *Criminal Woman* in all this, but, above all, there is an influence from Gina Lombroso who, as part of her polemic against mechanisation and industrialism, argued for a return to the land as a form of moral regeneration that could resolve both the problem of unemployment and the women's question.

Leo Ferrero was not so much interested in the realistic representation of the social conflicts of his time as in devising symbolic variations of male–female relations, a crucial cultural tension of the epoch. The subject became highly evolved in *Poids d'Or*, which he reworked many times between 1924 and 1928. The plot came very close to the bone, if one considers the lives of Leo's parents and grandparents. In the play, the scientist Jean-Sébastien discovers a serum that can save the life of many miners, but he comes up against his colleagues' hostility. His wife, Natalie, who makes great sacrifices for him, arranges for the family, including little Pierrot, to move to her cousin Maggie's villa on Elba where they can test the new serum on miners. But on Elba the scientist runs away with Maggie, while Natalie manages to gain the confidence of the miners and complete the experiment. She accepts her contrite husband back and allows him to take the credit for a scientific discovery largely based on her own work.

It is possible to read the play as topical and realist with marked autobiographical references.[53] However, an overly biographical interpretation would not be convincing, partly because the fortitude of Leo's father and grandfather is not reflected in the moral weakness of some of the male characters in the play. On the contrary, an interpretation from the point of view of cultural history perceives a twin reversal of stereotypes in the play. The first reversal demonstrates that of a great man and his wife; she has the only real claim to be great. In the perspective projected by the play, moral weakness is more attributable to men than to women, thus contradicting the assertions made in *Criminal Woman*. However, the second reversal reestablishes the sexual roles that had been overturned and reveals Leo Ferrero's ambivalence over relations between the sexes: Natalie, putting the new certainties and a year-long autonomy behind her, takes her husband back and adopts a decidedly antifeminist stance.

The play points to a revolt against the traditional way of interpreting the masculine and the feminine, a subject close to Leo's heart, torn as he was between the old and the new perceptions of relations between men and women, and between an impulse to appropriate the feminine and anxiety over whether he was up to the public demands for manliness. The play is characterised by this contradiction: contempt for women runs through the whole play, which also has Natalie as its 'true protagonist', another superior woman (Lombroso-Ferrero 1943: 154).

The background to the conflict between the sexes in *Poids d'Or* is the conflict between the elite and the people. The latter, who are represented as miners, are corrupt and blinded by self-interest, and are portrayed in a very negative light. Are they an image of the Italian people? The play suggests that the people are not entirely in the wrong, given the elite they have been landed with. This theme is also found in *Angelica*, considered the most mature of Leo Ferrero's plays and not staged until after his death.[54] *Angelica* is based on a simple but effective *coup de théâtre*. The characters are the masks of the *commedia dell'arte*, which constitutes a significant shift back to the Italian tradition. This reflected Leo's conviction that only decadent art was incapable of following the well-trodden paths of expression in its desire to indulge in supposed freedom. The plot concerns a young woman who is about to marry, and the demand by the country's dictator to exercise *jus primae noctis*. Orlando, a free man who came from outside the community, confronts and defeats the dictator, but immediately afterwards encounters difficulties with the working class and the bourgeoisie when he insists on free elections based on universal suffrage. Angelica kills Orlando, after having declared that she had flirted with the dictator and was not at all displeased by his attentions.[55] In this play, conflict between the sexes is subsumed into the struggle for freedom, and sham freedom is represented in the allegory by a beautiful and 'egocentric' woman, flattered by being courted by the powerful, and piqued by the lack of attention paid to her by Orlando.

Recalling the first time he read the play as he was travelling by
train to Leo's funeral, Garosci explained some of the reasons why
Italian antifascist exiles identified with the work: '[T]hose people of
Italian stock characters – were our people – and the generous deeds
of a modern Rienzi against dark oppression, soon to be rejected,
abandoned and lamented, were our destiny, and our feelings were
not shouted out but touched on almost by a background music or
reflected in a few bitter sentences' (L. Ferrero 1984: 7).

Silvio Trentin, another antifascist exile, wrote from Gers in July
1934, 'this book turned up with its words of advice and consolation
at the most desolate moment of my exile'. Garosci quotes two
passages from *Angelica*: the hero's question to a passer-by, 'What do
you think of liberty? – It is a sweet thing, Monsieur', and the final
comment, 'Disorder is better than injustice'. Garosci recalled that
another final scene was added to the work in the version staged by the
Pitoeffs: after the hero's death, the lights were turned on again and the
Italian masks that had followed the tragedy with detachment began
to sing 'our ancestors' anthem', *Fratelli d'Italia* (ibid.).[56]

Leo's writing for the theatre is interesting in its ability to dramatise
thoughts and words.[57] No sooner does Leo bring a matter up on
stage, be it a particularly bitter or arid one, than the ideas take on
substance and demonstrate their vitality in an exchange between two
or more characters. He had taken the propensity for this
expressiveness from his father, as Guglielmo Ferrero declared in
conversations with Bogdan Raditsa in Geneva against the
background of the 'bloody twilight of Europe' (Raditsa 1939: 23).

Leo's involvement with the theatre did not stop him from
developing a passionate interest in cinema and an awareness of its
innovativeness. He thought that cinema was the art of dreaming,
capable of portraying what the imagination conceives in those
moments in which it is on holiday ('Cinema Nuova Forma d'Arte', in
Ferrero 1940: 143). In Paris, Leo frequented cinemas, including the
more avant-garde ones, and was rather sceptical about the films they
put on that 'served no purpose because the wider public is slowly
developing in the great Hollywood studios' ('Cinema d'Avanguardia',
ibid.: 144, 147). He considered cinema as the art of representing
man's passions through pure mimicry, whereas theatre was the art of
fusion and evocative atmosphere ('Limiti del Teatro', ibid.: 166).

Leo Ferrero's fiction and non-fiction are closely intertwined, just
as the public and the private were for him strongly interconnected.
As was noted by a critic in the *Nacion* of Buenos Aires,[58] *Angelica*
was simply the transposition of the second chapter of *Paris* into

another medium: both presented his list of Italy's woes and of the intellectuals and champions of liberty that Italy had killed over the centuries. These theatrical works inspired by social issues had a potential European dimension. A markedly European outlook is adopted in *Angelica*, which 'with a bold, firm but light touch confronts the fundamental question in modern European tragedy: humanity's inability to use freedom' (Ratel, in L. Ferrero 1936: 38–39). Simone Téry, Leo's friend and lover, observed that *Angelica* is a satire that takes revenge on all fascisms in the world (ibid.: 41) and, therefore, cannot be seen as a satire exclusively of Mussolini.[59] The incipient European dimension in his social and historical plays is consistent with the importance Leo attributed to the theatre in Europe and its capitals such as London, Vienna, Berlin and, above all, Paris. There it was the core of the whole city along with the salons, whereas theatres were half empty in Italy because they had been abandoned by intellectuals.[60] Leo's passion for the theatre was based on the conviction that the theatre and the novel require liberty, which is not true of poetry.[61] In his opinion, the contrast between the latter form of expression and the first two corresponded on the political level to the contrast between dictatorship and democracy that was dividing Europe at the time.

Europe, and Love

The European question was central to Leo Ferrero's non-fiction work. In Florence, Leo and Nello Rosselli took part in Jean Luchaire's initiatives aimed at creating European associations for young people,[62] and his publication of magazines such as *Vita* and *Jeune Europe*. The manifesto to mark the launch of the latter periodical (November 1921) made references to Mazzini's Young Europe movement, without actually acknowledging his name. 'We feel profoundly European', Luchaire would write, while pointing out that Coudenhove-Kalergi also belonged to their generation (Luchaire 1929: 56).

Leo was later to be one of the protagonists of the intellectual 'meridian' (Manacorda 1979: xxi) that linked Florence and Turin. This role was enhanced by his involvement in *Solaria*, which was intense from the magazine's foundation in 1926 until his death in 1933. Even when in Paris and at Yale, and in spite of a few disputes with the editors, he continued to send articles and letters, and to spread awareness of the magazine successfully. During the period

1926–27, he published poetry, dialogues, articles and reviews on works by Saba, Svevo, Alvaro and Pirandello. From 1928, he sent not only articles from Paris but also reviews of French books and plays. Leo Ferrero was rightly considered one of the 'three main links between *Solaria* and Europe', the other two being Arturo Loria and Nino Frank (ibid.: xxxv).[63]

Solaria carried on the intellectual commitment that had existed in *La Voce*, the European slant of *La Ronda* and, above all, the inspiration of Gobetti's thought that united both these traditions. For *Solaria*, as had been the case with Gobetti's *Il Baretti*, being European meant introducing foreign literature and opening its pages to twentieth-century literature, particularly from France but also other countries (Alessandrone 1985: 130). It was a work of 'extreme European popularisation' (Luti 1995: 67). The Europeanism was often more implicit than explicit and, as in the case of Gobetti's publications, it was mainly intended as cultural open-mindedness: '*solariano* was a word that in the literary circles of the time meant antifascist, supporter of European integration, universalist and antitraditionalist', wrote Elio Vittorini, adding, 'they called us dirty Jews because of the hospitality we gave to writers of the Jewish religion and for the praise we heaped on Kafka and Joyce' (Vittorini 1957: 174).[64] In the autumn of 1932, Carocci entered discussions with many correspondents on the possibility of founding a magazine with the explicit purpose of debating the European question, but the project came to nothing (Manacorda 1979: xl).

Leo Ferrero attempted to articulate a more specific meaning of Europeanness. In January 1928, he published an article in *Solaria* entitled 'Perché l'Italia abbia una Letteratura Europea' ('In order for Italy to have a European Literature'), in which he outlined his vision of Europe. What Leo meant by claiming to belong to Europe was above all – as with Gobetti – redeeming one's own national literary tradition. Leo had learned from his father that a literature expresses a people's moral character, and like him he strongly associated literature with the theatre. The link between morality and artistic expression leads back to universal values, which count as *sottintesi*, a term often used by Leo to mean the undeclared and underlying assumptions on which collective life is founded. Italian intellectuals lacked moral sentiment, and while 'wrapped up in their illustrious, splendid but dead cities, and their venerable and slow-paced cafés', they appeared not to notice the 'hurricanes that have devastated Europe'.

Leo Ferrero's appeal for European integration had a global dimension: '[E]very book that portrays the grandeur of Italy must contain a sense of the world'. This was exactly what the literature in the service of the fascist regime lacked; it was incapable of setting Italy within its international cultural context, and could only fulminate about fascism's return to the traditions of ancient Rome.[65] The transition from Europe to the 'world' occurred implicitly, with a leap that recalled De Sanctis, who considered humanity and Europe to be great nations as opposed to the small ones, and Mazzini, who considered Europe to be only an intermediate term along the scale that rises from individual nations to humanity.[66] Leo Ferrero was influenced by Giuseppe Mazzini, unlike Gobetti, who was critical of him (Bagnoli 1993: 55–64). In her introduction to *Diario di un Privilegiato sotto il Fascismo*, Gina Lombroso wrote that Leo became passionately interested in Mazzini's writings in 1920 and was very moved by them. The article 'Perché l'Italia ...' was particularly influenced by Mazzini's article 'D'una Letteratura Europea', which asserted that Europe possessed 'an agreement on needs and desires, a common thinking and a universal soul that propels its nations along similar pathways towards a shared goal; there exists a European tendency' (Mazzini 1994: 11). Although Mazzini did not define the content of this tendency exactly, he suggested its broad direction in the part of the article on 'European civilisation' in which he rejected theories on the influence of climates on literatures and all other forms of materialist determinism.

Mazzini's historical account (inspired by Vico) attributed particular importance to the development of chivalry, the 'only sign of an intellect tending towards civilisation' before the degeneracy marked by the 'folly' of the crusades. When the spirit of liberty manifested itself through confederations of cities in different European countries and feudalism came to an end, there was a return to intellectual development and the politics of nationhood.

The first attempts at poetry had more or less the same features everywhere. The Arabs had transmitted to Europe their good taste, their wealth of descriptive skills, and their aptitude for the mystical and the ethereal, and this trend was assisted by the widely held Platonic opinions in Christianity. Invasions by the Normans, a people always in search of adventures, revived chivalric elements. Because of these factors, the 'gay science' (*gai saber* or Provençal poetry) spread to every part taking on a lively and amorous form, as though a universal anthem of joy had opened up to greet the dawn of a new life, 'thanks to minstrels, troubadours and *minnesaengers*'.[67]

Mazzini acknowledged 'a fervour, an admirable harmony in scholarship and intellectual progress throughout Europe'. He was not referring to any specific existing literature, but rather to a potential – an ideal civilising process (Mazzini 1994: 32).[68] The only feature of this literature that is defined a priori is its 'eclecticism', a reference to European pluralism whose roots go back to the philosophical sects of the ancient world. This overview of Europe's cultural genealogy does not overlook the importance of love: it perceives it not only as a historical stage constituted by the gay science, but also as a sentiment that runs through all eras as an extra-institutional force (ibid.: 10). It therefore makes it possible to go beyond cultural and national divisions; hence 'Italian, Persian and Arab love songs occasionally appear to have been inspired by the same afflatus under the same sky'. There had been a centuries-long dispute over the Arab origins of Provençal poetry, and Mazzini rejected the views of those who claimed it and declared the sentiments expressed in it were exclusively European.[69] Mazzini concluded his essay by asking young people 'to arouse and spread this spirit of love everywhere they go' and pleading, 'study therefore the literatures of all the nations'.

Mazzini's influence on Leo Ferrero was principally in his way of perceiving Europe and the link he saw between literature and morality. This can be found not only in the previously discussed article but also in *Trasfigurazione dell'Amore* (published by *Solaria* in July–August 1929), and in some passages of *Secret de l'Angleterre*, in which he wrote that Europe was undergoing unification (L. Ferrero, 1941: 156), and wondered whether the sleeping soul of England would reawaken with integration into Europe. But Mazzini's influence is particularly noticeable in the importance attributed to love as a distinguishing feature of European civilisation, although Mazzini did not so much put emphasis on the distinctiveness of European love as on the unifying and intercultural potential of undiscriminating love. For Leo, 'love has become entangled with civilisation', as he wrote in *Trasfigurazione dell'Amore*.[70]

According to this article, civilisation is based on love. Although love is passion that almost always involves the desire of a physical union, it has real importance only when it becomes a discourse, that is, when it is 'transfigured into art, literature, ambition and action'. All civilisations implement a transformation of this sentiment of some kind, but some achieve greater results than others: in Europe this is true of France, where love is the fulcrum of social and intellectual life, whereas this does not occur in England and Italy for opposite reasons: in Italy because, although always the subject of conversation, love is no more than the fulcrum of individual life and therefore 'rudimentary, tempestuous and all-consuming' (words that echo Stendhal's observations on Italians in his treatise *De l'Amour*), and in England because 'it is of no importance'.

In other writings, Leo reflects on love in the context of a classification of civilisations undergoing change during his lifetime. In *Secret de l'Angleterre*, Leo took up his father's ideas, but modified them in a remarkable manner: his father Guglielmo had argued that the English people were capable of better social organisation because they were not oppressed by the burden of love, whereas Leo emphasised that in reality the English were weaker because they were not acted upon by the 'leaven of love'. *Secret* insists upon an interpretation of the sentiment of love in terms of the history of civilisation: for those who have not reflected upon it, love is nothing more than physical desire mixed with a nebulous moral confusion. Pain is the true measure of love's depth, and love cannot be considered a struggle between the sexes, but the struggle of each person with themselves (L. Ferrero 1939b: 166). All this contrasted with Guglielmo's biological determinism, although Leo did retain some of his concepts of evolution.

In this context, the role attributed to women was fundamental, as they were considered love's representatives in society – its experts and its administrators. This was why Leo defined Englishwomen as 'the unhappiest women in Europe' in spite of their intelligence and beauty (Ferrero 1941: 135). In no other part of the world did you see so many women in public spaces with important secretarial, management and political roles (ibid.: 129–30), but English civilisation was a male one, and men remained in charge, because women had given up on being 'powerful as women' in order to become equal to their 'bosses' (ibid.: 131–32). On the other hand, Frenchwomen, who had less freedom, held the only real female power: that secret and individual power that makes the French civilisation a female one. In France, women carried out the role of the elite, because the influence of nobles and intellectuals had diminished, whereas the influence of a certain kind of woman remained unchanged under all regimes and throughout all centuries.[71] Moreover, Frenchwomen, in Leo's opinion, presided over a veritable social organisation of happiness (L. Ferrero 1932: 123). Leo's arguments mix some insights with an underlying male chauvinism (L. Ferrero 1941: 138).[72]

The question of female potency, as coupled with the renunciation of the power that can derive from equality, was developed by Leo in *Paris Dernier Modèle de l'Occident*,[73] one of his few works that was published during his life. Paris occupied a fundamental position in Leo's concept of Europe and embodied the myth of a 'Jerusalem of the secular world' – a capital of Europe and humanity, and a 'refuge for the universal intelligence'.[74] In Paris, his most significant exchanges of ideas on Europe were with Paul Valéry, who wrote a long introduction to his thesis on Leonardo, which was published in Italian and French, and also with Drieu la Rochelle whom Leo frequented in 1929–30 ('Drieu awaits papà in the way that people await the Messiah') (L. Ferrero 1999: 223). In Paris, he met exponents of European unity such as Ortega y Gasset and Salvador de Madariaga, and he was a contributor to such magazines as *L'Européen* and *Europe Nouvelle*, edited by Louise Weiss, another exponent of European unity, although his articles were never on the European question: he introduced readers to such Italian authors as Montale, Quasimodo and Loria, and expounded his theories on France, England and, later, New York and the United States. Leo never drew on the political implications of his interest in the European dimension, in spite of his contacts with active supporters of European unity. When he was in Geneva, Leo would go to the League of Nations, for example in December 1931, to listen to a 'very sombre' Briand (ibid.: 272), but there is no trace of the political idea of United Europe in his writing. He restricted himself to the cultural implications of Europeanness.

During this period, the idea of Europe was being pulled in opposing directions: it was subject to the efforts of fascists and Nazis to appropriate it, and to attempts to revive not only its political sense but its utopian one, as a new force between the United States of America and the Soviet Union. Two definitions of Europe were fighting it out, but not without some ambiguities, such as the attempts by Coudenhove-Kalergi, the founder of Paneuropa, to flirt with Mussolini. During the late 1920s and early 1930s, however, the French premier Aristide Briand attempted to establish the United States of Europe in agreement with the German chancellor Stresemann, and the appearance of European visions led in some countries to the foundation of groups interested in the spiritual regeneration of Europe, such as New Europe in England (Passerini 1999: 105–48), and Ordre Nouveau in France. Leo Ferrero took part in the debate on the cultural renewal of Europe, in which the emotive aspects of European integration played an important role. It was the cultural climate that produced Denis de Rougemont's *L'Amour et l'Occident*, and attempted to redefine people's sense of being European and create a new European identity in the vain hope of avoiding the polarisation between fascism and communism. In this light, the regeneration of Europe no longer took the form of literary and poetic experimentation, but was based on the attention to psychological processes within an inner existence in which the individual and the collective come together. Both Leo Ferrero and Denis de Rougemont believed that this could be achieved by joining love and religiosity together (see Part II, Chapter 4).

Love Stories

We have now come to the heart of Leo Ferrero's work. This does not mean that his intellectual positions can be inferred directly from his experiences of love, but rather that we are on the terrain where the public and private come together and generate attitudes and ideas, in particular the emotional components of its new vision of love. Guglielmo Ferrero, in the preface to *Espoirs*, observed that 'the problems of love and the devastation that it can produce in youth were of great concern to Leo during the last years of his life' (L. Ferrero 1935: 9). In reality, Leo's obsession went much further back: he said himself that a recurring thought had always been 'the love / that I dreamed in vain from the birth / of my inner life' (poem 'Mio cuore!' in L. Ferrero 1939b: 136).

His unfinished novel, *Espoirs*, is centred on this obsession. The protagonist, Bernardino, whom we have already discussed, 'appeared to be interested in many things, such as literature, art and music, and he could talk on all these subjects intelligently, but in reality he could only think about love' (L. Ferrero 1935: 68). His young friends 'were [also] all obsessed with love, because none of them knew what it was except in theory'. In the novel, some of the men sought out their first sexual experiences with prostitutes among the homely squalor of small brothels on the outskirts of Florence.

As far as Leo was concerned, his eagerness to be loved was not assuaged, indeed it was exacerbated, as Montale observed, by his being 'his family's emotional centre' (Montale 1946), because it was accompanied by his urgent need to become his own man. This need then became muddled up with his desire to write great works. Given the history of his family, Leo could not help putting all his efforts into creating his own identity through writing. Anything less would have risked his cultural existence and put him in the shadow of his father, his grandfather and even his mother. The recognition he received on the basis of this family background brought him advantages, often pleasures, but also some burdens. During his military service, he discovered that his background was not always effective, as it counted for little in the army. Leo was obsessed with creating his own public profile and his own personal and intellectual identity. He applied most of his energies to this task, particularly when he was in Paris, where he made a 'tremendous effort' to be 'intelligent all day long' (letter to his family dated 16 January 1928 in L. Ferrero 1999: 89). But he also realised the misleading nature of his imagined association between creativity and success on the one hand, and love on the other – an association that he found extremely stressful. Success did not satisfy his need for love; indeed, he felt that destiny was mocking him (L. Ferrero 1937: 26).

During his early twenties, Leo had his first experiences of love, in particular a troubled relationship with Yone who was a few years older than him. In two of his poems to her, Leo portrays himself as being the passive partner in their relationship: like the autumn sun, 'you sink so sweetly in me' (June 1926) or 'I am the open earth to be sown / and await that the grace of your beauty / rains down on my spirit' (November 1926) (L. Ferrero 1939b: 71, 75). Does this reversal of the traditional male–female relationship reflect the difficulty he had in identifying both himself and the object of love? In any case, these expressions and observations that appear elsewhere in his works suggest that he expected too much from love. He was aware of his own inability to bring his expectations of the object of his desires back down to more reasonable proportions, and because of these expectations he ended up being overwhelmed by his lover and having to accept a pact with a destructive dynamic:[75] '[O]ur words and our behaviour are never proportionate to the gravity of our feelings', he wrote.[76] Hence the inability to satisfy expectations, which was particularly pronounced for someone brought up as the centre of attention and used to seeing all his desires met or even predicted for him. His poetry continually refers to love as expectancy and impatience: '[A]mour, amour, attente, impatience' (L. Ferrero 1937: 31). Waiting, which Roland Barthes considered one of the 'figures' of the lover's discourse (Barthes 1990), became for Leo torment, deep insecurity, fear of being an outcast and almost the desire not to exist, and this removed any possibility of happiness in love.

The connection between love and pain leads in the courtly tradition to an understanding of the path of love as an education that inflicts very hard trials, but also develops the character as a whole. Leo observed that love taught him compassion for human suffering and also brought him towards God. Later this would become an original argument in Leo's poems and Notebooks: the link between the suffering of love and praying to God. In February 1925 on the Abetone Mountain, he spoke directly to God, 'I have started to believe in You':

> [F]rom the day in which I began to fear Yone, I shouted to You (on my knees, as I remember, and with my hands together) that I would believe in you and would give you my life, if you restored her to me. Not only therefore did I attempt to blackmail You, but I also asked you to grant me the sinful love of a woman.[77]

There are signs of the torment that tested Leo's moral principles: when his prayers were met, he immediately became ashamed of having asked God's intervention, except when he relapsed into a confusion of conflicting feelings.

Leo's attitude to love has been considered immoral because of his multiple adventures (Kornfeld 1993; see also Ciferri 1993). I find this judgement moralistic and partial, because Leo's principal interest in the relationship between love and morality concerned his relationship with himself (which included his relationship with God) and not his relationship with another self. This attitude is typical of a male cultural tradition, although not unknown among women and not purely European. In Europe, it found its most celebrated form in Don Giovanni and Casanova – but also Madame de Merteuil – and its brilliance in libertine novels. Given that in this context an amorous conquest is perceived according to the principle of pleasure and self-creation, the moral question can exist only as a polemic and explicit revolt against widely held principles. The entire game of love is understood as a challenge to religion and contemporary morality. Elements of the libertine tradition can also be found in feminism, and echoed through the twentieth century in Europe, in debates on sexuality and love in which women took the lead, such as the debate on 'dual love' (Arni 2004). Leo came somewhere between this tradition – or what remained of it – and the courtly one that associated love with the search for God.[78] These European traditions of love are the two sides of the same coin (Passerini: 1992: 17–38), but even in the courtly tradition, the moral question was not posed in terms of contemporary morality, given that the Provençal tradition often (but not always) contrasted marriage with love (and we know that Leo absolutely rejected the prospect of marriage). Both traditional forms of love discourse are all encompassing and radically change the way we see the world. If anything, it is the flirt who could be considered 'blasphemous' in this context, and this was very much Leo's case.

Leo Ferrero vacillated between his efforts to discover new forms of the male–female relationship and his acceptance of his society's and his family's stereotypes concerning women and gender. His was the story of a young European male whose background pushed him in opposing directions: it encouraged him to search for an intelligent but subordinate woman, but caused him to be attracted to emancipated women. He wanted to conform to the inherited idea of the strong and authoritarian man, which he did not find congenial ('I find that I have to make an effort in order to take up the superior and dominant position that is due to the man'),[79] but above all he wanted to follow his desire for happiness. His writings alternate self-critical passages with smug passages that fully accept the role of mirror attributed to women by male narcissism – 'I often think of myself with a woman at my side who says to herself, "Look how he walks well! What a smart observation! How sensitive he is!"'[80]

Leo Ferrero's secular upbringing and the Jewish tradition safeguarded him against the sense of guilt typical of Catholic education in relation to sex. For him, sexuality had clear significance, and it even managed to raise him up above his torments. His was 'a delicate and timid sensuality' (Pézard 1941), and this led him to reflect not only on sexuality but also on sensuality. He was very alert to physical manifestations of virility: he observed in his Notebooks, in 1925, that when he suffered over matters of the heart:

> [T]he most painful moment is the one in which the senses have a release. Then I wake up in the night feeling crushed into a state of utter despondence, because I feel that all my ills come down to the question of sex, and I reflect upon the disproportion between sentimental desperation and what appears to me to be a bodily function. (Ferrero 1984: 182)

Later, in 1932, he would observe changes in his 'male potency': 'I must acknowledge that my adolescence is over. My male potency has not diminished; on the contrary, it is more solid and judicious. This calm is linked to a vegetarian regime: I have stopped eating meat, eggs and wine'.[81]

Leo's insistence on his unhappiness in love should not lead us to think that he had no success: '[H]e was always in love and women liked him', his sister recalled (Ferrero Raditsa 1984: 11). When he went to live in Paris, this propensity reached dizzying heights due to new enticements and his success in Parisian society. Leo had many adventures in Paris, sometimes with married women, of which he wrote to his friends in contradictory terms: 'I am half buried in a frenzy of work and love. Every day I die from emotions [*je me meurs*] and dream of complete calm'.[82]

The letters provide a typology of the relationships open to a young, educated and sensitive European man in that period: the teenage loves full of obsession with sex; the youthful love for Yone; the loving friendship with Marion; the potentially stable relationship with Simone Téry, an older, emancipated and professional woman who was involved in politics; and the romance with Ginetta, which was typical of encounters during travel. This range of relationships with women is coupled with a concurrent development towards greater emotional stability. Leo was not always the victim. By experimenting with the various types of European male behaviour in love, he displayed elements of male dominance. For example, in his relationship with Irma, an American who was his contact with *Cosmopolitan* for the series of interviews with 'the last European kings', he was unsure of his feelings and the ensuing toings and froings proved disastrous for the relationship and for Irma herself. It would appear from their correspondence that their relationship started in 1931, when Irma was visiting Paris. In the spring of 1932, Irma returned to Europe to work with Leo on the interviews, but the resumption of their relationship was not a success. In October 1932, when Leo was at Yale (and *Cosmopolitan* had in the meantime rejected one of the interviews),[83] Irma replied lucidly to his proposal to meet up, 'why should we see each other again? Our last meeting was such a failure that I do not see any reason for having any mutual expectations', and she concluded unequivocally, 'I am not good for you; and you are not good for me'.[84]

It is not only the content of the letters that provides us with information, but also the handwriting and the material on which it is written. These evoke different kinds of relationship: for example Ginetta Diaconescu used lilac envelopes lined with purple, which gives the impression of tasteful frivolity, and remind us of her lovemaking with Leo in a Bucharest park. In these cases, the love letter 'acts as a metaphor for the body of another person' (Lyons 1999: 232–39; Cornille 2002: 296). In August 1930, Leo himself described the letters sent him by Hélène Serpeille de Gobineau: 'Your letters are like yeast: they are small, brief, perfumed and they cause all that immensity of dough to rise. They bring me the heavy sensual pleasure of your perfect body – the pleasant and bizarre/fantastic subtlety of your spirit – and the tender vigour of the exquisite hand I kiss.'

This stylistic gesture of a devoted *cavalier servente* presupposes a love relationship based on a play of gallantry. But this is very different from another amorous game, that of the flirt. In 1922, Leo argued: 'I consider the flirt to be not only a blasphemy in love relations, but also the most stupid way of meeting and encountering people. The absolute contempt I feel for this grotesque parody of love makes me shun anything that resembles or supports it in a conversation with an intelligent woman and above all with a beautiful woman.'[85] The term and concept of flirt at that time referred to the Americanisation of love, and its rejection was consistent with Leo's anti-Americanism.[86]

Something of the game of gallantry can also be found in the friendship between a man and a woman in which sex is discussed but does not take place. This was the case with the relationship between Leo and Marion Mitchell (later Stancioff), an American of his own age who remained in touch for many years. The correspondence started after a meeting in Florence at the end of 1922 on a formal note: Marion wrote from London, 'Mon cher Monsieur Ferrero-Lombroso', and Leo replied using 'Dear Miss Marion'. Discussions on love, Leo wrote, 'are fundamentally the substance of my life', but he acknowledged with self-irony his own false steps in experimenting with the range of amorous relationships.

At the beginning of 1924, Marion announced that she would now call him 'Cher Léo', and the correspondence became more intimate, although it retained its tone of camaraderie. Leo treated his correspondent as a *femme supérieure*[87] and he told her that he had realised that the woman he was in love with was 'silly and bourgeois'. Marion, in turn, presented herself as a 'plain-speaking American', and she provoked him by talking of 'all the young men who paid *her* court', and the 'stupid ones' who remained indifferent to her declared belief in free love, but she immediately added that love is never free. Leo wisely replied that if those youths had responded to her appeal, she would have tired of it very soon. However, the compliments exchanged by Leo and Marion were not very flattering to women: '[Y]ou are the first young woman I have met who thinks and judges with her brain. You have some ideas, young woman', and his conclusion is mindlessly sexist, 'But of course you prefer to be prized more for your physical qualities than for your intellectual ones'.[88]

Leo and Marion were engaged in a genuine exchange of ideas and criticisms of each other. A deep sense of complicity was established between the two, and this would last, in spite of the crisis caused by Marion's marriage in 1925 to a Bulgarian diplomat, with whom she would have five children. On that occasion, he expressed resentment, enviously pronounced that she would not be happy and accused her of shifting their correspondence into English to purge it 'of the unconscious tenderness of the French language'.[89] With time, Leo and Marion made their peace, and when she passed through Florence, she invited the whole Ferrero family to supper at the Hotel Palace. He accepted and called her 'my old friend',[90] and later he would define her as 'the most delightful of my women friends'.[91] Leo confessed to her his difficulties and sufferings at the beginning of his stay in Paris in a very different tone to the reassuring one he used for his family:

> I feel crushed by a burden of sadness and bitterness that is truly far too heavy. I am a legal exile. I left Italy with a passport but with my heart full of disgust and indignation for what is happening there – determined to put off my return for as long as possible. For me there is nothing more to be done back there. ... Now I am in Paris and my heart is bursting. Forgive me for this lack of restraint, but you are the only person to whom I can write all this and I need to write because I cannot talk about it.[92]

It would be memory that would prolong the imagined relationship, restore its value and turn correspondence into a place of amorous memory. One day in 1928, Marion noticed in a restaurant 'the blond nape of an Italian's neck' that immediately reminded her of Leo. She wrote to him that she had kept 'in her heart an immense tenderness for our romantic friendship', and recalled what may have been their only amorous meeting in a tea room on the corner of Bond Street.[93] Marion, who converted to Catholicism, fully understood Leo's anguished path towards religious consciousness in 1931–32 and wrote to him about the crucifixion, God and suffering as growth. A final letter, which was probably not posted, was written by Leo on board the *Corinthia* which took him to the United States, and in it he accused her of not understanding that 'universal suffrage is a government's only source of legitimate authority (this I got from my father)' and that 'political freedom is the main problem in today's world (I say this at the risk of invading my father's patch)'. He reminded her that 'at the moment there is a small elite that will fight for this idea, which is a matter of life and death for Europe'.[94] The letter tells us a great deal about Leo: although he had no political commitment, he did have a clear vision of the European situation.

The range of relationships that we are examining could be interpreted as an attempt by Leo Ferrero to engage in the myth of Don Giovanni within a kind of 'mythbiography', as Ernst Bernhard intended the term, as a psychological type in the Jungian sense on which to exert individual variations (Bernhard 1977). While such a reference figure might have been Don Giovanni for the young Leo who wrote his friends letters about his adventures and misadventures, it was always mixed with its opposite – the unhappy lovesick type. Leo's relationship with Simone Téry produced a new attitude in his love life, which attempted to overcome this combination of opposites, although the anguish remained. This relationship continued with its ups and downs from the spring of 1930 until May 1932, and after that it transformed into an affectionate friendship. Simone Téry was the daughter of two great journalists and was herself a journalist and novelist.[95] In 1928, a journalist who interviewed her for *Nouvelles Littéraires* described her as having 'an almost childlike face modelled with gentle lines under short hair, large, bright, aquamarine eyes which display careful reflection and thoughtfulness, and remain vigilant while the mouth smiles' (Normand 1928).

Simone was another woman a few years older than Leo (she was thirty-three and he twenty-seven), but this time she was an intellectual *engagée*, who frequented the left-wing cultural circles of Paris. Leo found himself dealing with a woman of a considerable personality and intelligence, who had rebelled against her family discipline and was used to taking independent decisions. She was a seasoned traveller in the East, which held such a fascination for Leo, and, like him, she was aware of the relationship between Europe and other cultures.[96] But she was also the woman of his dreams, who admired him and satisfied his narcissistic needs: 'How well you write! How intelligent, ever more intelligent!' she wrote to him from Marseilles. But Simone felt emotionally insecure because she had just come to the end of an unhappy relationship with a man who 'was not free' (like in the relationship described in her book *Passagère*), and at times she was uncertain of Leo's existence, still less convinced that she loved him.[97]

Leo was unable to reassure her. As she would point out, he swung from a crisis of feverish activity to a crisis of apathy and back.[98] Some of Leo's letters to her place Leo in the epistolary tradition that goes back to *Nouvelle Héloise*, in that they represent an attempt by men to occupy the feminine genre of the love letter (Cornille 2002). Such letters are in some ways self-referential and declare the difficulty in their being written and the unusual situation of the author as a man. A letter that expresses emotional torment is primarily written for the writer, but the suffering acquires meaning by being seen by another person. It is an extension of the body, which exposes a wound to another's eyes and dramatises the silence, and does not go beyond the utterance of inarticulate sound, shouts and screams.

Leo and Simone projected demands for salvation on each other. Leo got depressed because the spring made him think about death and he wrote to Simone, 'You will help me to get through it safe and sound, won't you?'[99] She believed that he did not return her love and specified pedantically, 'Je vous aime, moi' ('As for me, I love you'). She continuously wanted to break off the relationship, but also wanted to be held back, 'Empechez-moi de m'en aller' ('Stop me going away').[100] Simone was often travelling because of her work and Leo was unhappy about it. But he was often on the move as well, and she reproached him for it. Leo's letters were full of daydreams, unrealised desire, and expectations that become bitter disappointments.[101]

The relationship almost foundered when Simone was invited to Ulivello and turned up 'all sparkling' after a holiday at Saint-Paul in the Maritime Alps.[102] While the two had previously known moments of happiness in which they were able to overcome their fears, now they were in the family environment, Leo displayed 'such a bizarre mood and such strangely frayed nerves'[103] that Simone once more felt that she was not loved. The two were unable to communicate, and the lack of space in which to be intimate possibly did not help. Leo recalled furtively holding hands.[104] On returning home, Simone sent a thank-you letter and then stopped writing to Leo, but continued to correspond with Nina, who had become a friend. When Leo realised the situation, he reacted with desperation and sent one of his anguished letters,[105] in which he spoke of God and their love in desolate terms.

They re-established an affectionate and even loving relationship, although they did not see each other until October. But now their expectations were much reduced, perhaps even too much so. 'Just a few weeks of happiness is not too much to ask', Simone wrote, but she added that sooner or later they would need to split up, partly because she wanted children and 'a woman who does not have children is a woman who has not fulfilled her destiny'.[106] It is significant that Simone, in spite of her polemics against men, shared these convictions with the whole Ferrero family with the exception of Leo, who did not want to marry and was not interested in children.[107]

The relationship continued for a few months and then finished. In Leo's eyes, Simone remained a symbol of Europe. At the end of 1932, he implored her from New Haven, 'write to me, Simone; I would like *tout de même* to convince myself that Europe still exists'.[108]

Simone's letter to Leo dated 9 July 1930 still contains a sprig of lavender, a sign of the lovers' need to share tangible symbols of beauty and perhaps also of unrealisable aspirations. This love, which both seem to have considered impossible, was not so much a genuine love affair as mutual acknowledgement of similarities. Simone provided a wonderful portrait of Leo, of his 'exquisite mixture of modesty and confidence, his affectionate, attentive expression, either serious or laughing, and overlaid with dreaminess, his delicate hand with which he modelled his words and that indolence that suddenly became animated and exploded in laughter, mischievousness and epigrams lacking malice' (obituary in L. Ferrero 1936: 42). The relationship was in some ways an equal one and, therefore, an important test for Leo. Perhaps this explains the tone of self-congratulatory pain he adopted in the correspondence when there did not seem any particular reason for it, if not the difficulty he was having in putting himself on the same level as his female counterpart.

Leo adopted a very different tone in a relationship that he considered an adventure from its very inception. The comparison throws light on his concepts of Europe and his love relationships. A committed relationship was only possible for him with a woman who belonged to the intellectual world of Western Europe, whereas he treated women from other European regions as exotica. Leo's fling with Ginetta Diaconescu occurred during his trip to south-east Europe as part of his series of interviews with the dwindling number of kings in a Europe increasingly given to either democracy or dictatorship. The first stop was Bucharest.[109] Ginetta and Leo met on the train and engaged in a protracted conversation that lasted into the night and continued in the parks of Bucharest. Leo kept a diary of his impressions of the city, 'gardens, the smell of trees, very beautiful women, the type I fall in love with, sensual city'.[110] Bogdan wrote to Leo from Athens, 'I envy you the Rumanian women: the best in the world'.[111] Leo's diary continued:

The first day: walk in the park with Ginetta. Had tea while listening to Rumanian music. Then kissed Ginetta when trees provided the opportunity. A Rumanian sung songs that Ginetta translated for me: 'You too are lying to me' or 'Why do you embrace me if you do not love me?' It was almost evening, day turning into night. A long evening, so long, so sweet. This music put me in an artificial and extremely pleasant state of mind. I felt I was faraway in Bucharest with a woman who was fascinating and whom I had met during the night on a train.

Both lovers retained a memory of their encounter of which the travelling emphasised the romantic and exotic aspects. In a letter dated 22 April 1932 (which arrived in Paris on the 24th!), Ginetta wrote of the conversation on a train that was bearing Leo 'towards an unknown country' and recalled 'the magic of your words imbued with tender music'. But she was under no illusions. The only real thing between them was his desire for her, which she had detected in his expression and the pressure of his hand. Leo's recollections in his Notebooks confirmed this impression:

> It is curious; I did not love Ginetta. I felt relieved on the day she no longer came to our appointments. ... I started to love her reciprocally (how odd!), when she started to love me. ... On the last day I really loved Ginetta. She was pretty in her morning clothes, and so tender.

Leo's attraction to Ginetta had a strong element of sensuality. His memory of this enabled him to assess himself lucidly and dispassionately. This revealed a desire for self-understanding, but the tone was that of a collector who catalogues his conquests:

> She fondled me, caressed me, held me tight and tenderly, stared at me with her beautiful, black, sad eyes, said little and was submissive in every way. I adored her submission. ... I love gentleness in women ... To dominate me a woman only has to be weak (frightening pride) ... Something that idiot 'I' did not understand.

The 'catalogue' approach recalls the myth of Don Giovanni and his triumphal lists, which, however, implied the seducer was equally attracted by all women, whereas Leo's attitude contained an element of comparison between his lovers in the manner of Casanova's detailed accounts and evaluations. For Hélène, 'a sensual, intelligent, brilliant, exciting, spiritual, but never happy woman', Leo made a careful analysis of their sexual relationship and commented, 'she is the woman I have most desired, but on four or five occasions I had to cool my desire and suppress it'.

Ginetta, not without an element of seduction, insisted upon her own ignorance, 'Je suis tellement ignorante! Il y a tant de belles choses dans le monde! Comme je voudrais être renseignée par toi!' ('I'm so ignorant! There are so many beautiful things in the world! How I wish you would teach me!'). Leo was attracted by the Pygmalion role and immediately fell for it. He added a European dimension to this new aspect of his love life – a strictly Western European dimension. He wrote in his Notebooks: 'Ginetta is aware of nothing; she has never left Rumania. This is enchanting: I have the impression that I am introducing her to Europe and that Europe will always bear my imprint in her spirit (pride)'. For Leo, then, 'Balkania', which included Rumania, could not be considered wholly European and he expressed this opinion to Ginetta as well.[112] She participated in Leo's exotic image of a fabulous European East.[113]

It is doubtful that Ginetta was really so ignorant; it is more probable that she played a game of seduction, having understood Leo's weakness. Her, albeit imperfect, knowledge of French, the tone of her letters, her interest in receiving his book and the fact that she consulted the entry for Ferrero in Larousse all suggest a woman with cultural interests. Although Leo fully accepts his role in this amorous game and does not hide his gratification, it is not at all clear who of the two was leading the love affair. It is true that Ginetta dreamed of going to Paris to see Leo, but she also expected to show him the churches, the Louvre and the Bois de Boulogne. In their relationship, he appears to have been much more the prisoner of stereotypes than she was, as she was capable of ridiculing clichés. Whatever the truth of the situation, the two played a game in which Leo assumed the role of Pygmalion, another European myth that exalted a man's ability to mould a woman spiritually and intellectually in his own image. Leo had written a short story on this theme of 'fashioning' a woman and putting one's own 'imprint' on her, and in it he depicted the incommunicability between teenage boys and girls ('Chassé-croisé', in L. Ferrero 1941b: 158–59). Attempts at dialogue in one adolescent couple ends in mutual incomprehension in spite of their love for each other. When they eventually separate, he thinks that all women are stupid and she wonders in her desolation whether this is a new 'fashion' whereby men and women go their separate ways.

Leo and Ginetta, too, went their separate ways. Theirs was an unequal relationship in which Ginetta seemed to rely on Leo much more than he did on her. She had just experienced an unhappy marriage and was waiting for a divorce. Her affair with Leo occurred during this limbo devoid of immediate hopes, and was projected onto a not impossible future. In a letter, she wrote of her return to the park in her imagination: 'You and I were there alone. You looked at me with soulful eyes, and I smiled with happiness. A dream, a wonderful dream for the spring'. Again imagination had an essential role in love and the writing of love letters. But Leo, who was very busy in Paris with his writing and social commitments, did not meet her expectations. 'Every day I go to the Post Office: nothing', Ginetta reproached him on 18 May. On 10 July, she spoke of her happiness at receiving Leo's book, and complained of the fact that her husband would not let her leave: she had to wait for the divorce proceedings before she could obtain a passport. In the meantime, Leo left for America, but Ginetta's life was also changing. On 10 September 1932, she was no longer thinking of suicide. On 13 December, she was no longer sad, she had put on weight and was going to see her brother in Bessarabia, but she had not heard any news from Leo. On 6 March 1933, she returned to Bucharest after 'three months of fun', and felt that she was cured and happy as Leo would have liked. The divorce proceedings finally came to an end: 'Amen' was all Ginetta could say. She received a letter from Leo that implied he loved her. 'What a wonderful lie!' she exclaimed. It was almost certainly the letter that she copied and sent to Gina Lombroso at her request.

His letter was sent from Yale and, therefore, must have been sent in 1933, 'Chérie, je n'oublie pas Ginetta encore qu'elle soit si loin qu'elle me semble un mythe' ('Dearest, I haven't forgotten Ginetta although she is so far away that she looks like a myth to me'). Leo told her that America was a cold and tiresome country, and that you cannot meet people and exchange a few words on the trains. He recalled their first encounter with nostalgia, and produced the stereotypes on European women and love in Europe when compared with American women and America:

Ah the sweet trains of Europe – of Rumania where you meet Ginetta and talk through to the dawn. Oh sweet, beautiful, warm-hearted, tender, sensual, intuitive, sensitive and intelligent Ginetta, where are you now? Why aren't you here … in place of these pretentious, unfeeling, cold-hearted and idiotic American girls who cannot understand anything? My heart beats faster when I think of Bucharest.

Europe included Rumania now that he was writing from distant and alien America. Leo promised to return to Europe and asked Ginetta to come a little closer to him – a reference to the postponed trip to Paris – and he ended the letter with a display of warmth, 'Embrasse moi comme je t'embrasse' ('Kiss me, as I kiss you'). This was the letter as a place of memory and regret, in which he evoked and yearned for the past and what could have been.[114] Ginetta replied with some irony: 'I would like to be the cold and foolish American woman who has the good fortune to converse with you and be kissed by you. … When are you coming back to Europe?' On 20 May 1933, she sent him a small photo of herself with a cigarette in her mouth, along with a brief note (which was forwarded from Yale to Leo in New Mexico), 'There is no other love'. The correspondence contains a postcard showing the Cismigiu Park with a note from Ginetta on the anniversary of their meeting: 'Silence ... oubli / Pas un reproche, chéri / seulement cette nuit tu dois penser à moi / c'est l'anniversaire de notre connaissance' ('Silence ... oblivion/ Not a reproach dear/ but tonight you must think of me/ it is the anniversary of our meeting').[115]

Leo did not lose his head in his love relationships, in spite of the sentimentality and orientalism. On occasions he felt that he had made progress: 'In 1932 I showed a certain degree of wisdom' in at least two relationships, but when he came to assess the overall situation, he had to admit that his original boundless need was still intact. 'I have a violent need for women, female tenderness and love'. The problem was transforming this need into relationships capable of establishing reciprocity and giving happiness, rather than pursuing many different opportunities. The only significant change was when Leo was in the United States and had a relationship with Thelma Sachs, which was the most mature of his relationships and coincided with his theorisation of European love. Thelma was Jewish-American. She did not allow Leo to monopolise suffering; indeed, she constantly deluged him with her own anxieties. She lived in New York, while Leo was at Yale. At the beginning of 1933, the relationship does not yet appear to have become a love one. On 7 March, Thelma wrote a long letter to Leo in which she expressed anguish over fears that the world was preparing for another war, while 'there would be food enough to feed the whole world if men were not so greedy'. But she was clearly making an advance in the letter, as in her declaration that she would like to know Italian or French so as to better understand what he was thinking.

The tone was that of a lament for herself and the world in general, 'My brain is too lazy and I simply haven't learnt to discipline it enough to study seriously'. It seems to echo Julie's entreaty in *Nouvelle Héloïse*: '[C]'est à moi, c'est à moi, d'etre faible et malheureuse. Laisse-moi pleurer et souffrir ... mais toi ... comment t'oses-tu dégrader au point de soupirer et de gémir comme une femme' (Cornille 2002: 293) ('It is for me, for me, to be weak and unhappy. Let me weep and suffer ... but as for you ... how dare you demean yourself to the point of sighing and groaning like a woman'). It was the right tone to take with Leo, who immediately accepted the implicit invites and suggested that they should study some philosophical problems together. In the general sense of apprehension, the only flashes of vitality from Thelma concerned her teaching work, when she spoke of how she enjoyed the audacious intelligence of the street children, but was exhausted at the end of a day with them. Leo sent her letters in a similar vein. Every day when he read the *New York Times* he was shaken by local and international events full of injustices and insanity, 'I have a deep sympathy for lost causes'.

The letters soon became more intimate and the forms of address more affectionate. Thelma shifted from 'Dear Leo' to less formal and standardised openings to her letters, such as 'Leo dear' or 'Leo Darling' or 'my sweet Leo'. At the same time, the relationship became increasingly complex and demanding. In response to Leo's reproach that she was 'selfish, full of herself, matter of fact', Thelma responded that this was a result of her past, as well as the intense depression she was going through, but reasserted her intention of 'belonging to [her]self'. In April, Thelma told him of the increasing distance between her and her cohabitant, 'who was locking the stable door after the horse has been stolen'.[116]

On 29 April, Leo wrote to her in New Haven a very important letter in which he expressed his new convictions on love, which we will examine in the last part of this chapter:

> [W]hat a marvellous but terrible thing is love. It is – I believe – a by-product of Christianity, the painful privilege of the West. I don't think that Chinese and Hindus know what is passion. I don't think that the Romans and the Greeks really knew it. This sentiment had no name and was, therefore, impossible to understand or express. Christianism for the first time has freed the monster, has given a name to this mysterious force that was sleeping in the man, and has tried to direct it towards God. But the consequences of that love have been enormous. When one has recognized in oneself the force and the need of love, if he cannot project it toward God, he will project it toward a human being. And passion is suffering, as it can be understood from the Latin meaning of the word: 'passion' comes from the Latin *patire*, 'to suffer'. So that it is impossible to have passion and not to suffer.
>
> Dearest mine, I am still very tired and preoccupied.[117]

On 1 May, Thelma announced that she had told her companion that their relationship was really over and she intended to go to Europe. At the same time, Thelma did not gloss over the serious problems caused by Leo's positions, '[E]xperience has been that the kind of relationship you propose works terrific hardship on a woman'. For his part, Leo was studying the questions of predestination, grace and freedom in Thomas Aquinas, and he attempted to involve her in this enterprise. Thelma had, in fact, expressed her doubts on the existence of absolute freedom. But Leo realised that this proposal was also a means to evade the wave of sentiments that could have overwhelmed him.[118] Anyway, on 20 April, Leo announced his firm intention of continuing the relationship that promised to change the meaning of his life: 'No, my sweet, I will not leave you here. Do not fear. Thelma, for the first time I feel that my constant secret desire is being realised, that my desperate conflict between women and love is over'. But the question of marriage divided them profoundly. Thelma suggested that they could always obtain a divorce if they married in accordance with American law. However, she learnt from a mutual friend that Leo thought she did not really love him but was only interested in marriage, and she reproached him in turn for only being interested in himself.

The dispute could not be reconciled. Instead of going to Europe together, Leo ended up organising the journey that would take him from New Mexico to Asia and, on 26 May, he wrote to Simone Téry with bitterness, 'Mes amours américains s'effondrent au dernier moment comme des décors mal arrangés' ('My American love affairs are collapsing like badly built scenery').[119] The relationship with Thelma was not the only one Leo embarked upon during his stay in America, but it was the one in which he placed his greatest hopes. However, it collapsed like a house of cards. The last letter from Thelma no longer entertained any amorous tones and returned to polite forms: 'Dear Leo' at the beginning and 'Sincerely' at the end. Thelma now appeared only interested in the return of two books he had borrowed, before he left for Mexico.[120] In spite of the promises of Leo's new equilibrium and his attempts to instil this into his relationship, his amorous dialogue had not succeeded in building bridges between differences.

Love of Self and Love of God: Comparisons between Civilisations

'He was preparing to become a great European', Albert Thibaudet wrote of Leo Ferrero.[121] The question of 'great Europeans' was a recurring one in the history of European culture. In general, it referred to highly cultured men who found themselves equally at ease in the continent's many capitals, because they knew different languages and could rely upon networks that made it possible for them to enter into dialogues with people in Paris, Vienna, London or Berlin. Their community was almost exclusively an urban one and based on contacts created through publications and/or cultural exchanges in the fields of art and music. It was a Europe of the mind, a territory crossed by cultured travellers who met up in cafés and salons. The term 'great European' was reserved for those who were most visible and active in spreading international solidarity. It was used by Stefan Zweig for Emile Verhaeren and by Jules Romains for Zweig. It usually applied to a man, even though the community that found it valid certainly included many women, given its position on the boundary between the public and the private and the role of women in this intermediary area.

The term is suited to Leo, in whose work and attitudes many people perceived elements of Europeanness.[122] As a young man, he gained a reputation as a 'European intellectual' and exponent of the spirit of Europe against the dictatorships and chauvinism (Ferrero 1936: 65). Simone Ratel, using the typical hyperbole of obituaries, even considered him one of the 'incarnations of Europe's genius', and provided the customary interpretation of this spirit as nothing more than the sum of the national parts: '[S]ensitive to the arts like a Slav, interested in philosophical arguments like a German, frank and malicious like the Latin he was, but a Latin with a share of Semitic blood that linked him to the profound Orient' (ibid.: 38–39). The subtitle of this chapter characterises Leo Ferrero as a 'young European' with reference to both Mazzini's Young Europe movement and the fact that he was young, European by education, and willing to accept change. Early influences came from his journey to London and the period he lived in Paris, and these integrated his sense of belonging to Italy within a wider identity. As we have seen, though, this was limited to Western Europe, which he considered different from 'Balkania'. The biggest change in his self-perception as a European occurred when he travelled to America, where his sense of being European was tested by intercultural encounters and developed profoundly. While in the United States living in Yale's multicultural environment, visiting New York, Chicago, Washington and Detroit, having love relationships with American women, Leo was able to make comparisons to an extent that was not possible in Paris and London. As with most migrants, European identity is triggered by living and working in another continent. For working people, this may be the first real occasion on which they are considered and consider themselves European, often in a defensive and even racist mode (the elites had shared a European identity for many centuries). The attitude of the 'others' is decisive in this process, as they view the migrant as a 'European' and put all the nationalities together, which lessens their significance.

The first signs of Leo's awareness of this enlarged identity appeared in his correspondence (in French) with Victoria Ocampo,[123] in which he displayed an acute sense of how she belonged to a culture that was European, but not solely European. Through Victoria, Leo perceived the relationship between Europe and other continents in a new light. They had met in Paris in 1930: 'I am lovingly and zealously cultivating South America,' he wrote to his parents, 'personified by an extremely beautiful, intelligent and powerful woman' (postmark 5 March 1930) (Ferrero 1999: 232). They quickly developed a friendship and a profound intimacy. He was grateful to Victoria for having provided him with the chance to write articles for *La Nación* and he admired her ability to establish friendships and contacts, which included Ortega and other famous intellectuals. For her part, Victoria, who had a difficult relationship with Drieu la Rochelle, confided in Leo that the 'propreté de votre jeunesse' ('the cleanness of your youth'), as against the 'sordid things' she saw in Paris, was good for her like green trees in the city.[124]

When Victoria left Paris for New York, Leo wrote to her and recalled something she had said: 'Je ne peux m'amuser à voir des nègres [it does not amuse me to see negroes], I am too much like them.' This probably referred to one of the black artists living in Paris at the time (but not Josephine Baker, who was touring in Spain in the spring of 1930). Leo further developed the idea contained in this sentence and found the key to the European success of Vic, as he called her, but also to her *ennuis parisiens*. He saw Victoria as a 'negro', or in other words someone belonging to a new and young civilisation when compared with the old European one, and he deduced the following:

> The Parisians were attracted by what was new and 'authentic' in you (to use an expression you like), but at the same time they couldn't believe in it entirely. ... There is a contrast in you (perhaps typical of young peoples) that makes you enigmatic for men of such an ancient civilisation in which all intellectual and moral qualities are now on a par. Intellectually you are very refined, complicated and mature, but morally and emotionally you are very simple. Your passions, desires and affections are as vigorous, clear cut and candid as those of a child or a savage.

According to Leo, a distinguishing feature of Parisian civilisation was precisely the continuous exchange between intellect and feeling, and it was on this basis that La Rochefoucauld could come out with his famous maxim that people would fall in love much less if they had never heard of love. But the maxim was not valid for Victoria who 'would have been able to love even if she had read nothing about love', because her inner worlds were completely separate; her intellectual system was clearly distinct from the 'kingdom of her heart'.

In this correspondence, Leo adopts Eurocentric tones informed by an essentialist perception of women, European culture and other cultures. Even Roger Caillois, who had one of his longest love relationships with Victoria, had no scruples about defining her as the 'carnivore of South America' (Caillois and Ocampo 2003: 41–42). Victoria Ocampo encouraged this view of herself: in her letters to Leo from New York, she told him about her visit to a Methodist church in Harlem and the film *Green Pastures* ('une fable jouée par des nègres' ['a fable acted by negroes']), and claimed that she shared the 'tremendous spiritual hunger that characterised one aspect of the negro soul'.[125] Leo showed sensitivity to manifestations of racism in other ways: some terms he uses, such as 'presunti primitivi' ('supposedly primitives') for the Mexican *indios* indicate a different position from his father's and grandfather's racial attitudes.

The relationship between Leo and Victoria continued to be intense. The possibility of Leo visiting Latin America was discussed, but was never to happen. However, Victoria remained someone whose views he wished to consult. On 25 August 1932, Leo wrote to her before leaving for America: 'When will I see you next? I no longer see, as would be normal, an endless stretch of time before me, but something cut short in I know not what manner, and I leave for America as though I were certain of shipwreck.' The premonition was immediately softened by an attempt to put it into a context, '[B]ut this mood is perhaps determined by the tremendous heat'. Guglielmo Ferrero told Bogdan Raditsa that Leo had been 'a little gifted with prophecy throughout his life' (Raditsa 1939: 83).[126] There are, in fact, other similar premonitions in Leo's work, for example a poem in *Catena* that refers to 'a future / that will always be unknown to me' (Ferrero 1939b: 135), and some of his letters to Simone Téry.

During his stay in America, Leo developed two threads of thought: one that continued the type of sociocultural observations he had done on England and France, and the other that studied the question of the divine. The first was documented by his collection of writings in *Amérique, Miroir Grossissant de l'Europe*, in which he concentrates on his examination of women as indicators of the profound nature of a civilisation. Leo noted 'the enormous prestige women enjoy in America' and found its origins in the absence of women from the frontier experience. However, he was extremely critical of American women, whom he considered to be dominated by 'selfishness' (L. Ferrero 1939a: 57).

We know from Leo's letters that he suffered from the lack of human contact in the United States, and idealised his memory of Europe, which became the continent in which love permeated the everyday relationships between men and women, even fleeting ones. While he observed the difference between the United States and Europe, Leo also pointed out the similarities that bring them together in the shared concept of the West. In a posthumous article, America was presented as an extreme example of Western civilisation, in the sense that both the Americans and the Europeans have renounced contemplative life.[127] At the same time, Leo started to develop a systematic comparison between the world's great civilisations, and returned to the question of self-love which had fascinated him in the past but which he now saw in a new light. From this new perspective, which concerned its connection to religion, the essential contradiction of existence was self-love. Christianity had tried to sublimate it by fusing it with the concept of God, without which the whole edifice comes crumbling down. This was why Westerners were descending into instinctive life and becoming slaves to their passions: the disorder of emotions shared by Americans and Europeans arose from an irresolvable dilemma, namely the perpetual presence of the Christian ideal of saintliness, which they no longer can or wish to live up to ('Où est le Bonheur', in L. Ferrero 1984: 97–98).

These ideas lead Leo Ferrero towards religious consciousness. This was an aspiration he had had for some time and had held at the margins of his secular upbringing, as can be understood from a brief dialogue with his mother when he was seventeen, 'You know, mamma, I would have liked to have a religion; a religion is useful'. – 'Would you like to have it taught to you?' – 'No, that would be useless, a pretence. I would like to have had one' (G. Lombroso 1935: 293).

Gina Lombroso's reply was open and enlightened, yet inadequate. Leo's spiritual journey did not abandon the principles he had been brought up with, but went beyond them. Leo loved Buddhism because it was closer to Greek philosophy than a religion and because it considers a sin of ignorance more serious than a conscious sin. He aspired to become a sage, because a sage is the saint of godless civilisations, and capable of reaching productive calm and winning the struggle against self-love and desire (L. Ferrero 1937: 114).

Leo's readings showed new interests: he was reading thinkers like Vivekananda, and studying Chinese and Indian philosophies as well as Aquinas, Augustine, Pascal, Spinoza and histories of European mystics. He was interested in belief systems such as the yoga of Patanjali, Buddhism, Taoism and Confucianism, and he compared them with Christianity. He introduced references to Judaism and made comparisons between Catholicism and Calvin's and Luther's Protestantism. Most importantly, he approached the European classics from a different perspective, because he was reading them in a Mexican village: here he touched the limitations of being European and the profound innovation resulting from contact with Europe's other.[128]

Leo Ferrero developed a concept of self (*moi*) based on the Hindu perception that it is made up of an infinity of selves, each of which can be continuously modified (L. Ferrero 1937: 158). Leo developed his thought in a new direction by combining oriental ideas – which he found in Schopenhauer and Spinoza – with the Western tradition. This made it possible for him to criticise twentieth-century Western civilisation as a glorification of self-love, which was produced by a degeneration of Christianity or passion–love, and large-scale industry. Salvation could only come from more selfless ideals (ibid.: 116, 175).

In his opinion, passion–love was incomprehensible to civilisations that had not been influenced by Christianity, which had deified womanhood, repressed sexual love outside marriage, created an obsession with sex, and released man's passions (ibid.: 176). Before Christianity, passionate men could not express their passion, as in their societies there were no words to express it (ibid.: 177), but afterwards the opposite occurred: everyone attempted to make their feelings live up to the words, and to feel what they say they feel. Leo specified that this was especially true of young people, in his notes for *Espoirs*. He, therefore, returned to an idea he had already expressed from a different viewpoint in the article published by *Solaria* in 1929, 'Trasfigurazione dell'Amore': '[L]'amour se complique avec la civilisation parce que l'homme commence à réfléchir' ('Love becomes entangled with civilisation because man has started to reflect') (ibid.: 179).

Leo asserted that the problems had to be resolved without recourse to God, but at the same time announced his conversion (L. Ferrero 1941: 181).[129] By this he meant that you must not believe in God out of a sense of need, but out of 'a gesture of love':

I came to believe in God from one day to the next; I do not know why. Because I woke up in the middle of the night and I heard the nightingale sing in the garden. And all of a sudden, without having time to reflect on it, I said to myself: this nightingale sings every night and I hear it this night for the first time because I have woken up. God has always existed close to me, and I couldn't know him because I was asleep. I got up and leant against the window: thousands of fireflies filled the valley and the fields sparkled lit up by the moon. Yes, I reflected, God exists.

His new conviction, which had much to do with aesthetic pleasure, was neither confessional nor linked to a system of Christian values. It was more a cosmic sentiment, powerfully informed by a sense of beauty (L. Ferrero 1939b: 39).[130] The relationship between Leo's acceptance of the divine and the development of his concept of love should be put in the context of his comparative analysis of the history of civilisations. On the basis of his own studies and also conversations with Chinese scholars like Motse and Liang, whom he met at Yale, Leo was increasingly convinced that in China the sentiment of love referred only to relations between a mother and son, and not to spouses, 'Chinese civilisation is founded on the family, and the family on the absence of love' (L. Ferrero 1937: 188). In the preface to *Espoirs*, Guglielmo quotes passages from Leo's Notebooks that refer to the American period and mention the young philosopher Binham Daj, whom Leo met in Chicago. He was attributed with the information that an English word, 'romance', was used to describe relations between lovers in China, and that there was no verb in Chinese to say 'I love you'. Thus the Chinese were happier than Europeans because they did not feel they had a right to love and were not obliged to pursue its shadow throughout their lives, as were Europeans, who had fallen prey to a veritable madness. Leo added, 'Alas I myself am the maddest of all madmen! But at least now I know it'. The frenetic activity of Westerners, including Americans, was nothing but sublimation of the passion triggered and exalted by Christianity; American life was an escape from love through work (ibid.: 192–93). Leo contrasted this with Vivekananda's affirmation based on Bhagavadgita, according to which calm is the highest manifestation of inner power, whereas movement is the expression of an inferior force.

It was his constant search for happiness that led Leo Ferrero to travel to the East in order to learn the teachings on this question. In the past he had believed that Paris had achieved a genuine 'social organisation of happiness', but now he changed direction completely. He discovered the signs of a different route to happiness during his stay in Mexico amongst the poorest and most unaffected of the *indios* he met.[131] The idea of a trip round the world and a return to Europe via Asia had a symbolic meaning for Leo and he wanted to use this journey, which was so tragically interrupted, to revisit the tradition of Western thought on love and God in the syncretic light of Eastern philosophies.

In spite of his persistent Eurocentrism, Leo adopted positions that diminished the Eurocentric triumphalism on the subject of love, which he conceived not as a sign of superiority over the world's other cultures, but as a symptom of a painful European syndrome. The primacy of the love discourse was central to Leo's thought, which took to its logical conclusion La Rochefoucauld's maxim according to which we would fall in love a lot less if we had never heard of love. European civilisation exalted its moods through the love discourse, exactly like young people who 'simulate the moods they actually feel'.[132] The implication was that it was possible to get out of this trap, the short circuit between the love discourse and love as a passion, something specifically European, and become happier. The comparison between civilisations demolished the biological interpretation of the different attitudes to love in favour of the cultural one, and stressed the priority given to the love discourse rather than love as feeling, as would be done more fully by Denis de Rougemont. It is striking that Leo came close to positions expressed in *L'Amour et L'Occident*, as Rougemont admitted in an appendix to this work which was published in 1939.[133] There was something in the Zeitgeist that pushed in that direction, and related to the passions unleashed by the First World War, the crisis in European consciousness and the renewed contacts with other civilisations.

Leo Ferrero made important advances along the road away from biological determinism and towards acknowledgement of the ways in which individual and collective characters are cultural constructs. The fact that he came closer to religion was an essential part of this process. This religiosity did not take the form of a return to Judaism because this was the religion of his fathers, and he had to break away from the patriarchal family for the sake of his own individuation process. The stages along this journey were a reassessment of women and the feminine, and the concept of an increasingly close relationship between love as sentiment and the love discourse.

Notes

1. For Piero Gobetti, the connection meant modernity saturated with the spirit of freedom and capable of providing intellectual and political opposition. In a leader for *Il Baretti* in December 1924, Gobetti linked Europeanness to an historical and ethical concept of enlightenment; see N. Bobbio (1977: 40). Gobetti's idea of enlightenment has been interpreted as a development of his liberalism (i.e., a political and intellectual attitude that prioritises individual rights and the role of conflict in the battle of ideas) and as an antidote to irrationalism. In this case, 'European style' means openness to an extensive exchange of ideas and coherence between one's life and one's thought (see Polito 1993).

2. To avoid endlessly repeating surnames, I will occasionally use only the forename for some of the people most frequently referred to, such as Leo Ferrero, Gina Lombroso Ferrero, Guglielmo Ferrero and Nina Ferrero Raditsa.

3. According to the account of Robert Michels, besides Italians like Gaetano Mosca, Achille Loria, Leonardo Bistolfi and Zino Zini, there were many visitors from abroad, including Max Nordau, Max Weber, the Swedish feminist writer Ellen Key and Anna Kuliscioff.

4. By way of example, we can recall the writings of Giovanni Agnelli and Attilio Cabiati, published in 1918. The authors criticised the League of Nations in the name of a European Federation that went beyond the principles of nationality and involved the masses as the premise for a Labour International (Agnelli and Cabiati 1918: 126). However, these arguments did not become part of the political debate at the time (Pistone 1975: 37).

5. Leo Ferrero was born in 1903 in Turin, where his parents lived in the same house as Cesare Lombroso. After his death, Gina was no longer tied to the city, and Guglielmo could move his family to Florence so that Leo could learn 'the best Italian' (Lombroso 1935: 185).

6. See Ferrero Raditsa (1984); Raditsa (1982); Calloni and Cedroni (1994); Bagnoli (1986, 329–38).

7. Guglielmo often travelled in Europe and America, and between 1893 and 1896 completed study trips to London, Berlin and Paris. He too was ostracised by the Italian university system, which denied him a professorship because of opposition from Benedetto Croce, but in 1930 he was given the chair of modern history at Geneva.

8. Piero Gobetti spoke admiringly of his bilingualism with Jean Luchaire, who recorded Gobetti's opinion in *Notre Temps*, 10 September 1933. Leo Ferrero's attachment 'to various motherlands' was mentioned by a review published in *Europe* after his death; see Hertz (1937: 405–6).

9. Nina, who attended courses of a technical and practical nature, felt that she exemplified her mother's theories of female education (although her mother had two degrees).

10. Leo's letters to his parents demonstrate his relief at escaping from 'deadly Florence' (letter written from Turin before leaving for Paris on 8 July 1919, in Kornfeld 1999: 33).

11. See also Scotti (1984: 19–26, 27–29); Scotti (1993: 135–46).
12. A series of illustrations show figures of brilliant European and American women who 'have masculine characteristics' (Lombroso and G. Ferrero 2004: 84, Table 3).
13. See Puccini (1981: 217–44, 187–238). On the criticisms by Italian feminists of positivist anthropology, see Gibson (2002: 79 ff.)
14. Published in 1897 and dedicated to 'Cesare Lombroso / This fruit of a tree / Cultivated by him'.
15. Gaetano Mosca (1858–1941) was a jurist, political scientist and the author of *Sulla Teorica dei Governi e sul Governo Parlamentare* (*Theory of Governments and Parliamentary Government*), published in 1884, and *Elementi della Scienza Politica* (*The Ruling Class*, published in 1896).
16. He upbraided Ferrero for a concept that acknowledged 'Jewish genius' but did not challenge the racial difference between Aryans and Jews. Lombroso had explained Jewish behaviour in part through environmental factors and not exclusively biological ones, which was exactly what he did in the case of black people (Gibson 2002: 106–7).
17. 'How Valuable Women Can Be', wrote Cesare Lombroso in the preface to *Criminal Woman*, 'is demonstrated by the honoured' ladies that provided him with documents and advice, 'and you demonstrate it most of all, my darling Gina, the last and only thread that ties me to life, my steadiest collaborator and inspiration, more stimulating than any of my books' (Lombroso and G. Ferrero 2004: 37).
18. See Bibliography in Calloni (1998: 273–94).
19. This is the title of the first part of *L'Anima della Donna*, the manuscript on which she began to work in 1917, and which was published in 1921 and translated into sixteen languages. Significantly, Gina dedicated it to her daughter Nina, 'in the hope that by reading it she would be spared some of the anguish that awaited her'. In a letter to Leo, held as 'A mother's testament' in the 'Leo Ferrero' collection at the Centro Studi Piero Gobetti in Turin (Folder G), Gina advised him to harmonise his interests and ideals, but admitted that 'she could have achieved greater wealth, glory and love by following the opposite principles'.
20. The friendship and affinity between these two women were deepened by the anguish of their sons' deaths within a few years of each other. Words of affections for Gina and Leo are to be found in Rosselli (2001: 120–21). For information on Amelia, see Miniati (2003) and Pugliese (1998: 2).
21. Leo wrote, 'God, art, science, an idea, an action, business are the absolute for men, and women don't understand' (Leo emphasised, 'this agrees with my mother's ideas') (L. Ferrero 1937: 190).
22. S. Ratel in *Journal des Nations*, Geneva, 29 August 1934, now included in L. Ferrero (1936).
23. *Espoirs* is the story of a group of young Florentines between the ages of fifteen and twenty, starting from February 1914. They include the children of the Resmini family, inspired by the Lombroso and Ferrero families.
24. Dated September 1922 by Gina.

25. Leo's aunt, Paola Carrara, broken-heartedly reflected on the fate that led to the early death of Luchaire and Pavolini – the first of whom became a Nazi collaborator and the second a fascist – and Nello and Leo, the first of whom was assassinated by French right-wing *cagoulards* and the second who died in a car accident (Dolza 1990: 158n.).

26. He was the son of Julien, the founder of the French Institute in Florence. Jean was a political journalist and worked for Louise Weiss's *L'Europe Nouvelle* and founded *Notre Temps – La Revue des Nouvelles Générations* in 1927, which was linked to Aristide Briand. The outcome of Jean Luchaire's vision was tragic: when the plan to revitalise and transform the Radical Party failed, he exchanged Briand's idea of Franco-German cooperation for the Nazi one of a 'new Europe'; see Bruneteau (2003). He became an official in the Vichy government and a collaborator with the Gestapo, and was condemned to death in 1946.

27. On either 12 or 15 February. Unless stated otherwise, the letters come from the Archivio Leo Ferrero at the Fondazione Primo Conti in Fiesole (ALFFPC), where they are categorised by addressee if written by Leo, or by sender if addressed to him. Letters by Leo are quoted here with the indication of the name of the addressee, and letters to him with the name of the writer.

28. Aldo Garosci (1907–2000), historian, and Carlo Levi (1902–75), doctor, writer and painter, were both antifascists. Giansiro Ferrata (1907–86), critic and writer, was initially linked to groups of fascist dissidents and then became active in the Resistance.

29. Claude Dauphin, the pseudonym of Legrand, son of the poet Franc-Nohain (Maurice Etienne Legrand). Claude Dauphin became a successful actor in Paris and on Broadway, and then moved from the theatre to cinema.

30. Letter to Claude Dauphin of 21 April 1922.

31. Letter to Dauphin of 11 May 1922.

32. Dauphin's letter from Paris, 5 February 1922.

33. In a letter dated 17 June 1923, Claude recalled his arrival at Ulivello in the rain. When he and Leo met, they looked at each other in silence: '[I]t is a look of joy and seriousness, an intense communion, an exquisite moment, the most precious of our friendship'.

34. Dauphin's letter of 12 August 1923.

35. Dauphin's letter of 23 December 1923.

36. 'I have had three marvellous suits made (which I hope you will not wear) and six silk poplin shirts, two pairs of shoes, one overcoat, etc. I am ready for marriage ...', undated letter.

37. Dauphin's letter of 10 September 1926.

38. Letter to Raditsa, July 1930.

39. Raditsa's letter from Split dated 17 May 1929. Among the other readings mentioned in the correspondence, Bogdan spoke about Erich Maria Remarque's *All Quiet on the Western Front* and Massimo Bontempelli's *Il Figlio di Due Madri* (both published in 1929). Claude advised him to read Jean Cocteau, Paul Morand and *Le Diable au Corps* by R. Radiguet (1923), which, however, he did not like.

40. Zweig (1981: 37); this is the famous novella *Twenty-four Hours in the Life of a Woman* (Zweig 2003).
41. Raditsa's letter from Athens, August 1929.
42. In the original version of *Espoirs*, Leo wrote that Bernardino 'était obsédé par le sein d'Ester' ('obsessed by Ester's breast'), but Gina Lombroso 'suppressed the word "breast" on several occasions' in the published version of the book; see Kornfeld (1993: 355).
43. Raditsa's postcard from Athens of 27 November 1931.
44. In November 1922, Leo wrote to Claude to express his mixture of physical and political disgust, 'at half past eight in the morning I went to present my body to the inspection of military gentlemen, in the midst of rowdy young fascists – as ever! – who undressed while narrating obscene tales. I cannot express the indignation I felt when a *carabiniere* explained how the previous day he had beaten a socialist and forced him to drink a purgative because he had a hammer and sickle tattooed on his arm'.
45. The French term means 'nice arse' and was originally used to describe the rear of a horse.
46. The part of *Espoirs* that concerns military service was very probably autobiographical.
47. An observation that Gina Lombroso and Guglielmo Ferrero took from François Franzoni (L. Ferrero 1942: 13).
48. See Lorenzer (1970).
49. In *La Favola dei Sette Colori*, written at the age of seventeen, the love story between the goddess Iris and a mortal minstrel is overlaid with a satire of the gods, represented by a shortsighted Juno and a crooked Mercury. *Il Ritorno di Ulisse* came out two years later and was a modern reinterpretation of the *Odyssey* with a few innovations: Gina Lombroso observed that his Penelope was no longer the sensible matron, but had more of a resemblance to Nora in *Casa di Bambola* (L. Ferrero, *Il Ritorno di Ulisse. La Favola dei Sette Colori* n.d., Preface: 10). In the rest of the notes it will be referred to as *RUFSC*).
50. L. Ferrero, *La Chioma di Berenice. Le Campagne senza Madonna* (n.d. but known to be 1924: 15). In the rest of the notes it will be referred to as *CBCSM*.
51. Ronzy in Lombroso-Ferrero (1943: 92).
52. It was the only one of his plays that he saw appear on the stage, in Rome in 1924, where it was well received. It was staged again in Florence in 1927, Geneva in 1940, and on Swiss radio in 1941 and 1942 (Lombroso-Ferrero 1943: 97–98). The first staging had a *parterre de roi*, as a result of Leo's activity as a cultural organiser: in 1922–23 he worked hard to set up an Italian sister organisation to La Chimère, which had been founded in France to revive the theatre (see Chapter 5).
53. Ernest Ansermet, conductor of the Suisse Romande Orchestra, wrote in *Sur* in 1942 that Pierrot signally evoked the memory of Leo when he was small, of whose 'precocious and mischievous understanding of human affairs' he had been told by Leo's mother (Lombroso-Ferrero 1943: 157). Even the clash between Natalie and her husband could recall the relationship between Leo's parents, who went through a particularly difficult period when Leo was nine

years old (Kornfeld 1993: 348). The scientist's character is a reference to both Cesare Lombroso and Guglielmo (L. Ferrero 1924–28: 34).

54. It was written immediately after Leo's move to Paris, but remained in his drawer until his death because Leo feared the consequences it could have had for his family in Italy (see letter of February 1929 to his sister and parents [L. Ferrero 1999: 153, 155]). The manuscript was found by Aldo Garosci in Leo's flat after he left for America, and was delivered to his parents when Garosci went to his friend's funeral at the Plainpalais cemetery near Geneva. The work had a considerable success in Paris: Valéry and Bergson were moved by the reading they listened to, and André Maurois wrote in the *Literary NY Times* of 8 July 1934, 'Angelica is the tragedy of the despot, but also of mediocrity and cowardice' (L. Ferrero 1936: 62). In London, on the other hand, it was staged in 1937 and considered too light and farcical to penetrate the question of dictatorship ('London Sees "Angelica"', *New York Times*, 13 April 1937, 31).

55. The original Italian version no longer exists. The version published by Capolago in 1937 is a translation back into Italian from the French version and then edited by Gina Lombroso, who changed the ending to make it more optimistic. The new ending completely falsifies Leo's thought. It was one of the very few significant changes made by Gina, who was generally scrupulous in her philological work, although she felt entitled to censure her son's writing 'in a few exceptional passages' (Kornfeld 1993: 354).

56. It has correctly been pointed out that *Angelica* is a portrayal of Italy's drama and how it sold itself out to tyranny, from which it cannot free itself because for the moment it was too pleased with it (Scotti 1984: 28). The critics saw the Italian masks as symbols representing different classes, and Angelica as false liberty in contrast with true liberty as perceived by Orlando; see P. Jeanneret, 'Leo Ferrero (1903–33)', *Nouvelles Littéraires*, 9 September 1933; Franc-Nohain's review of *Angelica* in *L'Echo de Paris*, 17 May 1934, republished in L. Ferrero (1936: 31–33).

57. Leo Ferrero, who was conscious of his theatrical abilities, devoted a great deal of time to studying the technique of playwriting. An entire critical study of *Romeo and Juliet* survives, and many observations on the theatre can be found in L. Ferrero (1940).

58. 4 December 1934; see L. Ferrero (1936: 51–52).

59. Actually, the dictator in *Angelica* somewhat resembles D'Annunzio, or rather any dictator who establishes a political aesthetics. This interpretation has been recently revived (Panzini 1999: 35–57) to support a less strictly political reading of the play than its traditional one.

60. 'Il Teatro e gli Intellettuali', *Il Piccolo della Sera*, 24 April 1929, now in L. Ferrero (1984: 83–84).

61. He felt that Italians were not interested in either the theatre or the novel, but only poetry, and they easily adapted to the conditions of dictatorship (article in *Vita*, 1924, now in L. Ferrero 1932: 33; 1984: 33–35).

62. Initially the Latin Youth League, which during the period 1916–20 reached a membership of 50,000, and later the International Union of Youth to Study

Social Questions, whose founding text was written by Nello Rosselli (Manacorda 1979: xxi).

63. Leo wrote the reviews with a view to 'launching grappling-irons into Europe in the hope that they catch onto something'; letter to Alberto Carocci in Manacorda (1979: 242).

64. The reference to Judaism and its European significance is implicit in both Leo Ferrero's cultural work and the family tradition. His engagement with the literary magazine *Solaria* contributed to its Judaism (Luti 1995: 97–98), and associated Judaism with an openness to Europe (see the reviews of Saba and Svevo, as well as 'Visita a Svevo', *Solaria*, March 1929: 3–4), but this occurred without Leo examining the question explicitly. However, he must have been familiar with the positions of Nello Rosselli, who lucidly explained his sense of being Jewish and his reasons for not being a Zionist to the Jewish youth conference held in Livorno in 1924; see Ciuffoletti (1979: 1–5); Manacorda (1979: xl).

65. It was precisely on this point that Guglielmo's studies of ancient Rome, which were translated into many languages, and Leo's own works dramatically diverged from the fascist position (Guglielmo and Leo wrote *The Greatness and Decline of Rome* together). However, the Ferreros found themselves under attack not only from fascism but also from Benedetto Croce, who was very critical of Guglielmo's historical works. He was a little kinder about *The Greatness and Decline of Rome* (original title: *La Palingenesi di Roma*), 'it is clear that Guglielmo Ferrero has profited from having an assistant [Leo]' (Croce 1960: 193–94).

66. See Morandi (1952) and Della Peruta (1962).

67. This recalls the Enlightenment interpreters of courtly poetry such as Thomas Warton and Jean-Baptiste la Curne de Sainte-Palaye; see Passerini (1999: 201–2, 204–5).

68. This grandiose utopia would be the basis for Young Europe's constitution in 1934, and Mazzini's constant references to the European dimension as the setting for revolutionary initiatives (*Dell'Iniziativa Rivoluzionaria in Europa*, 1835) and future democracy (*Manifesto del Comitato Centrale Democratico Europeo*, 1850).

69. On this dispute, see Menocal (1987).

70. The ideas contained in 'Trasfigurazione dell'Amore' constitute a synopsis of a manuscript Leo produced in 1928, and which would form the basis for many of his writings, such as the first part of *Paris* and various articles ('La Faillite des Femmes Anglaises' [1928] and 'Il Destino delle Donne Inglesi' [1929b]), whereas the main part on English civilisation would be published only after Leo's death under the title *Secret de l'Angleterre* (1941).

71. Leo provided a lively sketch of 'omnipotent Parisian women' who behaved as an elite.

72. Leo's articles on Englishwomen, which were previewed in newspapers like *Il Lavoro* of Genoa, provoked a 'craving for argument' in Marion Cave, Carlo Rosselli's wife, as Carlo wrote from internment on Lipari to Gina Lombroso (Calloni and Cedroni 1997: 60).

73. Nicola Chiaromonte, who wrote a cautious and unpersuaded review of *Paris* for *Solaria* (Chiaromonte 1933: 59–62), accepted the beauty of the passages in which Leo expresses his love for Paris's sophisticated civilisation. The book received a brutal panning from the fascist magazine *Antieuropa*, which in the July issue of 1930 published a lengthy accusation against Leo under the title 'L'Occidente dei Rinnegati' ('The Turncoats' West'). The reviewer, who used the byline *Cunctator*, countered the 'idiocies' and 'servility' of 'Ferrero II' with his own interpretation of French culture (521–22).

74. The expressions are taken from Macchia (1965: 341–44).

75. Leo spoke of 'the need to violate the concept of being loved' within oneself: this is why 'a terrible struggle, which is called love, is triggered between the lover and the concept of the lover' (L. Ferrero 1927a: nn. 7–10, 56–59).

76. *Il Baretti* (February 1925), now in Leo Ferrero (1984: 52).

77. Notebooks, now in L. Ferrero (1984: 180–81).

78. There are a few traces of this in his correspondence: Leo jokingly signed a letter to Line Aman, sent in April or May of 1929, 'Le troubadour L', while Claude Dauphin referred to himself in his letters to Leo as a minstrel and referred several times to Don Giovanni.

79. Letter to Claude, n.d. but probably written between 18 October and 2 November 1929.

80. Notebooks, May 1932.

81. On 22 February 1932, he wrote to Bogdan that he was 'reborn' since he had been feeding on 'plenty of fruit and raw and cooked greens'.

82. Letter of 15 July 1929 from Paris to the Bernards.

83. As a result two interviews, one with King Carol of Rumania and King Albert of Belgium, were published by the *New York Times*, on 8 January 1933 ('Portrait of a King Who Likes His Job') and 16 April 1933 ('A Modern King and a Democrat as Well'), respectively.

84. Irma's letter of 14 October 1932.

85. Letter to Marion Mitchell, late 1922.

86. The term, which in English goes back to 1700, entered Italian literature in the twentieth century. It was used by Pea (1931) and Bacchelli (1932) in the sense of 'to court briefly as a pleasant pastime without the occurrence of any transport of sentiment or passion' (*Grande Dizionario della Lingua Italiana*, UTET).

87. Letter to Mitchell, 18 February 1924.

88. Ibid.: 1922.

89. Ibid.: 10 December 1924.

90. Letter to Mitchell Stancioff, December 1926.

91. Ibid.: February 1928.

92. Ibid.: 28 October 1928.

93. Marion Mitchell Stancioff's letter of May 1928.

94. Letter to Mitchell Stancioff, 11 September 1932.

95. Simone Téry (1897–1967) had a career in journalism and political reporting which took her to China, Japan and the United States. Téry also wrote novels, such as *Passagère*, which was published in 1930, and *Le Cœur Volé* (1935), loosely based on her relations with Paul Nizan.

96. Her novel *Passagère* (1930) had some influence on Leo, who turned to Simone once again in 1933 for a letter of introduction and advice for the trip to the East he was preparing. It was the story of a woman who leaves Europe to get away from the man she loves and the impossible relationship with him because of the presence of another woman. The novel follows the traditional progression of a journey to the East, marked out by the ship's ports of call from the Mediterranean to Japan and Indochina. The protagonist retains her yearning for Paris and Europe ('Europe, ma Patrie', 87).

97. Téry's letter of 11 July 1930.

98. Ibid., 11 October 1930.

99. Letter to Téry, 28 February 1930.

100. Téry's letter of 30 June 1930.

101. Leo was obsessed, almost prophetically, with the life that could have been and yet did not translate into reality (letter to Simone, 27 January 1931).

102. Téry's letter of 10 September 1930.

103. Téry's letter to Gina Lombroso of 20 November 1933.

104. Letter to Téry, 26 August 1930.

105. Ibid., 15 September 1930.

106. Téry's letter of 18 October 1930.

107. Simone wrote a letter to Gina Lombroso on 20 November 1933 in response to Gina's request for copies of Leo's letters: she was worried about the fact that Leo was much younger than her; moreover, she desperately wanted a child and Leo never talked about it, just as he never talked about marriage.

108. Letter to Téry, 19 October 1932.

109. Apart from the correspondence, we have the diary he kept during the journey; see the Notebooks, particularly the one that starts on 18 December 1931 and ends on 30 May 1932 (ALFFPC).

110. Leo also presented Bucharest as a 'strangely fascinating city' in one of the interviews published by the *New York Times* ('Portrait of a King ...'). Bucharest still retained its fame from the previous century for being 'Little Paris'. It was a cosmopolitan city, whose elites travelled to Paris and Vienna and dressed in accordance with Western fashion, and where a declining aristocracy and a rising middle class competed for prestige and elegance (Ioanid 2000: ix–x).

111. Raditsa's letter of 15 April 1932.

112. 'When it comes down to it, I get a great kick out of the fact that you haven't seen anything: I could introduce you to Europe' (from Hôtel du Roi Serbe, Belgrade, 19 April).

113. In a sense, Leo perceived the trip to 'Balkania' as a form of regression: 'In Zagreb I had a relapse into lyricism ... It was two o'clock, and groups of teenagers were going to the upper secondary school.' All this reminded him of his time at secondary school and his teenage loves: 'This need for love, this violent desire for a woman took hold of me and made me unhappy, and along with this need came my ancient yearning for death. "To kiss Ginetta, or one of these teenage girls, and to die in Zagreb"'. (Notebook December 1931–May 1932).

114. Undated letter copied from one sent by Leo, in the Diaconescu folder.
115. Ginetta's last letter is the one she sent to Gina Lombroso (30 August 1934). This correspondence, which resembles the one between Gina and Simone Téry, shows the lengths Gina was willing to go to bring together her son's papers and have them conserved for posterity. Such an act of love was in some ways heartbreaking, but it was also an act of extreme interference by a mother in her son's life.
116. Sachs's letter of 13 April 1933.
117. The quotation reproduces the original language mistakes. Leo uses 'he', and it is clear that he is thinking of a male subject, even though he started with the impersonal pronoun 'one'.
118. Letter to Sachs, 17 April 1933.
119. Letter to Téry from New Haven, 26 April 1933.
120. Sachs's letter of 2 June 1933.
121. Obituary in *Athénée de Genève* (20 November 1933), now in L. Ferrero (1939c: 223–24).
122. For example Costa Ouranis (Athens: *Nea Estia*, 15 December 1934) in L. Ferrero 1936: 64–66.
123. Victoria Ocampo (1891–1979), who was born in Buenos Aires, wrote in Spanish, French and English, and was editor of *Sur*, which she founded in 1931. An untiring traveller, she discovered many talented people and was friend to many intellectuals around the world. She also founded the Unión Argentina de Mujeres.
124. Ocampo's letter of 17 May, probably 1930.
125. Ocampo's letters of 25 May and 1 June.
126. There is a connection between the belief in communication with spirits as practised and studied by Lombroso (on his encounters with his dead mother in different séances, see Pick 1989) and the perception of 'affinity, telepathy, synchronism of soul and thought' between Leo and his mother (according to his aunt Paola Lombroso Carrara; see Kornfeld 1994: 51) and even Guglielmo's hope of meeting 'Leo, our dear Leo' again after his death. All these extrasensory experiences refer to family relationships across generations.
127. Published in *Revue Juive de Genève* in February 1934.
128. It was in the light of his contact with the *indios* that he discovered the contradictions in Pascal and the unpleasant aspects of his attitude, such as his ignorance of India and China and his anti-Semitism. However, the root of his criticisms of Pascal was that he was unable to achieve the true happiness and peace that Leo was searching for, '[T]o find peace in God you need to imitate not Pascal but Maria de la Mesa, an old and unmarried native American who prepares my lunch and who since childhood has lived with God as if with a respectable husband' (L. Ferrero 1937: 213).
129. Further evidence of this conversion can be found in a letter to Max Ascoli from New York, 27 October 1933; see 'Leo Ferrero' Collection, Centro Studi 'Piero Gobetti' di Torino, Folder I.
130. In relation to Christianity, Leo veered between attraction and rejection of membership of a church. He acknowledged that the question of sacrifice

was Christianity's fundamental contribution to Western civilisation, but he did not accept the concept of sin in relation to sexuality (L. Ferrero 1937: 184).

131. In spite of the considerable difference of tone, there is a striking similarity between his attitude and that of Antonin Artaud, who three years later went to Mexico to escape European civilisation and 'the eternal betrayal by white people'; see Artaud (1980: 133 ff.).

132. Number 8 of the 'Notes on the Novel's Technique' that appear as an appendix to *Espoirs*.

133. See Part II, Chapter 4, n. 68.

EUROPE'S ROOTS IN LOVE

Chapter 3

Mediterranean Love

When he chose to start the magazine in the heart of the old town and port of Marseilles, on ground that may have been trodden by his distant and not-so-distant docker forefathers, Jean Ballard was more or less knowingly searching for, far from the great docks that continued to grow along the other shore, a promising, very individual, snug spot that harked back to the perfect and intricate links that had connected the port and the city of Marseilles a century previously. He set up the magazine near to the old granaries in the east, with their salvaged stones, flooring and beams that were often made out of recycled ships' masts, so evocative of the great warehouses on the ancient inland lake that was the Mediterranean. (Paire 1993: 68)

The link between Europe and love was explored by the magazine *Cahiers du Sud*, which was published in Marseilles for more than forty years, from 1926. The periodical and the surrounding environment marked an attempt to extend and, at the same time, to limit the idea of Europe by connecting it to the Mediterranean, to love and to poetry: according to this view, twelfth-century Provençal culture lay at the origins of the European conscience and was the crux of the relationship between Arab culture and Europe; between Islam and Christianity. The magazine's view of Europe was strongly skewed towards the Mediterranean, and the magazine devoted a regular column to the topic during the second half of the 1930s, 'Vers une Synthèse Méditerranéenne'. This constant reference to the Mediterranean meant that *Cahiers* could see, at least partly, the limits of the European world through its exchange with that of the Arabs. A Mediterranean dimension was already apparent, in the form of an attachment to the city of Marseilles and to its multicultural seafaring traditions, in *Fortunio*, a small magazine started in 1914 by Marcel Pagnol.[1] One of that magazine's contributors was Jean Ballard, who later became editor of *Cahiers*.[2] When Pagnol moved to Paris in 1922, Ballard became editor of *Fortunio* and moved its headquarters to the old port area of Marseilles, a significant and symbolic location: a magazine is 'a product of its soil' (Paire 1993: 86), as Ballard was to write later. The title chosen for the new magazine introduced a reference to the South and alluded to a mixture of old and new, with a critical nod to modernity. Significantly, a special issue of *Cahiers* was dedicated to Marseilles in 1928.

Most of the magazine's long-term leading contributors were based in the south of France, 'true southerners, sensitive only to the reborn part of every lasting thing', according to Bousquet.[3] Its most important contributors included Gabriel Audisio in Nice, and Joë Bousquet, René Nelli and Pierre and Maria Sire in Carcassonne.[4] The magazine also attracted great writers and artists as well as authors from Paris and abroad, from Marguerite Yourcenar and Paul Eluard to Walter Benjamin, from André Masson to Paul Valéry. *Cahiers* was a magazine without any manifesto and without any literary or political axe to grind (Fabre 1987b). Despite its surrealist influences, it did not share the political tendency of the movement and became the exception to the rule whereby the French literary and artistic world flocked to Paris. It focused on literature and poetry from Europe and elsewhere, devoting most of its space to reviews and criticisms. The feature of *Cahiers* that set it apart from its fellows was that it combined an international and European outlook with an idea of love as the basis of European civilisation, and emphasised the role of pure poetry and faithfulness to the text as a higher ideal than the intellectual *engagement* championed by Julien Benda.

Europe and the 'Meeting between Civilisations'

The topic of Europe is woven into *Cahiers* as a recurrent theme along with its other theme of France. The diatribe against France is frequent, demonstrating the bitterness of Provençal culture towards the French culture that absorbed it (Brion 1933a: 631–34), and stating its determination to break out of national boundaries and project the idea of regional autonomy on a continental scale. One sign of the magazine's Europeanness was its closeness to Paul Valéry, a European activist and also a champion of the Mediterranean perspective. The concept of the Mediterranean underpinned the affinity between *Cahiers* and the poet, for whom 'Europe and the Mediterranean ... due to the effects of the intellectual qualities that developed there' became elements of the human universe.[5] One of the contributors with the most distinctly European outlook was Marcel Brion, who for a long time wrote the columns *Lettres Etrangères* and *Revues Etrangères*, which helped to set the international tone of the magazine.[6] Brion travelled often in Europe and was in contact with Joyce, Rilke and Thomas Mann. He wrote about Miguel de Unamuno, Pirandello, D'Annunzio, Yeats, Benjamin and many others. It was due to him that *Cahiers* published translations of mainly European authors. During the years 1930–38, Brion – who dreamed of a magazine as vast and diverse as Europe itself – supplied *Cahiers* every month with reviews, news and texts containing literary references from the entire continent (Paire 1993: 163). In a piece that he wrote in 1935, he quoted a definition of Europeanness taken from Troeltsch, according to which the specific feature of Europeans in the history of the world is the 'uninterrupted assimilation' of their relationship with antiquity. Only the link with the past, commented Brion, can lessen the sense of instability of the current human condition in the universe.[7] Brion numbered amongst the 'great Europeans' Theodoric (on whom he wrote a biography), Charlemagne and Napoleon, who were all, in his opinion, aware of the fact that Europe can be nothing else but united (Harrel-Courtes 1936: 158–62).

In *Cahiers*, the term 'Europe' is often used interchangeably with 'Western', but not in the sense of an opposition with the East. In a long review of the French translation of Spengler's *Decline of the West*, the poet Jean Audard defines the opposition of East and West as 'superficial', reminding us that of the two forms of Christianity the schismatic form was the true heir to the spirit of Christ, and that original Christianity was profoundly Eastern by nature. These attitudes reveal an intention to reclaim the heritage of Provence and its heresies (Audard 1932: 804–8). Both Audard and Léon Pierre-Quint – in a criticism of the 'great and miserable' Europe that was hurtling towards ruin, threatened as she was by the colonies she had subjugated in accordance with her principles of reactionary authority and racial superiority (Pierre-Quint 1933: 169–70)[8] – saw, echoing Gide, a new culture growing up in the European East and Soviet Russia. *Cahiers*, nevertheless, displayed an extremely critical attitude to Russia in many other articles. A report on a cultural congress organised in 1935 by the French Communist Party registers disappointment over the Soviet contributions, which were deemed uninteresting compared to those of the European intellectuals, who made an effort to reconcile their defence of individualism with their support for the USSR (Minet 1935b: 607–10).[9]

In *Cahiers*, the sense of a Europe in crisis deepened as the years went by, until they were forced to make the painful admission that unity of the European spirit – defined as 'enfant douloureux et fragile' – had become temporarily impossible to achieve, as occurred at the end of the decade, when the magazine was forced to announce the closure of T.S. Eliot's *Criterion* (Fluchère 1939: 181–84).

Before that, the hope of helping to renew the European spirit was alive and well in the contents of *Cahiers*, as is demonstrated by the reviews of works on Europe. Glowing reports were written of books such as *Analyse Spectrale de l'Europe* by Count Hermann de Keyserling[10] and *Synthèse de l'Europe* by Count Carlo Sforza.[11] Both these works hoped for European unity in their own different ways: the first through a form of 'supranationalism' that would not eradicate individual nations, and the second through a new European ideal that would go beyond nationalism. Despite a nod to lines of thought that attempted to connect the intellectual world to the political world, the main thrust of *Cahiers* was to provide a cultural interpretation of the European ideal, which began to become established from the 1920s in literature, poetry and essays (Chabot 1978: 225 et seq.). For example, *Cahiers* deliberately displayed a consistent devotion to the work of Denis de Rougemont, even though he contributed only sporadically. The reviewer of his book *Le Paysan du Danube* took for granted that the 'Europe of sentiment' of which the author spoke existed and that the roots of Rougemont lay mainly in French-speaking Switzerland, where artists and writers attempted to reconcile the Latin and Germanic cultures: perhaps this very tension between the two cultures could create a 'new European style' while preserving their differences (Trolliet 1933: 724).[12]

In 1930, Max Rychner observed, quoting Valéry, that Europeans succeed in developing a feeling of supranational solidarity only when they place themselves between America and Asia and their relationship with the United States comes into play. Europe becomes annoyed or ecstatic when faced with the vitality it attributes to Americans, with their aggressive optimism and with their 'youth'. It feels old, and it says so in the hope it will be contradicted, which does not happen. Rychner claimed as European values the intellectual independence of the individual and metaphysical intelligence but, above all, a particular tension between the community and the individual that prefigured a universal sentiment. A new collective feeling was indeed developing, an investment in the world: the first glimmerings of an ability to feel and understand the world as one unit, the heralding of a new life in which events are no longer assessed in terms of a continent, but the earth as a whole (Rychner 1930: 174–85).[13]

A trawl through the magazine in search of intercultural and intercontinental relationships throws up frequent references to Arab culture, Sufism, and the links between Muslim and Christian mysticism (Dermenghem 1931: 135–141), not only in articles and translations from the Arabic[14] but also in a monographic issue on the relationship between Islam and the West.[15] Jean Ballard dreamed of this issue for years, perhaps due to his peregrinations across the Mediterranean during frequent trips to Morocco and Algeria, where he had acquaintances and friends. In 1932, he entrusted Emile Dermenghem,[16] at that time the magazine's 'correspondent' in Algiers, with the task of drawing up a monographic publication on the relationship between Islam and the West. The issue was to be inspired by hopes of a better, mutual understanding, leaving aside movements of opinion and political influences, and setting itself the task of seeking out cultural values instead. It was to 'reinforce an extended notion of Mediterranean culture', a meeting place between various cultures as opposed to a restricted viewpoint inspired by the 'Latin spirit' or the 'Greek miracle'.[17] The Introduction opened by recalling a sentence that Valéry wrote in 1918 ('Nous les civilisations …'), in which civilisations acknowledged their own mortality, 'at a certain point of their life cycles, civilisations seem to be beset by self-doubt and come to an awareness of their possible fate'.[18] Ballard was confident of the prospect of a broad-ranging 'Mediterranean neoclassicism', in which Islam would play a part in refining the Graeco-Latin intelligence and helping to create a new syncretism.[19]

The pamphlet was based on two essays (by the Frenchman Bonjean[20] and the Egyptian Haykal)[21] on the lack of understanding between Europeans and Muslims (Bonjean 1935: 5–27; Haykal 1935: 28–36). Bonjean asserts that 'most Westerners are unimaginably ignorant of Muslim life and psychology'; he also observes that the lack of 'Westernists' (academics studying the West) in the East is a sign of inequality and a serious obstacle to mutual understanding. Another limitation lies in the fact that European freethinkers have contact only with Easterners who consider themselves 'liberated'. Bonjean believed that the divisions between Westerners and mutual forms of fanaticism bore the brunt of responsibility for the divide, but concluded by characterising the East as 'a lover of the night' and the West as 'migrant, high priest of the dawn' (Bonjean 1935: 27). Haykal's article contains all the hallmarks of the shift that took place in his beliefs between the end of the 1920s and the beginning of the 1930s, from a heroic vision of an admired West to an image of the West as an 'imperialistic civilisation', although with an effort to find a hope of understanding.[22] Haykal, who defended the Muslims against accusations of fanaticism, was highly critical of the responsibilities of Europeans and had a specific historical view of the opposing positions of East and West, adversaries for thirteen centuries throughout the Muslim expansion and the Crusades: in his opinion, European colonial politics were the true cause of the lack of understanding. However, even Haykal declared his faith in achieving 'a universal understanding', based on the two religions and through men of good will, although he believed that the opportunity would arise only in the future and would be linked to the coming of a 'world resurrection' greater than the European Renaissance (Haykal 1935: 35–36).

Another not very optimistic view was expressed in an article by Claire Charles-Géniaux on women and Islam that does not conceal elements of discord between the cultures regarding the condition of women, although maintaining that the Koran does not prescribe servitude and ignorance for them. Claire Charles-Géniaux considers that the merging between peoples will take place only as 'unity' – through the general introduction of mechanisation or on a spiritual level, both distant prospects (Charles-Géniaux 1935: 120). The author was the wife and colleague of the writer Charles-Hyppolyte-Jean Géniaux,[23] with whom she travelled to North Africa, particularly to Morocco and Tunisia. In 1934, Claire Charles-Géniaux published L'Ame Musulmane en Tunisie, in which she referred to her husband's work Les Musulmanes.[24] This text, representative of their ideal of assimilation, alternates social observations about cloistered girls who had just reached puberty with the story of Nijma (Star) who undergoes a traditional marriage to a Tunisian doctor. The couple, open to new ways of living and to abandoning the veil, experience the violent hostility of the Arab community and are forced to move to the French part of the city. Their choice is encouraged by the groom's grandmother, but during a return to the Arab town, the young woman is cursed by her father, who threatens to have her imprisoned. The ending is encouraging, however, because Nijma is said to be 'still shining in the great free sky' – a sign that Tunisian women are beginning to wake from their long sleep (Géniaux 1909: 266, 281).

Claire Charles-Géniaux returns to these themes in *L'Ame Musulmane*, in which she recounts conversations with Tunisian friends and describes the lives of some well-to-do women who wanted for nothing except the tenderness, trust and companionship that Frenchwomen supposedly find in marriage. The book contains fine passages on the landscape and terraces of Tunisia, which belong to the women, and discusses examples of both Tunisian women who love their traditional lifestyles and the much freer wives of nationalists, as well as the French wives of Muslims or converts to Islam who have adopted a Muslim lifestyle by choice. The author is openly outspoken against the submission of women, but also criticises Western civilisation, where social cohesion is in ruins. Charles Géniaux observes that this situation arises out of a mistake that mirrors the error committed by Islamic society, because the West encloses its women in factories and workshops instead of allowing them to live in their homes as respectable mothers. Both writers criticised the condition of women in Western society in a novel whose feminist heroine exemplified a lifestyle new to women. She was, however, destined to be faced by an irreconcilable dilemma because her destiny required her to give up the devotion to a man that constitutes a woman's ultimate raison d'être (Géniaux and Charles-Géniaux 1924).[25]

Charles Géniaux dreamed of a coming together of the two civilisations and their respective guiding principles – toil for the West and wisdom for the East – and Claire Charles-Géniaux hoped for a dialogue between East and West. Her article in *Cahiers* of 1935 establishes a difference between Tunisian and Algerian women, on one hand, and Moroccan women (less emancipated), on the other, and envisages an 'infinitely desirable coming together', when all women will be 'as highly evolved as European women'. Géniaux expresses the fear that reforms such as that of Mustapha Kemal in Turkey, which are 'purely lay, rationalist and materialist', would impoverish Islamic culture (Charles-Géniaux 1935: 121). Hers are 'moderate' attitudes,[26] since, though she longed for emancipation and progress, she did not wish to lose the cultural heritage of ancient civilisations that she admires in an aesthetic manner.[27] After considering the fate of Islamic women and that of Western feminists, she suggests that the only road to salvation lies in a limited form of female emancipation, in the service of a husband. From this perspective, full knowledge of love, while it is open to all regardless of religious or geographical belonging, is the sole preserve of Europeanised, hierarchical couples.

Significantly enough, the article that was to replace that of Clare Géniaux in the 1947 republication of *L'Islam et L'Occident* was written from a male Muslim viewpoint. While acknowledging the 'serious nature of the intellectual and moral misery' in which Muslim women 'struggle and sometimes even wallow', the author contents himself with the observation that the Koran and the Sunnah represent progress compared to previous times, when a father held the right to decide life and death, particularly over his daughters. He was to agree with Géniaux over her disapproval of Kemal's measures for Turkish women, but to deplore the feminists who were concerned only with satisfying their thirst for independence, thereby discrediting women who wish to liberate themselves yet remain within the framework of tradition (Benabed 1947: 211–19). The two articles exemplify the opposition between a male community viewpoint and an emancipatory and assimilatory viewpoint, neither of which represents the voice of women.

Although the special issue on Islam and the West of 1935 boasted well-known contributors, it was patchy overall.[28] An article by Probst-Biraben on the continuity between Spain and Islam is somewhat superficial, as Brasillach observed, while the article by René Guénon on Islamic esotericism – which claims that Sufism does not have foreign origins – is overspecialised in tone (Guénon 1935: 37–45; Probst-Biraben 1935: 46–54).[29] The recurrent theme of many essays is the convergence between civilisations: the similarity between Arabic and Persian music and European music of the eighteenth century suggests that Eastern musicians are heirs to the Greeks in this field (Borrel 1935: 98–100),[30] as does the use of the Hippocratic oath by Arab doctors in twelfth-century Andalusia (Faraj 1935: 95–97). The issue, written from a strongly Eurocentric viewpoint, expressed hopes that Christianity would help to increase and preserve the spiritual values of Islam while adding the dimension of incarnation, and, at the same time, defend Islamic values against the seductions of modernity (Guiberteau 1935: 84–94). This approach was countered by an invitation to Westerners seeking a return to a more spiritual path to follow the way propounded by Islam, typified by clarity and purity and aiming towards an awareness of the transcendent Being

(Gleizes 1935: 101–6).[31] The most important contribution to the issue came from Massignon, who centred his discussion of Arabic as the liturgical language of Islam within a more broad-ranging framework, namely, by comparing it with the three monotheistic Mediterranean religions (Massignon 1935: 71–77).[32] The issue concluded with an article by Emile Dermenghem, who stressed a need for a meeting between Europe and Islam to ensure the salvation of both cultures. He perceptively analysed the specific nature of the meeting between both worlds, so different from the meeting of fifty years earlier, and now based on two forms of nostalgia, each for the past of the other. The author warns Muslims not to refer to decaying Western traditions and notes that Europeans are no longer certain of their superiority, but look instead to the East in a quest for transcendental wisdom.[33] The Muslims, as intermediaries between extreme Eastern and Western viewpoints, may borrow the inductive method of the West and give back the sense of metaphysics and spiritualism watered down by the specialisation of recent centuries (Dermenghem 1935: 141–44). This is the opposite of the idea of 'assimilatory regeneration' that, according to Amsell, conveyed an idea developed in France at the end of the eighteenth century concerning mixed marriages between Jews and Christians: according to this view, physical regeneration was seen as the first step to assimilation. If we adopt this analogy, sick Europe may be envisaged as regenerating itself spiritually through syncretistic contact with 'Eastern' religions (Amselle 1996: 151 et seq.).

The issue met with limited success. Specialist reviews such as *Revue des Etudes Islamiques*[34] did not cover it, and of the general reviews only *Revue Universelle* mentioned it at all by carrying a review by Robert Brasillach, who defined the issue as interesting but disappointing, because it had failed to strike the right balance between over-popularisation and over-specialisation. Brasillach, who particularly admired Massignon, observed that it would have been better to concentrate on Mahommed and the Crusades rather than the Persian tragedy, which had already been discussed in a more interesting fashion by Gobineau.[35] *Les Nouvelles Littéraires* praised Ballard's premise, considering that this issue of *Cahiers* made a very important contribution to the study of the permanent values and current problems of Muslim civilisation in its relations with the West, though admittedly viewed mainly from its perspective as a Mediterranean civilisation.[36]

Ballard consoled himself for his lack of success by writing to Bonjean that the issue had been a long shot, particularly in an apathetic land that was so slow to react, but that in any case *L'Islam et l'Occident* had found its audience (Paire 93: 238).[37] This issue of *Cahiers* was significant for its specificity: while interest for the East had been a veritable fashion in Germany and France during the ten years following the First World War, it had later dwindled (Trebitsch 1998a). The magazine's renewed efforts in this direction showed that *Cahiers*, at least, was not dealing with orientalism on a superficial level but felt a deep-seated interest for the fate of Europe in relation to other cultures. The overall tone of this special issue is, however, often similar to the form of orientalism analysed by Said, in the sense that the experiences of war, colonialism and imperialism are filtered through metaphysical and rose-tinted spectacles that present us with an image of the object stripped of its history. For example, the anticolonial, nationalist movements that arose during that period within Maghrebian Africa have been glossed over. The prevalence of assimilatory European views in the issue was, however, perceived as a problem by *Cahiers* itself, to the point that it was decided to republish the issue to make more room for Islamic contributions.[38] All this merely makes for a more detailed criticism of Eurocentrism within a form of orientalism that was simultaneously ethnocentric and passionate about the other culture.[39]

The topics chosen for special issues of the magazine in the 1920s and 1930s confirm a concept of the European and Mediterranean space that extended from the earth to the sea:[40] the city of Marseilles (1928), Elizabethan theatre (1933), German romanticism (1937), Islam (1935) and Portugal (1940). In the 1940s, this space included Provence (1942), Switzerland (1943), Greece (1948) and extended to India (1941 and 1949). In 1950, a special issue was dedicated to 'The Spirit of Israel'. In *Cahiers*, the hoped-for 'meeting between civilisations' is, therefore, wedded to the development of a Mediterranean ideology, a position that reached its most rarefied form in the writings of Gabriel Audisio, who dreamed of unifying a new world around the Mediterranean, which would link southern Europe and North Africa. Audisio dreamed of a people with many different faces, whose allegiances were local more than national (Tuscans, Catalans, Corsicans, Berbers, Provençales) and who spoke many languages that were understandable to all (he recounts how he spoke Piedmontese in La Ciotat, Bouches-du-Rhône, to a man who responded unhesitatingly in Catalan). He believed in 'Mediterranean unity' with a strongly independent flavour: Maghreb is not yet Africa, which starts in the Sahara, just as Turkey and Syria are not yet Asia, which starts in

Iran. Audisio did not go so far as to say that southern Europe is not yet Europe (Audisio 1933: 601–9). The limits of Europe must be found in an incessant cultural exchange, against the expansionist aims of fascist and Nazi viewpoints, against the 'foolish ambitions of Mediterranean imperialism', and against all forms of racism (Audisio 1936b: 520).

From the beginning of 1936, Audisio stepped up his efforts to clarify the misunderstandings surrounding his book *Jeunesse de la Méditerranée*. He declared his mistrust for the claims of 'Mediterranean humanism' that represented a blend of Mussolinian (or even Hitlerian) conservatism. He railed against the idea of Latinism and the 'Latin race' and the claim, encapsulated by the slogan 'mare nostrum', of reducing the Mediterranean to Rome. Returning to the spirit that pervaded the issue of *Cahiers* on Islam, he took up a stance against the policy of the Italian government in Ethiopia.[41] As far as Audisio is concerned, the 'Mediterranean homeland', open and 'maternal' to all its offspring, should engender a brotherly coming together and not opposition (Audisio 1935: 15, 23).[42] It represents something more vast and plural than mere nationalism: all the peoples of the sea, including Jews, Arabs, Berbers and Moors, are citizens of this 'liquid continent' (Audisio 1936b: 273–76; 1936c: 427–29).

The Jews and the people of Marseilles had a fundamental part to play in the Mediterranean because they were 'eternal agents of connection' (Audisio 1933: 608). This view embraced a reassessment of Carthage, disfigured by the butcher Scipio. In his book *Sel de la Mer* (1936a), Audisio showed that a difference of opinion over Semitism lay at the root of the conflict between Carthage and Rome, and strongly disapproved of Roman imperialism while extolling the peaceful mercantile ambitions of the Carthaginians. Audisio's contribution prompted *Cahiers* to redefine its concept of the South, giving it a symbolic marine dimension that took Valéry's viewpoint one stage further.

Another loyal contributor to *Cahiers*, Armand Lunel, maintained the urgency of doing away with all prejudices founded on race, to return the Mediterranean to its original role. Only in this sense was it the cradle of European civilisation, 'the Mediterranean area has shown itself to be better placed than any other area in the world to promote the birth of a material and moral civilisation that may be described as "Western" or "European"' (Lunel 1936: 403). Although this Mediterranean is a boundless sea whose waters lap the walls of the University of Rome and the Sorbonne, of

Cambridge, Oxford, Upsala and Harvard, European civilisation and white humanism are very far from representing all humanity and all civilisation. This stance highlights two lines of thought: on one hand the openness of the idea of Europe and on the other its resolute limitation. Even Audisio, who agreed that the eastern part of the Mediterranean world was the quintessential incubator of European culture (Audisio 1937a: 133–36), wrote a favourable review of George Sarton's work *The Unity and Diversity of the Mediterranean World*, which anticipated the ideas of Martin Bernal in *Black Athena*, maintaining that Greek culture was permeated with Egyptian and Mesopotamian influences. At the same time, Audisio sympathised with the Maltese poets who wished to rid themselves of the dominant Italian tongue (Audisio 1937b).

This view of the Mediterranean must have been shared by several contributors to *Cahiers*, since in 1939 a special issue on myths and legends opened with the question, 'Are we at the dawn of a Mediterranean renaissance?' (Fuzellier 1939: 11). The view was certainly shared by Bousquet, who saw the revival of Provençal culture as encouraging a form of total humanism, well suited to the spirit of the age, by accomplishing an active regeneration and opening a new era towards the light of the Mediterranean character.[43] This was an idea that ran counter to the exaltation of the North in a Nazi sense, seeing as the same issue takes up a stance against Alfred Rosenberg's *Il Mito del XX Secolo*, entirely rejecting the racist inspiration. The view of the Mediterranean that emerges from *Cahiers* is not, however, free of stereotypes and sometimes strikes a tone that to our ears seems almost racist, as in *Le Concerto Européen* about a village of workers from all over the world, or in an immoderate piece by Georges de Santillana, which claimed that the 'Mediterranean spirit' had passed from Parmenides to Plato and from Leopardi to Valéry (Santillana 1936: 754–60). There were, however, also arguments against Félibrige[44] mannerists and their self-congratulatory exaltation of a South made inflexible by local rhetoric.

Despite these highs and lows, the concept of the Mediterranean described in *Cahiers* added a utopian dimension to ideas of Europe, or that 'constant desire for mirage' that Jean Paulhan recognised in the magazine (Paire 1993: 130), but above all the values set out by Ballard as typical of the Mediterranean civilisation: tolerance, personal respect, intellectual curiosity, a tendency to swing the balance of community in favour of the individual, and a creative relationship with Islam. It also assumes a certain concept of love to be an essential element of Provençal and European culture. This image of the Mediterranean embraces not only climate, indolence and *loisir*, but also a way of loving (Audisio 1938: 574–75).

Love as a Form of Intersubjectivity

Love was the third element of the constellation, after Europe and the Mediterranean, as a recurrent and characteristic theme of *Cahiers du Sud*. Two significant pieces by René Nelli and Joë Bousquet – who shared a deep affection for one another and an intellectual friendship – appeared together in May 1933 (Bousquet 1933: 340–49; Nelli 1933: 326–37). Nelli's article was dated, in the author's distinctive fashion, 'Montségur 1931', in a reference to the rock destroyed by the crusade against the Cathars, which became a sacred place in Provençal memory. The article opens with an entreaty addressed to a *gitane*[45] he had encountered in childhood, referring to the excruciating memory of 'your all too evident flesh'. The central theme was 'male love', defined as the joy that is felt by a limited being in going beyond his individual being. An unmistakably male subject addresses his amorous discourse to a woman, who represents that being in whose love he seeks oblivion. The man wishes to become confused inside the womb of the unconscious mother, whom he will find fully only in death. This is the reason he feels attracted by boundless love, which allows a form of oblivion. Nelli established an equation between sleep, religion, love and death, comparing rest in God to rest in absolute femininity. While man's typical erotic attitude is sleep, that of woman is 'maternal' or watchful, in the sense that the essence of her love is the joy of watching over the being whose folly she contains for an instant (Nelli 1933: 332). The beloved woman is the 'foreign' shape that man always awaits; she is the quintessential other. By contrast, an 'invert' rejects the woman because he deceives himself that he himself is the mother in spirit, in a form of sterile exaltation and spiritual rebellion.[46] Homophobia is the inevitable by-product of the insurmountable and hierarchical division between the genders thus established.

A woman dressed in the costume of a *gitane* also won the heart of Joë Bousquet in his elegant piece 'Amour qui parle en ma pensée'. The lovely Annie is described stealing away from a masked ball at midnight in the winter to meet the poet. Autobiographical touches, such as a reference to the pictures of Max Ernst and

Tanguy and an African mask in the poet's room, hint at Bousquet's own story: the writer, confined to a wheelchair following a severe injury sustained during the First World War, remained surrounded by loyal friends and central to the intellectual and artistic debate of his day. His condition becomes a metaphor for the idea that waiting in silence and in solitude is a fundamental aspect of love. Once the woman finally arrives, verbena-scented like his much loved Provence, she calls him 'mon enfant' and promises him that she will rock him to sleep in her arms – a sleep in which the poet will not find rest but rather a sense of nonexistence. It is the sleep of which Nelli spoke, with the ability to dispel a sense of anguish similar to a feeling the poet remembers from his childhood. Annie in fact reminds him of when his long-dead wet nurse used to breast-feed him and sing songs of Montségur. He sees in Annie's moonlit nudity the image of his own death, a conclusion that reminds him of the *assag* in which, according to Nelli, the troubadour looks on a naked woman, but does not break the pact of limiting himself to contemplation. Love is seen as waiting and contemplation, not yearning or the consummation of desire.[47] Bousquet writes as a poet rather than as an essayist, but this and the previous piece on love chime strongly with one another and reveal echoes of Provençal verse or, rather, a particular interpretation of this form of poetry and the sentiments it expresses. The two authors agree particularly on the subject of the otherness of women and the essential unhappiness of a loving relationship.

These themes are central to *Cahiers*. The magazine often published articles and reviews that depicted women as foreigners. This idea was widespread in the literary culture of the day and evident in many of the romantic novels reviewed by *Cahiers*. With its central theme of the love between a German woman and a French man, *L'Etrangère* by René Jouglet, for example, offered 'a most eloquent argument in favour of Franco-German rapprochement and a sense of European awareness' (Pillement 1930: 71–72). In *Frieda ou le Voyage Allemand* by the same author, the heroes are another 'mixed couple' – the young, athletic woman represents 'present-day Germany' driven to the limit of desperation and on the brink of revolt, while her sentimental and bewildered lover is reminiscent of France, in all its 'innocence – or ignorance?' (Petit 1933: 307–8).

The heart of another unspecified foreign woman is also won by the Basque hero – who lives in Brittany – of the novel *L'Amour de Vivre* by Frédéric Lefèvre (Lafont 1933: 392–94). The beautiful, treacherous young woman who seduces her Swiss cousin in *Victor et l'Etrangère* by René de Weck is Russian – arguably the very essence of foreign womanhood (Petit 1934: 253–54). The reviewer of *Les Cloches de Bâle* by Louis Aragon criticises the Russian heroine of the book as being too similar to 'our own modern, bourgeois and recklessly bold young women' (Minet 1935a: 153–54). Forms of behaviour that are irresistible in male eyes can be attributed to foreign women: in one of the short stories in *Les Aveux Complets* by Jacques Chenevière, a young Englishwoman undresses before the eyes of a young Swiss man (Petit 1932: 645–47). Non-European woman are even more foreign. One example is the young Creole woman in *La Créole du Central Garage* by Jean Pallu (Blin 1935: 691–92), whom everyone loves because she has the ability to make her admirers forget who and where they are. Or Lupé, who 'embodies all the passionate and mysteriously alluring magic of Mexico' in *Absence* by Marc Chadourne (Brion 1933b: 726–30). Or again, C.B. (colonial born), a character unhappily married to an Englishman who appears in the narrative part of a travelogue by Guy de Portalès, *Nous, à Qui Rien n'Appartient* (Missac 1931: 461–62). The device of foreignness, embodied also by adolescent women (Odic 1936: 24–29), is a way of saying that women and men really cannot understand one another and that a woman is, after all, a force of nature. Before her, the only subject worthy of this name, namely, the male, is left with no alternative but to look on her in awe.

The theme of love recurs in a special issue of autumn 1942, dedicated, after years of gestation, to *Le Génie d'Oc et l'Homme Méditerranéen* (*Cahiers du Sud*, 249; Fig. 3).[48] We can imagine the difficulties involved in publishing this issue (which exceptionally ran to 7,000 copies) during the Vichy regime in France, with its severe shortages of paper, ink, glue and cardboard – and also the restriction of censorship.[49] The issue revisits the work of some great writers and the themes covered in the special issue on Islam and the West: the idea of Arabic poetry as a forerunner of Provençal poetry (Dermenghem 1942: 26–38); the topic of Mediterranean unity (Probst 1942a: 161–72) – 'Mediterraneans have the same mental basis' (Benoit 1942: 313; see ibid.: 312–23; Bonjean 1942: 326–31);[50] the geographical extent of the Provençal area of influence or of derivation, which stretched from the world of Andalusia and Catalonia to that of Germany (El Fasi 1942: 39–43; F. Soldevila 1942: 173–81; Singer 1942: 209–14);[51] and the 'eastern basis' that lay behind the flowering of Provençal poetry and Catharism (Sire 1942: 292–300).

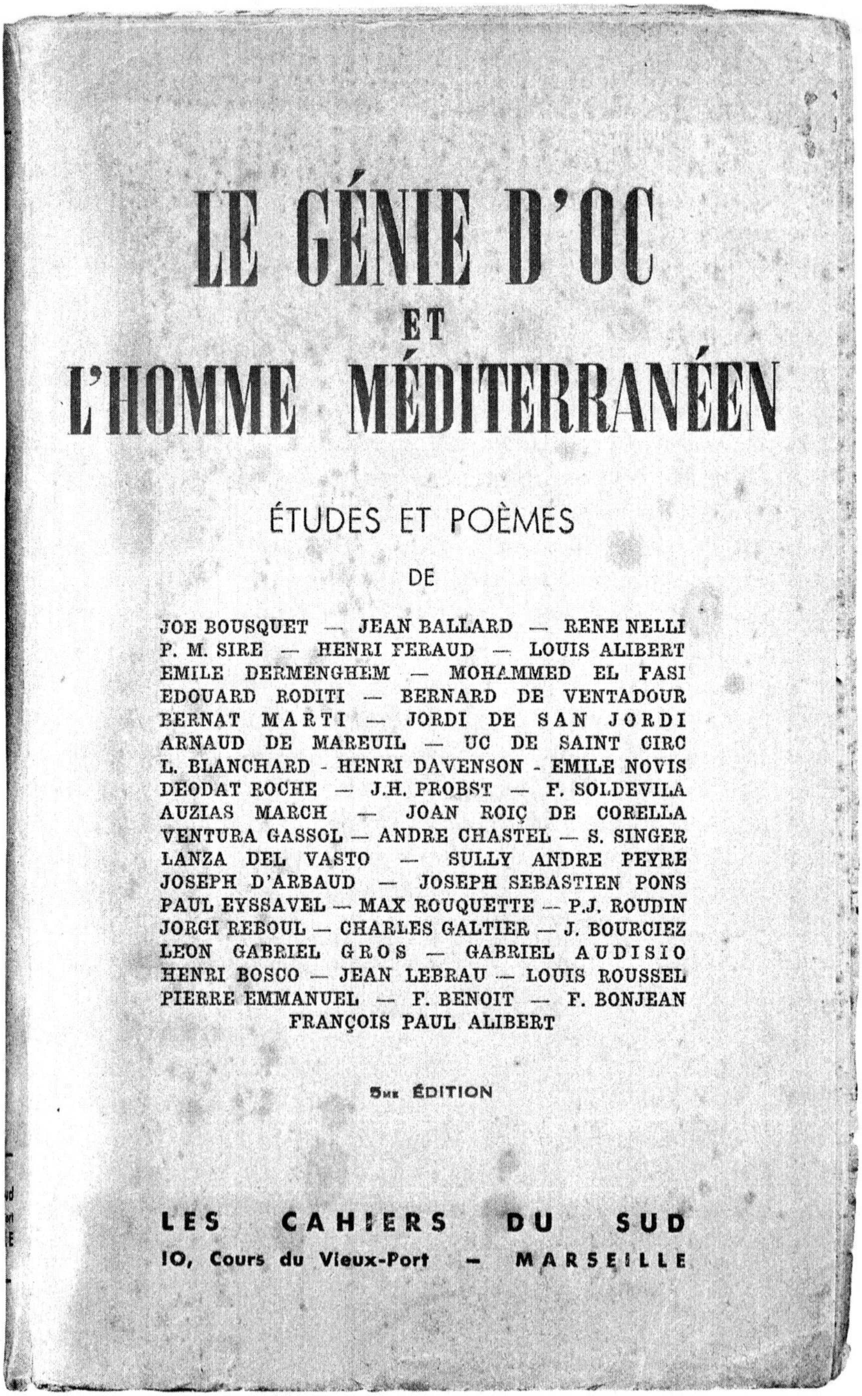

LE GÉNIE D'OC

ET

L'HOMME MÉDITERRANÉEN

ÉTUDES ET POÈMES

DE

JOE BOUSQUET — JEAN BALLARD — RENE NELLI
P. M. SIRE — HENRI FERAUD — LOUIS ALIBERT
EMILE DERMENGHEM — MOHAMMED EL FASI
EDOUARD RODITI — BERNARD DE VENTADOUR
BERNAT MARTI — JORDI DE SAN JORDI
ARNAUD DE MAREUIL — UC DE SAINT CIRC
L. BLANCHARD - HENRI DAVENSON - EMILE NOVIS
DEODAT ROCHE — J.H. PROBST — F. SOLDEVILA
AUZIAS MARCH — JOAN ROIÇ DE CORELLA
VENTURA GASSOL — ANDRE CHASTEL — S. SINGER
LANZA DEL VASTO — SULLY ANDRE PEYRE
JOSEPH D'ARBAUD — JOSEPH SEBASTIEN PONS
PAUL EYSSAVEL — MAX ROUQUETTE — P.J. ROUDIN
JORGI REBOUL — CHARLES GALTIER — J. BOURCIEZ
LEON GABRIEL GROS — GABRIEL AUDISIO
HENRI BOSCO — JEAN LEBRAU — LOUIS ROUSSEL
PIERRE EMMANUEL — F. BENOIT — F. BONJEAN
FRANÇOIS PAUL ALIBERT

5ᵐᵉ ÉDITION

LES   CAHIERS   DU   SUD

10, Cours du Vieux-Port   —   MARSEILLE

Figure 3 Cover of the special issue of *Cahiers du Sud* on Provençal culture

After a short introduction by Ballard, the issue opens with a piece by Bousquet (1942: 9–13), which returns to the topic of the 'annexation' of French Languedoc and refers to its European vocation. The Nelli–Bousquet partnership is again in evidence, but the differences between the two have increased. Nelli contrasts the Provençal idea of the erotic, where carnal urges and male instincts are turned into a quest for perfection, with Christianity (which dispenses with a body altogether) and with the eroticism of ancient Greece, where perfection was symbolised by the male body (Nelli 1942). Love also lies at the centre of the concluding piece by Bousquet (1942: 374–89), which is of a literary and poetic nature. Here love is seen as the tool of redemption, although it succumbs to the temptation of seeking the eternal in human happiness. Bousquet believed it essential to accept a form of revelation that places the laws of love at the service of salvation. Love is the quintessential form of intersubjectivity, whether it is between human beings or between mortals and the transcendent.

Significantly enough, the few women's voices heard in the review suggest otherwise. Thérèse Aubray wrote at the end of 1940 that 'love must be reinvented' to get away from an erroneous idea – that of burying oneself alive, suffering nobly and giving without expecting anything in return, because real love is 'essentially an exchange of forces' that requires mutual consent. Love is a symbol for a form of balance: when not repaid, it loses its effectiveness. In physical love, no desire, however great, can really be sustained if repaid by coldness. We must, therefore, replace the common notion of unhappy love with the idea of love as a mutual exchange, particularly in the hearts of young girls (Aubray 1940: 521–22).[52] Her opinion finds no echo in the stance adopted by the magazine, although her work is appreciated and praised because it explores one of its recurrent themes – that the drama of love is identifiable with the problem of poetic creation and prefigures it (Hourcade 1938: 308). The symbol of the great lover remains male and is embodied in the person of André Gaillard, who had played an active role in *Cahiers* alongside Ballard and Bousquet and died young after a life lived to the full.

One exception is found in 'Soirée Languedocienne', which is set in the house of Pierre and Maria Sire in Carcassonne. This piece of writing by Ballard closed the issue on *Génie d'Oc*, thereby completing a circle that began with the editor's preface on Bousquet and his group of friends. Amidst their spiritual atmosphere, he had appreciated 'different resonances, with a dominant Eastern note –

not the fanatical East of the nomads, but that of an Islam softened and refined by culture' – and also a taste for a good story, for intellectual recreation and for friendly debate (Ballard 1942: 5–8, 390–405). 'Soirée Languedocienne' is an unusual piece that mixes autobiographical references with philosophical dialogue. It is unusual first and foremost because women were present and played an active role: Maria Sire opened the discussion by asking light-heartedly what 'the Languedoc spirit' represented and what of it remained. Few traces – was Bousquet's reply – save in ourselves, in our hearts and in our memory. In general, women were not very visible throughout the history of *Cahiers*. The editorial secretary, Marcelle Ballard, wife of the editor and indispensable 'superintendent' of *Cahiers*,[53] did not have a voting right in decisions taken by the magazine. Other names that appeared in the background were Georgette Camille, who came up with the idea of having special issues, and Thérèse Aubray, a member of the editorial board but mainly active in Paris (see 'Oreille et Porte-parole à Paris', Guiraud 1993: 70). During the Carcassonne soirée, it was left to Claire Charles-Géniaux to explain that the Languedoc spirit had been created by bringing together different races and by bringing the eastern Arabic, Persian and Indian cultures into contact with the Graeco-Latin culture and Christianity. A Languedoc man does not associate the joys of the flesh with sin or live in terror of death and he has sober and moderate appetites. All in all, he is a Mediterranean in the full sense of the word – while men of the North 'work hard and eat hard' (Ballard 1942: 393).

In the issue on *Génie d'Oc*, another woman, Simone Weil, suggested a bold interpretation of the Europe/love/Mediterranean constellation.[54] In her two pieces, published under the pseudonym Emile Novis, an anagram of her name, to escape the Vichy censors, she clearly stated the connections between Europe's past and present/future. Her belief that Europe's fate could have been different if the Languedoc civilisation had survived reveals Weil's burning regret for the loss of this potentiality, which she sees as a magnificent opportunity crushed by the aggression and terror of the anti-Albigensian crusade – a regret that sounds very like a warning against the threat of Nazism. In Weil's writing, strict contrasts between the genders and homophobia are muted to give way to a kind of zero-point for the love discourse and for political and social creation. We certainly cannot describe Weil's attitudes as conventional femininity, although her own gender did not pass unnoticed in the magazine.[55] The negation of the body practised by

Weil throughout her life and beyond, to the point of death itself, prevents us from claiming her to be a subject incarnated in the body of a woman, despite the fact that she perceived the meanings and risks implicit in that body.[56] For these reasons, I return to the idea of neuter as a place of all possibilities (Blanchot 1977: 398–408; Barthes 2002; see also Boella 2001: 36), beyond or before the dichotomy between male and female, to observe that the love subject of which Weil speaks is neither a female object of adoration nor a subject modelled on the male. All the signs indicate an idea of the love subject that goes beyond the dichotomy of gender, towards the neuter. This unprecedented subjectivity reaffirms the value of courtly love yet distances itself from it (at least in terms of the love described by Nelli and Bousquet), and excludes the theme of the woman as the quintessential Other.

Weil's two articles, written about one year apart, set the tone for the special issue,[57] representing as they did 'an act of spiritual resistance of rare scope' (Paire 1993: 277). Simone Weil's interpretation is based on her view of history as freedom: according to her, every individual and every civilisation at any stage in history is free to choose between all the moral notions available to them. The choices made in twelfth-century Provence were characterised by the highest level of spiritual freedom that had ever been achieved in Europe: they were the choices of intelligence, of tolerance and of the free circulation of ideas. There was a will to combine the greatest freedom with the greatest sense of order, a deeply felt sense of civic duty and loyal obedience to the legitimate masters. According to Weil, this allowed the Provençals to embrace very different cultural influences – from the Nordic to the Arabic, from the Platonic to Buddhism, from the ancient classics to the Druids – which resulted in a cultural flowering that was cut down by Christian fundamentalism. The greatest crime that Simon de Montfort and the Roman Church were guilty of was that of destroying a seed of European civilisation and liberty that could have grown to the same heights as Greek civilisation, the culture that had been most successful in interpreting the Mediterranean spirit as a melting pot of traditions from Nordic countries and the East. Weil, 'a Christian without a church' (Freixe 1987: 398), found it 'infinitely painful' that those crimes were committed by the Catholic Church (Weil 1960), a sign of the lack of faith that reigned over the extermination: the Catholic Church had introduced a totalitarian form of spirituality, which was in itself degenerate and anti-Christian. Though no one can bring back Provence, a dead country, 'killed off all too thoroughly' (ibid.: 28), our contemplation of the beauty of that period should make us at least partly immune to the baseness of the present and guide us in the quest for a new spirituality. Weil's approach was rigorously antihistorical. Her interest lay in a direct relationship with the texts, from which she derived 'nourishment'(Weil 1997: 42)[58] in her resolute actualisation of the past in respect to the present. She fully accepted the idea that Catharism was the ultimate expression of pre-Roman antiquity, because this reflected her own feelings,[59] yet she still acknowledged Catharism 'its rightful place amongst the authentic and pure expressions of Christian spirituality' (Zambon 1997: 25).

The renunciation of violence so typical of the Provençal civilisation was centred on a concept of love. According to Simone Weil, courtly love was extremely similar to love in ancient Greece, despite the different role of women. In other words, it was an impossible love that required chastity.[60] Courtly love was not determined by lust: it was an expectation directed towards the beloved being, which always required consent, and its fullest expression was love of God through the beloved. The Cathar religion practised non-violence and held an almost evangelical view that anything that came within the domain of force was bad, whether that force was carnal or social. Simone Weil's viewpoint added a heterodox and innovatory perspective to the magazine. Despite the regard in which her opinions were held, however, and the evident affinity between her voice and that of Bousquet, a male heterosexual viewpoint was generally privileged in *Cahiers*.

The 'Languedoc soirée' was no exception to this rule and men accounted for the lion's share of the debate on Provençal culture and its concept of love. Once the various contributors to the magazine had taken the floor to emphasise the tolerant, self-ironical values of the Languedoc culture, it fell to Bousquet to conclude the first part of the conversation by recalling that the concept of womanhood was all important to the Languedoc culture, though female individuality counted for nothing. This was reinforced by a long speech credited to Nelli on love as it was perceived by the 'male conscience' (Ballard 1942: 399), since in Provençal love the woman was an object of mystic adoration, but on a social level she was kept in dependency and humiliation. Here we may discern the implicit sense of superiority of someone who was living through a period in history when women had won greater recognition and emancipation, but this did not conceal a nostalgia for the past. According to Nelli, in the modern idea of love, lovers are liberated from one another, the woman socially and the man metaphysically. This results in women becoming more like men and means that 'Femininity' is in crisis, because women can find no other way of expressing their transformation than in the language of male reason. Nelli deplored the results of this masculinisation: twentieth-century women seemed to him to be like men without dreams. They had been delivered from self-idealisation but this had led to them losing love, given that one does not exist without the other. Woman's social being, which is responsible for her liberation, is illusory and divorces her from her deeper nature. Nelli, therefore, felt a pressing need to take up the strand that runs from Plato to Lamartine, passing through the troubadours, Dante and Petrarch, to return to a situation where the love subject creates the love object and renders it unassailable, thus building the idea of the eternal feminine through the power of love. At this point, Nelli departed from the poetic and transcendent ideas of Bousquet and also the dramatic view of the impossible love relationship proposed by Weil.

The subject of incommensurability is a constant theme in Nelli's writings. The woman as Other is an imaginary figure who first appears to the male subject in childhood, when she is confused with the figure of the mother, as part of an imaginary oneiric picture that depicts the beloved as 'all naked, emerging in real life from my hallucinations' (Nelli 1935: 531). In his writings after the Second World War, Nelli attempted to code the eroticism of the troubadours, where a key role is played by inhibition, present in the two rites of contemplating a naked woman and the *assag* – the trial of love that marks the difference between the attitude of the troubadours and that of the knights.[61] In his opinion, Provençal culture had regularised the sexual urge, thus exalting and giving a new sense to love, in response to new feelings about emotions that gained currency in chivalrous circles at the beginning of the twelfth century. While Nelli fully acknowledged Arab influences in the field of literature, he did not accept that they applied to customs, which include the *assag* (Nelli 1942). Nelli agreed with Weil that Provençal love translated the values of idealised homosexual friendship into those of love between the sexes. In this sense, it established a kind of camaraderie between lovers and engendered an equally shared passion – although he does not deny its nature of affirming the male vital urge. This type of passion has helped liberate men from misogyny and from the mother complex that drove them to appropriate the desired object instead of establishing familiarity with it (Nelli 1963). Nelli differs from Weil in affirming that courtly love has made love marriages possible in the long term. Impossibility, which was the distinguishing trait of this form of love in Weil's tragic and religious view, is softened in Nelli's interpretation, whereby happiness is possible within a passionate love where spiritual communion acts as an agent of sexual arousal. Women are thus required to perform a dual role, as a *camarade* and as a 'stranger' at the same time.

This theme is central to the Mediterranean ideal extolled in the magazine, which reconnects the 'contemporary male conscience' to the romantic myth that equates Woman with Nature. It mirrors the action of the troubadours, who 'created' woman so that she could be rescued from the emancipation which would lead her towards maleness. Nelli's characterisation of Provençal love as a choice, and not a passion to be succumbed to, presupposes the domestication of male instincts, which is a valuable exercise for those who wish to know the temptations of the flesh in order to overcome them. According to this view, the contemplation of eternal beauty is exalted by the metaphysical value of the female body (Nelli 1942). Such traits may be predicated for a *Homo europaeus* still able to master the hardships of civilisation. This view stresses man's isolation, and gives women a supporting part as a 'bonne petite seconde', as Marcelle Ballard described her role under her husband's editorship of *Cahiers* (Paire 1993: 150). Considering the array of male types that we have encountered in this book, this attitude is very different from views that included contempt for the feminine, as advocated by Lombroso and Ferrero. *Amour fou*, to which these attitudes are related, requires a certain type of camaraderie combined with the acceptance, by both lovers, of a mysterious female nature that makes 'Woman' like a goddess and hence a source of physical and spiritual creativity, but also a full subject of love.

Poetry as the Foundation for Relationships between Cultures

Another aspect of the Europe/Mediterranean/love constellation has so far been relegated to the background, but without it the arguments of *Cahiers* would be meaningless: poetry is an absolute spiritual priority according to the ideal of Mediterranean humanism. *Cahiers* always gave it great prominence in their cultural enterprise, understood as refinement of language and of the feelings it expresses. Simone Weil said that the Provençals 'had a word to designate their country: they called it the language' (Weil 1997: 22). The 'language' in which Weil recognised the 'homeland' of the Provençals was the language of poetry and it is no mere chance that her greatest aspiration was to write poetry.[62] She did not mean *engagée* poetry, even in a surrealist sense, but 'pure poetry', as it was termed by Valéry, which was often love poetry: poetry as the 'versant caché de chaque objet', the hidden aspect of every object, as Bousquet described the Languedoc spirit (Bousquet 1942: 13); poetry as an oral and musical tradition. According to this viewpoint, the poet is always in revolt against society. He protests against society (Ballard 1935: 852), but also has an important part to play in society: young poets, above all, burn with an inner fire that illuminates the chaos of their age and paints a less negative portrait of it (Ballard 1938: 62). Poetry acts as a form of secularised religion or amateur psychoanalysis, setting itself at the basis of spiritual regeneration.

Poetry is the foundation of the relationship between cultures. The view of love outlined in *Cahiers* is based on a recognition of the link between Provençal love and the concept of love in pre-Islamic and Islamic Arabic poetry. In the special issue on Islam and the West, published in 1935, an essay on the Muslim poets of Cordova maintained that the origin of courtly love was in Baghdad, at the Persian-influenced Abassid court, and then transferred to Cordova, from where it inspired the 'gay science' of the troubadours (Pehau 1935: 55–70). The crucial point of contact between Islam and Christianity lies in Provençal love poetry, which forms the basis of a non-autochthonous European identity that fully acknowledges its debt to Arab culture. By the new 1947 issue of *L'Islam et l'Occident*, interest in the topic had grown and two major essays were included on the role of Arab Andalusian poetry as a link, transmitting courtly values and feelings between Muslims and Christians (Pérès 1947: 107–30; Sallefranque 1947: 92–106). As far as the secular argument was concerned, the special issue on *Génie d'Oc et l'Homme Méditerranéen* again plumped in favour of an Arabic influence, accepting that the sentiments and ideas of the troubadours were directly inspired by Arabic sources, but ruling out the idea of slavish imitation (Dermenghem 1942: 26–38).[63]

The interpretation of the troubadour culture outlined in *Cahiers* – such as the views propounded by Denis de Rougemont – insists on its relevance to the present day, in the conviction that our age faces spiritual problems extremely similar to those faced in the twelfth century, with its Manichaeistic polarisation of good and evil. Many essays in the *Génie d'Oc* issue dwell on the links between the Manichaeans and the Cathars. The Cathars offer us the example of a form of understanding based on love and encouragement for an age in which the victory of good will be assured, 'a great era of peace after our tormented age'.[64] Bousquet believed that the Languedoc spirit was passed down through oral tradition (Bousquet 1942: 9–13), outside the official canons. This fact increases its potential for innovation, which acts through literature and poetry first and foremost. During the tragedy of the Second World War in Europe, the only hope was to recover that legacy and the commitment it involved. In his introduction to the June 1940 issue, Ballard wrote that in a France that had already been invaded, the main task of *Cahiers*, during those days laden with misery and mourning, was to struggle against 'the corruption of the meaning of words', to reinstate language in all its dignity and its truth (Ballard 1940: 356), as an essential aid to saving Mediterranean and European civilisation from the catastrophic fate to which Nazi fascism had condemned it. It is not by chance that the special issue on *Génie d'Oc* provoked a negative reaction from Provençal regionalist groups, with their scholarly approach to folklore, who were protected by the Vichy regime. Conversely, the progressive Languedocian movement espoused by young political firebrands such as Robert Laffont saw that issue as an invitation 'in the night of war' to rekindle the fire of independence and commence a critical reappraisal of the Albigensian past, partly for the very reason that the fire had been set by 'a non-Provençal, a Jew and a member of the Resistance' such as Simone Weil (see Paire 1993: 309–10; Canciani 1996; 2002: 271–72).

Poetry lies at the basis of the historical development of civilisation, in the same sense that the troubadour culture lies at the root of Europe and the relationship between Europe and Arab culture. Yet it also sets itself beyond present-day European civilisation, since it prefigures its possible regeneration in a relationship of tension with the past. Poetry sowed the seeds of the new in that catastrophic age. It saw beyond dissolution towards a rapprochement between peoples. Only poetry is able to speak of love in a convincing manner, on a level that transcends its boundaries to reach out towards the mystic and the heretical. Poetry, therefore, makes it possible for love to form the basis of cultures and potentially help them emerge from barbarism, as represented by Nazism. In this sense, the influence of *Cahiers* took on a political flavour that was deliberately outside politics, such as when the special issue on German romanticism, in 1938, was said to have inspired cultural understanding between France and Germany.[65] Similarly, the special issue on *Génie d'Oc* vindicated the values of the ancient Languedocian civilisation and also aimed to make it 'the symbol of all Western humanity threatened by Hitler' (Fabre and Piniès 1987a: 22). It was left to Claire Charles-Géniaux to express the feeling of history coming full circle, when she visited her friends, the Sires, in occupied Carcassonne in 1940: in the evening, when she saw some officers passing in their grey uniforms, she did not know whether they were De Montfort's crusaders or German barbarians. *Cahiers* maintained a consistently antifascist and anti-Nazi stance, with rare exceptions, and the Vichy censors shut their eyes to their transgressions.

The cultural approach of the review, heedless of accusations of anachronism and aware of its isolation in a 'world that pressed all its great thinkers into action', looked forward to a time when 'culture would be a synonym for happiness to all men' (Ballard 1938: 62). From the headquarters of *Cahiers* this argument was directed at Europe at the time of its greatest destruction. It gave an interpretation of Europeanness that did not stop at the topic of intellectual decline and went beyond the militarisation of politics.

Cahiers du Sud established a parallel connection between the geographical pairing of Europe/Mediterranean and the literary pairing of love/poetry, and then proceeded to give the former combination an interpretation (i.e., stressing the aspect of intercultural relationships) that took it out of its geographical context,[66] and to twist the latter coupling to focus on the expressive side of love. In this regard, too, *Cahiers* emphasised the historical aspects of relations between East and West, between Christianity and Islam, and then took their exploration one stage further to outline possible future scenarios.

Notes

1. Marcel Pagnol (1895–1974), playwright, film-maker, poet and novelist.
2. Jean Ballard (1893–1973), while editing the magazine, was also a lifelong verifier of weights in the market of his city.
3. Quoted by A. Freixe (1987: 402).
4. Gabriel Audisio (1900–1978), poet, essayist, novelist and high official in the Algerian government, studied Muslim law and civilisation. Of Italo-Rumanian extraction, he was born in Marseilles, where he became director of the Opéra. He also spent long periods in Algiers, where he was director of the municipal theatre. Joë Bousquet (1897–1950), was a poet, critic, essayist and novelist.

After a wound sustained at the age of seventeen in the First World War, he was sentenced to a life of immobility and suffering. His figure is central to many relationships: he signed the Surrealist Manifesto in 1925, played a leading role in *Cahiers* and maintained close contact with the *Nouvelle Revue Française*. He was a close friend of René Nelli (1906–1982), a student of Romance philology and the Middle Ages as well as a folklorist and author of works on the Cathars, Provençal culture and love. Pierre and Maria Sire co-wrote novels such as *L'Homme à la Poupée* (1931) and *Le Clamadou* (1935).

5. *Rapport d'Organisation* by Paul Valéry for his appointment as Chief Administrator of the Centre Universitaire Méditerranéen of Nice, 1933, quoted in Guiraud (1993: 72). 'For us, Valéry remained the ideal Mediterranean type – and also a symbol, a guide', wrote Ballard, quoted in Guiraud (1993: 258).

6. Marcel Brion (1895–1984), solicitor, art historian, essayist and novelist.

7. This essay is based on a lecture held at Maggio Fiorentino in 1935; see Brion (1935: 574).

8. In this article – initially conceived as part of his book *André Gide, Sa Vie, Son Oeuvre* – the author reviews and interprets Gide's assertion that all Europe was hurtling towards ruin. Pierre-Quint (1895–1958), essayist and literary critic, took part in the surrealist movement.

9. The convention was attended by André Gide, André Malraux, Julien Benda, Aldous Huxley, Heinrich Mann and Gaetano Salvemini, whose denunciation of the concentration camps in Siberia aroused 'an indescribable tumult' according to Noth (1935: 611–16).

10. A 'thrilling' book that gives a 'comprehensive and original explanation of the natures of the various European peoples', according to a review by M. Brion (1930: 559–60).

11. 'A book full of thought and faith' that seeks the birth of a modern Europe in the historical forces acting in the Balkans and in an Italy that is capable of returning to its traditions and escaping fascism. Review by H. Bénac (1937: 446–47).

12. Gilbert Trolliet (1907–1980), Swiss writer, poet and editor of magazines in France and Switzerland.

13. Max Rychner (1897–1965), Swiss journalist, literary critic and writer. On the anti-American attitude of French culture during that period seen as a humanistic vindication and 'defence of man'; see Roger (2002: 481–83). *Cahiers* did not, however, go all out for the stereotypical approach: a review by Gabriel Bertin of *Scènes de la Vie Future* by Georges Duhamel, one of the most representative books of this trend, advises the author to thank America for having offered him such a fine opportunity for him to vent his spleen; see Bertin (1930: 629–31).

14. For example in a mystical-erotic poem, 'Poème', by Ibn Al Fâridh (1932: 180–83).

15. *L'Islam et l'Occident*, in *Cahiers du Sud*, 175, August–September 1935; the volume was republished and extended in 1947.

16. Emile Dermenghem (1892–1971) archivist-paleographer and librarian in Paris and Algeria, author of *La Vie de Mahomet*, 1929; *Vies des Saints Musulmans*, 1942; *Culte des Saints dans l'Islam Maghrébin*, 1954.

17. Letter from Ballard to Dermenghem in 1933–34, in *Rivages*, 320–21.
18. J. Ballard, Introduction, *L'Islam et l'Occident*, 7.
19. Ibid., 4. The ethically inspired humanism of Ballard claims a Graeco-Latin heritage, unlike that of Audisio; see M. Coulet (1993: 242 et seq.).
20. François Bonjean (1884–1963) lived in Egypt, Algieria, India and Morocco, where he married a young Muslim woman and pursued a syncretism between the Muslim world and Christianity.
21. Muhammad Husayn Haykal (1888–1956), Egyptian intellectual and politician, author of various novels and a biography of Mahommed. His constant focus was the role of reason in the European heritage, even at its time of crisis, and hopes for a new world based on an Islam able to promote science and reason; see Johansen (1967). His novel *Zanayb* (1914) illustrates the difference between two forms of love: *hawa*, the passion that a man can feel even for 'backward' women, and *hubb*, a refined form of emotion with educated women. See Smith (1983).
22. The complex development in the thoughts of Haykal was analysed by I. Gershoni (1991: 209–51; 1997: 21–73). Haykal turned away from an assimilative model of social progress dependent on the West in favour of a pathway to modernity based on an independent Egyptian and Islamic identity.
23. Both natives of Rennes, but later settled in Provence. Charles Géniaux, pacifist and Christian, was a successful novelist whose books received many literary prizes; see Dufour (1936: 27–31). For her part, Claire Charles-Géniaux wrote many romantic novels, partly autobiographical and with a historical setting.
24. *L'Ame Musulmane en Tunisie* (1934) was dedicated by the author to her dead husband. His *Les Musulmanes* (1909) was meant to contribute to the emancipation of Muslim women.
25. The ending of the novel is tragic: the ageing heroine drowns herself in the sea because she does not wish to choose a life of marriage, yet, at the same time, she can not tolerate the solitude of her old age.
26. The definition is that of Coulet (1993: 240).
27. In *L'Ame Musulmane*, the author praises the beauty of the Muslims and Bedouins. This categorisation does not include the Jewish community of Tunisia.
28. A good part of the issue is devoted to literary documentation: it includes the translation of poems, a review of contemporary Persian literature and a reassessment of pre-Islamic poetry.
29. René Guénon (1886–1951) devoted himelf to occult and theosophical studies and converted to Islam.
30. Eastern influences on European music are evident from the 1930s, in an attempt to introduce new musical languages, according to P. Bois (1991: 437–55).
31. Albert Gleizes (1881–1953), art historian and essayist.
32. Louis Massignon (1883–1962), was an advocate of the communion between Islam and Christianity. His will to open a dialogue with Arab culture was based not merely on his studies but on his own spiritual development: he

converted from Catholicism to the Byzantine church and became a Malachite priest in 1950; see Trebitsch (1998a: 546–47). Edward Said accepted him as a representative of French orientalism, acknowledging his value, but criticising his view of the Islamic East as 'spiritual, Semitic, tribalistic, monotheistic, non-Aryan' (Said 1979: 271).

33. Amongst the many examples we could cite, note the case of Leo Ferrero (Chapter 2).

34. A check through the following reviews for the period from October 1935 to September 1936 showed no reaction to the special issue of *Cahiers* on *L'Islam et l'Occident*: *Esprit, Journal Asiatique, Revue des Etudes Islamiques* (formerly *Revue du Monde Musulman*); similarly, a check of the period from October 1935 to the beginning of 1936 drew a blank for the following: *Revue Africaine, Revue Tunisienne, Revue des Deux Mondes, Afrique Française, L'Information de la Quinzaine, Questions Nord-Africaines*.

35. *Revue Universelle*, 63, 14, 15 October 1935, 253–54. The *Revue Universelle*, ed. Henri Massis, was Catholic and neoscholastic, and generally hostile to Eastern philosophies and religions.

36. 'L'Islam et l'Occident', in *Les Nouvelles Littéraires Artistiques et Scientifiques*, 685, 30 November 1935, 9, entitled *Revue des Revues*. His review, much more eclectic than the first, both politically and intellectually, supported the possibility of regenerating the West through contacts with Eastern religions and philosophies.

37. The normal print run of *Cahiers* was between 1,900 and 2,200 copies, of which 1,000 were distributed free of charge and 350 were subscriptions. The special issues ate into the review's reserves, which show a deficit of 40,000 francs in 1936. The magazine was distributed to many provincial towns, abroad and to the French colonies; see Guiraud (1993: 75). It was placed in the ships and hotels that worked for the shipping companies (E. Temime 1993: 102).

38. The publication reissued in 1947 reveals differences compared to that of 1935, especially because the number of pieces written by Arab authors has increased. Massignon opened the 1947 issue with a worried analysis, 'Situation Internationale de l'Islam', 13–18, in which he states that the Muslim world is caught between social communist and Western pressures. It has rightly been said of Massignon that he expressed that part of the Western conscience that had been wounded by discovering its limitations, while at the same time Massignon placed his knowledge at the service of French colonial politics (239); see T. Hentsch (1988b: 237). The 1947 issue revealed a greater effort to bring together Islam and the West, as evidenced by the extension of the final essay by Dermenghem, whose title was changed to 'Témoignage de l'Islam. Notes sur les Valeurs Permanentes et Actuelles de la Civilisation Musulmane' (372–87).

39. As Hentsch wrote about Massignon (1998b: 241).

40. Joutard suggested that the dual belonging, to the earth and to the sea, underpinned an ability to reconcile a sense of belonging to a place with a tendency towards cultural hybridity (*Rivages*, 361).

41. Audisio was engaged in a fierce debate with some members of the Mediterranean Academy of Monaco who were in favour of Italian fascism

and/or Hitlerism. He spoke out against the laws against concubinage in Italian Africa (1937a: 133–36), and dreamed of an 'impure race made up of all incomers and all mixtures' (1936a: 11). He took great satisfaction in quoting Albert Camus who, when he opened the Maison de la Culture in Algiers, gave a lecture which declared the Mediterranean to be the very antithesis of Rome (1937b: 457–60).

42. According to E. Temime (2002: 118–23), Audisio considered the liberal development of the French empire to be necessary.

43. Quoted in Freixe 1988, 11, 2: 167–69.

44. The aims of this Avignon-based movement, which dates back to the mid-nineteenth century, were to promote the languages and expressive forms of Provence. Its main proponent was Frédéric Mistral (1830–1914), who was awarded the Nobel Prize in 1903.

45. On the figure of the *gitane* as a symbol in romanticism of extreme emotions, the object of an *amour fou*, who teases and then turns away, see L. Piasere (2002).

46. The conflict between heterosexual and homosexual love is not present in the troubadour culture, but the topic of male homosexuality is dealt with in disapproving tones elsewhere in *Cahiers*. In a review of a novel by Breitbach, the author claims that homosexuality 'always has something sadly miserable' (G.D. 1936: 268). In another review, of a novel by Georges Portal, the author complains that 'our literary inverts' are monotonous and boring (Haedens 1936: 857).

47. His insistence on the mask of the woman in the love scene is reminiscent of the topic of masking in Lacan's writings on female sexuality. 'For Lacan, a mask is not an identity but a set of significant features, it is a stylisation that conceals nothingness', in other words, the lack of a phallus (Francesconi 2003: 101–8). On the relationship between Lacan's ideas and courtly love, see Part II, Chapter 4 .

48. The issue actually came out in February 1943, due to printing problems. The essay on the *langue d'oc* by L. Alibert (1942: 17–25) bears the sign of the times, because it ends by welcoming the promise made by Marshal Pétain to introduce the *langue d'oc* in primary schools and reconstitute the former provinces – an unusual concession in *Cahiers*, given that many of its contributors took part in the Resistance. The issue contains a documentary section and a considerable anthology of poems. Provençal poetry is presented as 'a rare example of an almost native European literature' (E. Roditi 1942: 69–76).

49. *Cahiers* operated as a host organisation in Marseilles for French and foreign intellectuals, particularly Jews, but also those whom the Vichy regime considered 'undesirable', such as communists, surrealists and stateless people. The refugees they welcomed included Simone Weil. The German invasion in November 1942 made the situation of *Cahiers* even more difficult and forced the closure of the Centre Américain de Secours, which had managed to get more than 1,000 refugees out to the United States, including André Breton, Marc Chagall, Marcel Duchamp, Max Ernst, Claude Lévi-Strauss, Hannah Arendt and André Masson; see Guiraud (1993: 80–84) and Paire (2002: 105–19).

50. Bonjean tackles the important topic of Eurafrica, which reveals the limits of European multiculturalism; see Ellena (2004: 326).
51. The Spanish influences on Provence and France are stressed in Probst-Biraben (1942a: 161–72; 1942b: 215–23).
52. Thérèse Aubray, born in Marseilles, was the author of several collections of poetry (*Battements I, II, III, IV*) published between 1933 and 1939, and translator of Shri Aurobindo and D.H. Lawrence.
53. The description of 'superintendent' was bestowed on her by J. Raymond (1993: 30), who also spoke of the 'lively nature, freedom, openness and practical good sense' of 'Marcou' Ballard.
54. Simone Weil (1909–43) was forced to leave Paris with her family in June 1940 due to the arrival of the Germans. From September, the Weil family moved to Marseilles, where Simone began to contribute to *Cahiers*, which published her essay on the *Iliad* in December 1940–January 1941. She took part in the magazine meetings, which she experienced as an 'outpost of the moral and intellectual resistance' (Canciani 1996: 256). A meeting with Bousquet sparked a deeply felt exchange of correspondence; see Fiori (1981: Ch. 16), Nevin (1991: 212 et seq.) and Pétrement (1973: Part 2, Chs 7 and 8). During the period from September 1941 to the end of the year, Weil wrote two essays on science especially for *Cahiers* and, in February–March 1942, those published in *Genie d'Oc*; see Gaeta (1982: 65 et seq.). On her Marseilles period, see Weil (2005).
55. Paire (2002: 113) noted that Weil's presence in *Cahiers* represented a break with the usages and customs of a mostly male review.
56. On Simone Weil's complex self-perception of gender, on her 'studied masculinity' in her youth and her observations on the vulnerability of female workers from her experience of factories, see Nevin (1991: 21, 34–35, 216–20).
57. Nelli quoted by Freixe (1988: 174).
58. Letter to Déodat Roché (Weil 1997: 42).
59. Such ideas, now abandoned by specialists, included the suggestion that the Cathar doctrine and the erotic ideas of the troubadours had a common source in Provençal thought based on Platonic ideas; see Zambon (1997; 1999); Brenon (2000). The topic is discussed in greater depth with reference to Rougemont, Part II, Chapter 4.
60. The same tone is adopted in *Quaderni*, written in Marseilles between the beginning of 1941 and May 1942: '[I]t is the *impossibility* of leading to God … The very reason Greeks praised homosexual love so highly was because it was impossible'. See Gaeta (1982: vol. 3, 124).
61. The theme, already present in Nelli (1963), is further pursued in Nelli (1974: 19–70): in the troubadouresque *assag*, which is radically distinguished from a conjugal sexual relationship, the decision is left entirely to the woman. The knight will never attempt to go beyond the limits of the trial, which is understood to be a loving relationship without penetration. The *assag* is ridiculed by the chivalrous attitude because a real trial must be military and heroic in nature and the virility of the knight is affirmed only through 'complete' sexual relations.

62. Weil returns to the theme of language as homeland in *Venise Sauvée*; see Veltri (2002: 39, 53). On her 'desire to be a poet', confirmed by Jean Tortel, see Paire (2002).
63. In another respect, the review upholds a Mediterranean idea of conjugal love, shared by Muslims and Europeans, whereby a man's only woman is his legitimate wife, mother of his children; see Audisio (1942: 271–82).
64. See D. Roché (1942: 112–40), who complements his writings with a selection of texts. See also H. Feraud (1942: 343–69), who maintained the relevance of Manichaeism (in a psychological rather than a metaphysical sense) to the present day.
65. Contributors to this number included Walter Benjamin. In October 1929, Ballard attempted to obtain the release of Benjamin from the Nevers internment camp. On contact between *Cahiers* with Germany, see Narbutt (1993: 813–25).
66. On the concept of deterritorialisation, see Deleuze and Guattari (1980); on its significance for today's Europe, see Passerini (2007b).

Chapter 4

The Heart of Europe:
Love in the Western World by Denis de Rougemont

Berne, February 1940
Climbed up to St Gotthard yesterday for matters of service.
I have never been able to come to this high place in Switzerland, this
true heart of Europe, without feeling an emotion that I am at a loss to
describe: it is like no other. I must have been thirteen or fifteen when
I came here for the first time, walking down from Andermatt and
going via the Devil's bridge. And the thing that immediately struck me
was not the almost lugubrious vastness of the landscape, but a train
chugging steadily along at its normal speed at the bottom of the valley.
As it snaked from one side of the mountain to the other, it
disappeared, reappeared, circled the hill at Wassen crowned by its
white church, climbed again around immense bends and finally reached
our level, only to plunge back into the rocks at the base of a vertical
wall blackened by water. I could read the words on the long, dark,
wagons: 'Amsterdam – Basel – Milan – Zagreb – Bucharest'. I
remember I wrote a poem about it. I had experienced Europe for the
first time. (Denis de Rougemont[1] 1982: 112)

Reading of the First Edition

'I have lived this book throughout all my adolescence and my youth;
I conceived it in the form of a written work two years ago, feeding it
with some readings; finally I put it together in four months', wrote
Rougemont in the Foreword that precedes *Love in the Western World*
(*L'Amour et l'Occident*), signed 21 June 1938.[2] The work was written
in a period of crisis, both for Europe, with the annexing of Austria

to Nazi Germany in March 1938, and for France, where Rougemont had lived since 1931: the beginning of April 1938 saw the resignation of Léon Blum and his Popular Front government. As the year went on, the Munich conference revealed the inability of the European democratic states to stand up to Hitler, with repercussions on the French situation, which saw the left-wing parties finally give up their support for the government in December.

Almost at the same time as his book on love, which came out at the beginning of 1939, Rougemont published his *Journal d'Allemagne* in November 1938, based on notes he made during his stay in Germany during 1935–36. The two books balanced one another out: *L'Amour et l'Occident* (referred to hereafter as *AO*) being a work of great cultural breadth on Western civilisation; the other being a personal work on the topic of Nazism. The publication of the German diary was important in highlighting the internal coherence of Rougemont's work, since *Journal d'Allemagne* contained some premises of *AO*. The latter book has enjoyed growing success from that time to the present day.[3]

Love in the Western World seduces the reader, in the same way as its subject must have seduced its author. Rougemont's seduction is evident in the lingering way he dwells on aspects such as the literary parts. The seduction is revealed by his initial appeal to his readers or rather, as Rougemont writes in the Foreword, to his female readers whom he thought would account for most of his potential audience, in addition to 'a few specialists':[4] 'My Lords, if you would hear a high tale of love and death …'. The author replies on our behalf, 'We know we could listen to nothing more delightful' (Rougemont 1939: 1. 1983: 15); Invited to share this answer, we comply, almost without realising it, with Rougemont's fundamental thesis, which he will use to lead us inexorably to his conclusion – that Westerners prefer stories that connect love and death to any other form of literature. They also allow themselves to be influenced by the same themes in life, in a contradiction between the exaltation of love and marriage and that which destroys them. From the first page, Rougemont draws us in by promising not only to tackle this enigma but also to reveal the hidden reasons of its appeal, which make up the 'European mind' (1939: 1; 1983: 15).

Many allowed themselves to be seduced by Rougemont's invitation. The writer Benjamin Fondane wrote to him that his theory and his demonstration of the Manichaean origins of courtly love had 'completely seduced' him.[5] Rougemont's friend Roger Jézéquel, a pastor and writer, expressed himself thus: 'As soon as your book arrived, I threw myself into it and I finished my first reading yesterday evening. I was literally enchanted by the first three books'.[6] Daniel-Rops included the manuscript in a collection entitled *Présences* that he was editing for Plon and wrote to Rougemont on 3 July 1938, '[J]'en suis enchanté'.[7] Others, such as Gustave Thibon, put up some resistance to the seduction, considering it 'erroneous' (Thibon 1939).[8]

Most of what follows the opening invitation – the first five books of the work – is taken up by a diatribe on passionate love, which is portrayed as an old and well-known friend, or enemy. Only Book 6 reveals the intention of the diatribe, which is evident from its very title: 'The Anti-marriage Myth'. The long historical preamble is determined by the needs of the present. The problem that lies at the root of the whole discussion is the crisis in marriage, a topic that was hotly debated in the period between the two wars and considered central to the crisis in Western civilisation in both Europe and the United States. According to Rougemont, the term 'Western' includes both, which are sometimes in conflict with one another.

In considering the crisis in marriage and heterosexual love to be central to the crisis in civilisation, Rougemont was in agreement with most interpreters of the time, including Freud and Jung (Passerini 1999: 81 et seq.). According to the diagnosis in *AO*, the crisis in marriage is the outcome of a conflict typical of the period, between two equally powerful forces: middle-class morality and passionate or romantic morality. Western middle-class adolescents are taught to believe in the idea of marriage, but at the same time they are submerged in a romantic atmosphere fed by films, books and everyday references, which suggests that life is not really lived without the supreme test of passion that is, nevertheless, considered to be incompatible with conjugal union. Yet consumer society maintains that even happiness can be bought: passion is touted as possible by the happy endings to those films, so numerous in Germany after the advent of Hitler, that suggest a gypsy can run off with a princess and a mechanic marry an heiress. Divorce allows the illusion of combining marriage with passion, and finding happiness in the next love. Modern man, who embodies these attitudes (Rougemont 1939: 283; 'The moderns, men and women of passion' [1983: 282]), cannot possess, because he has lost the sense of fidelity and finds it repugnant to set his own limits voluntarily, which are sure signs of personal decadence and of a kind of sickness of being.[9] The diagnosis of a crisis refers to Rougemont's personalistic ideas, connected with his reworking of

Kierkegaard and Barth,[10] and relates to contemporary discussion: personalism is in fact one of the roots of *AO*.

In 1930s France, personalism was supported, in its various guises, by the intellectuals who moved between the 'spiritualist with a political perspective' review *Esprit*, with a strong Catholic component, edited by Emmanuel Mounier (Loubet del Bayle 1969: 125; see also Touchard 1960: 89–118),[11] to which Rougemont contributed; the federalist and pro-European *Ordre Nouveau*, of which he was a part of the editorial team together with Alexandre Marc, Robert Aron, Arnaud Dandieu and Daniel-Rops; and *Hic et Nunc*, a magazine founded by him and edited with Henry Corbin, the bearer of a wave of theological and ecclesiastical renewal into Protestant environments.[12] In the 1920s, the influences of dialogism, or the philosophy of encounter, which rejected an abstract and isolated subject in favour of a social constitution of the individual (a line of thought pursued by Martin Buber,[13] amongst others), had been grafted onto the French tradition started by Charles Renouvier, characterised by a view of the world based on relationships between people and supported by a nonconfessional god. *Ordre Nouveau* proclaimed itself 'against capitalist disarray and communist oppression, against homicidal nationalism and impotent imperialism, against parliamentarianism and fascism', ideas which lay the basis for a critique of the decadence of French and European civilisation and launched an appeal for its recovery in opposition to the form of modernity represented by the United States (Aron and Dandieu 1931a, b).[14]

According to the generally accepted view, personalism represented a third way between bourgeois individualism and communist collectivism. Differences were, nevertheless, present between those who claimed to be personalists, in particular between the *Esprit* and *Ordre Nouveau* groups, although some people, such as Rougemont, took part in both.[15] The personalist doctrine of Rougemont (Rougement 1934, 1972b) translates and develops his ideas on 'modern man', exemplified by the arrogant technician, who has lost the 'human measure' (1934: 15–16). The concept of 'person' for Rougemont is the basis of every true and sound revolution: 'The person, the man in progress, the man consciously and voluntarily engaged in the vital conflict that joins him to and sets him against his fellow man' is the foundation of the community. The human being is depicted as 'neither angel nor beast: neither right nor left', in Rougemont's constant striving to accept dualisms but go beyond them (1934: 159–60, 240 et seq.).

In *AO*, he adds a dramatic coda to his personalistic theses of the first half of the 1930s that specifically concerns the crisis in love and marriage. He considers the Church's efforts to redefine the institution of marriage honourable yet useless and takes an ironic look at Jung's suggestion of analysing the psychological conflict that lies at the basis of sickness, 'from which you should deduce that mental medicine is able to heal everything' (1939: 291; 1983: 288). At the same time, he recognises the huge extent of the disaster. Indeed, for him recent European history recorded a changeover from permanent anarchy to totalitarian cleanliness: after the sexual revolution triggered by the Soviet revolution, and the phase of freedom in relationships between the sexes in Weimar Germany, the dictatorships of Stalin and Hitler set themselves the task of cleaning up the resulting anarchy, and Mussolini's dictatorship imposed draconian measures against unmarried men. Rougemont points out the dangers of these totalitarian developments: if eugenics wins the battle, Europe will have stopped living (1939: 26; 'The Europe of passion would be no more', 1983: 291) and a new threatening West could take shape in the laboratories.

The first five books of *AO* attempt to find the origins of the current crisis, and find them in the medieval myth of Tristan and Iseult. The origins are admittedly indirect, but no less meaningful for that. This is Rougemont's starting point for his examination of the five versions of Tristan, 'a kind of archetype of our most complex feelings of unrest' (1939: 5; 1983: 18).

The myth of Tristan has dominated the cultural and emotional scenario of Western civilisation for almost a millennium. Rougemont uses psychoanalytical tools and techniques of literary analysis to decipher its hidden content, but his definition of the myth is underpinned by the debate held at the Collège de Sociologie from November 1937 to July 1939, in which he played a part.[16] According to Rougemont, myths express the rules of conduct of a social or religious group since they proceed from the sacred element around which this group is formed. The 'obscure' origin of the myth is a mark of its profoundness and thus its rooting in the subconscious, which allows it to act on us without our full awareness.

These theses echo those of the Collège, as formulated by Bataille, Leiris and Caillois.[17] Bataille believed that the myth cannot be separated from the community that experiences it: '[T]he myth lived ritually reveals nothing less than true being'. There are radical differences between Bataille's view of the myth – which emphasises aspects such as the dual nature of repulsion and attraction typical of the sacred, cruelty, sacrifice, excess (waste), violence and blasphemous desecration, the Nietzschean anti-Christ (Pearce 2003: 3) – and Rougemont's view, which relates every religious phenomenon to his own Protestant faith. Their concept of *eros* also differs, which for Bataille includes references to the excremental, the coming together of the divine and the scatological, the bedroom as a 'sinister' holy place, madness and death; to him, the loving relationship is convulsion and perdition in a sort of single sacred beast,[18] a concept poles apart from that of Rougemont, who uses all his intellectual energies to oppose the idea of fusion between lovers. As a consequence, their views of women are extremely different. Bataille sees them as simultaneously victims and saints, while Caillois believes that the male collective must cleanse itself of its female element (Sweedler 2001: 55, 61); despite his contradictory views on the subject, Rougemont's concept of woman is as man's equal. One thing he shares with the founders of the Collège, however, is their interest in the sacred in everyday life and their repudiation of the hegemony of utilitarianism, economicism and Marxism, which were held to be responsible for the reductive view of modern man (Richman 2003: 31). They also shared an interest in rituals able to create unity in the collective, though for some members of the Collège, such as Bataille, this could reach the point of longing for human sacrifice to be perpetrated in a secret society.[19]

They also agreed on the reason for the opposition between myth and art. As far as Rougemont is concerned, myth expresses a collective reality, unlike a work of art, which is individual. Bataille believed that myth, even when a fairytale, is the opposite of fiction if one takes into account the people to whom it is a living reality. The reason for the opposition between myth and literature was developed above all by Roger Caillois, who believed that myth loses its moral power at the point at which it becomes literature and the subject of aesthetic enjoyment.[20] This opposition is not original, since it was introduced at the time of German romanticism. In a review of *AO*, Sartre suggested that the concept of myth had been inflated to the point that 'one fears that nowadays there exists a myth of the myth' (Sartre 1939: 243–44). For Rougemont, however, the expression 'myth' is meaningful, because it goes back to the *engagement* of the Christian intellectual, whose commitment must be to 'deconstruct' the myths of his or her period (Rougemont 1934: 19–20; Ackermann 1996: 349).[21]

In the case of Tristan, the myth is associated with the rules and rituals that governed chivalry, which are equivalent to a sacred mystery. This connection is also consistent with the theses of the Collège de Sociologie, and particularly with the link between love and war. It is no mere chance that the volume of *AO* that Rougemont chose to present to the Collège was Book 5, which is specifically concerned with this link. When the institution of chivalry disappeared, according to Rougemont, the passion for the original myth became part and parcel of everyday life, bringing about the return of what had been removed through a quintessentially Freudian process. *AO*, therefore, draws a distinct difference between the two contents of the myth, its manifest meaning and its latent meaning.

According to the manifest content (Rougemont 1939: 14–18; 'What the Tristan Romance Seems to Be About', 1983: 26), Tristan is born marked by misfortune, as his name suggests. He loses both his parents and is raised by his uncle, King Mark. His first feat is to kill the giant Morholt, but he sustains a poisoned wound in the struggle. He is then healed by Iseult the Fair, Queen of Ireland and sister of the giant, who does not realise she is saving her brother's killer. When King Mark decides to marry her, Tristan is charged to bring her to him. Tristan is again injured in a fight against a dragon and again healed by Iseult, who, however, discovers that he is her brother's killer and in turn threatens to kill him. She has a change of mind when she becomes aware of Tristan's mission and the two set sail for Cornwall, but during their voyage the handmaiden Brangäne offers them the love potion destined for the newly-weds by mistake. The fact that they consequently fall in love does not deter Tristan from taking Iseult to the king, but during their wedding night it is Brangäne who replaces the legitimate bride in the royal bridal chamber. The lovers are discovered due to a trap set by a dwarf, an accomplice of the villainous barons, who scatters flour between their beds. As he clears the space that separates him from Iseult in one bound, Tristan leaves traces of blood from a recent wound. The two take refuge in the forest where they remain for three years – the time the love potion takes to wear off – leading a hard and primitive life. During this period, King Mark finds them there one day sleeping in a cave, but separated by Tristan's unsheathed sword, a sign of chastity. The king is moved and spares their lives, replacing Tristan's sword by his own. When the two at last return to court, their love survives, this time without the potion, rearousing the suspicion of the barons, who order them to submit to Divine Judgement. Iseult overcomes this by swearing that she has never been in the arms of any man except those of the king and the peasant who helped her out of the boat (Tristan in disguise) and is, therefore, able to grasp the red-hot iron without harm. Further adventures take Tristan overseas, where he agrees to marry Iseult of the White Hands (because she has the same name as his beloved and also because she is his friend's sister), but he does not consummate their union. Wounded again, he calls Iseult the Fair to him, and she arrives in a ship with white sails, a sign of hope. Out of jealousy, however, Tristan's wife tells him that the sail is black. Tristan dies. Iseult the Fair arrives and expires on the body of her lover.

This love is very strange, comments Rougemont, noting that Tristan did not have to take Iseult to the king: it is a love that conforms to the rules that condemn it, in order to preserve itself. The two lovers never miss an opportunity to separate, and when there are no obstacles they invent them (the unsheathed sword, Tristan's marriage). All this must be understood in accordance with dream logic, however, which is not the same as real life and expresses that of 'the demon of courtly love', 'i.e., the very demon of *the novel* as we in the West like it to be' (1939: 26; 1983: 37). All this is so enigmatic that Rougemont feels entitled to ask a bold question: does Tristan love Iseult? His answer to the paradoxical question is also the answer to the enigma of the West: the two love without loving one another, because '*what they love is love and being in love*' (1939: 31; 1983: 41). Unhappy mutual love – the Western paradox – is falsely reciprocal, because it masks a dual narcissism and an ascetic opposition to earthly life. Tristan loves the awareness that he is loving far more than he loves Iseult (1939: 31; 1983: 41) and Iseult does nothing to hold him back when he goes away, because the dream of passion is enough for her. The lovers 'do not need one another as they are' but rather they need the other's absence (1939: 32; 1983: 41–42). The real object of their passion is impediment, which they recreate incessantly. If there were no impediments, they could marry to create a situation that Rougemont considers absurd: that of a 'Mrs Tristan', a perfect recipe for killing passion.

The impediment driving the fatal passion becomes the purpose, or rather the desired end in its own right. The end of passion is indeed death, which extinguishes it. At a deeper level, the active passion of Night, as Rougemont calls the death wish, is at work. We have thus penetrated the latent content of the myth, which allows us to perceive aspects that are normally hidden. The Western psyche is characterised by a threefold link between passion, the taste for death and a form of consciousness that closely connects consciousness and suffering. Rougemont calls 'our sadistic genius'

(1939: 42; 1983: 51) a repressed wish for death and for absolute self-knowledge, which he claims also lies at the root of the instinct for war in Westerners. The quoted passage also reveals the equivalence between the West and Europe: the persistence of the secret that the West has never dared to reveal – namely, its desire for suffering – brings us to a highly pessimistic view of the future of Europe.

Rougemont chooses to explain the origins of the set of links he has brought to light by setting the myth (Book 2) in its historical and religious context, a problematic choice because he himself repeats several times that his work is not really historical. The operation hinges on a syllogism (or a paralogism, if we deny the relationship between the two premises): all European poetry, including *Tristan*, is derived from the poetry of the troubadours; this was imbued with Catharism of Eastern origin, so that European consciousness is imbued with this heresy and its consequences. According to Rougemont, the troubadours were actually inspired by Catharism, a belief that he judges to be of Manichaean origin and very close to Eastern religions such as Christian Gnosticism, Buddhism, Essenism and Jainism.[22] This equivalence, which is central to Rougemont's argument, was also the belief that aroused most criticism. As we will see, there are fluctuations and changes in the various versions of *AO* in this respect, but there is no doubt that Rougemont's main achievement was to treat very different cultural entities as one: the story of Tristan, which is part of northern French culture; the troubadour poetry and culture of Provence (at that time poised on the brink of becoming a mass tourist destination instead of the favourite place of various sects) (Passerini 1999: 213 et seq.); the Cathar heresy; and 'the East'.

The East of which Rougemont speaks is more a psychological concept than geographical: 'by "East" I mean in this book an attitude of the human mind which has reached its highest and purest expression in the direction of Asia' (Rougemont 1939: 62; 1983: 69), in the sense that Eastern dualism, between light and shade and between good and evil, can allegedly be resolved in the quest for a fusion between human beings and God or between two lovers. So-called 'Eastern' asceticism tends towards complete union with God or with the universal One Being, as in the case of Buddhism. Rougemont wishes to remove himself from geographical determination and he emphasises this by reminding us that a cardinal rule of theological thought that he upholds – the belief in the existence of an essential gulf between God and man, defined by Kierkegaard as 'the infinite qualitative difference' – has triumphed only in the West despite its origins in the Near East. He refers to the biblical concept that rules out the possibility of essential union and allows only communion, 'the *marriage* of the Church and her Lord' (1939: 63; 1983: 70). Western tendencies exist in the East, and vice versa, since 'everyone must stand to the East of someone else' (1939: 139; 1983: 156). In the history of emotions, the Eastern question arises in terms of the debate over the Arabic derivations of Provençal poetry, which was the subject of a long drawn-out *querelle* in the nineteenth century.[23]

Rougemont's 'orientalist' argument is continued in Book 3, which analyses the relationship between passion and mysticism with the intent of overturning the dialectic between the two. Orthodox mysticism is epithalamic – that is, it focuses on the spiritual marriage between God and the soul in this life – while 'oriental' heretical mysticism places its hope in total fusion after the death of the body. The former case reflects the situation of Tristan's passion: because the soul can no longer join with God in an essential manner, we are left with a case of unhappy reciprocal love, which is expressed in impassioned language – that of the Cathar heresy debased in literature. The Cathars are the main target of Rougemont's polemic because they did not accept incarnation. For them, profane love was absolute unhappiness, attachment to an imperfect creature, while divine love for a Christian is restorative suffering and profane love may be sanctified in marriage. The lovers in the myth of Tristan ignore the movement of return to the world that is a characteristic of Christianity, as Christians do not throw themselves into the illusion of a transfiguring death.

Rougemont's theses on mysticism allow him to overturn ideas of materialism, whereby courtly love is an idealisation of carnal love and male and female mystics are cases of sexual deviation. Rougemont considers these ideas to be vulgar and ridiculous, since Teresa of Avila and John of the Cross were deeply aware of the dangers of spiritual lust and spoke of it freely enough to quash any suspicion of repression. At the same time, their language should not be confused with their experience. Teresa was well aware of tales of chivalry and she used this type of language as a rhetorical resource. This device amounts to another twist of dialectic: a rhetoric such as courtly rhetoric, formerly directed against the Christian church, was taken up by Christian saints, but in order to express *agape*, conjugal love, rather than *eros*, fusional love.

Rougemont's diatribe against materialism, which pervades his entire work, is not merely directed against every Marxist-inspired interpretation, which considers economic realities to be the underlying conditioning factor of cultural realities, but also reveals the limits of his Freudianism. Rougemont mocks 'materialistic prejudice' (1939: 93; 1983: 97),[24] setting against it the entire genealogy of beliefs that ultimately led to courtly love: this includes the Iranian and Orphic origins of the Platonic concept of *eros*, the Gnostic and Hindu myths, and the religion of the Celtic bards. Rougemont gives great prominence to the latter, 'the basic religion of Europe' (1939: 51; 1983: 63), in particular to its assumed conception of woman as a divine and prophetic being embodying *eros*, and to the dualistic distinction it draws between light and dark beings – a concept it shares with Manichaeism. Paganism, which weds East and West, is overcome only by Christianity, which sanctifies the duality between earthly night and transcendent day through the incarnation of the Word in the world – of light in the darkness. This is the basis of Christian love, *agape*, and of its reaffirmation of life. Love is no longer flight and refusal to act, but a positive action of transformation.

Rougemont's theses on mysticism centre on the way he sets East and West in opposition to one another, which should not be interpreted as a general form of Eurocentrism or, still less, a Hegelian system of thought.[25] Rougemont's orientalism is more complicated than appears at first sight. He drew on references taken from Islamists of the age, particularly Henry Corbin, from whom he took the idea of the 'lyrical' structure of the Manichaean faith (Corbin 1937).[26] According to Rougemont, a mixture of Iranian Manichaeism, neo-Platonism and Islamism was at work from the ninth century in Asia Minor in a form of religious poetry with erotic metaphors. He refers to mystic poets such as Al-Hallaj, studied by Louis Massignon, and Suhrawardi of Aleppo, translated with an introduction by Corbin[27] – both accused of Manichaeism and heresy and executed, because Islamic orthodoxy, like Catholic orthodoxy, could not accept that man contains a divine part that merges with his creator. Their language is similar to that of Christian mystics in that it uses erotic and religious metaphors that appeal to death. Rougemont, who gives to an indefinite 'East' attributes that in Corbin's studies were limited to some Arab mystics, points out many analogies between Arab mystics and the troubadours. He nevertheless maintains a radical difference between their concept of death and that of Teresa of Avila.[28] When he quotes Teresa's utterance: 'I die of not being able to die!' (Rougemont 1939: 105; 1983: 105), which apparently echoes that of Arabic mysticism, he means that Western mysticism has borrowed the language but not necessarily the sentiments of *eros*. That cry should not be understood in the commonplace sense of a desire for death, but in a dialectic sense since 'death' has two meanings: the death induced by sin (as in Kierkegaard's 'sickness unto death'), much worse than carnal death; and death in Christ, which in reality is life. Teresa 'means that she is not able to die to the old life enough to become alive in the new', in the very context of a return to the world (1939: 131; 1983: 149).

Rougemont's other source for distinction between East and West is a book by Rudolf Otto that was published in German in 1926 (Otto 1926),[29] and which deconstructs the over-facile differences between East and West using as their representatives the Hindu mystic Sankara and Johannes Eckart, respectively. Otto's thesis is twofold: on the one hand there exists a primary feeling of the numinous, the totally other, which characterises a fundamental human and spiritual experience and enables us to speak of a unifying essence of mysticism, regardless of differences of climate, region or race between East and West (ibid.: 7–8). On the other hand, a great variety of expression may be found in mysticism within the same ethnic and cultural environment. According to this view, Sankara and Eckart are both opposed in the name of consciousness to the rival form of mysticism – emotional or voluntaristic mysticism (ibid.: 36). Yet the two mystics differ over love: Eckart believes that love is the Christian virtue of *agape*, which has nothing to do with the *eros* of Plato and Plotinus; Sankara recognises an affective unity based on the essential unity, which does not resemble Christian *agape* or *bhakti*, a form of unitive mysticism.

Rougemont's reading of Otto is simplistic, because he reintroduces the distinction between East and West and connects them respectively to *eros* and *agape*. In a similar way to his treatment of Corbin, this path leads to an undifferentiated idea of the East opposed to the West, which was the very opposite of what Otto was trying to convey, that is, the attribution of characteristics opposite to those that the Europeans claim as their own, obtained by putting together the most diverse 'Eastern' types.

Lastly, Rougemont also refers to Leo Ferrero in developing his notion of the East. On the basis of his reading of Ferrero (too little, as Sartre rightly observed),[30] Rougemont attributes to 'Orientals' a characterisation of Europe based on the importance that Europe is believed to confer on the forces of passion as a result of its Christian legacy. Rougemont concurs with Ferrero in his belief that Christianity, passion and dynamism are the dominant traits of the

Western psyche. Yet Ferrero, certainly no stranger to orientalism, blamed Christianity for having generated both the passion and the catastrophic spirit of the West.[31] Rougemont believed that love–passion is not a 'by-product of Christianity', as Ferrero had written, but the product of a heresy.

Over and above these specialist references, Rougemont came up with his own general definition of the East,[32] as many of his correspondents observed, whether they agreed with him or not. This is echoed in some letters from readers of *AO*, such as the one from a Swiss friend – citing René Guenon, Raja yoga, theosophy and the anthroposophy of Rudolf Steiner, but also St Paul and St John's Gospel – which accused him of ascribing aspects that specifically concern the Vedic East 'a little too generally to the entire East'. His correspondent asks questions that highlight the absurdities of Rougemont's dichotomisation of East and West, '[I]s Ghandi corrupted by idealist aestheticism?'[33] Another letter from the Crédit Foncier Egyptien of Cairo devotes several pages to arguing the doubt that the dogma of incarnation could really be 'the expression of Western paganism', as the fundamental characteristic of the West is the glorification of man as the sovereign expression of the world.[34]

Rougemont believed that Eastern wisdom pursues the abolition of the different, while Western wisdom seeks the density of being in the individual person. This attitude, which he calls 'my West', 'amounts to defining the ultimate conditions of fidelity, the person, the marriage – and of the rejection of passion' (Rougemont 1939: 321–22; 1983: 318). The identification between the West and Europe appears in such passages. Such an expression of Eurocentricism in passion in its pure state – almost identical to that claimed by C.S. Lewis in 1936 in *The Allegory of Love* (Passerini 1999: 188–213), and also Leo Ferrero's opinions on the subject – seems to constitute a distillate of the beliefs of the age. This expression was reflected in the common consciousness of many, reassuring them and guaranteeing them an identity of their own while they recognised the state of crisis in Europe and its civilisation.

The Europe that Rougemont discusses in *AO* is, nevertheless, not clearly characterised. Rougemont's Europeanist commitment dates from 1946, after his return from the United States, and certainly owes something to his better understanding of the contrast between the cultures of the two poles that make up the West, gained during his stay.[35] During the earlier period of his life, his attitudes veer more towards Europeanness than towards Europeanism. Foremost among these attitudes is the theme of 'Europe of sentiment', mentioned in writings that date back to the years from 1926 to 1930, during the course of Rougemont's travels in Central Europe and Italy.[36] He conjures up an idea of a Europe of nostalgia, 'of farewells', 'a slow country', 'a lost paradise', 'that no longer exists any more', but that 'we carry in ourselves like the memory of an evening from our adolescence' (ibid.: 20). The feeling of *finis Europae*, which becomes more marked in Rougemont with Hitler's conquest, reveals a nostalgic, backward-looking overtone, but constitutes a significant basis for his emotional identification with the area of Europe which he was to develop in his Europeanist commitment after the Second World War. His belief that Switzerland was the 'true heart of Europe', the basis of the federalism in which he believed the salvation of the continent lay, is also rooted in this sentiment.[37]

Another element of Europeanness, connected to the former but couched in political and philosophical terms, is federalism as the basis for a society inspired by a 'new order'. Rougemont's meeting with Alexandre Marc in 1930 was crucial in his development of the link between federalism and personalism.[38] Personalists such as Marc rejected the idea of a united Europe that would maintain nationalism and an internationalism founded on it. He dreamed of a global federalism, partly inspired by Proudhon, which would profoundly reshape the political and social alignment of the continent (Vuillermoz 1999–2000: 21–42; Hellman 1999–2000: 139–50).[39] The personalist revolution does not require centralisation but the principle of federation, in order to respect the diversity of personal, local and regional expressions within a democratic framework.[40] In the first half of the 1930s, federalism was the watchword in Europe. It was believed that this was the only path to peace, potentially constituting a third way between the United States and the Soviet Union, between capitalism and Sovietism. One other factor that illustrates Rougemont's Europeanness and contributes to his Europeanism is his admiration for Goethe, the centenary of whose death he commemorated in 1932 (Rougemont 1938: 43). Goethe represented the messenger of peace who fought nationalism in the name of a universal humanity, and a man capable of restraint, to be offset against Kierkegaard's restlessness.[41] For Rougemont, these elements of Europeanness would form the basis of a better constructed and politically specific idea of Europe after the Second World War. In *AO*, the elements are brought together to define a cultural Europe with somewhat vague boundaries, that needs to define itself inwardly with reference to the concept of the West current in the United States, and outwardly with reference to an ill-defined East.

In 1939, *AO* played a political role as 'a great act against every ideological fanaticism', which saw death as ultimate fulfilment, but in particular against fascism, which was now raging at its height.[42] *AO*'s interest is to establish a link between public and private, political and personal, in that historical context. The speculative grounds adopted by those who assert that *AO* is 'the product of an interior rather than a theoretical debate' (Roy 1998: 426), and those who interpret the work as a mainly public act are equally weak. Though the 'public' interpretation is unfounded, it does reveal a glimmer of truth when it acknowledges *AO*'s merit for its idea of Europe as a third way that could provide a historical response to Rougemont's interests (Keller 1998: 345). By the end of the decade, the spirit of the 1930s had nevertheless run its course. The schism between *Esprit* and *Ordre Nouveau* had taken place at the beginning of 1936, and hope had faded of creating a group that would transcend the differences between right and left which had characterised these intellectuals during the first half of the decade.

While *AO* operates at the level of a link between the individual and the collective, this necessarily implies a relationship between divine and mortal. It is no coincidence that Barthian roots are evident in its discussion of unifying mysticism and the dialectic concept of the history of myth.

Rougemont had translated from German the first volume of Barth's *Church Dogmatics*, a text that served as a basis for the French translation of the full work that appeared in the 1950s in Switzerland.[43] That first volume set out the conception of transcendence put forward by Barth against the historicism propounded by supporters of liberal theology, whereby God is immanent to the human consciousness. It contained, amongst other things, the Barthian doctrine of the incommensurability between the divine and human.[44] Anyone who wishes to overcome the relationship between God and man in the name of unity would fail in the biblical and Christian sense. Barth considers the course adopted by those mystics who seek such unity highly dangerous (Rostagno 2003: 47), and Rougemont takes up and develops exactly this point. Barth repudiates the dualism between matter and spirit, but not that between human and divine (Selinger 1998: 157), which remains fundamental and insuperable. Barth believes that the only way to overcome dualism is incarnation, which exemplifies dialectic on a historical level. This form of dialectic involves a return to transcendence and the possibility of a paradoxical interruption of history through incarnation, in a manner opposite to that of historical materialism.

Dialectic is at work in the way the myth of Tristan is debased through literature. The book on mysticism in *AO* is followed by an investigation of the influence of literature on customs. Book 4 makes reference to a whole series of works ranging from the writings of the Sicilian court of Frederick II to Dante and Petrarch, through Shakespeare's *Romeo and Juliet* to Corneille, Racine, Rousseau and German romanticism. One noteworthy passage in this overview is the small section on Don Juan, whom Rougemont considered to be the absolute antithesis of Tristan even though they shared the same war-like nature (Rougemont 1939: 201 et seq.; 1983: 209 ff.). Don Juan embodies spontaneity of instinct and perpetual infidelity, but also the insolent avidness and the secret weakness of one who cannot possess.[45] Don Juan is the demon of pure immanence, slave to worldly appearances, while Tristan is a slave to transcendence.

One constant reference point is Wagner's opera *Tristan and Isolde*, which harks back to Europe's pagan roots. Wagner takes the myth to its ultimate conclusion, in the sense that he restores its lost meaning. For this reason, interpretations of the opera as a drama of sexual desire and productions that use realistic set designs are committing an error.[46] As a result of Wagner's treatment, the myth is no more than a ghost, and the period of its existence only in poetry and literature commences. In making it contemporary, the myth has been debased by customs (or perhaps morals), in paperback novels, in popular theatre (a three-sided comedy, where Isolde becomes the dissatisfied bride, King Mark her cuckolded husband and Tristan the lover), and lastly in cinema. We have reached the final stage of the myth's decline. Rougemont perceives the possibility that consciousness will help show a way out of the crisis, '[I]t may be that Europe, after a *crisis* of totalitarianism (and assuming that this is not fatal), will recover the significance of a fidelity that is secured by substantial institutions – to the person's measure' (1939: 323; 1983: 319).

Rougemont's criticism is directed also against the rhetoric of the happy endings typical of U.S. films of the first few years after the war. Only in the second edition of *AO* does Rougemont develop his comparison between Europe and the United States. His concept of the West was influenced by the works of authors such as Aron and Dandieu, who considered 'the American cancer' to be a hegemony of rational mechanisms on sentimental realities (Aron and Dandieu 1931b: 16–17).[47] Aron and Dandieu, therefore, launched an appeal to the 'different and one' Europe, calling on it to reawaken and become again 'the youngest hope of the world' (ibid.: 244–45). From the viewpoint of *AO*, the extreme illusion of the fusion of lovers triumphed in the United States along with a forced exchange of the protagonists, considered not as people but as equivalent atoms, which is accentuated by market forces.

This passage takes us to Book 5 and the start of Rougemont's discussion of war, presented to the Collège de Sociologie on 29 November 1938. It is based on his first-person observation of Nazism, as is evident from *Journal d'Allemagne*. This is written in accordance with the conventions of the diarist's genre; Rougemont excelled at this form of writing and it was a tried and tested medium for him.[48] The *Journal* effectively describes the spread of Nazism into daily life: the parades, the songs and also the ghettoisation of the Jews. The author is dissatisfied both by the view of the socialists (Nazism as the salvation of the middle classes) and that of the reactionaries (a bulwark against Bolshevism). In his opinion, Nazism is a type of Jacobinism, which speaks only of duties and not of rights, in order to impose spiritual control, rationalist levelling, deification of the masses, and suppression of the person.

Rougemont's diary records (9 March 1936) Hitler's occupation of the demilitarised Rhine area in contravention of the Versailles agreements, an event that aroused a 'bizarre euphoria' in the city air (Rougemont 1938), as if it were a sort of sexual act. The high point of the *Journal* (11 March), though, is the author's report of his participation in a 'sacred ceremony' (ibid.: 46 et seq.),[49] a speech by Hitler delivered to one million listeners. Rougemont, who attended with them – workers, militiamen, young women dressed in shabby clothes – standing for more than four hours, felt alone, while they were united in their ecstatic support for their leader. Hitler saluted 'with a slow, episcopal gesture, in a deafening thunder of rhythmic *heils*', and Rougemont finally intuited something that one cannot appreciate unless one has experienced it: the sacred horror, the chill and the racing heart in celebration of a new cult. He would never forget the collective uproar at the announcement that a new era had begun. He realised that 'it is about love', the heartfelt attraction of Hitlerism seen as a nascent religion, 'I felt the loving intake of breath in the soul of the masses, the dark and powerful gasp of a nation possessed by the Man with the ecstatic smile' (ibid.).

According to Rougemont, he was witnessing the beginning of the 'true struggle' for Christians: it was time to go back to the catacombs and muster the resistance. He must have been thinking of Karl Barth and the *Bekennende Kirche*, the confessional church – the non-denominational sect of Lutheran and Calvinistic Christians who refused to give in to the orders of the regime – and

Figure 4 Denis de Rougemont, Simonne Vion and Emmanuel Mounier in Frankfurt, 1935–36 (*Nouvelle Revue Neuchâteloise*, 47/XII, Autumn 1995, special issue: *Denis de Rougemont, De Neuchâtel à l'Europe*, p. 37)

Pastor Martin Niemöller, arrested in 1937.[50] Barth himself, having refused to swear loyalty to the Nazi regime, was suspended from teaching at Bonn University in 1934. He was 'rested' in 1935, and his writings were banned, so he left Germany and moved to Basel. Rougemont found it difficult to make his interpretation of the events understood in France to those who were not 'initiates' and who immediately accused him of being a Hitler sympathiser.[51]

Rougemont was aware of the baseness of the Hitlerian 'religion', but believed that this very characteristic corresponded to the needs of the masses, who had been worn down by centuries of individualism. Hitler was a genius in the demonic sense of the term. Because of the love that the majority bestowed on him, only a prophet could have stood up against him. Rougemont believed that resistance was possible only by believing in a truer faith and being able to demonstrate it. The only ones who stood up to Hitler were those who communicated in the faith in which Kierkegaard had lived, and who were living it at that present moment, *hic et nunc*.

Book 5 of *AO* assumes this analysis and complements it. It supports the parallelism between forms of love and war, and illustrates this not only in its language but, above all, with reference to the rituals, such as in a tournament. The connection between love and war is death, although in classic war there was much less loss of life than in modern war. In revolutionary war after 1789, a transposition of passion took place on a collective level. Nationalist ardour is also a form of self-exaltation, a narcissistic love, but this time of the collective self, just as love is much more an exaltation of the lover than the relationship with the beloved. Nation and war are linked like love and death. After Verdun, however, we see a new type of war, all-out war, due to the intervention of an inhuman technique: no longer only violence but assassination, an act that destroys the object instead of taking possession of it. In this way, the parallelism that gave rise to chivalry between *forms* of love and war is broken because there is no longer form and there is no longer convention.

When Rougemont writes that if the rules are ignored, war is no longer an act of violence between nations but the act of a sadistic crime, we cannot fail to remember the words he was to write immediately after Hitler's invasion of Paris: the invader has entered the city, 'but it is no longer Paris ... it is snuffed out'.[52] In *AO*, Rougemont observes that after the world war passion was neutralised and 'a kind of vast castration of Europe' took place (1939: 268; 1983: 266). Individual relationships between the sexes have ceased to be the ideal place for passion, which invades the theatre of mass politics as a continuation of all-out war by other means.

The author concludes his discussion by stating that Europe has only two possibilities: either war or a peace in which the problem will arise again. *AO*'s final two books are based on the latter eventuality. The final book of *AO* opens with a declaration of humility: the author confesses that the meaning of his work eludes him, before going on to state that he has reached conclusions that he did not expect at the beginning. This declaration is more than a rhetorical artifice if we interpret it as Rougemont's acknowledgement of his own personal contradiction. One reviewer observed that the author was himself 'inhabited' by the myth which he resisted, and the book was the confession of an interior tension (Béguin 1939).

The crisis in marriage in the twentieth century is rooted in the conflict between two religious traditions that demands a subconscious *decision*. The appeal to Kierkegaard is explicit in the attempt to deal with this impasse. Rougemont takes from the philosopher the theme of alternation between the aesthetic stage of life (when the passion embodied by Don Juan reigns supreme), the ethical stage (in which the figure of the husband triumphs as a 'conjugal hero') (Cantoni 1976: 78 et seq.), and the religious stage. Rougemont observes that Kierkegaard incessantly moves from one to another of the stages, which are separated by gulfs and chasms. Though Rougemont himself had experienced all three in his own way[53] – and thus their incompatibility – he now opts decisively for the second stage, quoting the famous passage from Paul's First Letter to the Corinthians, '[I]t is better to marry than to burn'. Rougemont disagrees with the apostle on one basic point: he affirms the equality of 'woman, a completely human person, not a half-goddess, half bacchante, a compound of dreams and sex' (Rougemont 1939: 314; 1983: 312). Equality cannot, however, be seen as a claim in the modern sense: it is demanded and created by truly reciprocal love. A man of loyalty sees even other women, those he does not love, as people who demand respect, which dispels his temptation and allows him to consider them as 'an independent, alien existence' (1939: 315; 1983: 313). All this saves him from erotic obsession, from identifying desire with love. These tones suggest that the author of *AO* is familiar with temptation and obsession.

On the figure of the husband, Rougemont took things one stage further by borrowing from Kierkegaard the idea of believing in the absurd, with reference to the figure of Abraham in *Fear and Trembling* (Kierkegaard 2006). The birth of Isaac to Abraham and Sarah at such a late age was absurd, God's request for him to sacrifice his son was absurd, and God's withdrawal of that request was absurd. The thing that appears exemplary in this affair to Kierkegaard, and later to Rougemont, is the movement from the finite to the infinite and vice versa: Abraham has resigned himself infinitely to everything and thus he has been able to have everything back by virtue of the absurd. He continually completes the movement of infinity, but with such correctness and certainty that he always obtains the finite and never does he wish anything else. This coming and going is precisely what Tristan and Iseult are not able to do since they remain prisoners of transcendence; Rougemont thus proposes placing them within the ethical stage. Fidelity, which either is not there or is without justification, just like passion, may only establish itself by virtue of the absurd, as profound nonconformism, '[F]idelity thus understood sets up the person … fidelity to something that before was not, but now is in process of being created' (1939: 308; 1983: 307–8). The difference with regard to the fidelity of Tristan is that here we are outside naturalness, which would lead to polygamy according to Rougemont. We are in a spiritual place, a revealed *agape*, that natural man cannot imagine. The application of faith in the absurd to marriage is taken to its ultimate conclusion by the idea of a wager, placed by an inevitably male subject, despite Rougemont's protestations of equality: 'choisir une femme, c'est parier' (1939: 302; 1983: 303),[54] since you cannot predict the future development of yourself or your chosen bride.

While Rougemont's thoughts about the relationship between men and women are derived from Kierkegaard, the apostle Paul and even Calvin,[55] the matter of his relationship with Barth on this score is of particular interest. In the 1930s, Barth had not yet written the pages on this topic in his *Church Dogmatics*, but in his *Ethics* of 1928 we may find the first glimmerings of his argument that the man–woman relationship is a paradigm of the human being–transcendence relationship. *Ethics* states that man would not be human without woman, and woman would not be herself without man, and both would not belong to themselves without the one belonging to the other (Barth 1981). On the various occasions when Barth and Rougemont met, the latter may have become aware of these attitudes.

In one of the documentary sections of *Church Dogmatics*, Barth discussed *Love in the Western World*, describing it as 'excellent, intelligent and instructive' (Barth 1963: 119–248; see 207–8 for discussion of *AO*). Barth believes it right that monogamous marriage will not be long-lasting in the context of an 'unqualified *eros*' such as that of the myth of Tristan and Iseult. However, he maintains that monogamy rests on a decision, that of fidelity, which is comparable with *eros* in its irrationality, although in his opinion to declare the decision superior in value and strength is simply 'changing the patient's sheets'. Barth, therefore, critically quotes Rougemont's assertion that 'choosing a woman is a wager' and voices strong doubts that monogamous marriage is guaranteed more effectively by this wager than by love. If the decision that lies at the basis of the wager is taken in the light of God's commandment, should not love itself necessarily be seen in the same light? Rougemont would thus be performing a capitulation to the theories and practices of marriage typical of the East, which are seductive because they simplify the problem in the extreme.

The manner of considering the man–women relationship in Barth is not idealised. There remains an insuperable 'incomprehension' between the two and a reciprocal freedom, since in Barth there is no finality, superior harmony or unity, the duty to be (Barth 1964: 213; Rostagno 2003). There is an anti-humanistic thread running through both Barthian and Rougemontian thought,[56] in their shared interest in maintaining an unresolved tension between finite human time and divine eternity. Kierkegaard had already ridiculed the humanistic illusion of imagining oneself to be infallible and in possession of the world. Traces of humanistic conceit may also linger, though, in the Rougemontian belief that it is possible to find a completely new way to win the wager of combining love and fidelity. This is particularly pertinent when we think of the discrepancies between the claims of *AO* and events in the author's own life.

Even if we overlook the reports that appear to suggest that he was somewhat of a Don Juan himself during his marriage to Simonne Vion, whom he met in 1931 and married in 1933, there remains the fact of their separation in 1949 and their divorce in 1951, and his second marriage to Anahite Repond. The presence of Simonne Vion in Rougemont's life had certainly been of great importance in two respects: in making the close relationship that he wove between his public and his private life possible on an existential level, and in projecting the theoretical repercussions of their relationship into the ideas that he explores in *AO*. As far as the former aspect is concerned, we need only remember the discreet yet indispensable role that Simonne Vion played in the experiment of poverty conducted on the Ile de Ré, a crucial passage in Rougemont's life and in his literary production.[57] As far as the latter aspect was concerned, it was during his marriage with Vion that Rougemont wrote in 1938 the apt lines that conclude *AO*, 'we are two in contentment' (Rougemont 1939: 327; 1983: 323), on marriage as a union between two people who are totally and perfectly equal in their reciprocal acceptance of the other in his or her otherness and in their acceptance of the world. In disagreeing with Kierkegaard's decision not to marry Regina Olsen, though he understood the choice very well,[58] Rougement observed: '[O]thers are endowed with some other vocation: they marry Regine, and passion lives again in their marriage, "by virtue of the absurd". And they are day by day astounded to find that they are happy' (1939: 326; 1983: 322).

We know that Rougemont's first marriage was afflicted by deep-seated tensions concerned with the matter closest to his heart – religion. Simonne Vion, who had not received any religious education from her agnostic parents, converted to Protestant Christianity for her marriage with Rougemont. Later, however, she developed such a strong leaning towards Catholicism (particularly around 1938–39) that she thought of converting, but her husband set her an ultimatum resolutely stating that he would divorce her if she did so.[59] In the absence of any documentation that allows us to explore this private aspect, I would like to make two points. The first concerns the consistent presence of similar contradictions in the relationship between public and private in the tradition of European thought. In this context we can hardly avoid mentioning the case of another great Swiss thinker, Jean-Jacques Rousseau, and the inconsistency between his thinking and his life, an inconsistency that does not diminish the importance of his claims, nor those of Rougemont for that matter. This inconsistency is situated historically within thought systems that acknowledge female equality only partly and in an abstract manner that has more form than substance. We need only think of Quartara's and Leo Ferrero's attitudes to women and love to find the same type of contradiction in various forms. My second point is a qualification of the first. Kierkegaard, Barth and Rougemont all acknowledge that women are due some form of equality, but this is limited in different ways by the way each man thought.[60] The equality between men and women before God acknowledged by Kierkegaard is not a reason for any social change (Sipe 2004), while Barthian anthropology does not doubt the subordinate role of women with respect to men.[61] Rougemont's own attitude was contradictory, since he upheld the absolute equality of women as people, but sometimes referred to them in discriminatory terms, as in the remark that Marrou had spotted in the opening passage of *AO*.

Both Simonne Vion and Charlotte von Kirschbaum had the task of typing out the great works of their life companions, a symbolic function of the female role in intellectual work of the past, although the two women differed greatly in their respective roles. Simonne acknowledged that she was self-taught and played a subordinate role in the intellectual processes in which Rougemont was the main protagonist,[62] while Charlotte von Kirschbaum played a leading part in the intellectual and political life of her day.[63]

To conclude, my discussion of the first edition of *AO* has traced some of the roots of this versatile work, namely: philosophical–political roots arising out of the personalist school of thought he shared with other contemporaries; theological roots, from Kierkegaard and Barth; historical–political roots, from his observation of Nazism; and anthropological roots, from the Collège de Sociologie. There were certainly also existential and personal components, which we have mentioned but which cannot be developed for the time being. Rougemont's achievement lay in combining in an original and innovative way the various sources and translating them in terms that struck a deep chord with his readers, while simultaneously arousing the criticism of experts.

Reception and Vicissitudes in the Life of the Work

Rougemont struck an immense chord both with specialists and a wider audience made up of not only intellectuals but also ordinary people. Within just eight days of the book's publication, the author had received numerous letters from women and men 'in unhappy marriages'.[64] The letters – often sent to publishers or bookshops, or to the author, simply addressed to a place name – include some that reveal Rougemont's growing fame, such as a letter from a Gaston Barbier, who signed himself 'manœuvre d'usine' ('factory worker') and declared himself to be unemployed, aged 38, 'pauvre paysan et profane' ('a poor peasant and layman'), asking Rougemont to send him a copy of the volume, even second-hand.[65] When *AO* came out in English, the year after the French edition, other letters arrived from the United States, such as that from the chief inspector of a company in Massachusetts, who considered the book 'one of the greatest and most noble of all the great books', at a time when 'humanity has strayed from the path that you have told us so clearly to return to if we wish to find happiness and peace'.[66] In 1943, a Mrs Wadsworth wrote from Virginia on the 'unconventional fidelity', achieved through 'a strenuous and passionate lifestyle', between her and her husband, first a diplomat and then a captain in the United States Army.[67]

AO acted as a mirror, according to Kierkegaard's saying that there are books in which the reader cannot fail but to see himself. Many readers were indeed prompted to confess the things that were closest to their own hearts. Théo Spoerri, then lecturer in romance literature at the University of Zurich, informed his 'venerable and dear friend' that *AO* was 'exploding' among his students and wanted to talk to Rougemont about how it would be possible to 'reawaken the soul of our country'.[68] Adolphe Ferrière, founder of the Lausanne-based International League for New Education, wrote to the author about a new science based on the premise that a particular psychological type prevailed during each stage of civilisation.[69]

The theme of the book and the author's treatment of it touched many readers deeply. 'Books should be useful' (Rougemont 1937) was a deeply felt conviction of Rougemont, who had already touched on sensitive areas of the relationship between public and private in previous writings, particularly his diaries. With *AO*, he was aware he had written a very stimulating book and he was pleased by its success. His readers, for their part, intuitively realised that the author was partly talking about himself despite the discretion of his tone. His Dutch translator admitted that the book had 'considerably changed my life, and not only my private life'.[70] Though he did not go quite so far, Gide confessed that *AO* had offered him an explanation of some of his mistakes, particularly the longer-standing ones (Delay 1956: 305 et seq.).[71]

One of the most felicitous examples of the emotional impact that the book was able to arouse came from the Italian translator of *L'Amour et l'Occident*, Luigi Santucci.[72] In a letter to Rougemont dated 1946,[73] Santucci remembers reading the book when he was acting as a clandestine courier between a band of patriots and the political centres of Lugano. Santucci had made a pledge to himself – 'a sort of vow' – to translate it and track down the prestigious teacher to inform him that his book had ended up 'in the knapsack of an unknown young man from the Italian *maquis*' and expanded his knowledge[74] to European dimensions. In his first letter to the author, Santucci introduced a personal note, thanking Rougemont for having guided his ideas on marriage at a time of life when he was experiencing a personal crisis on this subject.

Santucci's tone echoes that of his contemporaries from other countries, such as the Englishman John Heath-Stubbs, poet and translator, also born in 1918, who read *The Allegory of Love* by C.S. Lewis and *Love in the Western World* by Denis de Rougemont in his first year at university. The books revealed to him the historically determined nature of ideas of love and helped to form a specific Western identity that did not claim to be absolute in nature (see Passerini 1999: 199). The slightly younger Swiss literary critic Jean Starobinski, born in 1920, read *AO* during his first year at university and was struck by the fact that it was 'structured in the form of a pathway', which influenced him to produce writing of the same type (Starobinski 1986: 92–93). These readers were separated from Rougemont by ten to fifteen years, an entire generation. Youngsters of the 1940s, engaged in their university studies or in the antifascist struggle, were particularly conscious of the problem of supranational and spiritual identity. The solution offered by *AO* made sense, particularly for those who shared the same religious faith, but Rougemont's ethical and civil commitments were also recognisable to lay readers.

Decades later, others recalled the impact of Rougemont's book on themselves at the time. The Mexican poet Octavio Paz (born in 1914) wrote in 1993 that he had long accepted the ideas expressed in *AO*, and finally realised that the love of which Rougemont spoke did not belong only to 'our civilisation', but also to the world of Islam, India and the Far East (Paz 1995). The book also had an emotional impact on Robert Malan, an Italian Waldensian who was not an intellectual. He claimed in his autobiography that his 'sentimental education with a view to marriage' had been greatly influenced by reading *L'Amour et l'Occident* (Malan 1996: 202–4).[75]

I would categorise as emotional also many reactions to the book from the world of art and communication, and Rougemont himself believed these to be important. *AO*, wrote the author in 1970 (Rougemont 1972a: 369; 1983: 327), had inspired choreographers and composers, novelists, poets and film-makers, for three decades. Jean Delannoy's 1943 film, *L'Eternel Retour* (*Love Eternal*), reveals indubitable resonances, through the medium of Jean Cocteau, who wrote the screenplay.[76] Barthélemy Amengual considered the film a secularised transposition of the myth of Tristan (Amengual 1952: 9). In the field of literature, one significant example is the novel by Bernard Pingaud *L'Amour Triste*, which includes a long reflection by the protagonist on fidelity, which goes beyond carnal fidelity and involves 'a veritable conversion', even without any faith in God (Pingaud 1950).[77]

A long letter from Rudolf Jakob Humm[78] may also be categorised as an example of the book's emotional and aesthetic reception. Humm, who was engaged in writing a romantic novel when he read *AO*, wanted to thank Rougemont for having offered him an explanation of the affinity between the magic of love and the 'spellbinding' of the fascist masses, but he directed a criticism against the author's theological concepts of woman and the feminine. In his opinion, where Rougemont claimed that marriage could end the anguish of being two separate individuals, he was really attempting to bewitch women by dazzling them with a theory of which he was the prophet. Humm proposed that Christian mythology should conceive not only Christ's incarnation 'but also the incarnation of a female divinity', anticipating points raised by contemporary feminist theology: 'Since this divinity is missing in our purely patriarchal religion, [women] can do nothing more at the end of the day than *submit to*' love that is supposed to be reciprocal.

Moving on to the book's reception by the press, *AO* struck a great chord in the academic and non-academic press in both France and Switzerland. Protestant publications used tones of enthusiasm and relief: 'At a time when Christians are crushed by their social and political defeat, at a time when they are close to despair, what a comfort it is to follow Rougemont', wrote an anonymous leader writer in the Swiss journal *La Vie Protestante*.[79] The student and critic of Barth, Jean-Louis Leuba, considered *AO* a theological work that stood as a milestone in the history of courtly literature, which Leuba believed to be more concerned with grammar and metre than thought (Leuba 1939: 59–61).[80] Jean Bosc acknowledged that *AO* had touched a sensitive nerve for its time with the clear-sightedness of unashamedly Christian thought (Bosc 1939: 471–73).[81]

The most popular newspapers and magazines often referred to the book to deplore the habits of the day, with the usual tirades against modernity, permissiveness and the breakdown in human relationships.[82] In the early part of 1939, the tone struck by academics was often positive, despite the criticisms.[83] We rarely see any recognition of the Western identity of which *AO* spoke,[84] while in some reviews Rougemont was actually the victim of literary patriotism by the French-speaking press, which emphasised the fact that the author was not from France, for example J. Fourès (1939) in *L'Indépendant*.[85] In later years, as Rougemont himself noted, the gulf between the enthusiastic non-academic reception of his book and criticism by the experts broadened constantly, but this was not the case in the foreign press.

As far as the book's reception by the English-speaking world is concerned, all the great newspapers and weekly magazines, from the *Daily Telegraph* to the *New York Times* and the *Herald Tribune*, from *Punch* to *Time*, published encouraging reactions with a few critical observations, but no arguments against it comparable to those published in France. W.H. Auden wrote a long review in the *Nation*, in which he directed 'only one criticism against the profound and brilliant study by Mr de Rougemont': it sometimes seemed that *eros* had a sexual origin and the distinction between *eros* and *agape* was dualistic rather than dialectic (1941: 756–58). Montgomery Belgion, who translated *AO* into English, wrote a positive review that included criticisms of Rougemont's presumed Freudianism, already expressed in his correspondence with the author (Belgion 1939: 205 et seq.).[86] C.S. Lewis's review drew a clear distinction between the book's moral stance and its historical stance. Rougemont had, nevertheless, written one of the most penetrating sermons he had ever read on the value of marriage (Lewis 1940; see Passerini 1999: 197–98).

In French-speaking Europe, three arguments became the objects of recurrent criticisms: orientalism, the attitude to women and the attitude to history. The third argument gave rise to a debate of considerable interest, which is still relevant today in many respects. The most significant criticisms came from students of medieval romance and from historians. The Russian scholar Myrrha Lot-Borodine, a student of Gilson and a specialist in medieval romance and theology,[87] considered *AO* a dangerous book to its unguarded audience due to its dogmatism. Her strongest criticism was reserved for the anachronism of *AO*: the Cathar heresy did not reach southern France until *after* the older versions of the myth. The review also took up the Eastern question, accusing Rougemont of 'forcing all the Orient into the bed of Procuste that is sentimental dogma', and making claims for an iconoclastic East without any shred of evidence, overlooking the worship of icons in the Greek Orthodox Church amongst other things (Lot-Borodine 1939: 365–72).[88]

Apart from its content and procedures, Lot-Borodine also criticised *AO* for its use of sources. Amongst these, the least reliable was the book by Otto Rahn,[89] who had invented the crusade against the Grail. Lot-Borodine considered the antinomy between *eros* and *agape* to be of Protestant origin and she defined it as historical nonsense that was not justified by Patristic texts.[90]

The liveliest debate took place over Rougemont's historical method and the nature of history. It started with a review of *AO* in *Esprit*, written by Henri Marrou under his usual pseudonym of Henri Davenson (Marrou 1939a: 70–76).[91] The reviewer acknowledged the originality of Rougemont's Protestant and Barthian personalism. He nevertheless was not convinced by the arguments in *AO* and reproached its author, who had not understood anything about the troubadours, '[C]ourtly love exists, Rougemont, and you do it the specific injustice of supposing that it never existed, except as a symbolic expression of Cathar mysticism'. Marrou follows his critical review of *AO*, not by chance, with an enthusiastic review of an essay on Heloise and Abelard by 'our teacher' Gilson:[92] Marrou shares Gilson's passion for philology, while *AO* is not a history book and Rougemont is no historian. Marrou, in his provocative way, was correct about this aspect, as the author of the reviewed work sometimes acknowledged himself.[93]

Rougemont replied to this 'friendly and ironic' review[94] that Marrou had attacked him as a historian who believes in history. He himself, however, did not believe in the 'objective facts' which the historian claims to take 'as a starting point'. In reality, a historian '*composes facts*, as a poet composes a poem' out of strange and wonderful materials. At the same time, Rougemont did not claim that his publication was a history book in the accepted sense of the term, even a literary history book: '[I]f I must give it a label, then it is a book on moral theology', and he immediately added, 'of Protestant theology'. The disagreement arose out of their different understanding of the essential dogmas of Christianity: the Catholic position aimed at encapsulating all reality within a transcendent synthesis, to save everything and everyone, while the alternative Protestant position aimed first and foremost at distinguishing the decisive element, that which saves, 'the only necessary thing' according to the Scripture.

Rougemont quoted a passage from the thoughtful and ironic letter that he was sent by Etienne Gilson: 'When I was young, I would have looked down on your casual way of resolving problems, but now I no longer know. Because patient historical analysis does not lead to certainty, it may be just as wise to trust your intuition'.[95] In his answer to Rougemont's reply, Marrou admitted that his disagreement was on a theological level, since he and Rougemont belonged to two spiritual families that were irreducible and yet equally essential to Christianity, but rebutted Rougemont's ideas on history point by point, with arguments well known to historians, 'It is not true that a historian builds facts from documents with a freedom equal to that of a poet composing a sonnet' (Marrou 1939b: 767). This argument was very close to Marrou's heart, and he wasted no opportunity to air it. He returned to it in 1945 and again in 1947 (Marrou 1947: 81–89). Even in his 1954 essay on historical knowledge, Marrou kept up his debate with Rougemont (Marrou 1954: 172). Their disagreement was never-ending – and even in 1970 Rougemont reserved his bitterest tones for Marrou when discussing the reviewers of *AO* (Rougemont 1972a, Postscript; 1983: 327 ff.).

Another difference of opinion, this time on a philosophical and existential level, continued through the decades – with Sartre. Sartre's review of 1939 had acknowledged that Rougemont's work had merits: the intelligence of his analyses, the finesse and the originality of certain juxtapositions, such as that between love and war, and also the fluent style; but he attacked the main thesis, stating that the link between the myth of Tristan and the Cathar heresy was not proven (Sartre 1939: 242–49).[96] Sartre was disturbed, above all, by Rougemont's spiritualism, just as Rougemont was annoyed by his insistence on the corporeal nature of passion. Sartre was not convinced by the argument that literature could influence customs and felt obliged to defend the concept of sexuality: 'I feel that Rougemont is saying to me: the sexual instinct is incapable of dialectic when abandoned to itself. If he wants to speak of that itch in the lower abdomen that nineteenth-century psychology calls sexuality, I agree. It remains to be seen whether sexual desire is really an itch in the lower abdomen' (ibid.: 247). Sartre proposed his idea of transcendence as a starting point for his argument that sexual desire is in itself transcendent.

Their antagonism was impossible to resolve; they were rivals struggling for the souls of their readers. In 1944, Sartre squared up to Rougemont when he met him in New York with the words, '[Y]ou personalists have won, everyone in France says they are personalists' (del Bayle 1969: 414–15). Still in 1972, Rougemont made fun of the arguments expressed by Sartre: 'Would not a dog's sexual desire be part of its "existential structure" – "canine transcendence"?' – accusing Sartre of drawing general principles from his own neurosis (Rougemont 1972a, Postscript; 1983: 367n.).

Such disagreements, coupled with the enthusiasm of the general public, helped make *AO* a success. This was not immediately evident at the outset,[97] given that, as Rougemont himself recognised, he was neither 'a popular paperback author nor an author who appealed to fashionable intellectuals in the fifth *arrondissement*', but at the same time his works had 'a long-term staying power that few French authors achieved'.[98] *AO* nevertheless represented considerable progress when compared to the print runs of previous works by Rougemont.[99] The first edition in 1939 ran to 5,000 copies. The two reprints in 1950 and 1952 were for 5,000 copies each. The revised and extended edition of 1956 ran to 10,000 copies. The 'definitive' version of 1972 was produced in 5,000 copies. The real leap in numbers came with the paperback version in the 10/18 collection, which ran to 85,000 copies from 1961 to 1979, taking the total number of copies sold in France over forty-three years to 125,000.[100] The translations were an intrinsic part of the book's success. In a list drawn up by Rougemont on 24 January 1983, he listed the languages into which *AO* had been translated: English, Dutch, Japanese, Italian, Spanish (which covered Latin America as well, particularly Argentina), Swedish, German, Portuguese, Polish, Serbo-Croat, Rumanian and Hungarian. Rougemont noted a total of 395,000 copies sold.

The first edition fuelled debate and influenced much that was written about love during the two decades following its publication – the 1940s and the first half of the 1950s. During that period, many interpreters, even if they were strongly critical, maintained a tone of great respect for *AO*.[101] The Jesuit Father D'Arcy of Oxford acknowledged his debt to the work's author and the step forward it represented compared to Lewis's *The Allegory of Love* (D'Arcy 1947). The historian Pierre Belperron, who strongly opposed Rougemont's arguments for the Cathar influence on the troubadours, defined Rougemont as a 'talented writer' and asserted that his mistake did not in the least reduce the value of *AO* (Belperron 1948: 222n.). The writer Claude Elsen, in his 1953 essay *Homo Eroticus* (1953: 132),[102] described *AO* as a 'maître livre', although he stated that he did not agree with all of Rougemont's ideas. Micheline Sauvage, in her 1953 book on Don Juan, treated Rougemont as an undisputable authority, referring to his book *La Part du Diable*, but also to *AO*, quoted repeatedly for its interpretation of Don Juan as a Western myth that was the mirror image of that of Tristan (Sauvage 1953: 93). All these works clearly show that *AO* is so multifarious that even when some of its ideas are refuted, others remain standing and even the rejected ideas prompt further research.

Numerous handwritten notes reveal that during the years from 1939 to 1955 Rougemont paid great attention to the reviews when preparing his revised version of *AO*. One important note that he wrote for the 1948 Dutch edition is a response

> to historians to explain that I was in search of an existential *meaning* and never dreamed of competing with them. The documents I quoted and the parallels I established were above all illustrations, not evidence as far as I was concerned. ... I had to clear the ground, underline fundamental contrasts and I have not always been able to tone down the picture.[103]

The development in *AO* over time reveals the incessant process of reflection that led Rougemont to make major changes at the same time as he continued to discuss the ideas in other writings and to plan future books that never came to fruition, despite the numerous preparatory notes in the Neuchâtel archive.[104] Reviewers did not take into account the great effort that the author had made to revise his work, but continued implacably to direct the same criticisms against him, often couched in harsher tones; this helped to instil in Rougemont the bitterness he expressed in his 1972 Postscript. The main changes appeared in the 1956 edition; the 1972 edition is not much different apart from the appendices and the Postscript.[105]

The changes reveal that Rougemont took into account many of the criticisms he received. Various reviewers and correspondents had observed that the way he contrasted East and West was vague.

He made various cuts and additions in response. Significant additions include those in the section on 'East and West', while some changes help to highlight the different way things were perceived in the period after Nazism and the Second World War.

Rougemont's main undertaking was, however, to repropose his argument for the parallels between Catharism and courtly poetry, now stripped of certain ambiguities and supported by new bibliographical references. This rewriting gives *AO* a new twist, both in the way it reads and in its spirit. The main thrust of the revised section on the Cathar doctrine is to underscore the relevance of his ideas to the present day, which categorically makes the point that his intentions are more contemporary than historical. The tragically contemporary aspect not only of Manichaeism but also of all dualistic religions is, in his opinion, the problem of evil, which is considered absolutely heterogeneous to good, as if there were two worlds and two creations, while Christianity resolves the problem through the dialectical paradox of reconciling freedom with grace. The new edition dwells on the function of Satan in dualistic religions and the role allocated to women in this context as an instrument of perdition, the opposite to Mary, symbol of the redeeming light (Rougemont 1956: 62–65). One of the most criticised points was the credit accorded by the first edition of *AO* to Otto Rahn's book *Kreuzzug gegen den Graal*. In his revision, Rougemont greatly reduces the number of references to Rahn, defines his idea as *maxima* in relation to his own and its author one of those 'venturous spirits' who 'damaged [this view] by trying to make too plain at a historical rather than a spiritual level' (1956: 66; 1983: 83).

One of the most substantial additions is a passage that stresses the significance of the 'psychical event' as not less 'real' than other historical events (1956: 75–76; 1983: 91), and the interpretation of the Lady as an Anima: 'If the Lady is not simply the church of Love of the Cathars (as Aroux and Peladan considered they were entitled to think) nor the Sophia Maria of the Gnostic heresies (the Female Principle of Divinity), why should she not be the *Anima*, or, more precisely, man's *spiritual* element?' (1983: 90).

Book 2 is extended to include a whole new chapter, Chapter 10, which is preceded by two pages of discussions on the influence of Arabic poetry on courtly poetry (1956: 93–94; 1983: 106–7) and includes an 'apology to historians' (1956: 108; 1983: 120). Rougemont, returning to the theme after years of work, cites backing of a 'psychic' nature, such as the revolution of the Western psyche in the twelfth century, which led to a radical change in emotional attitudes and the way of considering women; the loosening of the feudal and patriarchal bonds and the impact of the Oedipus complex on society; the birth of the cult of the Virgin and the change made to the game of chess by the new importance attributed to the Queen; and René Nelli's ideas on the *assag* or test of love as a method of chastity of tantric origin. This new aspect is spelt out to his readers: 'The criticism, plus the numerous discoveries made in the last fifteen years by authorities on courtly love, Catharism, and Manichaeism, as well, possibly, as the experiences I myself have had and my own research – all that brings me today to a conception of *cortezia* hardly less "historical" than the one I sketched above, but far more psychological' (see 1956: 94–95; 1983: 108–9).[106]

His 'psychological concept' is evident in his interpretation of the physical and ethical revolution of the twelfth century as being the emergence of the female to counter the Oedipal character of patriarchal society, and the appearance of the cult of love as an 'epiphany in history' of this great change (1956: 99; 1983: 113), even in the absence of "material" reality' (1956: 108; 1983: 120). This interpretation is reminiscent of certain Jungian influences, that explain the reappearance of the archetype that had too long been ignored (the *puer* which emerges against the *senex*, the female against the male) and heralds a 'digestion' of the historical facts in their psychological meanings (Hillman 1983).

By situating the first five books of *AO* in a psychological light, Rougemont is anticipating the psychoanalytical interpretation of courtly love, although his own approach may more accurately be described as psychological. I have already mentioned the limits to Rougemont's Freudianism imposed by his antimaterialism. He refers in *AO* to Freud with regard to the death wish and the taboo of incest, but includes him within a tradition of 'materialist superstition', which traces everything back to the sexual instinct.[107] Although some interpreters have detected a similarity between the analysis of desire in Freud and that of Rougemont (Belsey 1994: 52–53), others have observed that when *AO* makes observations on the psychological genesis of love in Provençal poetry, it tends towards philosophy rather than psychoanalysis (Cholakian 1990: 6, 10n.). In actual fact, despite its references to Freud, *AO*'s approach is more in sympathy with Jung. This applies not merely to the passage quoted above on the Anima, which in Jungian thought represents the female part of the male psyche, but also in handwritten notes to the 1956 edition: 'Freud's abuse seems to be that of individualising the meaning of these symbols and taking from them a key to dreams that is purely sexual. C.G. Jung is undoubtedly closer to the truth when he discovers fundamental religious symbols created in ancient times in the contents of our dreams'.[108] In a piece written in the 1960s, after describing Barth and Jung as 'two great incompatible masters', he gave the latter the credit for having rediscovered the phenomenon of religion in all its psychological, ethnographic and evolutionary dimensions, for having given importance to universal myths, and for having paid homage to the *Sophia aeterna* of gnostic mythology, concluding, '[O]ne day, perhaps, I will try to understand *myself* how much I owe as much to one as to the other of these incompatible masters' (Rougemont 1989: 240–41).

AO prefigures the future most of all in its psychoanalytical interpretations of love as a discursive structure. I find resonances between *AO* and recent analyses that stress the narcissistic structure of the courtly relationship. According to H. Rey-Flaud, who bases his thought on the Freudian theory of narcissism, whereby the sexual ideal possesses an unattainable perfection, courtly love does not express the historical relationship between men and women in the twelfth century. To understand it, we need to adopt a synchronous approach that sets historicity in parentheses. In narcissistic passion, there is no true otherness: each of the pair is lost in their own image of the other and this imaginary annihilation leaves no space for third parties (Rey-Flaud 1983: 66).[109] According to this viewpoint, the story of Jaufré Rudel, who falls in love with a woman he has never seen, crosses the ocean to find her and dies when he reaches her, is an example of the incompatibility between the desiring subject and the unattainable object. We may remember that Rougemont had a strong sense of Rudel's fascination for unreachable distance.

In his own mocking and irreverent way, Lacan was also to touch on the subject of narcissism in courtly love.[110] Lacan did not deny the historical basis of courtly love: this is rooted in the matter of medieval loyalty to a person and appeared at a time of political degeneration of feudalism. It shone out through history like a meteor, then returned to obscurity, and courtly love remained enigmatic. Lacan defines courtly love as a sophisticated way of making up for the lack of a sexual relationship, a male discourse that men use as an elegant way of compensating for this lack. The strength of courtly discourse is that of being fully aware of, even emphasising, the impossibility of sexual relationships in the full sense of the word, because pleasure, being sexual, is phallic, that is, it is not related to the other as such. What conditions the analytical discourse is the truth that there is no sexual relationship, even though there has been no need of an analytical discourse to discover this. Courtly discourse had already postulated love as the impossibility of a relationship with the other and proclaimed that speaking of love constitutes a pleasure in itself.

Lacan's presupposition is, as he says in a piece that he decides to read to his listeners 'for relaxation', that in analytical discourse you speak of nothing but love. Love letter, anima, alma, almore, amore: Lacan's ebullient word play is designed to lose you, entertain you and irritate you. Despite the criticisms of Luce Irigaray, I think that the men come off worse from Lacan's mockery, while he says of women that 'in the end it is always they who possess the men' (Lacan 1999: 73). Irigaray is correct when she highlights the will to dominate evident in Lacanian psychoanalytical discourse over all others (Irigaray 1977). Yet if we are to believe her, this discourse is identified with the ritual of courtly love seen as an elegant and impotent way to ensure women are kept in a submissive role. Irigaray accuses the Lacanian approach of being unable to accept in its discourse the idea of female pleasure. I prefer to translate the accusation into the challenge of accommodating female pleasure through the act of talking about love, with reference to the trobairitz, and to reintroduce the idea of the female subject in Provençal love (Rieger 1991).[111] In the psychoanalytical field, the challenge has been taken up by the Lacanian debate on the specific nature of female pleasure, which includes as one of its fundamental aspects the pleasure in speaking of love (Mangiarotti 2003: 96–97n., 241).

Supporters of a psychoanalytical interpretation of courtly love have deliberately not taken into account the fact that the output of the troubadours cannot be reduced to these contemporaneous arguments. Mario Mancini, while acknowledging 'Dominance, Absence, Desire as constituent moments of *fin'amor*' (1984: 13), observed that we cannot treat courtly love only as an existential, metahistorical and metaphysical metaphor but need to see it in the specificity of its tangible aspects: the emergence of an aristocratic materialism in troubadours such as William IX and Raimbaut d'Arenga; the existence of courtly idealism at the same time as a base, obscene way of life; and the great subject of make-believe (ibid.: 30–31). According to this approach, 'an entire series of possible behavioural analogies between courtly love and analytical discourse – the role of the symbolic, removal, transfer – reflect the impasses, the happiness and the illusions of love perhaps more than the wish to perpetuate dominion' (ibid.).

I do not intend to attribute an *ante litteram* Lacanism to Rougemont, rather to highlight the resonances between psychoanalytical interpretations of courtly love and *AO*, and open up another understanding of the work, that Joë Bousquet foresaw when he asserted that Rougemont was not interested in situating the myth but in assessing its spiritual fatalism. This interest led him to a 'psychological view of history', whereby 'every historical fact is nothing more than an inward sign of its deeper reality' (Bousquet 1939: 217, 530).

Returning to a philological key, the changes made to the last two books of *AO* complement each other in their psychological emphasis, because they stress aspects of subjectivity. At the end of Book 6, in 1939, Rougemont suggested three possible hypotheses for the future of Europe: the resurgence of passion with a new language; war – a passionate discharge at collective and national level; and eugenics. He considered the second possibility most probable, which is effectively what ensued (Rougemont 1939: 295–96). In his update of 1956, Rougemont notes that Stalinism and Nazism now belong to the past, but that totalitarian temptation persisted and eugenics could also reappear. He then adds an entire chapter on the 'Sense of Crisis', which dwells on the relationship between Europe and the United States. Rougemont uses the United States as a starting point, on the basis of his own experience. He defines it, using an image that comes directly from the period between the world wars, 'America – that other Europe which has been released from both the routine practices and traditional restraints of the old' (Rougemont 1956: 274; 1983: 291).[112] In the United States, as in no other civilisation, the term *romance* is aired on a daily basis because love and marriage are considered completely equivalent, and the urgency of falling in love is translated into the urgency of getting married, Hollywood style. Divorce in the United States is more normal than in Europe, but the answer is not to make divorce more difficult: it is marriage that is too easy. The causes of the crisis in marriage include female emancipation and the popularisation of psychological knowledge, which increase expectations and demands in married life. Rougemont's analysis of the situation in the United States concludes with the observation that the current crisis is similar to that which took place in the collective psyche in the twelfth century. Thus the psychological approach comes full circle as it is consistently applied to the past and to the present.

The final page of Book 6 is particularly significant if we consider that it was written after Rougemont's separation in 1949, his divorce in 1951 from Simonne Vion and his marriage to Anahite Repond in 1952. Rougemont does not change his position on fidelity and divorce in the slightest, but emphasises his decision of abstaining from offering any solution (1956: 278; 1983: 295). Instead he maintains the importance of deciphering the crisis, which offers us an insight into ourselves, calling on the Absolute, who only judges and raises up the person (1956: 278; 1983: 296). Thus Book 6 closes with an admonition to keep the general principle that will be propounded in the next book – fidelity – separate from individual specificity, and with the resolution of submitting to divine rather than human judgement. This is an invitation to discriminate between the autobiographical relevance of the work and its literary and philosophical independence.

In the final book, 'The Myth against Marriage', we see a further important change: in marriage, fidelity is no longer devoted first and foremost to the other, but to the other at the same time as to the true and proper self. The change moves in the direction of advocating that the subject should be responsible for the choice. In the same book, a section on fidelity is added in Chapter 4, which introduces the distinction between the state of falling in love and the act of loving: the first is something that is undergone, the second is a decisive action; thus the former belongs to the world of *eros*, the latter to that of *agape*. The latter is not a state of feeling, but a structure of active relationships, as in the First Commandment, 'love the Lord thy God', while you cannot command anyone to fall in love (ibid.: 291–92; 1939: 312).

The changes to the 1972 edition were few and almost all formal. In the 'Unscientific Postscript to Philosophical Fragments',[113] written in 1970 and published in the 'definitive' edition of 1972, the tone changes radically compared to the 1956 edition. Rougemont vindicates his approach, and does not acknowledge the changes added in the second version, although he states he had corrected many errors in the new version. Even on the subject of Otto Rahn, he stubbornly insists that his mistakes are more productive to an understanding of courtly love than so-called serious works. His tone is much sharper than in the past, even displaying a certain exasperation and almost a desire for revenge.

In many aspects the Postscript seems to be a settling of accounts. First and foremost with *Cahiers du Sud*, towards which Rougemont harboured a grudge for the special issue on *Génie d'Oc*: he is convinced that that issue was composed on the basis of his book or around it,[114] and he bemoans the fact that on his return from the United States, he found the issue 'bel et bien paru' ('well and truly out'), with his ideas all over the issue but without any true acknowledgement. Denis de Rougemont's relationship with *Cahiers du Sud* had always been good. The review had paid great attention to his books, from *Paysan du Danube* (Trolliet 1933: 723–30) to *Politique de la Personne* (Bousquet 1935: 875),[115] *Penser avec les Mains* (Breuil 1937: 218–22)[116] and *Journal d'un Intellectuel en Chômage* (Bousquet 1937: 741–43).[117] For *AO*, Joë Bousquet wrote a review himself (Bousquet 1939: 529–32).[118] In their private correspondence, Bousquet (who had written enthusiastic letters to Rougemont in the past about *Paysan du Danube* and letters of appreciation about his 'sense of the invisible') after reading *AO* told its author about 'an undertaking' in which he wished to involve him.[119] Rougemont, in turn, had contributed to *Cahiers*,[120] albeit less frequently than to other reviews, such as *Nouvelle Revue Française*. He was not entirely wrong to complain about the treatment reserved for him in the special edition of *Cahiers* on the *Génie d'Oc* (see previous chapter), in which his name was quoted only in passing or in the course of irrelevant observations, while the most important contributions of *AO* were not acknowledged.[121]

Rougemont took issue with everyone in his Postscript. Amongst others, with René Nelli (whom he praises elsewhere) on the matter of the non-noble social origin of the troubadours, which went against his own theory of their aristocratic origin. He takes issue, above all, with Marrou. He feels himself to be the object of intimidation, which forces him to lose his balance and take up untenable positions: for example that only the emotion that he felt reading Jaufré Rudel could be the arbiter in his difference of opinion with Marrou (Rougemont 1972: 389; 1983: 340 ff.); that the number of Cathar troubadours 'matters little as long as there is at least one' (1972: 391; 1983: 346); and that the troubadour–Cathar relationship 'exhibits a kind of spiritual evidence that no so-called objective method will ever adequately grasp' (1972: 392; 1983: 346).

His 'final imprecation' attacks his adversaries who still believe in a relationship of cause and effect, while nuclear physicists abandoned this long ago and now attach more importance to concepts such as relationship clusters, interaction structures and force fields. Fortunately the tone of the Postscript is tempered by a humorous comparison that describes love as being very similar to an allergy. The final part vigorously rejects the accusation that *AO* proposes the obliteration of passion to save marriage and hints at the possibility of a third type of love that combines *eros* and *agape* in the quest for the other. Rougemont takes leave of his work by summarising his ethical, erotic and political views, '[A]ll my morals, my passion, and my politics derive from the composition and tension of opposites' (1972: 423; 1983: 378).

AO attracted criticism from many quarters, from historians studying the idea of love, who considered it superficial and distorting,[122] to young scholars who noted the lack of references to a new role for women or sexuality in a work that upholds the idea of formal respect for the other, even in the 1972 edition (Cirulli 2002–3: 67). More recent interpretations of the poetry of the troubadours have also condemned Rougemont's ideas. Historical perspectives on Catharism have been totally revised, if not altogether overturned, and the Cathar phenomenon is no longer seen as a medieval resurgence of ancient Manichaeism, but as part of the Christian culture of the age. The hypothesis of any relationship with ancient Eastern dualism is, therefore, rejected (Brenon 2000: 13–15), while the troubadours and Cathars are considered to be two constituent parts of the same medieval Provençal civilisation that need not necessarily have come into contact much (Zambon 1999: 31).

Despite these criticisms, *AO* remains a 'book with staying power', to use a term of Starobinski's (Starobinski 1988–89: 27–33), outside the canons of university life, and able, like other great books, to take account of the present in the field of knowledge, literature, customs, politics and the links between them. Unlike Sartre, Starobinski believed that Rougemont was not the victim of the myth of a myth, but instead excelled at analysing mythology. Sartre was, nevertheless, correct when, despite his criticisms, he allowed *AO* the fundamental merit of eliminating the naturalness of loving passion and restoring it to a cultural construct. This resolutely historical treatment of the subject helped to lay the basis for a European identity that no longer appeared essential and eternal but the outcome of many influences, including those from the East. The network of relationships that grew up around the book suggests that it interpreted a common sentiment, in the sense of recognising oneself to be at the same time European and able to love, with all the contradictions of its day.

Notes

1. Denis de Rougemont was born in 1906 in Couvet, in the canton of Neuchâtel in Switzerland, from a family of ancient lineage with European ramifications. His father was a pastor. He studied at the universities of Neuchâtel, Vienna and Geneva. In 1931, he moved to Paris, where he contributed to various magazines and wrote numerous books and articles. After a period in the United States (1940–47), he returned to Switzerland and became actively engaged in the European Federalist Movement, in campaigns for cultural liberation and in the Green movement. He died in 1985.

2. According to Simonne Vion Sinclair (1908), his wife at the time, who typed the manuscript of *L'Amour et l'Occident*, he probably took six months. Her interview, recorded by myself in Paris on 14 June 1996, confirms that he wrote the book extremely quickly, with few corrections.

3. This reading of the original edition of *Love in the Western World* is based on *L'Amour et l'Occident* (1939), indicated in the text as Rougemont (1939). The other two French editions used are *L'Amour et l'Occident* (1956) (indicated as Rougemont 1956) and *L'Amour et l'Occident* (published 1972) (Rougemont 1972a). The quotations are followed by a comparison with Montgomery Belgion's English translation, *Love in the Western World* (1983), first published 1940, based on the French edition of 1939, revised in 1954, and updated partially with reference to the latest French version (1972a). The UK title is *Passion and Society* (1956).

4. As Henri Marrou observed in *Esprit*, April 1939: 'Why does Rougemont draw a distinction between his female readers and the specialists? There will be more history graduates amongst his female readers than amongst his male readers'.

5. Letter from Paris dated 20 June 1939, Fonds Rougemont, Bibliothèque Publique et Universitaire, Neuchâtel. Fondane, born in Romania in 1898, moved to France, where he wrote poems and essays. Arrested and sent by the Germans to Auschwitz, he died in 1944.

6. Letter from La Chartreuse dated 19 January 1939, Fonds Rougemont, Bibliothèque Publique et Universitaire, Neuchâtel. Jézéquel (1898–1948) wrote his novels under the pseudonym of Roger Breuil, and his essays under his own name.

7. Letter of 3 July 1938, Fonds Rougemont, Bibliothèque Publique et Universitaire, Neuchâtel. Henri Daniel-Rops (1901–65), historian and novelist, active member of Ordre Nouveau.

8. Thibon (1903–2001) was a conservative Catholic writer.

9. The term echoes that of Kierkegaard, 'the sickness unto death', in the sense that desperation is a disease that threatens the destruction of the spirit and is, therefore, much more serious than biological death. See Rocca (1999: ix–x). In the 1930s, French studies and translations of Kierkegaard underwent a great revival; see Spera (2002: 159–61).

10. Rougemont established a connection between the two thinkers; see Ackermann (1996: 381–83).

11. Mounier (1905–50) faced hostility from certain Catholic quarters, including the Vatican, during the course of his editorship of *Esprit*. The Second World War with the German invasion of France led to the suppression of the review and the imprisonment of its editor, who resumed publication after Liberation.

12. The reference to *hic et nunc* in the magazine title echoes both Kierkegaard and the Barthian idea that reform is decision for the present.

13. In *Penser avec les Mains*, Rougemont indicates the following genealogy of personalism: Renouvier, Maritain, Berdiaeff, Buber, Aron and Dandieu, Mounier, Marc, and his own *Politique de la Personne*. He also added Jean Wahl, Gabriel Marcel, Georges Gurvitch, Lévinas and the translations of Kierkegaard. From the perspective of this chapter, it is useful to remember that Buber constituted the main interlocutor for Barthian anthropology of the man–woman relationship; see Gallas (2002: 299–322).

14. Robert Aron (1898–1983), essayist and historian, worked with Dandieu on studies that constituted one of the bases of the Ordre Nouveau movement, whose magazine he edited from 1933 to 1938. Active with de Gaulle during the Second World War, he took part in European federalism after Liberation. Arnaud Dandieu (1897–1933) cultivated a variety of interests: poetry, philosophy, psychopathology and sociology.

15. Despite his close relationship with *Ordre Nouveau*, Rougemont (now absent from Paris because he had moved to the Ile de Ré) did not help write the Letter to Hitler published by *Ordre Nouveau* in 1933, which aroused controversy and led to a split between *Ordre Nouveau* and *Esprit*; see Ackermann (1996: vol. 1, 263 et seq.). Both groups displayed an ambiguous attitude to fascism in the 1930s, which was to lead to polarisation between members, some of them to sympathise with the Vichy regime and others to take part in the Resistance.

16. Interview by Hélisse, 1939, in the weekly magazine *Tribune de France*. Eugénie Hélisse (journalist, film producer) was part of the second generation of Ordre Nouveau; see Roy (1998: 458). 'Sociology' from the viewpoint of the Collège, influenced by Durkheim and Mauss, is not distinctly different from 'anthropology' and develops a critical attitude towards the specialisation and fragmentation of disciplines; see Richman (1988: 81–82, 84).

17. The intent of the Collège was to develop a moral community whose activities could be defined as 'sociologie sacrée' (Hollier 1995: 27), the 'sacred' being understood in the 'violent and devastating' sense of Bataille (ibid.: 303), but also as a communication between beings that presides over the formation of new beings. The speakers, apart from the above, were Jean Paulhan, Jean Wahl, Alexandre Kojève and Pierre Klossowski. The participants included Jacques Lacan, Georges Dumézil, Jean-Paul Sartre, Claude Lévy-Strauss, Max Horkheimer, Theodor Adorno, Walter Benjamin, Julien Benda and Pierre Drieu la Rochelle.

18. In the final meeting of the Collège de Sociologie, on 4 July 1939, Bataille emphasised the essence of his positions on the sacred: 'two beings of opposite sex lose themselves in one another, forming together a new being that is different from each one of the two'; see Hollier (1995: 805–6). See also Sweedler (2001: 57).

19. Such as that which was called Acéphale, like their journal; see Blanchot (1983: 28–30).
20. See Caillois's (1937) contribution to the international convention on aesthetics 'Le Mythe et l'Art'. He expanded on his position in *Le Mythe et l'Homme* (Caillois 1938).
21. On the importance of the concept of *engagement*, Rougemont maintained in the introduction to a new edition of *Penser avec le Mains* (1972b: 14) that while the term was new at the beginning of the 1930s, by June 1938 he found it overused and hackneyed. In actual fact, the idea of intellectual engagement had been at the centre of an extensive debate since the second half of the 1920s, with the publication of works such as *La Trahison des Clercs* (1927) by Julien Benda (Eng. tr. *The Treason of the Intellectuals*) and *Regards sur le Monde Actuel* (1931) by Paul Valéry (Eng. tr. *Reflections on the World Today*). The personalists took issue with both for their concept of intellectual engagement; see Aron and Dandieu (1931a: 68 et seq.). On Rougemont's concept of *engagement* or *tâche*, in his work as a writer, see Starobinski (1987: 19–28).
22. The last two were respectively a Jewish ascetic sect of eschatological inspiration (second century BC and first century AD) and an Indian religion that arose in the sixth–fifth century BC, which practised an ascetic attitude to life.
23. On the Eastern origins of the courtly spirit, see Vadet (1968).
24. Rougemont saw a vein of materialism running from Voltaire to Freud (1939: 144; 1983: 160).
25. Thierry Hentsch (1988b: 231–39) maintains that Rougemont's thought must be cleansed of traces of a Hegelian view of history whereby the West is set up in opposition to the Muslim Mediterranean East. *AO* recognises the Arabic influence on Provençal poetry, however, and condemns those who reject this view. Besides, it is not convincing to attribute an out-and-out Hegelian stance to Rougemont, who considered Kierkegaard to be his master.
26. Corbin (1903–1978), orientalist and philosopher inspired by Heidegger and Husserl, taught in Paris at the Ecole des Hautes Etudes and was head of the Iranology department of the Franco-Iranian Institute in Teheran. His works include: *Histoire de la Philosophie Islamique*, 1968 (Eng. tr. *History of Islamic Philosophy*, London: Kegan Paul Int., 1993), and *En Islam Iranien*, four volumes published from 1971.
27. In particular, the treatise *Familier des Amants*; see Corbin (1932–33: 371–96).
28. Keller was over-hasty in interpreting a short passage in *AO* on Teresa's approach to the Arab mystics, without comparing it with other longer passages; see Keller (1998: 457; 2001: 345).
29. Otto (1869–1937), theologian, student of Luther and author of *Das Heilige*, 1917 (Eng. tr. *The Idea of the Holy*), had a thorough knowledge of Sanskrit and the history of religions.
30. Sartre wrote 'to support his cause, Mr de Rougemont needs to demonstrate that the Chinese know nothing of love–passion. So he says it and I would love to believe it. But I soon start thinking that China has five thousand years of history behind it and huge numbers of very different peoples. So I go

straight to the appendix in which de Rougemont justifies his claims and I see that he bases his entire psychology of the Chinese on a short passage from *Désespoirs*, a posthumous collection of Leo Ferrero's writings. Is he really being serious?' (Sartre 1939: 242–43).

31. Rougemont quotes *Désespoirs* by Ferrero in these terms: 'the problem of passion is admirably defined by this little book in its psychological data', referring to Appendix 4 (1939: 318n.; 1983: 316n.). Among the correspondence received by Rougemont there is a note from Gina and Guglielmo Ferrero sent from Geneva on 8 February 1939, to thank him for having sent them 'such a fine book with its precious dedication' and for having mentioned Leo (Fonds Rougemont [F.R.]; see References).

32. Rougemont sometimes used the expression 'Orient' in a commonplace acceptance of the way Europeans represent themselves; he writes in 1926, 'to give a consciousness to the age or merge with it and go off at a tangent towards an East of oblivion' (Rougemont 1977: 26). In this sense, Rougemont's stance could be categorised as a reaction to the quest for new forms of spirituality in the East in the wake of the First World War; see Trebitsch (1998a).

33. From Guy de Wurstemberger, writing from Ain Aicha in Fez, 9 April 1939 (F.R.).

34. Letter of 11 March 1939, signed Emile Simon (F.R.).

35. He told Silvio Locatelli that in the course of his stay in the United States he had thought for the first time that if Europe survived the war he would devote his life to European unity; see Locatelli (1965: 18, 27). His writings on Europe date to 1946; see Rougemont (1995). On Rougemont's Europeanism from 1946, see Brugmans (1988: 109–16); Izard (1988); Valentino (1990); Deering (1991) and Ackermann (2000).

36. Writings collected in a 1932 work, *Le Paysan du Danube* (Rougement 1982).

37. The term 'heart of Europe' to describe Switzerland was to become the title of his book *The Heart of Europe* (1941), co-written with Charlotte Muret, where Switzerland is considered an example for a European federation. Here we find the clear formulation of the analogy between marriage and federalism, '[M]arriage is a federal union because it does not presuppose the identity of those who are joined together, but is based on the diversity of the sexes' (Rougemont and Muret 1941: 252).

38. Marc is the pseudonym of Alexandre Lipiansky (1904–2000), a Jewish exile from Russia, active in the European Youth Movement in which Jean Luchaire (see Chapter 2) was also engaged. He was active in the Resistance and then in European federalism; see Roy (1998) and Saint-Ouen (1997: 229–71; 2000–1: 155–62).

39. Federalism received a lot of attention in the review *Ordre Nouveau* throughout the lifetime of the publication from 1933 to 1938, but the same did not apply to the theme of Europe: in the contents page to the reprint of the entire collection of the review, the entry 'Europe' does not appear on its own, but only in relation to 'nation state'.

40. The theme appears in some of Rougemont's articles in *Ordre Nouveau*, which adopted federalism as one of its leading principles; see 1, 2 June 1933, 2.

Examples included 'Communauté Révolutionnaire', 15 February 1934, and 'Les Jacobins en Chemise Brune', 15 December 1935. See also *Penser avec les Mains* (1972: 140). In the Preface to the 1972 edition of this book, he specifies that federalism is based on regions and not nation states (ibid.: 11).

41. In that year, Rougemont wrote an essay on Goethe for *Nouvelle Revue Française*; see Ackermann (1996: 206–7).

42. According to P. von Matt (1989: 71), in *AO* the much denigrated institution of marriage was to Tristan's love as the denigrated institution of democracy was to the fascist state in the Europe of 1939.

43. Rougemont translated the first section of the first volume, *Prolegomena to Church Dogmatics*, in 1934 on the Ile de Ré. A typescript of the translation is filed in the F.R. The translation was included in the French version of the entire *Church Dogmatics* begun in 1953 by the publishing company Labor et Fides of Geneva. A statement in vol. 1, t. 1*, acknowedged the debt to Rougemont; see Barth (1953).

44. The part on Barth in this chapter owes much to the writings and advice of Sergio Rostagno, to whom I offer my warm thanks. For this first point, see Rostagno (2003: 34–35). According to S. Selinger (1998: 80), Barth's preoccupations changed from theorising on the total otherness of God to a concern with his own being together with that of other creatures. This change coincided with his meeting with Charlotte von Kirschbaum in 1926 (ibid.: 81–82).

45. Rougemont develops the theme of Don Juan in *Doctrine Fabuleuse* (1947).

46. In *Journal d'une Epoque*, Rougemont evokes a performance of 21 June 1938, the day on which he finished writing *AO*. Later in the evening, he went to see Wagner's *Tristan* at the Paris Opera House. The magical atmosphere of the evening contributed to his special feeling of emotion; see Rougemont (1968: 366).

47. On the critique of American modernity in French culture, see Nacci (1996).

48. This was included among the books prohibited in Nazi Germany. Bruno Ackermann has highlighted the nature of the literary construction of *Journal d'Allemagne*, written in spring 1938 (exactly the time when Rougemont was writing *AO*) on the basis of notes and articles dating from 1935 to 1936; see Ackermann (1996: 910 et seq.).

49. Starobinski (1995: 62) notes that the description of Nazism in the *Journal* is the source of Eugène Ionesco's *Rhinocéros*.

50. Martin Niemöller (1892–1984) was imprisoned by the Nazis until 1945. In the relationship between the churches and Nazism, Catholicism was shielded behind the 1934 agreement that required the bishops to swear an oath of loyalty to the Nazi regime and banned priests from taking part in political activities. Despite this agreement, there were Catholic opponents to the regime. As far as the Protestants were concerned, in April 1933 a 'German evangelical church' was set up which – or so the regime intended – was to connect local churches at national level. This lasted until 1945. From July 1933 Barth and others set up a resistance movement, and in May 1934 Barth presented Barmen's declaration, which stressed the independent nature of Christianity; see Barth (1983: 51–52; 1986) and Rostagno (1984).

51. The same accusation of ambiguity has been made again by Jean-François Fourny (1985: 535). It is impossible to attribute a similar ambiguity to Rougemont if we take into account the support he expresses in the *Journal* for Barth and Niemöller.

52. This is taken from an article written on 15 June 1940 and published in the *Gazette de Lausanne* on 17 June, now in Rougemont (1982: 115–16). The article caused him to be sentenced to fifteen days of isolation, after which the Swiss government sent him on a mission to the United States for a set of lectures on Switzerland. He left on 15 August with his wife and two children, Martine aged six months and Nicolas aged five, and reached New York on 20 September 1940.

53. As far as the aesthetic stage is concerned, Rougemont himself spoke of his 'great loves particularly during a trip to Austria and Yugoslavia', referring to the years 1926–30; see Bignardi (1983). Various relationships were attributed to him in Argentina and Europe, which date from the final period of his first marriage. Simonne Vion also had other relationships at the same time.

54. The English translation tones down the maleness of the statement, '[C]hoosing a man or woman for the rest of one's life … to choose is to wager'.

55. Calvin believed that God's intention was that the woman should be man's companion and not his subordinate, and nothing prevented women assuming the highest offices in the Church; see Bouwsma (1992).

56. In *Politique de la Personne*, Rougemont defines 'humanisme' as a 'general concept of life, political, economic, ethical, founded on *a belief in the salvation of man through his own human efforts*' (see Rougemont 1934: 112), and sees communism as the humanism of the age (ibid.: 116).

57. Rougemont, who had been unemployed for three months, decided to take up the offer of living in an unoccupied house on the Ile de Ré. He and his wife lived there from November 1933 to the start of July 1934, according to an ideal of poverty.

58. In breaking off his engagement to Regina Olsen, Kierkegaard had renounced forever the marital bliss of the ethical stage by making a negative decision that gave preference to the religious stage of life.

59. Recorded interview (SVS 1): 'Si tu fais ça, je divorce'. Simonne Vion repeats it a little later: 'He told me: "if you become a Catholic, I will divorce you"'. He found Catholicism horrifying'. Whether or not this did lie at the root of their separation, they had nevertheless started to grow apart from one another due to their different religious persuasions.

60. In feminist theology, Kierkegaard's anthropological model was criticised for its binary opposition between male and female; see Kamitsuka (2004). Feminist philosophy has judged Kierkegaard's contribution positively, despite his misogynist attitude, since he opened up spaces that feminism has been able to use; see Léon and Walsh (1997).

61. Also according to Charlotte von Kirschbaum, who nevertheless tempered Barth's idea/opinion that feminists were either lacking in sex or male, and his strictly patriarchal view of history, with man as the only agent and advocate of human events; see Selinger (1998: 172, 101).

62. In the interview quoted, 'I am self-taught, I have shared many things'.
63. Active in the opposition to Nazism, she played a leading role in the Freies Deutschland movement founded in 1943 in Zurich and contributed to the feminist movement with writings that took issue with the ideas of other feminists, including Simone de Beauvoir; see Munz (2000: 202–26).
64. Interview with Jeanine Delpech, 'Non, Tristan et Iseult ne s'aimaient pas, nous dit Denis de Rougemont', in *Les Nouvelles Littéraires*, 11 February 1939.
65. 11 May 1939, from Flexanville, Seine-et-Oise (F.R.).
66. Illegible signature, letter of 29 September 1940 from Lawrence, Mass. (F.R.).
67. 12 October 1943, Wellington Villa, Alexandria, Va. (F.R.).
68. Letter from Zurich dated 9 February 1939 (F.R.). Théophil Spoerri (1890–1974) was the author of numerous works of romance literature. The convergence between both men was the basis for the setting up in June 1940 of the League of Gotthard, clandestine in its operation and public in civil opinion, which set out to act for the defence of the country and the renewal of Swiss political life; see Ackermann (1996: 650 et seq.).
69. A. Ferrière (1879–1960), Swiss pedagogue, set up experimental educational institutions and in 1921 the Ligue Internationale pour les Ecoles Nouvelles.
70. P. Hymans from Rotterdam on 21 September (1946?).
71. Gide knew Rougemont and had lent him and his family an apartment in Paris in 1939. See Rougemont 1961 (republished 1996: 161 et seq.).
72. L. Santucci (1918–99), writer and essayist of nonconformist Catholicism.
73. Letter of 1 May 1946, from Milan, typewritten, with a handwritten note by the recipient: 'rép. 5.VII' (F.R.).
74. Note by Luigi Santucci, Italian translator of *AO: L'amore e l'Occidente*, 1977, Milan: Rizzoli, 9.
75. Roberto Malan, proprietor of a major travel agency in Turin, was born in Catania on 25 March 1920 and married Bianca Revel in 1945 (1996: 202). He was active in the antifascist resistance.
76. The film tells the story of a young man, Patrice, played by Jean Marais, in search of a wife for his Uncle Marc. He finds, on an island, the young, fair Nathalie (Madeleine Sologne), who follows him to escape from a coarse and violent suitor, with a name reminiscent of the myth of Tristan: Morholt. The uncle's castle is also inhabited by the uncle's sister, with her husband and child, the dwarf Achille (Pieral). The latter, another direct reference, plays an active part in the events, which borrow from the myth the ideas of the love potion, the discovery of the lovers, and the moving away of the young Patrice, who seeks in vain a new relationship with a brunette Nathalie. In an attempt to see the fair Nathalie again, he is mortally wounded and the two lovers die together. Some aspects of the film are particularly successful, particularly the link between myth and modernity represented by the character of the dwarf, the journeys to and from the island, and the final scene when the two lovers die together.
77. Pingaud, born in Paris in 1923, acknowledged the influence of *AO* on his novel; see Cirulli (2002–3: 71).
78. Humm (Modena 1895–Zurich 1977), Swiss author of novels, plays and essays, wrote on 10 February 1939 from Zurich (F.R.). There are other similar

examples in Rougemont's correspondence, for instance Victoria Ocampo wrote to him that she had reread some pages of *AO* and found certain contradictions: 'I do not love the absurd, I do not find fidelity absurd. But we can be faithful to a being only if this fidelity agrees with what we owe to ourselves'. The letter is headed 'Villa Ocampo/San Isidro/F.C.C.A.' and the author repeats that they would be able to speak of such things if her correspondent was less absent and absorbed in his thoughts. All this suggests that the letter, undated, was written during Rougemont's stay in Argentina, between July and November 1941.

79. 17 November 1939.

80. Jean-Louis Leuba (1912–), Swiss theologian and pastor, was editor-in-chief of *In Extremis* – the review of the Swiss Students' Christian Association.

81. Jean Bosc was part of the *Je Sers* group and editor after 1936 of the journal *Semeur*, the mouthpiece of the French Federation of Protestant Student Associations. A review of similar tone can be found in *L'Essor*, 1940. These were all Protestant-inspired journals published in Switzerland.

82. One example was Gaston Rageot (1872–1940), literary critic and novelist, who wrote in *Le Temps*, an independent newspaper of the governing elite during the Third Republic.

83. Gabriel Marcel (1939) found the book 'systematic to excess' and 'a little over-ingenuous'. André Rousseaux in *Le Figaro Littéraire* (1939), a journal in the tradition of liberal conservatism, alternated praise and criticism for *AO*. A similar tone was struck by Ernest Seillière (1939) in *Journal des Débats*, a conservative evening newspaper, and Albert Béguin in *Journal de Genève* (1939). These men specialised in similar fields: Rousseaux (1896–1960), a major Catholic literary critic, was a regular contributor to *Le Figaro Littéraire*; Seillière (1866–1955) had written on the passionate mysticism of the romantics amongst other things; Béguin (1901–1957), a Swiss Protestant, translator, publisher and critic, became editor of *Esprit* after Mounier's death in 1950. The writer Charles-Albert Cingria (1883–1954, born in Geneva of a father who was originally from Ragusa and a Polish mother) defined the book as a capital undertaking (1939: 495–98).

84. An exception was Armand Petitjean writing in *Marianne*, a left-wing journal with a circulation of 100,000 copies in the mid-1930s.

85. *L'Indépendant* was the regional newspaper of Perpignan.

86. See the copious correspondence between Rougemont and Belgion, who put him in touch with C.S. Lewis and T.S. Eliot (F.R.). The translator sent Rougemont passages from *The Allegory of Love* by C.S. Lewis that were relevant to *AO* (letter of 6 July 1938).

87. Letter of 24 February 1939, from Fontenay-aux-Roses (F.R.).

88. Lot-Borodine nevertheless admitted that she had admired previous works by the same author, particularly *Penser avec les Mains*; letter of 24 February 1939 (F.R.).

89. In effect, in the 1939 version, Rougemont praised Otto Rahn's book, *Kreuzzug gegen den Graal*, a book of esoteric inspiration, which mixed Cathar, neo-Manichaean and Celtic legacies in a Germanic mythology of ancient and contemporary seekers of the Holy Grail. Rahn (1904–39)

claimed to be on the trail of the Holy Grail and the presumed treasure trove of gold. His book, which interpreted the Cathar heresy as a Germanic religion derived from the Celtic druids, was appreciated by Heinrich Himmler, who used it to support his ideas about Aryan superiority. Rahn joined the SS, where he experienced problems due to his homosexual tendencies and alcoholism. He was found dead in a wood in the Austrian Alps in March 1939; see Zambon (1999).

90. Letter of 5 March 1939 (F.R.). Lot-Borodine observed that the important book by Anders Nygren, a Swedish Lutheran, was quoted in *AO* only in the bibliography. The work by Nygren, *Agape and Eros* (1982), came out in Sweden in 1930. The difference established between the two terms by Nygren is different from that suggested by Rougemont, since Nygren believed that the former term referred to the Platonic tradition, which tends to the deification of man, the latter to God's love for humanity and human love for one's neighbour.

91. Henri Marrou (1904–77) was a historian, antifascist and author of works on the history of Christianity and the theory of historical method, such as *De la Connaissance Historique*, 1954.

92. Gilson (1884–1978) taught medieval philosophy at the Collège de France. He was the author of many works, including the fascinating study *Héloïse et Abélard*, which was first published in 1937.

93. In a letter to Lot-Borodine-Rougemont wrote, 'it is certain that the historical argument *is not central* in my book'; 19 March 1939 from La Celle Saint Cloud (F.R.).

94. 'Autour de *L'Amour et l'Occident*', *Esprit*, 84, 1939, 1 September (see Marrou 1939b); contains letter from Denis de Rougemont (ibid.: 760–65) and reply from Henri Davenson (ibid.: 765–68).

95. Letter of Etienne Gilson from Paris dated 1 April 1939 (F.R.). He concluded, 'I owe you too much pleasure, and pleasure is something too rare not to recognise it, particularly when it is an intelligent pleasure'.

96. In *Situations II*, Sartre resumes his discourse in his introduction to *Temps Modernes* and significantly uses *AO* to rebut the argument that love–passion is a constitutional affliction of the human spirit.

97. A letter from Plon to Rougemont dated 11 April 1939 (F.R.) informed him that it had not yet been decided to reprint *AO* because numerous books remained unsold and remaindered copies were beginning to come back.

98. Notes in Rougemont's handwriting at the top of a prospectus (dated 1982) on the distribution of his works (F.R.).

99. *Paysan du Danube* in 1932 ran to 500 copies, *Politique de la Personne* in 1934 to 3,000, and *Penser avec les Mains* in 1936 to 4,000.

100. The first edition, published in 1939, was reprinted five times, and the same was true of the 1956 edition, while the 1972 edition had been reprinted eleven times by 2002.

101. Not Paul Zumthor, who presumptuously spoke of *AO* as a 'livre naguère célèbre' ('book that was famous a few years ago') (Zumthor 1952).

102. Pseudonym of Gaston Derycke (1913), Belgian writer and poet.

103. Note used as a basis for the revised French edition of 1956. Note de l'auteur, 1948 (F.R.).

104. Rougemont returned to the theme of love in works postdating *AO*; see Rougemont 1961: 8, Note liminaire, in which he proposes a monist view of love, mentioned also in his 1972 Postscript. Successors to *AO* that discuss other themes are: *La Part du Diable* (1942), which analyses the theme of passion as a diabolical aspect of love, and passion as a sort of neurosis; and *Doctrine Fabuleuse* (1947), which takes up again the topic of Don Juan, in which he sees the diabolical and the desire for perpetual change.

105. In the 1956 edition, some books contain a few corrections, mainly formal in nature, while Book 6 reveals a few changes in content. The most radically amended is Book 2, on the religious origins of the myth.

106. He uses a new bibliography for this part, considerably extending that of 1939.

107. In the first two editions of *AO*, no work by Freud is specifically quoted. The only title that appears in the 1972 Postscript is *Civilisation and Its Discontents* (Rougemont 1972: 412n.; 1983: 367n.). The analogy between the influence of the Cathars on the troubadours and that of Freud on the surrealists (Rougemont 1939: 98–100; 1983: 100 ff.), often misunderstood by his critics, may be found in a brilliant digression in which Rougemont imagines that future historians, in the absence of any decisive evidence, do not accept the second influence and that only one 'not very serious' academic airs the hypothesis according to which the surrealists were influenced by Freud.

108. Notes for *AO* II (F.R.).

109. Rey-Flaud (1983: 66). J.-C. Huchet (1985: 223–33) confirms the structural sympathy between medieval romance and psychoanalysis, and indicates that, on a literary level, the comparison with psychoanalysis highlights the structural function of death in the universe of courtly love.

110. Lacan alludes to the 'orgy of literature' that has been produced on love and that is incapable of speaking of pleasure, Christianity having invented a God who keeps all the pleasure for himself (Lacan 1999).

111. G.E. Sansone noted that when a woman changes from being an object to a subject in the trobairitz discourse on love, the idealist connotations seem almost to disappear (Sansone 1984, vol. 1: 17).

112. In the period between the two world wars, there was a tradition of French writings on love in the United States, which had lost its fascination and mystery in the name of sexual liberation, female emancipation and divorce. It often took the form of travel writing, as in one significant example by C.-A.-A. Ferri-Pisani (1927). See, for other examples, Nacci (1996: 37–39).

113. 'Inconclusive and Scientifico-polemical Postscript' uses Kierkegaard's title: 'Concluding Unscientific Postscript to Philosophical Fragments'.

114. In actual fact, Jean Ballard had already announced his intention of publishing a special issue on Mediterranean man in January 1938 (Ballard 1938: 61–64) and in September 1938 he addressed the same idea in a letter to Bousquet; see Paire (1993: 286).

115. The same book was again reviewed by B. Fondane (1936: 334–35).

116. The name of the reviewer, a friend of Rougemont, was actually Roger Jézéquel (see first part of this chapter).

117 See also the review signed by 'G.D.' (perhaps Gaston Derycke?) of *Journal d'Allemagne* ('G.D.' 1939: 543–44).

118. A new review of *AO* appeared in issue 222 of *Cahiers*, March 1946, signed by Roger Breuil (1946: 209–10), to mark the first reprinting of the 1939 edition.

119. These were two letters of 12 and 13 March 1933 (on *Paysan*), a letter of 1934 and another of 25 or 29 March 1939: in the latter, Bousquet tells Rougemont about what appears to be the special issue on *Génie d'Oc*, 'which will not come out without you' (F.R.).

120. For example, he contributed to the review an extract from *Penser avec les Mains* entitled 'Décadence des Lieux Communs' (*Cahiers du Sud*, 189, December 1936, 898–905), an article on Chamisso, *Cahiers du Sud*, 194, 1937, 282–91, and a long review of *La Révolution Nécessaire* by Aron and Dandieu, *Cahiers du Sud*, 162, June 1934, 386–91.

121. In the special issue, Rougemont was only quoted by Nelli for his attempt to restore credibility to the institution of marriage (*Cahiers du Sud*, 249, 1942, 57) and by André Chastel à propos of the analogy with surrealism (189).

122. I. Singer (1984, 1987) demonstrates in both publications the historical inaccuracy of the ideas in *AO*.

PART III

CONNECTING JEWISHNESS, EUROPEANNESS AND LOVE

Jewish culture has long been typecast as a stranger to courtly and romantic love. This stereotype was taken to extremes by the Nazis, who simultaneously denied the Jews both their Europeanness and their ability to feel courtly love, represented by the 'song of the troubadours as an expression of those higher feelings that distinguish us from Jews and jazz-playing American negroes'.[1] The matter is complicated by the ambiguity of the term 'love' that may or may not refer to sexuality, a sore point of the meeting between cultures. Nazi propaganda and Italian fascist propaganda certainly dwelled on the 'lubriciousness' of the Jews, but the oversexed Jew was a common cliché even outside the racist regimes.

This detachment from romantic love was also confirmed in various ways by Jewish authors and sources. Emmanuel Lévinas spoke of the 'rejection of the courtly myth' by the Jews, maintaining that the romantic dimension, where love is an end in its own right is alien to Judaism though it may coexist with a religious civilisation, as is the case with Christianity. Lévinas adds that poetic images of a loving life are few and far between in the Bible, except for the Song of Songs, though this is most commonly interpreted in a mystic sense (Lévinas 1988–89: 40–48). However, it may also be argued that the Bible contains forms of love that can be traced back to romantic forms, for example in the story of Jacob and Rachel (Riveline 2000).[2]

The *Encyclopaedia Judaica*, after discussing the various meanings of the term 'love', from the love between engaged and married couples to the love of God for Israel, goes on to stress the link between divine love and human love, with particular regard to the esoteric teaching of Jewish mysticism.[3] The *Encyclopaedia* reminds us that while love between a man and woman in the Jewish culture is almost always with the purpose of marriage, the ideal of courtly love spread through the Jewish community during the eleventh and twelfth centuries, although 'unrequited passion never became a major topic of interest to the Jews'.[4] The note to the Italian edition of the *Dybbuk* maintains that the 'Eastern Jewish mentality still did not contain the idea of romantic love even at the beginning of the century', although it goes on to stress that fatal love is the key to interpreting the play (Freschi 1997: 101–24).

These reductive arguments arise as a result of considering Jewish culture as a monolithic whole instead of a complex set of different traditions and languages. They reflect clichés and prejudices in intercultural relationships and perpetuate the prejudice that communication between cultures is not possible. Examination of the thirteenth-century Ashkenazi text *Sefer Hasidim*, however, has revealed a patriarchal and semi-puritan Jewish tradition mixed with a chivalrous, romantic and semi-hedonistic tradition typical of the higher strata of Christian society. The parallels and differences between *Sefer Hasidim* and *De Arte Honeste Amandi* by Andrea Capellanus are not accidental. The fact that thwarted love between men and women is a constant theme of the former text indicates that, for certain Jews, the traditional Jewish attitude had become tempered by the courtly ideals that spread through the German Ashkenazi community from the thirteenth century (Monford 1959–60: 13–44).

This cultural mix must be taken into account if we are to see the historical nature of emotional phenomena. David Biale (1997) has given us an in-depth discussion of 'Eros and the Jews', which examines the theme of intercultural relationships and differentiates between the various Jewish traditions. Biale claims that Jewish culture cannot be categorised as simply affirming or repressing the erotic element. Instead, the culture is deeply ambivalent, as is evident from Freud's contradictions over Jewish sexuality. Biale devotes particular attention to the attitude of the Maskilim, proponents of the Jewish Enlightenment (Haskalah), who reacted against ascetic forms of Hasidism and accused traditional society of stifling erotic desire.[5] According to Biale, although there is no definitive answer to the question of the relationship between Jewish cultures and romantic love, it is certain that in the nineteenth century some young Maskilim expressed feelings similar to this form of love, attacking the custom of early marriages and the ban on couples meeting before marriage.[6] This condemnation of early unions by the Maskilim helped promote an image of a Jewish marriage as a union devoid of love and based only on financial considerations. On the other hand, Ben-Sasson claimed that in the nineteenth century the ideas of love propounded by the troubadours had been transferred by the Hasidim to the family circle – the new aspect being that they were extended over several generations: love for an irreplaceable woman, or at least love approved by God, could be a sign passed down to descendants who were destined to wed (Ben-Sasson 1976: 553).

The complexity of the issue of love in a Jewish environment makes it impossible to accept oversimplified ideas, for example that erotic feelings between Jews were modernised to imitate the romantic revolution in feelings – or the existence of an exclusive link between modernity and an end to arranged marriages (Biale 1983: 1–17). Pre-Enlightenment Jewish society offered a broad range of possibilities, which included forms of romantic love within arranged marriages and even during the period of engagement. The Haskalah, on the other hand, offered an idea of love that was at odds with traditional marriage and saw adolescence as a period of study, according to an ideology that had filtered into Jewish and Yiddish popular romantic novels[7] of the 1870s and 1880s. In the twentieth century, the world of the Jews in Eastern Europe was infused with popular literature and love songs that referred to medieval folk traditions, transforming traditional customs into romantic love stories. Due to the intermingling of traditional ideas and romance in Yiddish story books and popular songs sold by itinerant booksellers in the nineteenth century – mostly directed at a female audience – the stories of young lovers often concluded with the discovery that their parents had made a pact at birth that sealed the fate of the couple (Biale 2002: 831). Thus the topic of predestination was combined with that of falling in love – just as in the *Dybbuk*.

The complexity described here provides a historical backdrop to the love stories that will form the subjects of the next two chapters. It particularly describes the background to the *Dybbuk,* because the play simultaneously calls on the innovatory attempts typical of the Jewish Enlightenment and the values of the pre-Enlightenment community. The next two chapters discuss forms of love and Europeanness in two different representative strands of Jewish cultures, that of popular East European tradition as retold by a revolutionary intellectual such as Ansky – and that of left-wing 'humanist' Jews in Western Europe as represented by Giorgina Levi and Heinz Arian. In both cases, we note the range of levels of integration between traditional Jewish cultures and other cultures. This occurs to such an extent that the components are indistinguishable in the new cultural product, further evidence of the fact that the Jews cannot be considered foreigners but protagonists in the cultures of Western Europe in the fullest sense.[8]

Chapter 5

'Between Two Worlds':

Ansky's Dybbuk in France and Italy

Paris, 1928, Studio des Champs-Elysées theatre, first performance of
Le Dibouk *directed by Gaston Baty:*

A white curtain, striped with black, surmounted by Hebrew letters, which triggers in us
– the Israelites of France – a strange emotion: perhaps because we are allowed to see
them at the greatest time of our life or perhaps because certain memories are
subconsciously linked to them? ... An ecstatic scholar raises the curtain, murmurs, like
the ancient prologue, some verses on the ascension and incarnation of souls and many
of us rediscover the heart of a Hasid, reincarnated in a Parisian of 1928. (Pierre Paraf)

The history of the *Dybbuk*[9] is so symbolic of the link between
Jewishness and Europeanness in the period between the end of the
1920s and the 1930s, particularly with regard to the topic of love,
that some considered it a kind of Jewish version of the myth of
Tristan and Iseult, defining the final scene as a parallel of the
Wagnerian *Liebestod* (Safran 2000: 761–81; Wolitz 2006: 164–202).
The play expresses the specificity and the plurality of Jewish
cultures in the continent and acts as a catalyst to both the attitudes
of other Europeans to the Jews and Jewish attitudes to differences
between their cultures. The *Dybbuk* is also an opportune example of
the relationship between public and private, as it was written in
Eastern Europe during a period when the two spheres were brought
into direct contact by revolutionary intentions and events, and then
the impositions of totalitarian regimes and concerns over changes
induced by modernity – particularly in the area of the family and
marriage – accentuated the links between the public sphere and the
private sphere.

Ansky's play also represents the way popular traditions were
mined for raw material in an incessant quest for new artistic

creation (Demonico 1993: 201–7). Its origins bear witness to the mix of Eastern European and Western European cultures, between new and traditional forms of Jewish culture, between expressions of high culture and folk culture. It is a story of love between two young people who are hindered by rich and powerful parents, a love affirmed beyond death in the union between their two souls. The dybbuk – the soul of the young man returning from beyond the grave to become incarnated in his beloved – acts as a go-between between two worlds, the earthly and the supernatural, until it is exorcised as a demon by the *zaddik* (a Rabbi capable of performing miracles). The theme of the play crops up frequently in Yiddish culture, particularly in poetry and narrative, and to a lesser extent in the theatre.[10] Yiddish literature from the seventeenth century on contains a wealth of stories of possession, usually of women, but sometimes of men, often with strong erotic elements, namely references to the bodies of the possessed young women or to sexual transgressions by the dybbuk in his previous earthly life.[11] Ansky's play combines these different subjects in a new way by combining a love story with a narrative on the dybbuk.

In Jewish folklore, dybbuks are evil spirits or damned souls that enter living people, attach themselves to their souls and speak through their mouths, maintaining their own separate personalities. According to Gerschom Scholem, the term, which means adhering, is of Yiddish origin and made its first appearance in 1680 in a text in Volhynia – taken from the spoken language of the German and Polish Jews – while it is not used in Talmudic literature or in the Kabbalah (Scholem 1978: 349–50).

The subject of the *Dybbuk* combines various narrative traditions passed down from the Hasidic legacy, which considers storytelling to be a spiritual art. The play opens in the synagogue in Brinitz, where three *batlanim* (wastrels from the Eastern ghettos who say prayers in exchange for donations) intone a chant about the soul, which may fall or rise, and recount examples from the Talmud which show that true greatness and wealth are not the same thing. They also tell of a saint who performs magic by invoking the ineffable form of the Name of God, but a mysterious Messenger arrives and warns of the risks of such practices, because saying the name twice is tantamount to calling on Satan. The young Hanan, student of the yeshiva (the school for the study of the Talmud), displays great interest, however, because he is engaged in magical practices to obtain gold from the powers of evil. He is, in fact, in love with Leah, daughter of a wealthy man named Sender, who is seeking a bridegroom for his daughter from his own social class. Hanan expresses his faith in the Kabbalah and the conviction that one should not declare war on sin, but correct it. Even lust, the worst sin, may be transformed into the greatest purity[12] as we are shown in the Song of Songs, from which Hanan intones a strophe. He also mentions the numbers that correspond in the Kabbalah to his own name and that of Leah. Leah arrives with a friend and her aunt Frade to see the embroidered curtain of the holy arch, an object that may have been part of the folk art collected by Ansky's ethnographic expedition.[13] The Messenger recounts the story of the rich and avaricious Hasid to whom the Rabbi shows first a window, from which the man sees other people outside, and then a mirror, in which he sees his own image. The meaning of the parable is that people no longer see others, but only themselves, when silver is at stake. Despite their poverty, the *batlanim* eat and drink the little they have with good cheer, a trait that illustrates their distinctive attitude of joy for creation. This is also apparent to Sender (Ansky 2000: 19), who arrives announcing that he has finally managed to arrange Leah's engagement. At this news, Hanan despairs, shouts that the secret of the repeated Name has been revealed to him, and dies.

The second act depicts Leah's marriage in the square of Brinitz, in which lies the tomb of a betrothed couple killed in the pogrom of 1648 (5408 in the Jewish calendar). The act is dominated by the frenetic and grotesque dance of the beggars with the bride, particularly an old blind woman who introduces the theme of death. Leah emerges distraught and makes, in turn, a long speech about the dead, namely, her mother and Hanan, whom she wishes to visit in the cemetery so that she can invite them to her marriage. Leah declares her belief that the soul of someone who dies before their time returns to the earth, and wonders about children who are never born and about things never achieved. The Messenger, in turn, propounds a theory of metempsychosis between human beings, animals and plants, and introduces the topic of the dybbuk. The bridegroom-to-be is hesitant and frightened, despite the encouragement of his tutor, with reservations that echo those of the Maskilim about early marriage. Leah at last returns from the cemetery, but when the wedding ceremony begins and the groom is about to cover her face with the white veil, she tears it away shouting, 'You are not my bridegroom' and begins to speak in the voice of Hanan. The Messenger announces, 'A dead soul has entered the body of the bride: a dybbuk' (ibid.: 31).

The third act is set in Miropol, in the house of the miraculous Rabbi Esriel. Some Hasidim listen to the Messenger's stories. The first, a legend dating from the end of the eighteenth century and translated into German by Martin Buber in 1906, tells of the heart of the world attempting to reach a clear spring on the mountain without which he cannot live.[14] Reb Esriel, in turn, tells of the saintly Baalshem's admiration for the acrobats who walk above the abyss, taking them as an example of both spiritual and bodily exercise, and sings the praises of Israel to the people. Leah–dybbuk is taken to the Rebbe; Sender says that his daughter has been entered by the soul of Hanan, who often, in life, ate at his table, but he cannot remember having done him any wrong. When questioned about her identity by Esriel, Leah–dybbuk answers, 'I am one of those who looked for new paths', and categorically refuses to leave the body of her beloved (ibid.: 37). Esriel then asks ten Jews representing the community for permission to perform an exorcism, which is granted. They prepare the penitential robes, the seven rams' horns, the seven black candles and the seven scrolls of law for the ritual. The elder Rabbi in the town is also called, and reports that he has dreamed three times of Hanan's father, Nissan, who revealed to him the pact made with Sender many years before: they had promised one another that if they had a son and daughter, they would join them in marriage. The exorcism is then postponed and the trial starts, which takes place in the fourth act.

The dead Nissan is summoned to court, but a curtain separates his space from that of the living. He speaks in a manner comprehensible only to the elder Rabbi, who translates his words. Nissan bears witness that after the pact his wife brought Hanan into the world but he, Nissan, died shortly after. From the world of Truth, he followed his son with joy for his progress in knowledge, but after the death of Hanan 'he has been cut off from both worlds. He is unremembered – without a name, without an heir, without a son to say kaddish for him' (ibid.: 45). Sender admits the pact, saying he had been ignorant of the sequel, but Rabbi Shimshon accuses him of having recognised Hanan deep down in his heart but not seeking confirmation because he wanted only to pursue his own gain. Esriel's sentence is exemplary: since heaven smiled on the pact by making the two young people fall in love with each other, even though it is not known whether the wives had already conceived at the time of the agreement, Sender must give half of his wealth to the poor and recite kaddish for Nissan. Sender agrees to the sentence, but not Nissan, who maintains an alarming silence. In a dramatic scene, Esriel exorcises Leah and asks God's mercy for Hanan's imprisoned spirit. After Sender has recited the first kaddish, everyone except Leah goes to meet the bridegroom whom Esriel has called in the meantime, and the aunt Frade sings a wedding refrain. However, the spirit of Hanan returns; Leah welcomes it lovingly and during their conversation sings a lullaby for their unborn children. Leah dies as the wedding cortege enters the scene and the two lovers are reunited. The final song echoes the opening theme: 'Why, oh why, / Did the soul descend / From the highest height / To the deepest end? / The lowest fall / Contains the upward flight ...' (ibid.: 52).

Hybridisations in Central Eastern Europe

The original title, *Between Two Worlds*, suggests the idea of intermediation between life and death, but the duality of the worlds is more wide-ranging and subtle than it appears at first sight. The work is underpinned by a series of hybridisations effected by its author as a result of his beliefs and his life itself, which was lived during the height of the revolution.[15] Ansky, who trained at Vitebsk in an orthodox yeshiva and in Hasidism, was expert in both conflicting branches of East European Jewish orthodoxy. By the age of fifteen, he had begun to read the works of the Haskalah movement and he had learned Russian, which allowed him to read the nihilist manifestos and also feminist and utopian writings. He was attracted by populist doctrines and went to live first with the peasants and then with the miners under very harsh conditions that ruined his health. He worked as a blacksmith, bookbinder, workman and teacher. In 1892, he escaped from the tsarist police and was forced to leave Russia and live in Germany, Switzerland and Paris. After a twenty-year gap, in 1901 he decided to switch from Russian to Yiddish when he discovered the stories of Y.L. Peretz, which represented a blend of modernity and tradition, politics and culture (Ze'evi-Weil 1994: xiii). In 1905, when freedom was proclaimed and the Duma was created, he returned to Russia to join the Socialist-Revolutionary Party, for which he composed the anthem. From 1912 to 1914, he headed an ethnographic expedition that collected a wealth of material in Volhynia and Podolia, to which he added the fruits of subsequent searches in Galicia during 1915–16.[16] During the First World War, Ansky devoted himself to the organisation of committees for the rescue of Jews who were victims of war. His lifestyle was consistent with his beliefs: he had no property or fixed abode, he wrote in restaurants and hotel rooms, he had only one suit and an overcoat to his name, and his suitcases were full of ethnographic materials (reported by A. Rechtman 1992–4: 12–15). Ansky married a Jewish woman, but the marriage was short-lived and soon ended in divorce (Roskies 1992a: xix–xx; see also Y. Petrovsky-Shtern 2006: 83–102). In 1917, he was elected to the Constituent Assembly as a Socialist-Revolutionary deputy, but the following year he was forced to flee Petrograd (the name given to St Petersburg from 1914 to 1924) to Vilnius when the Bolsheviks took power and hunted out members of the Socialist-Revolutionary movement, of which he was one. In 1919, he founded the Jewish ethnographic society in Warsaw. He left fifteen volumes of works in Yiddish, including the *Dybbuk*, written between 1912 and 1919. He died in 1920 in Warsaw due to complications arising from pneumonia.

Ansky is considered paradigmatic of the cultural figure of the Jew who retrieves aspects of tradition for modern purposes, while slipping in and out of Jewishness. He intended his folk art collection to be a reconciliation between past and present, between the elite and the masses, between local and universal: he believed that certain stories awaited 'their redeemer' to return to full life. Biale dedicated his chapter on East European Jewish culture from the partition of Poland to the Holocaust to the *Dybbuk*, considering that the four stages of Ansky's biography: orthodoxy, Haskalah, acculturation to Russian and the revolution, and, lastly, his return to the people represented markers of the cultural directions that the Jews could take in relation to the specific forms of modernity in Eastern Europe (Biale 2002: 800). In particular, the theme of return has an archetypal resonance in Jewish culture that has now become even more pronounced than it was in the 1920s (Roskies 1992b: 243–60). Ansky's biography is also an example of the individualisation that the Maskilim called for, through subjective transformation and within interpersonal relationships, revolution-ising the private sphere to change the Jewish people (Biale 2002: 830).

The ambivalence or even the multivalence of the *Dybbuk* is evident from the very first draft of the play, of which various versions exist. It is not possible to establish categorically whether the first draft was written in Russian or in Yiddish, languages that Ansky spoke and wrote fluently, but now the first hypothesis has become more plausible, because a 1915 text in Russian approved by censorship has been found.[17] This version was submitted to

Stanislavsky, who suggested the introduction of the character of the Messenger.[18] This figure hinted at the role of Ansky himself, a mediator between two worlds, but in a form submerged in the material aspects of life (see Noy 1994: xvii). This text would have been translated into Yiddish by Ansky (Safran 2006: xxvi) and into Hebrew by the poet Hayim Nahman Bialik.[19] According to a tradition accepted by almost all scholars, Ansky retranslated the *Dybbuk* into Yiddish in 1918, after having lost it in his flight from Petrograd.[20] Ansky was convinced that trilingualism (Russian, Hebrew, Yiddish), customary among Jews in that area, and the coexistence of many facets in Jewish literature could form the basis for a recognised collective identity in Russia.[21] Ansky gave readings of the work, sometimes in Yiddish and sometimes in Russian, in many cities – in Petrograd, Odessa, Kiev, Moscow and Vilna. Sometimes he received critical reactions and altered the text accordingly. He added revisions that brought the text closer to colloquial language while maintaining a linguistic tension between the dialects of different regions, and he took out the German-sounding expressions.[22] The Yiddish text we have is probably a second-degree translation – a translation from the Hebrew that was, in turn, a translation from the Yiddish and/or from the Russian. Lastly, the work was passed on to those who do not speak those three languages through an additional translation as it was transposed to the Western languages.[23]

On an expressive and narrative level, the *Dybbuk* has been compared to a postmodern collage. Its first translator, the poet Bialik, observed that the work resembled a patchwork of fragments of different traditions, including folklore. One of the main present-day translators and interpreters discerns a different genre in each act: the first a love story with an unhappy ending, the second a musical with dancing, the third a ghost story, and the fourth a depiction of a trial and an exorcism (Neugroschel 2000: xiv). The *Dybbuk* is strewn with stories and parables and also historical and anthropological facts learned or observed during the ethnographic expedition.[24] For example, at the table of a rich Jew in Yarmolinetz, Ansky witnessed a silent exchange between the man's daughter and a yeshiva student who regularly ate with them. Later, he heard the girl crying in the night (Werses 1986: 110–12).[25] The most important historical element for contextualising the play was the tomb in the middle of the village near the synagogue: Ansky actually saw in the town square of Anapolia in Volhynia the tomb of a betrothed couple massacred by Chmielnicki in 1648, and an old man told him the story.[26] The link between the love stories, the hereafter and the pogroms is significant on a symbolic level: possession may be interpreted as interiorisation of the massacres, the rabbinic rite as an expulsion of evil spirits from the Jewish body, or the vulnerability of the maiden as the impotence or passivity of the Jews in the face of their slaughterers (Neugroschel 2000: 61). In the play, the mention of the Cossack hordes was the only hint at the existence of Christians: all the characters are Jewish – a prevalent device in Jewish literature, which allows attention to be focused on the Jewish community. Ansky created in the *Dybbuk* the illusion of a fully Jewish life that he dreamed of longingly after having lived as a Russian for so long.

The appeal of the work lies in the fact that it succeeded in maintaining the tension between its components without emphasising one to the detriment of the others: the awareness of the works of the Maskilim and the criticism of orthodox Judaism; the universality of the Russian revolutionary movement; and the Jewish tradition both in popular belief and in mystical thought and Hasidic culture. On a theatrical level, the *Dybbuk* represents a coming together of two trends: the need of the ethnographer to collect fragments of a threatened culture and reassemble them in artistic form, and a modernist aesthetic that turns theatre into a religious rite.

The choice of the theatrical genre was necessary to maintain the oral nature of the original culture. Ansky's interest in the oral tradition has been interpreted as a vindication of an 'oral Torah' of the Jewish masses of Eastern Europe: just as the written Torah is the source of creativity, the oral Torah represents the language of symbol and memory (Roskies 1992b: 244, 258).[27] Ansky's play is also part of the tradition of theatre shows held for Purim at the beginning of spring. This genre applies to a limited time period that is also able to reach out to a non-Jewish audience (Sandrow 1977: Ch. 1).[28] Theatre was a practically forbidden genre, given the traditional disapproval of the rabbis and the ban on women acting and men dressing up as women.[29] The vitality of popular Yiddish theatre was such that it lived on even in the Nazi camps, though the Nazi regime banned public performances (Biale 2002: 348 et seq.). Yiddish theatre is believed to be the last flourishing of the nineteenth-century romantic tradition due to the emphasis it placed on feelings and also to its tendency to mix expressive genres or even poetry and prose, serious and grotesque, as well as words and music, and folklore and high culture (Sandrow 2003: 47–59, 54–55).

The *Dybbuk* was first staged in Yiddish in the Vilna theatre of Warsaw and in Hebrew in the Habimah ('The Set', 'The Stage') theatre of Moscow. The production staged by the Vilna Troupe, which opened on 9 December 1920 in Warsaw – then cultural capital of the Yiddish world – was directed by David Herman, one of the young directors considered 'European' during the 1920s in Poland because he was engaged in a theatre that extended beyond national boundaries. His production rhythmically combined intonation, lines and colours with a strong sense of stylisation in the pantomime and dance, the abstract scenery and the simplified, far-from-realistic costumes (Lo Gatto 1952: 59). The Vilna Troupe's *Dybbuk* met with outstanding success. Its audience included Hasidim, despite their proscription of theatres and circuses, and many spectators went back to the theatre more than once (Steinlauf 2006: 232–51). Twenty-five years later, a spectator recalled, '[T]hey were more than actors ... it was something that I had never seen or heard before' (Sandrow 1977: 219). The Vilna theatre production, in fact, had something in common with a religious experience. Part of the *Dybbuk*'s success was due to the fact that, at that juncture in history, it was a poignant representation of the point of passage between two worlds. Six years of war, revolution and pogroms that had devastated hundreds of Jewish communities were giving way to the promise of a new existence in a modern parliamentary state that would include civil and cultural rights for the three and a half million Polish Jews. For them, the *Dybbuk* constituted an affirmation of the national and cultural identity that was so much more powerful because it was implicit; an affirmation that appealed simultaneously to the masses and to the Jewish intelligentsia. In 1922, the Vilna Troupe took the *Dybbuk* on tour through Europe. The troupe split in 1923 and was no longer in existence by 1927, but the 1937 film *Der Dibek* was filmed using some of the original cast.

The production by the Habimah theatre of Moscow was the most important in the history of the theatre and brought the *Dybbuk* world fame, making radical changes on an artistic level. During the summer of 1917, a group of young actors with different social origins began to work together and turned to Stanislavsky, who, struck by their commitment and devotion, asked his pupil Vakhtangov to direct the play. The founders of the Habimah theatre believed in education for the masses and they thought that the relationship between theatre and audience had to be sought not so much in social themes, as in pathos. The company put up with hunger and cold under conditions that were described as heroic, and they worked with an all-consuming fervour, sharing work, family and entertainment. Although Vakhtangov's direction was not inspired by dialectic materialism, it nevertheless tended to produce a people's theatre in the spirit of the revolution.

The *Dybbuk* opened in Moscow on 31 January 1922. The work was performed in Hebrew, with a strong emphasis on the rhythm between gesture and language. The Habimah company, with its Zionist sympathies, played a significant role in the rebirth of modern Jewish nationalism and the spread of the Hebrew language. The performers did not use Ashkenazi pronunciation, however, but Sephardite, which was more common at that time amongst Jews in Palestine (Levy 1979: 22).[30] Part of the company moved to Tel Aviv permanently from February 1931, and the *Dybbuk* remained in their repertoire for forty-three years (ibid.: 110). Their success in Palestine did not go unopposed. In 1926, the work was subject to an intellectual 'trial' in Tel Aviv, during which Zionist poets and writers took the witness box to speak for the prosecution and for the defence. The 'sentence' handed down accused the play of being a pastiche of legendary, realist and symbolist elements, and completely rejected the figure of the Messenger as a foreign addition (Roskies 1992a: xxvi, 212).[31] The work was criticised because it was considered to be overfull of folklore. There were vehement protests from religious extremists who even refused to say the name of the play, claiming it was written by a heretic (Werses 1986: 101–3, 105–6).

Vakhtangov, who was ignorant of Hebrew, as, incidentally, was most of the audience, stressed the musical aspects of the language and the performance. The result was a theatre of gesture and sound, able to convey meaning even without using words. One spectator remembers that his excitement built as the play gained pace, even though he could not understand Hebrew (Levy 1979: 35). The director staged a grotesque folk tale with the actors portraying the common Jewish people reciting in strident singsong voices with agitated gestures, and the exhibition of infirmity and deformity.[32] The expressionistic approach was evident in disjointed gestures alternating with complete immobility, contrasting tones of voice and make-up that distorted the actors' faces (Richetti 1962). The performance attributed a strong social significance to certain scenes, focusing on the central dance of the beggars, the oppressed of the world, as an expression of the spirit of the revolution (Kampf 1984).

The Russian Revolution did not, initially, attack Zionism, proclaiming the free development of national minorities and ethnic groups in Russian territory. In autumn 1919, however, the Zionist journals were closed down and their leaders arrested. Only Yiddish was legitimate. Habimah was left untouched and even acknowledged as a state theatre. Though criticised by young communist Jews who considered the struggle for identification with other members of the public a priority, it was defended by Russian intellectuals and artists such as Maxim Gorky (Richetti 1962). In the end, those who attacked the Zionist spirit won through and the government persuaded the company to tour abroad, though subsidised as a national Soviet theatre. Therefore, at the beginning of 1926, the Habimah company left Russia for a triumphant tour of European cities, including Vienna, Berlin and Paris. The tour continued to the United States in November and its influence has reverberated down through time. Kantor, who saw Habimah's *Dybbuk* in Crakow, was affected not only by the images in the scenery but, above all, by the ventriloquism of the dybbuk, which enabled him to portray the relationship between the dead and the living.[33]

The *Dybbuk* has been interpreted in many different ways. In general, the pair of lovers is taken to embody a criticism of the old Jewish world and the story is linked to progress and light (perhaps with reference to the Enlightenment) to a quest for new roads that lead away from superstition and obscurity. At the same time, the couple also stands on the side of 'superstition' and 'obscurity'. In any case, the losers are the father and orthodox Jewishness with all its rules and laws, which proves unable to separate the lovers, so that the world of folk belief triumphs in the end. In this primordial universe, good and evil, dead and living, are intimately linked and mystery is implicit in everyday life; a beggar may be the prophet Elijah or a demon reincarnated, which is at odds with the order imposed by the official religion (Steinlauf 2006: 232–51). According to Biale, Hanan is a Kabbalist, but his Kabbalah is a camouflaged form of modernist eroticism, as the character – now in the form of a dybbuk – tells the Rabbi, 'I am one of those who seek new paths'. The play is contemporary because it comments on the power of a system that opposes the counterculture of the people and revolutionary doctrines. The two worlds are not only those of the dead and the living but also, on one hand, of the universe of values that were threatening to disappear and, on the other, the universe of new values that was struggling into existence against the backdrop of the pogroms (Biale 2002: 850 et seq.). Among the emerging values was the role of women, central in the *Dybbuk*, while in traditional Jewish plays all the important roles were reserved for men (Deutsch 2006: 266–80; Wolitz 2006: 198). The *Dybbuk* was, therefore, radically anchored in the historical context in which it arose and in which it was staged for the first time, despite its recourse to the imagination and the subconscious. In Western Europe, though, the play, particularly the story of love and death, was treated as an exotic and primitive folk tale.

Reception in Western Europe

Audiences in the great cities of Western Europe were able to see the productions staged by the Vilna Troupe and Habima when they toured during the 1920s and 1930s. In London, the *Dybbuk* was staged in Yiddish in October 1922 by the Vilna Troupe, by Habima in Hebrew in 1926, and by the Forum Theatre Guild in English in March 1927 (Ansky 1927b).[34] Habima's version made a great impact in Berlin and Vienna: on Albert Einstein it made the greatest impression he had ever experienced in the theatre. Arnold Zweig compared it to the songs of the great Jewish festivals and Chagall's paintings – and also to the masked dances of South Sea Island savages. Joseph Roth spoke of the "Dionysian Jews" of Eastern Judaism being as distant and mysterious as the inhabitants of the Himalayas or the Indian fakirs (Bechtel 2002: 169–71). However, the reception was not always favourable and some reactions were inspired by anti-Jewish or anti-Semitic feelings. When the Habima production was staged in Berlin in 1928, even an appreciative pamphlet contained statements of this nature: 'Something that, nowadays, European theatrical art no longer possesses: a setting with a vision of the world, religion and universal law – these Jews create directly from their culture. We poor Europeans are forced in the opposite direction by cultural desperation: to turn art into culture and religion' (Diebold 1928: 7–8). In a subsequent tour by Habima in 1929–31, Nazi pickets protested in Würzburg against what was defined a 'cultural shame' (Levy 1979: 109).[35]

At the same time, productions of the *Dybbuk* began to be staged in Western languages. A recurrent motif of the reception (Jewish and non-Jewish) was the debate of how 'Jewish' the play actually was. In London in 1927, one reviewer, after dwelling on the 'disgusting vitality' of the 'Yiddish company' (evidently the Vilna Troupe), hoped that the entire cast was made up of Jews

(MacCarthy 1927: 797–98). The English staging was considered a 'refreshing change from the current production' for its religious and revolutionary fervour, despite a few weaknesses ('T' 1927: 414). In New York, too, with its large number of Yiddish-speaking residents, it was possible to compare three productions. One reviewer, who claimed to be an East European Jew, declared himself to be disturbed by two performances, both the Habima performance and the 'Oxford' English production directed by David Vardi,[36] who had been a member of Habima: particularly in the former, the beggars were dehumanised, and the malevolence they directed against Reb Sender could not have been 'Jewish', but must have been Russian or Bolshevik. The English performance was not 'Jewish', not merely because of the language, but because of 'the entire atmosphere' (Samuel 1927: 65–66). The best performance was deemed to be that of the Yiddish Art Theatre of New York, directed by Maurice Schwartz, who succeeded in recreating the mixture of Jewish Eastern Europe, of romance and filth, of exaltation of the East and the economic ferocity of the West.

Habima's Italian tour was preceded by the publication of the first translation from Yiddish of Ansky's play by Mario De Benedetti and Leo Goldfischer in 1926 – 5686 in the Jewish calendar – with a preface by Benvenuto Terracini, who eloquently expressed the contradictions in the attitude of enlightened Jews to the *Dybbuk* and to the world it revealed (Ansky 1926).[37] He emphasised the local colour and the exotic nature of a play that he believed had a place in 'the theatre of dialect', stating that 'the world of the Jewish riots in the ghettos of Poland and Russia are more archaic and foreign to us, men of the West, than our medieval past'. He considered Yiddish to be a 'vehicle whereby the first rudiments of European civilisation penetrated groups that were so isolated in their life of exile that they were even ignorant of the language of the country where fate had called them to live'. He believed that the work set out to demonstrate the vitality of ancient customs that refused to 'dissolve in our own civilisation'. Some scenes, he concluded, could appear 'either grotesque or sacrilegious to our own audience', but gave plenty of food for thought (Introduction by Terracini in ibid.: 6, 8).

In Italy, the translation of the *Dybbuk* was part of a general movement of interest in East European Jewish cultures and the Yiddish culture in particular. January 1929 saw the first performance in Rome by the theatre company directed by Tatiana Pavlova, which presented the world of north-east European

Ashkenazi Jewishness. A few months later when the Habima company reached Italy, even *L'Illustrazione Fascista* described their arrival as one of the greatest theatrical events of the month (Richetti 1961: 9). The tour began in Naples and travelled on to Rome, Florence, Genoa, Turin and Milan. They staged the *Dybbuk*, Leivik's *Golem*, *The Crown of Absalom* by Calderon de la Barca, *The Eternal Jew* by Pinski and *The Treasure* by Shalom Aleichem. On 16 October 1929, the Milanese audience was able to watch their production of the *Dybbuk*. Renato Simoni, who later wrote the libretto for the composer Rocca, was enthusiastic about this 'play of unique imaginative appeal and beauty', but had a few misgivings about the production, although he appreciated it for its pathos, acting and expressive strengths. He reproved it because it lacked 'the gift of measure, that harmonious attribute of the Latins' (Simoni 1955: 259–60).

The performances staged in Turin were of particular significance because they took place in the theatre founded by the industrialist Riccardo Gualino, with a very small elite of intellectuals and artists. The Teatro di Torino was given a permanent orchestra and became an avant-garde theatre of European standing (Tamburini 1966: 157 et seq., 211–13; Bernardi 1970).[38] It did not stage its own productions but imported the very best theatre that the international scene could offer at that time (Morteo 1978: 244–69). It opened with Rossini's *The Italian Girl in Algiers*, and the first concerts in 1925 included eighteenth-century and contemporary music, inspired by Wagnerism and late romantic melodrama, marking a break with the prevailing musical climate in Turin at the time (Fubini 1978: 228–43). During barely six years of activity, it occupied a unique place in the life of Turin as an up-to-date theatre of cultural information rather than an 'experimental' theatre. The greatest theatre in the city, the Regio, was a conservative institution that pandered to the taste of the lower-middle and middle classes of Savoy tradition without trying anything new, partly due to a fear of appointing musicians who were out of favour with the fascist regime (ibid.: 228). The Teatro di Torino swam against this tide by launching a serious cultural broadside against the fascist autarchy, through its openness to the international scene (Bernardi 1970: 43 et seq.). Public response was lukewarm, though: the theatre suffered from an attitude of indifference or even outright hostility. In 1931, Mussolini used the pretext of a financial irregularity to stop Riccardo Gualino's activities, accusing him of fraudulent bankruptcy and sending him to be interned on the island of Lipari.

Gualino had found Habima's performances 'stupendous in expression and measure, marvellous in colour, true magical transformations' (Gualino 1966: 102–3). The performance of the *Dybbuk* at the Teatro di Torino, followed by *Golem*, met with entirely the opposite reaction from the Turinese press. The *Gazzetta del Popolo*, above all, revealed a total lack of understanding not only of the Hebrew language but of the play itself: it described it as a 'strange, dark, grotesque fairytale, hallucinatory and comic', pervaded by 'stifling anguish' and 'mortifying sadness … inert and painful'.[39] The article in *La Stampa* signed 'fb' (Francesco Bernardelli[40]) considered the text 'almost nothing, fleeting, anecdotal', pervaded by a 'strange, tormented, burning and suffocating mysticism … vacuous, deformed and unbalanced', incidentally confessing that he had only a 'vague recollection of the text, which he had read in translation'. These press reactions reveal the contrast between the warm applause from the Teatro di Torino's enthusiastic upper-crust audience (including the Prince of Piedmont in the central box) and the city's incomprehension or outright hostility to the theatre.

There was a strong Jewish interest in the play. Paolo Milano and Dante Lattes[41] wrote a pamphlet published by Teatro di Torino,[42] which contained a history of Habima in the context of the Jewish theatre and emphasised the wish of the Russian company to achieve moments of theatrical perfection (Bertolone 1996: 341–44). The opinions expressed in this pamphlet are particularly interesting when we remember that Dante Lattes was not only a translator who introduced a wealth of East European Jewish literature to Italy between the two wars, but also an organic part of the Zionist movement and recognised by the fascist government as a representative of that movement in Rome. His acknowledgement of the value of the *Dybbuk*, even in the Hebrew version, therefore, had particular value as an assertion of the plurality and universality of Jewishness.

The performances of the Vilna Troupe and Habima, in particular, stayed in the memory of their audiences and were later compared with the performances in West European languages. The two most famous reworkings of the *Dybbuk* were a prose version produced by Gaston Baty in Paris in 1928 and an opera set to music by Ludovico Rocca with a libretto by Renato Simoni in 1934. These works were in French and Italian respectively – languages that were understood by the audiences to which they were addressed. The hybrid aspects were accentuated in these versions since the variety of languages was increased (both versions retained Yiddish terms) and the interpretations of the directors and actors reflected other cultural traditions. In the case of the opera, the musical dimension – present from the beginning of the play in the form of music by Yoel Engel based on the ethnographic collection – represents an additional contamination.

In France, Baty's version of the play staged at the Studio des Champs-Elysées made history.[43] Baty had seen Habima's version, which would resonated with him due to its strongly religious tone, although his own production was quite different: the Habima production interpreted the divine omnipresence as a source of liberation and translated it into light, using pale tones such as white and blue. Baty, on the other hand, set his show in almost total darkness, since he saw it as expressing the hand of human fate (Burko-Falcman 1967–68: 90). The thing that may have struck him in Habima's performance was the insistence on gesture and the expressionistic tendency, which revealed the subconscious and dark forces (Picon-Vallin 1973: 121–22). The play was part of an innovative programme staged by the 'youth theatres', particularly the Cartel des Quatre, founded in 1927 by its four directors, Louis Jouvet, Georges Pitoëff, Charles Dullin and Gaston Baty. The four were united by their concept of a total theatre, where all factors played a part in the show, and which reintroduced the communion between audience and actors. The end of the First World War had been marked by such a renaissance in the French theatre that Paris could boast more than sixty theatres by the mid-1920s, some of which were engaged in the work of renewing their resources and style, partly to meet the challenge of the cinema. The flourishing theatrical life during the years 1919 to 1920 in Paris was part of the revolution that took place in European theatre from 1910 onward (Blanchart 1939). In 1921, Gaston Baty[44] had founded Les Compagnons de la Chimère theatre, named after the bird–woman, symbol of balance between spirit and matter (Cogniat 1953: 13).[45]

According to Baty, the time had come to take the commercial theatre by storm and ring the changes for the European and international avant-garde theatre; his aim was to present the classics in a way that would move the audience and reawaken the spirit of the past. Baty was the right person to stage the *Dibbouk*: with his Catholic background, dominated by Thomist views, he also possessed a good knowledge of Germanic folklore. In practice, his theatre was not strictly Catholic but open to a host of European influences. Baty was an omnipresent and omnipotent director and to him the most important thing was the set design, whose every detail he personally attended to. He possessed an acute sense of the fleeting nature of a theatrical performance, similar to a 'lightning flash, magnificent and short', of which 'nothing will remain' (Baty n.d.: 5).

Critical reactions to the *Dibbouk* were unanimously positive. Everyone praised the production as admirable (Kemp 1928), defining it as Gaston Baty's finest triumph (Strowski 1928), the outcome of great theatrical artistry (Berton 1928), which succeeded in giving the impression of a huge set on a small stage (Brillant 1928). The critics reserved particular praise for the atmospheric lighting, a technique for which Baty was famous (Kemp 1928). Some critics had to admit that despite their disagreement with Baty's inspiration – which in their opinion devoted too much attention to the plastic side of theatre, to the extent that he referred to the authors by the pejorative term 'textiers' – the director had made up for weaknesses in the psychological characterisations of the characters and the dramatic action in the *Dibbouk* by the skill of his settings and the impeccable acting (Carsin 1928: 242–44). Antonin Artaud observed that if the script was only one of the elements of the scene, a form of theatre such as that of Baty preserved the memory of another language, able to use lighting, movements and sound simultaneously (Artaud 1980: viii, 9).

The theme of silence emerged to emphasise that man's conscious life is an intrinsic part of his subconscious and half-waking life (Daniels 1977: 103–12). The fact that the script was forced to adopt a secondary role in an attempt to bring out the subconscious and the invisible[46] aroused the disapproval of certain critics. Others, however, recognised an overall coherence in Baty's work and admitted that everything – the style of the scenes, the timbre and rhythm of the voices, the music and the psalm singing – chimed with the dialogue and the action to express the air of mystery and thus determine a simple and powerful tragedy (Salomé 1928: 465–71). They also mentioned the inclusion of subtle touches of humour in the performance (Brillant 1928), which were true to the original spirit of the work.

The long success of the *Dibbouk* (the production ran in 1928 for 134 performances, and in 1930–31 for another 62) (Blanchart 1952: 35–36, 42) is evidence that Parisians liked the production as much as the critics: the audience being 'surprised at first but soon enthusiastic' (Brillant 1928). This fervour was disconcerting to the critic of a Jesuit review, who was not persuaded by the play's enormous success. In his opinion, what attracted many 'youth theatre' fans to the *Dibbouk* was not at all the religious substance of the play but a theme that was of obsessive interest to new generations: a split personality as it operates in the character of Leah, to such an extent that part of her intimate substance identifies with Hanan. The exorcist Rabbi – wrote the critic contemptuously – followed procedures reminiscent of stage hypnotists and certain 'Freudists', which were really only of interest to 'those jumping on the bandwagon of the subconscious' (Salomé 1928: 471).

However, none of the spectators in the audience found the work unbelievable and it succeeded in immersing the onlookers in a supernatural environment. 'All Paris will tremble with religious anguish and terror', wrote the great critic Strowski (1928). All, but how many of them were Jews? The Jewish theatre-going audience was divided into at least two parts. Immigrants from Poland, Russia and the Baltic states (numerous in the 1920s), who were often tailors or milliners by profession, would have been able to recognise some of their traditions in the play. Such people usually only had a tenuous command of the French language, however, and in any case they mainly attended the numerous Yiddish theatres, and not avant-garde theatres such as Baty's studio (Salomé 1928).[47] The 'Israelites of France' audience, as the integrated community described themselves, would have been attracted only by the first performances because the work described beliefs and rituals unknown to them, which must have appeared heretical to traditionalist Jews and extravagant to secular Jews (Salomé 1928).[48] This was, however, belied by the positive reactions of the Jewish French-language journals, which were a voice for integrated Jews and the attempt to find common roots to both French and Jewish identities (Trebitsch 1998b: 169–95).[49] The Jewish audience was happy to be present at a performance by good French artists in an 'elegant setting', ultimately accepting the exoticisation of Hasidism currently fashionable in Paris (Biélinky 1928: 591–92). The reviewer of *L'Univers Israélite*, a journal set up to defend 'the conservative principles of Judaism',[50] considered Baty's staging 'a great event in the history of Jewish theatre', evoking Habima's version of June 1926 in Hebrew and 'the startled faces of the Israelites in France when faced with the revelation of a new aspect of the Jewish spirit'.[51] Even under such circumstances, the audience hoped that one day it would be able to understand the secret of the *Dybbuk* in French. When the same reviewer had this opportunity, he found that the strangest superstitions were mixed with the most noble faith and feared that the 'neurotic atmosphere' would convey a distasteful and incomplete idea of Hasidic culture. Alongside the 'hysterical, superstitious and – let's admit it – barbaric' element, the reviewer was also, however, aware of a sense of solidarity between all human beings, which prompted him to sing the praises of the 'nation of Israel' (Paraf 1928: 649–51). *Les Archives Israélites de France*, a journal with a distinctly reforming tone, confessed to be quite taken aback by the success of the *Dibbouk*, '[O]ne would have thought that this gloomy play, located in such a strange environment, so far from ourselves in space and mentality, would have repulsed the Parisian public which is so *éclairé* and *frondeur* in temperament'. The fact that this had not occurred was perhaps due to the slightly morbid curiosity of the age for 'the strange and the metaphysical' (Cahen 1928: 23).

When Baty's *Dibbouk* was restaged in 1930, Edmond Fleg[52] – who also considered the prevailing theory underlying the *Dybbuk* to be that of metempsychosis 'originally foreign to the Jewish mentality' (Fleg, '*Le Dibbouk*', in *Masques*, 22) – wrote of the play with enthusiasm, comparing it positively to the Vilna Troupe and Habima productions. Baty, acknowledging Fleg, conferred on the play a universal meaning, despite his success in producing a 'pièce ultra-juive' (Fleg 1930: 428–29). This universalisation was felt as a relief, as though the distance of the particularity of the East European Jewish culture in the previous versions was upsetting to Parisian Jews. Of particular interest was the reaction of the main Yiddish daily published in Paris during that period, the Zionist-sympathising *Der Parizer Haynt*.[53] A long article was written in praise of Baty's production, which was judged to be closer to that of the Vilna Troupe than that of Habima. The reviewer mentioned the 'strangeness' of hearing the play performed in French, but acknowledged that the French actors and director had gone to great lengths to learn gestures habitual to Jewish actors, noting that the very mystic world of Hasidism was to some extent strange. He singled out Marguerite Jamois, the actress who played Leah, for particular praise due to her talent and conscientiousness. His only objection was reserved for the scene with the elderly woman who cries in front of the Torah scrolls at the beginning of the scene in the synagogue, who 'did not seem like a Jewish woman at all'. The play had been a true meeting between cultures, with the French audience becoming infused by a mystical Jewish work and the Jewish audience showing their interest for the performance of the French artists.[54]

In general, the reviews of Baty's *Dibbouk*, which all the critics praised as a perfect depiction of the environment and culture of East European Jews, displayed some knowledge of works fundamental to Jewish culture, quoting Edmond Fleg (Fleg 1928), the Tharaud brothers and Paul Vulliaud (Vulliaud 1923; Tharaud and Tharaud 1927). Sometimes, however, non-Jews revealed contempt for, or a will to distance themselves from, East European Jews, who were perceived to be radically different to Western Europeans. The contrast between the theatrical value and its content accentuated this attitude: the play is 'sad and other-worldly' – wrote a critic – it inspires pity for the 'unfortunate Hasidic Jews who, poor things, have accumulated all these mistakes and organised imposing and horrible rituals ... these ceremonies, these superstitions are odious to our Western souls ... it is something savage ... but what allure! What style!' (Kemp 1928). In the period between the two wars, the anti-Semitism dampened by the First World War resurfaced, but at the same time it became fashionable to display Semitic sympathies. The Yiddish culture made only a minor contribution to this trend. The series *Judaïsme* edited by Fleg and the review *Europe* were two of the rare forums open to the cultural contribution of Eastern Europe (Trebitsch 1998b: 190).

Philo-Semitism was an ambiguous phenomenon. The process of exoticisation that causes certain cultures to be seen merely as picturesque curiosities was constantly at work in the case of the *Dibbouk*: the adjectives most commonly used to describe the text are 'curious', 'strange', 'savage', 'other-worldly'; the music is 'ingenuous, barbaric, striking' (Kemp 1928); the Jews praying in the synagogue are described as having 'greasy robes, hanging locks, pointed beards' (Brisson 1928), while they 'pray piously, swaying backward and forward' (Kemp 1928). Yiddish is defined as 'slang' or a 'curious language, slightly made up and artificial' (Brillant 1928; Salomé 1928). The process of turning art into folklore tends to be a great leveller of everything that is not high culture, absorbing the most disparate traditions: Ansky was referred to as 'a Jew from Vitebsk, gifted and self-taught', while the stage music was alleged to reveal an undeniable parentage between all 'popular' forms of music and with Gregorian chants (Brillant 1928). Part of the exoticism was also a nod to the genre of horror: one of the show's attractions was deemed to be the promise of thrills and nightmares for the ladies (Kemp 1928). This process went hand in hand with that of aesthetisation: the final scene, when a great Rabbi in white satin rants between the judges in black robes, was highly praised for the colour contrast (ibid.).

The appreciation expressed for the actress Marguerite Jamois is significant: reviewers repeatedly stressed the risk to her voice of being forced to cover all the female and male ranges during the scene of possession, when the actress was able to switch suddenly from a soft, husky, almost childlike voice, to a 'cry from the heart, a shriek of terror that stretches her mouth and face while a tremor passes through her body, which twists and is beaten down' (ibid.; Carsin 1928). Antonin Artaud considered that the *Dibbouk* was her greatest creation and that the voice that emanated from her during the 'extraordinary scene' when she spoke in the voice of her dead lover was 'one of the most terrible things' ever heard (Artaud 1980: viii, 178–79):

> The young woman arrives, wrapped in a black shawl, shaken by fits of shivering, short and sharp as though in the grip of tetanus, speaking in a broken, hoarse, frightening voice – an other-worldly voice – her face closed, her mouth twisted, first on her feet, then on her knees, bending before the hail of curses fired against her by the Rabbi (Brillant 1928).

The Jewish press noted the anti-Semitic tones present even in the favourable reviews. Some newspapers went on as if 'the witchcraft of the miraculous Rabbis' was still rife in Eastern Europe and spoke of the *Dibbouk* in the same breath as the repertoire of the Yiddish theatre, whose 'more than mediocre' productions could be seen in the establishments of Belleville and Montmartre (Biélinky 1928a: 591–92).[55] One reviewer deduced from the life of Ansky that the Russian Revolution was in essence a 'Jewish' revolution, in other words destructive, as opposed to the Western revolution, which had been passionately constructive – and went on to draw a distinction between 'our modern world' and 'these prattlings of the Israeli popular spirit', a century behind contemporary Judaism.[56]

Habima, now based in Palestine, returned to Paris for the Paris International Exhibition of 1937 and presented various pieces from its repertoire, including the *Dybbuk*, thus revealing the birth of a new Jewish awareness. The 'dybbuk', who had been wandering through Europe for the past fifteen years, had become the cursed soul that haunted all humanity. Christians and Jews came to see the play to rediscover the authentic atmosphere of Jewish rites and beliefs that they sought in vain in the most orthodox European 'choules' (Goll 1937: 119).[57]

The *Dybbuk* was a good catalyst of attitudes towards Jews and towards Europe, because it was appreciated for its beauty and liveliness, and depicted the world of the shtetl in all its richness but also in its repressive aspects. While secularised Western Jews were accepted, feelings of exoticism and racism or at least a closed form of Eurocentrism were directed towards traditional Jewish cultures, in the sense that they were not considered European. The theme of love acted as a litmus paper that revealed differences and similarities. In New York, it was found absurd that Hanan should fall in love like a 'Western hero', raising his eyes expectantly with his heart beating, pressing the garment touched by his beloved to his breast, because a yeshiva student 'is incapable of this type of expression', as he is 'shy, clumsy, impotent, ridiculous, pathetic, never dramatic' (Samuel 1927). In Paris, it was said that the *Dibbouk* was the Yiddish theatre's great play of love and death, equivalent to Daudet's *L'Arlésienne* for the French. Critical attitudes of this last type presuppose historical and cultural differences in the portrayal of love but accept that essential underlying human feelings are the same. The stress laid on Jewish authenticity, however, accentuated the divide between the cultures, almost as though they were different spheres, and caused the hybrid nature of the work to be overlooked. Far from recognising the *Dybbuk*'s crossover nature, the growing climate of racism in Europe during the 1930s caused the play to be pigeonholed as Jewish, thus denying its claims for the universal nature of passionate love. The attribution of an authentic Jewish character would have taken on particularly dramatic overtones in Italy.

The Musical Dimension

Music was an essential part of the *Dybbuk* from the very beginning (Izaly 2006: 203–31). One of the members of Ansky's ethnographic expedition was Yoel Engel, a composer and collector of Jewish popular songs.[58] Some of the music he composed on the basis of his folk music collection became part of the play, particularly the 1922 Habima production. Engel was responsible for introducing the Hasidic melody on the soul's fall and reascent that constitutes the thread running through the theatrical work and reappears in his suite *Hadibuk* op. 35 (Bardi 2002–3). Engel emphasised dance and choreography in his score. It comes as no surprise that some of the artistic productions of this subject were ballets, because traditional or ritual dance is an intrinsic part of the *Dybbuk*.

In Italy, Lodovico Rocca composed the opera *Il Dibuk*, which won a prize at a competition held between 180 new works at La

Scala and was staged the following year at the same theatre.[59] The Italian composer held off competition from other prominent musicians who applied for the rights to write works on the same theme. These included Alban Berg, who submitted his application in 1927–28, perhaps after seeing Habima's *Dybbuk* in Vienna,[60] and George Gershwin, who saw it in New York and in 1929 signed an agreement with the Metropolitan to set it to music with a libretto by Henry Ahlsberg. Gershwin had already made notes for a folk-opera, and was planning a trip to Eastern Europe to obtain more information about Jewish music, attracted by its essential harmony and an exoticism that combines elements of classical, folk and jazz music. In New York, home to millions of migrant Jews from Eastern Europe,[61] the Diaspora created a fertile environment for the reworking of Jewish music into new forms. Many musicians, singers and folksingers gravitated towards the Lower East Side Yiddish theatres. Works dating from the same period between the two wars include the trio for piano *Vitebsk: Study on a Jewish Theme* (1928) by Aaron Copland, inspired by Ansky's play, and Vladimir Heifetz's soundtrack to Waszynsky's film of 1937; later the ballet *Dybbuk* (1974) and *Dybbuk Variations* for orchestra (1980) by Leonard Bernstein also emerged from the same environment. In the period after the Second World War as well, the theme of the *Dybbuk* was used in many operas and ballets in Europe and the Americas.

The reasons why Rocca was able to snatch the copyright deal from Berg and Gershwin are documented by material in his archive. Until this documentation came to light, various sources had suggested that Rocca had become acquainted with the *Dybbuk* by watching the Habima performance at the Teatro di Torino in 1929.[62] In fact, he came across the play earlier, as Rocca himself had occasion to remark on several occasions.[63] In 1982, he dwelt on the matter at greater length when the *Il Dibuk* was revived at Teatro Regio in Turin:

> One evening in 1927, as I was walking through Turin, I stopped to browse in a small bookshop that used to stand in Via Sant'Anselmo, but is no longer there. I came across *The Dybbuk* by Ansky, a writer who had died in Warsaw in 1920.[64] I felt mysteriously drawn to the book and took it home with me. At first reading, I was fascinated by the play, which resonated with the eternal elements of human pain. 'Were you inspired by the Jewish musical tradition?' 'Not at all', said Rocca, 'everything in my play is made up. The themes, the motifs, the phrases, even those that seem most typical of a certain popular tradition and environment, sacred and profane, are from my imagination. I also made up the choral prayer, using Hebrew words.' (Allegri 1982)

As early as September 1927, Rocca contacted Izaac Grünbaum, a member of parliament in Warsaw who held the rights to the *Dybbuk*. A final contract (in French) was signed by Grünbaum and Rocca on 3 April 1928 in Warsaw. The opera was almost complete by 31 July 1931, despite the trauma suffered by Rocca due to the death in 1930 of his mother, to whose memory he dedicated the work.[65] An exchange of correspondence between the composer and the Italian Society of Authors and Publishers documents his copyright application for the *Dybbuk*.[66]

The composer had asked Renato Simoni to write the libretto, and on 2 January 1928 Simoni signed an agreement to complete the task by June of that year. A few days later, Rocca sent him a closely typed five-page letter in which he expressed his feelings on the *Dybbuk*. Three aspects of the play exercised 'an unusual fascination' on him: 'death, fate and distance'. The composer disclosed his sympathies with Hasidism: 'I have the deepest devotion for everything that is God's creation: I see the sign of divine creation even in plants and the humblest beasts. This atmosphere reigns in the Dybbuch.' Rocca was entirely aware of his intentions, with no historical or philological concern: 'I will use very few Jewish themes: two or three at most. I have no wish to write as an archaeologist or rebuilder. The Jewish atmosphere will come to me "subconsciously", i.e., naturally inspired by the play itself'.[67] Information on the characters in the work followed: Rocca wanted the choir not to be on the stage in the 'melodramatic' sense of the word, but 'offstage like a second distant orchestra at the beginning and end of the work'. The annotations underwent modifications as he worked through the opera with the librettist.

The correspondence between the pair reveals that Simoni consistently failed to meet his deadlines during the years 1928–31. When the libretto was finally completed and published,[68] critics were divided over its worth. According to some, the work was a success only due to Rocca's music, while the librettist's failure to share the poetic values of the original text was harmful to the 'cohesion of the poetic fabric with the musical embroidery' (Gatti 1934: 12). Others thought that Simoni's libretto was a model achievement because it emphasised the wedding ceremony, the dance with the Blind Woman and the final joining of the souls, while suppressing 'superfluous detail', such as the summoning of Nissan's ghost and the intervention of the community Rabbi (Bruni 1935: 1–12).[69] Such aspects were actually very important and their removal altered the spirit of the play,[70] as a comparison between

Ansky's play and Simoni's libretto shows. Simoni reduced (in accordance with the instructions given by the composer) the thirty-three characters to seventeen and added the voice of Nissan, Hanan's father, who is present as a ghost in the play but not as a sound comprehensible to the audience. The librettist made one major change, the addition of a Prologue, which is only spoken in the opera, to explain the background to the story – the pact made between the two fathers before God. Thus the opera anticipates Waszynsky's film, which opens with a sequence depicting the pact between the fathers and the death of one of them.

Simoni removes some of the Hasidic stories from the first act, thus reducing its folkloric documentation value, and Hanan's speech on the magical numbers of the Kabbalah, and also the speech on sanctity in sin, while the quotation from the Song of Songs remains unchanged. The second act is also shortened, but remains essentially similar to the original. The third act was changed the most because it combines what were originally two different acts. Two stories recounted by the Messenger are no longer present, as well as Reb Esriel's speech in praise of Israel. The biggest cut, however, was the trial scene when the rabbinic court sits in judgement of the dead Nissan's charge against Sender and the former makes his presence felt. As a consequence, the character of the Rabbi who translates Nissan's story in the play is also cut. The cuts do away with one of the points where both worlds come into almost physical contact: in Waszynsky's film, too, Nissan is present at the trial as a breath of wind that moves the curtains and the doors. Lastly, Simoni adds lines to the end of the final duet: while the play ends with the song 'the sad soul sinks', the opera continues with a finale that accentuates the glorious rejoining of the couple in God:

> Voices from heaven: ... The pact was made in the presence of the Lord!
> Elohim! Elohim! Holy is the Name! Israel! Adonai!
> And they are married for eternity!
> The holy pact was made in the name of the Lord!
> (Mist and clouds gather in a heavenly vision.)
> Voice of Leah: Let us go, let us go higher! I love you!
> Voice of Hanan: I love you! You are mine!
> Voice of Leah: I am yours!
> Voice from heaven: Still higher! In the name of the Lord!
> And for eternity!
> Elohim! Elohim! Elohim! (Ansky 1957: 61–62)

This type of finale lent itself to Italianisation in a traditional musical sense.

The performance of the opera at La Scala and the production that toured during the period 1934–38[71] met with largely positive reactions. All the reviewers praised the production and emphasised the public success, which saw nine curtain calls at the Milanese first night and up to twenty in other cities.[72] Gianandrea Gavazzeni considered this production to be the most important artistic event of the season, although he criticised the Habanera rhythm that accompanied 'the dance of the spectral shades' as out of place (Gavazzeni 1934b: 222–25). Ildebrando Pizzetti, who had heard the first two acts, sent the author a note of approval.[73] The composers Ghedini and Malipiero also sent their congratulations.[74]

Special Dopolavoro (workers' social organisation) performances were staged at reduced rates, for example in 1937 at the Carlo Felice theatre in Genoa.[75] One particularly interesting case was that of Trieste, where the La Scala production of the *Il Dibuk* was performed in February 1938 (see Fig. 5). Rocca himself was present on the first night and granted an interview to *Il Piccolo*, in which he reminisced about his participation in the 'unforgettable war' and declared his 'wish for his work to be worthy of our wonderful Italy and worthy of Mussolini's age'.[76] On the first night in Trieste, the opera received no fewer than twenty-two curtain calls. While *Il*

Figure 5 Scenery from *Il Dibuk*, La Scala, Milan 1934 (courtesy of the Toso family, owners of the Ludovico Rocca archive)

Piccolo considered the *Il Dibuk* an attempt to reconstruct 'the fundamental elements of a nation's art for a people that wishes to express its own soul' ('v.t.' 1938), the organ of the local Fascist Party spoke of 'a world so far removed from us Westerners (Jewish or non-Jewish), a life so closed in on itself' that 'only those who are born there can understand it'.[77] The performance of *Il Dibuk* in Trieste, a town of great Jewish tradition – a few months before the race laws were introduced – highlighted the fascist regime's contradictory attitude to the Jews and Jewish culture.[78] On the afternoon of Saturday 19 February, a repeat performance was held for the Dopolavoro organisation.[79] This was watched by workers and employees 'with rapt attention', which supposedly revealed the educational role played by the Dopolavoro organisation with regard to modern opera. The *podestà* and the provincial party secretary were present to lead the salute to the Duce from the gallery.[80]

In most cases, reviewers took the authentically 'Jewish' nature of the work for granted,[81] and this gave rise to praise or condemnation according to which side the reviewer was on. *Corriere della Sera* emphasised the will to renew traditional melodramatic forms to 'create a Jewish atmosphere of the people' in a manner that was extremely faithful 'to the practice in surviving ancient synagogues' ('g.c.' 1934). The national Fascist Party newspaper, *Il Popolo d'Italia*, expressed forceful anti-Semitic views, asserting that the legend of the dybbuk was 'a typically exotic expression that has no full reflection in our spirit'. The reviewer compared the Mediterranean spirit to the 'world of misery and spiritual deafness' in which the *Dybbuk* had developed, and contrasted 'two peoples': on the one hand 'a crowd that seethes like filthy worms of different shapes and sizes on the inhospitable, sunless earth beyond our mountains', and, on the other hand, the Italian people, whose art 'is something else entirely' and who must find their way again without being led astray by foreign imports ('g.s.' 1934).

In actual fact, the 'Jewish' nature of the work was the result of exoticising invention rather than of research and revival. This aspect was left ambiguous at that time. For example, Rocca stated that the music in *Il Dibuk* remained 'decidedly Italian in clarity and melodic expression', despite 'penetrating the Jewish soul with passion'.[82] Later, though, Rocca stated that everything was the product of his imagination. According to Pugliaro, Rocca's modal system was based on Eastern themes, sometimes inspired by Jewish touches of generic mid-European origin rather than Hebrew liturgy itself. The reference to Jewish melodic lines passes through intermediate forms such as that of the Jewish musician Ernest Bloch[83] rather than basing itself on a specific reference to the Jewish musical heritage. In general, performers agreed in acknowledging Rocca's ability to absorb the lessons he learnt from Russian opera, using a choir that is reminiscent of Mussorgsky, but they also agreed that he was a unique musician who trod an independent path. Massimo Mila notes that Rocca found in *Il Dibuk* a solution to the problems in which his theatrical vocation had become entangled, and praised the fact that 'the Jewishness of the typical local scenes was entirely made up and idealised' (Mila 1982).

By the mid-1930s, even the Italian Jewish population accepted the authenticity of this version, partly out of ignorance or because the original music was foreign to them.[84] One letter sent to Rocca by a listener in Ancona who had heard *Il Dibuk* on the radio stated, 'I am a Jew and I know the customs and ways of eastern Jews only through literature',[85] but he referred to the 'deep feelings' aroused in him by the music (quoted in Ferro 1998–99: 198). Mario De Benedetti, from Cuneo, probably the translator of the first Italian version of the *Dybbuk*, expressed his deep-felt emotion.[86] The other translator, a medical doctor named Leon Goldfischer, also wrote from Shodnica, Poland, congratulating him 'on the success of your Dybbuk'.[87] A letter from Rocca's brother stated, '[A]ll my Jewish friends are enthusiastic and moved and most of them have listened more than once, nearly always praising above all the faithful sincerity of the synagogue choruses and songs'.[88] Even a Jewish musician such as Max Ettinger fell into the same trap; after listening to the work on the radio and admiring it, he confessed his wonderment that the composer was not Jewish, 'seeming to him impossible that an artist of another race could have penetrated the spirit of the play so well'.[89]

According to the weekly review *Israel*, 'Jewish circles, pleased at the announcement of the performance, are waiting impatiently to listen to the music' at the imminent performance of *Il Dibuk* at La Scala.[90] The next review heaped praise on the work, stressing Rocca and Simoni's reworking of the original story: this was defined as 'a set of apparently heterogeneous and dissociated elements', to which Rocca 'has given a perfect stylistic unity', 'with a noble and religious sense' (Finzi 1934: 5). The preference expressed is significant of the 'integrated' attitude of many Italian Jews and their distance from the cultural universe of Eastern Europe. This was followed by an unsigned piece, the only article from the period to make a specific comparison between Simoni's libretto and the work of Ansky, but to the detriment of the latter: Simoni had stripped bare the play, wrote the author, so that the central message could reach the spectators more directly. The contact with the world of the dead seemed too direct to the Jewish reviewer, who also added, '[M]any Hasidic legends that adorn Ansky's text do not appear in Simoni's libretto which, for its very lack of embellishment, may be said to be a higher drama, from a theatrical viewpoint, than that of the Polish Jewish writer'.[91]

The newspapers in all the cities where *Il Dibuk* was performed in the years from 1934 to 1938 reported the event, publishing detailed summaries of the libretto[92] and reviewing the performance sometimes more than once. Particular attention was devoted to the theme of love, in two different directions: rarely as a reason for connection between the cultures and as the basis for a universal humanity (Bruni 1935: 10);[93] more often as a discriminatory factor. In the former sense, this implied a comparison with the Western tradition of love, which also justified the Jewish story of love and of death: according to Modesto Bruni, the central theme of the drama was not the dybbuk, but love as a spiritual force that fights against evil. It did not matter that the force driving the two protagonists together was not determined by their will, 'because, in this case, the love of Tristan and Isolde, magically aroused by the love potion, would not be the dramatic force behind the Wagnerian work' (ibid.: 10). In the second sense, the love poetry in the *Dybbuk* was linked to the 'gloomy exotic background' and the 'deep and picturesque expressiveness' (Incagliati 1935). 'The eternal theme' of love was translated into the specific theme of Jewishness through the 'transfusion' between two souls in the body of one: '[T]his transfusion ... is known in Hebrew as "*dybbuk*"' (Barbieri 1937). 'It is a sentimental drama', a reviewer stated dryly, although accepting that Rocca had also a strong sense of the grotesque (Ciampelli 1934: 135–38). This term was often used as a substitute for the adjective 'Jewish', because it referred to the world of the synagogue and the beggars in the shtetl. According to Gavazzeni, love was the prime motivating force behind the opera; love expressed 'with a certain very delicate lightness of touch that appeared to us extremely new and unusual', to which the grotesque – aka the Jewish character – is connected albeit on a subordinate level (Gavazzeni 1934a).

Il Dibuk enjoyed huge success, partly due to the numerous radio broadcasts, as we learn from several letters, including one from Camogli dated 15 March 1936 written by a 'parish orchestra leader and organist' who had 'enjoyed it on the radio' and asked for a copy of the work.[94] From a musical viewpoint, however, *Il Dibuk's* success was limited. In Turin, Andrea Della Corte, despite praise for the 'compact, pulsing harmonies, incessant, aggressive chromaticism', reported that the inventive parts 'did not add up a coherent whole' ('a.d.c.' 1935).[95] Audiences sometimes found the work very difficult to understand and sometimes expressed their dissatisfaction with the final scene (Barbieri 1937). Opinions diverged about this: some expected 'a more markedly lyrical language' while instead the expressive tone remained mysterious and solemn to the final note (ibid.). According to others, such as Della Corte, the love duet broke away from the style maintained to that point, 'without rising to the lyricism that would be more appropriate to the drama' ('a.d.c.' 1935).[96] Malipiero wrote to Rocca that in the final act 'there was a little of that divine melody that I consider somewhat too conventional'.[97]

The reservations were confirmed by contemporary critics, who believed that the final duet in the third act harked back to a somewhat conventional model of musical theatre in the ratio between singing and orchestral music (Pugliaro 1986: 95). Mila spoke of 'a Puccinian falling head over heels in love' at the end, which nevertheless seemed to him 'more a lapse in attention than a sign of true stylistic affiliation' (Mila 1982). Waterhouse has underlined the contradiction between the gloomy style of the choral parts with Bloch-like oriental inflections and the dissonant language in the dramatic episodes, while the final duet returns to a more traditional and sentimental Italian style (Waterhouse 2001: 478–79). The finale is definitely at odds with that 'increasingly taut, dry, less lyrical vocalisation' noticeable in Rocca's work and in many other twentieth-century operas, which reveals an aversion for the aesthetics of bel canto and the custom of putting the singer centre stage (Landini 1986: 108). All the critics emphasise – today as in the past – the massive presence of the choir and the tendency to superimpose the melodic line of the choir over that of the soloist, a typical feature of Italian opera in the first decades of the century. In *Il Dibuk*, however, the choir plays a leading role while also serving the purpose of projecting the dramatic perspective of the protagonists (Pugliaro 1986: 100–2).

The influences in Rocca's music have been repeatedly debated. From 1934, Mila observed that his ideal models were Wagner and, above all, Mussorgsky when he wanted to add a colourful picturesque touch. Rocca himself stated that he had been impressed in his formative years by the following operas: Strauss's *Salome* and

Der Rosenkavalier; *Tristan and Isolde* and *Twilight of the Gods* by Wagner; *Falstaff* by Verdi and *Boris Godunov* and *Ariane et Barbebleue* by Mussorgsky (Allegri 1982). Contemporary musical criticism has sometimes overlooked Rocca, dismissing him hastily as a 'composer of original exotic and primitive inspiration moderated by the study of Mussorgsky, Bloch and Pizzetti' (Nicolodi 1984: 457n.). However, Rocca displays a certain originality since he represents a sort of third way between the two main strands of twentieth-century Italian music: realist melodrama and its opponents. In general, Rocca is categorised among the eclectic composers, because he did not come to a decisive and wholehearted turning point.

A few years after the first performance of *Il Dibuk*, the confusion between exoticising inventiveness and 'authentic' Jewishness became extremely dangerous due to the race laws proclaimed by the fascist regime. The composer's relationships with the regime had been good, although not excellent. On the one hand, Rocca was one of the artists (along with Franco Alfano, Alfredo Casella, Giorgio Federico Ghedini, Gian Francesco Malipiero, Ermanno Wolf-Ferrari and Riccardo Zandonai) from whom the Ministry of Popular Culture commissioned theatrical works (ibid.: 20). Other musicians from the same post-Puccinian or 'Eighties' generation – the group who wished to distance themselves from nineteenth-century melodrama in favour of 'pure' instrumental music (Sachs 1987: 19)[98] – were linked in various ways to the regime. These included Pizzetti, signatory to the Gentile manifesto of fascist intellectuals; Malipiero, who dedicated his *Giulio Cesare* to Mussolini in 1936 despite the fact that the latter had banned one of his works in 1934; Luigi Dallapiccola, who changed from a 'fervent fascist' to an antifascist after the race laws (his wife was Jewish) (Petrassi quoted in Sachs 1987: 189) and Casella, who repeatedly expressed his sympathy for fascism despite his polyglot, cosmopolitan nature (Nicolodi 1984: 245 et seq.).

Rocca declared himself to be fascist in opportunist letters aimed at obtaining auditions of his works. On 21 December 1935 he wrote to the Duce's personal secretariat announcing the first night of *Il Dibuk* at the Teatro dell'Opera in Rome, expressing his 'deepest fascist devotion' and 'his greatest desire', as a combatant and artist, that 'our beloved Duce would give him the pleasure of attending this performance' (Nicolodi 1984: 458–89). His wishes were not granted, but the composer received a telegram of congratulations. As early as April 1927, he had asked the Prefect of Bologna to help him in his ambition of bringing one of his works to the attention of the Duce. The Prefect had written to Rome describing Rocca as a 'fascist of extremely pure faith', but the attempt was not successful.[99] In 1937, however, the Ministry of National Education appointed him a member of the Royal Academy of Santa Cecilia in Rome.

Despite his devotion and his status as a former combatant, the race laws were to affect Rocca as well. Circular no. 181 from the Minister for Education, Giuseppe Bottai, on 12 December 1938, established that 'given the views underlying the recent measures on racial protection, it is advisable to avoid the use of classical and modern musical operas by authors of the Jewish race for teaching purposes and in concerts held at royal conservatories and similar musical institutes' (Preti 1968; Basso 1971: Ch. 8). The Turin Conservatory reacted immediately by notifying musical societies that it could not approve concert programmes containing music by authors of the Jewish faith, whether living or dead (Basso 1971: 173). The means by which *Il Dibuk* fell into the category of prohibited works is not entirely clear. Rocca stated later, in 1946, 'the Germans put my name on the list of Jewish musicians (and as you well know, I am not Jewish) for having written *Il Dibuk*: much has happened since then, with possible grave consequences'.[100] In actual fact, this inclusion on the list, though taken for granted by some,[101] was not supported by any firm evidence. According to Leopoldo Zurlo, commissioned by police chief Bocchini to take charge of theatrical censorship in 1931, *Il Dibuk* was forbidden 'simply because the subject was Jewish', without any reference to the origins of the author, who was acknowledged to be 'Aryan' (Zurlo 1952: 242).[102] The list of Jewish composers (cited by Segre 1995: 71; Fabre 1998: 329n.; and Capristo 2002: 378), which mainly contains the names of foreign composers, does not include the name of Lodovico Rocca. Neither does it appear in the German list contained in *Judentum und Musik. Mit dem ABC jüdischer und nichtarischer Musikbeflissener (Jewry and Music. With index of Jewish and Non-Aryan Musicians)*,[103] to which the Italian censors also referred. The composer attempted twice to remove the ban on *Il Dibuk*, the first time by appealing to the then Minister of Popular Culture, Dino Alfieri, and the second time in January 1940, when he appealed to the new minister, Alessandro Pavolini. In both cases, the attempt was unsuccessful, because a note sent by Pavolini to Mussolini on the subject was rejected by the Duce (Zurlo 1952: 244). In January 1938, Mussolini had sent Alfieri an order to 'reduce

Jewish music on the radio' (Fabre 1998: 50–51). The Duce's answer to the statement that Rocca would be 'willing to introduce any changes necessary to remove the appearance of Jewishness was a categorical "no"' (Zurlo 1952: 244). Rocca's flexible attitude was confirmed by his response to the census carried out in the cultural institutions, which he had to respond to in his capacity as a member of the Academy of Santa Cecilia; in the personal record card he completed on 8 September 1938, after stating that he did not belong 'to the Jewish race', he added the wording, 'belongs on both father's and mother's side, *going back many generations*, to a family of Aryan race and Catholic religion'.[104] Others assumed an attitude of resistance to the same racial census, which was aimed at the expulsion of Jews.[105] In any case, the fact that Rocca was appointed the director of the Turin Conservatory in June 1940 confirms the fact that he was considered 'Aryan'. He could not take up his post until October because of bureaucratic problems created by the law on bachelors (Basso 1971: 177 et seq.). He, nevertheless, had to leave the post of director because he did not wish to swear allegiance to the Salò Republic, and did not take his job back until after Liberation, when he remained in office until 1966.[106]

After the Second World War, Rocca's *Il Dibuk* was hardly heard in Italy. In 1947, it was broadcast by radio and revived six years later. In 1949–50, it was performed at the Teatro Nuovo in Turin,[107] with repeat performances at the San Carlo theatre in Naples and Teatro Massimo in Cagliari; in 1957, it was performed at the Teatro dell'Opera in Rome and again in Florence in 1962 and in Turin in 1982, this time at the newly rebuilt Teatro Regio. On this last occasion, a medal was presented to Rocca, who by then lived alone and forgotten, and the work met with great success.

The *Dybbuk*, Link between Different Cultures

This chapter uses the *Dybbuk* as a marker of European attitudes towards Jewish cultures and as a case study of intra-European relationships during the comings and goings from Eastern to Western Europe and back that were common at that time. Such peregrinations were typical of the life of Ansky and were, to a certain extent, also apparent in the attitude of Europeans – Jewish and non-Jewish – who, when they came into contact with the *Dybbuk*, wished to get back to its origins and understand it. The play actually left the confines of Europe, in the wake of the East

European Jewish cultural Diaspora: while theatrical touring companies took it to the United States and Palestine, the medium of cinema took it to a wider audience.

Various film versions of the *Dybbuk* exist, some of which have been lost.[108] The most famous is the film by Michal Waszynsky, *Der Dibek*, shot in 1937 in Poland and produced by the company Fencke Film (Feniks/Phoenix), set up partly with American capital but based in Warsaw (Goldman 1983). In its country of origin, the film was successful at the box office and won critical acclaim, but we cannot discuss its reception in the countries we are concerned with because it was not distributed in Italy and no reactions to the film can be traced in France, where it was shown in May 1938.[109] *Der Dibek* has had as adventurous a life as Ansky himself: it was lost, refound and restored. The film that has been handed down to us today is the result of a recent restoration carried out upon the initiative of the National Film Centre for Jewish Cinema, through an international cooperative venture between various institutes in the United States and in Great Britain. In 1989, the restored *Der Dibek* was shown in New York, where it met with new success (Skorecki 1981: 50–51). The first showing in Paris after the Second World War was of a shorter version: while the restored version is 123 minutes long, the version that the Parisians were able to see from 9 February 1949 at Les Reflets cinema lasted only 100 minutes and prompted a few disgruntled comments about the 'heavy pace, the overly long dialogues and the over-mathematical machine-like movements' ('J.H.' 1949: 14).

The film was shot in a studio in Warsaw and also in a shtetl community, Kasimierz, that often cropped up in Polish Yiddish films due to its precipitous castle: the Vilna Troupe had used it for a performance of the *Dybbuk* in the 1920s. The director Michal Waszynsky,[110] author of the first Polish talking film and of many other successful productions, was commissioned to direct the film.[111] *Der Dibek* is part of the tradition of Yiddish cinema, even though this was not the language spoken by Waszynsky, whose mother tongue was Ukrainian.[112] Anti-Semitism was prevalent in the surrounding environment and the extras were picketed almost every day by hooligans who waited for them on the streets around the film studio. The film's first night was held on 25 September 1937 in a leading Warsaw cinema, the Sfinks. The film's run lasted for nearly three months and it attracted an audience of both Jews and non-Jews. Although many critics were enthusiastic, Waszynsky was also accused of displaying 'the nauseating dregs of pathetic kitsch'

(Hoberman 1991: 284). The film was shown in New York for seven weeks from 27 January 1938. Here, too, it aroused mixed reactions, ranging from enthusiasm to hostility.[113]

The film *Der Dibek* was able to include enactments of events that were technically impossible to stage in the prose play. It was a work of great cinematic strength that differed considerably from the play, which begins in the middle of the story, when Leah and Hanan are already a couple. A substantial Prologue was added, which set the scene for the story: the pact between the two young men who were to father Leah and Hanan; the death of Nissan by drowning (which concludes with a scene of a black hat floating on the waters of the river)[114] and the pain of his wife; the birth of Hanan and of Leah; and the death of her mother. The differences did not end here, however, because the Prologue did much more than introduce a linear progression: it is picked up again at the end when the tale comes full circle. At the end of the film, the Rabbi we saw in the beginning reappears (now visibly older) with the same characters from the community, who wear the same ritual garments. In cinematic language, the visual circularity expresses the theme of predestination. The second difference between the play and the film version concerns the strong erotic impact of certain images, such as that of Hanan naked in the ritual bath invoking the powers of evil, and the two scenes in which the unconscious Leah is carried first by Hanan, who lays her on her bed and looks on her lovingly in a scene of great intimacy, and then by the Messenger, who takes her from the cemetery once she has addressed her invitation to Hanan's grave. The film also indulges in certain stereotypes that are less obvious in the play: we are struck, for example, by the film's insistence on the stereotypical depiction of the wealthy and miserly Jew who repeatedly rejects his daughter because he needs to count his money. When the dead girl or dead people appear, the music predictably becomes typically oriental. This stereotyping reveals a lack of flexibility towards the issue of Jewish characterisations and a dangerous concession to the climate of the period, though the Jewish characters are not as sinister in tone as they were to become a few years later.

Lastly, Waszynsky's *Der Dibek* uses non-realistic cinematographic techniques to represent the supernatural: the Messenger – who opens the film – appears and disappears many times and Hanan emerges from his grave in a similar manner. During the *danse macabre*, the face of death changes into that of Hanan. Some felt that Waszynsky was too free with his use of movie magic (Hoberman 1991). According to others, the use of fade effects does not simply imply a sense of the supernatural and the miraculous but makes the film more specifically Jewish, because it alludes to nomadism (Fink 1996: 375–86). The fade in and out effects used for the character of the Messenger could be seen as film versions of the treatment given to the prophet Elijah's disguises in the theatre. In any case, the fade effects are less important than some of the other visual effects typical of cinema, such as the recurrent theme of the window as a medium between different environments and worlds: it is through a window that we see Hanan in his fatal bath, or Leah looking out from inside her house. Lastly, a window is used to represent the mirror of the rich man who can no longer see others but only himself. Overall, however, the film version follows the play closely and may be categorised as an example of expressionist cinema: gestures are exaggerated, the actors move their whole bodies to express their emotions, with slow and almost discrete movements that the camera freezes into pictorial attitudes. The slowness is accentuated by the music that gives the gestures their pace (Scheer 1986: 74). Distinctly theatrical aspects also remain in the film, such as the series of dances and the numerous songs. Lastly, Waszynsky retains Ansky's ethnographic approach in scenes of religious and domestic ritual: candlesticks, drapes, meals at home and in community settings – and references to folk superstitions.

It is difficult to evaluate the film's impact in contemporary Europe. The diary of Joseph Goebbels, then Minister of Propaganda and Information for the Third Reich, contains the following entry on his reactions to *Der Dibek* on 18 February 1942:

> This film is intended to be a Jewish propaganda picture. Its effect, however, is so anti-Semitic that one can only be surprised to note how little the Jews know about themselves and how little they realise what is repulsive to a non-Jewish person and what is not. Looking at this film, I realised once again that the Jewish race is the most dangerous one that inhabits this globe, and that we must show them no mercy and no indulgence. This riff-raff must be eliminated and destroyed. Otherwise it won't be possible to bring peace to the world.[115]

Naturally, *Der Dibek* could not be shown in Europe between the end of the 1930s and the first half of the 1940s. However, during that period, it was distributed in North America and seen by a young Jew of Eastern European origin who lived in Winnipeg, Canada: even today he remembers his feelings and those of others on seeing this depiction of a conflict that affected him because it set the young against the rich and powerful. He was particularly moved by the scene of the mirror turned into a window.[116]

The film's subsequent reception dwelt on the differences between the prose play and the film, maintaining – in my opinion unjustly –

that the film partly destroyed the original dramatic structure to restore the events to their chronological order (Ertel 1979: 54–56), and did not tie in with the action in the play again until the scene of the *danse macabre*. The 'over-folkloric' use of songs and artificial references to a Christian heritage in the subtitles were also criticised: 'Sind' is not 'sin' and 'Herem' is not equivalent to 'exorcism' (Marienstras 1981: 58–60). The entire film reveals the way the story weaves in and out between the play script and the visual action: from the play written by Ansky to the oral tradition of the theatre, with repercussions on subsequent literature, particularly on a short story entitled 'Austeria' written in 1966 by Julian Stryjkowsky, a Polish Jew. This story, in turn, forms the basis of the 1982 film *The Inn* by Jerzy Kawalerowicz (also Polish, though not Jewish but brought up amongst Jews) whose film reflects the cinematic vocabulary of Waszynsky's *Der Dibek* (Safran 2000).[117]

The link between love and death is also at the heart of the film in a visual sense. Waszynsky took the *danse macabre* from the version performed by the Vilna Troupe, which had made a strong impression on previous theatre audiences,[118] and made it central, bringing together love, death and dance. The Dance of Death, which originated in France as a response to the Black Death in the fifteenth century, was then introduced to Germany and to Jewish marriage ceremonies. The custom of staging a *dance macabre* – *toytntants* in Yiddish – at a wedding was shared by Christians and Jews during the Middle Ages, when it was used to symbolise the final struggle between love and death (Safran 2000). The oral tradition dates back much further; the film choreographer Judith Berg still remembered her grandmother's stories on the subject (Hoberman 1991). According to this tradition, death and marriage are connected and the respective rites strengthen this analogy (Goldberg 1996). By depicting the image of the young bride dancing with the figure of death, Waszynsky's film does not simply refer to a ritual within which love and death are inseparable, but sends out a more general message that life leads inevitably to death. The film image is more poignant because it shows us, through fade effects, that when Leah dances with death, she is actually dancing with the image of the man she loves. Unsurprisingly, the most striking and famous scenes in the film are those of the marriage ending in the *danse macabre*, when Leah dances with a figure in a skull's mask that gradually changes into the face of Hanan (Bartov 2005).

According to Konigsberg, *Der Dibek* is a kaddish, a prayer for the dead, that calls on us to remember them by looking beyond the world's limits and losses. Above all, however, it affirms the eternal presence of death and the way that death permeates the world of the living (Konigsberg 1997: 22–42). *Der Dibek* presents us again with the dilemma between duality and unity, polar opposites that are reunited in the two scenes of the wedding party and the dance with death. The dance is a symbol of the combination of unification between the 'two worlds' (Poma 1982: 215–18). Several commentators have emphasised that the film reveals features of the horror film genre – in the claustrophobic visual style created by 'closed-frame imagery' (Konigsberg 1997: 26)[119] – which is in general dualistic because it depicts the struggle between good and evil, where the victory over evil is always short-lived. The Devil is the product of Christianity's binary world view; in Hasidism, which is pantheistic, the dybbuk represents the drive towards fusion. Fusion between man and woman, between human and the divine, taken from the Platonic myth on the two parts of the original androgyne that strive to be joined together. *Der Dibek* is a film about the overcoming of separations and divisions, which instils particular terror for the very reason that it represents the realisation of something that is both desired and feared (Konigsberg 1997).

This spirit of connection persists in versions of Ansky's play that date from after the Second World War, which, nevertheless, do away with or reduce the direct relationship between the love story and the story of the dybbuk. In the last sixty years, the theme of the dybbuk has been employed several times to represent the conflicting relationship between cultures and their reciprocal influences. The best-known instances are that of the dybbuk invented by Romain Gary[120] in his 1966 novel *La Danse de Gengis Cohn*. This triumph of the grotesque is the story of a Yiddish-speaking Jewish comedian who was exterminated in Auschwitz and then appears as a dybbuk to one of his assassins, a former SS officer who became a police chief. The dybbuk, Gengis Cohn, makes the police chief's life impossible, appearing to him day and night in what he calls his stage costume: striped pyjamas, a black cloak with the yellow star very visible, hair standing on end above his waxy face, his body stained with the mud in which he and his companions had had to dig a pit before they were massacred. He has become 'the immanent, omnipresent, latent, assimilated Jew, who is intimately mixed with every atom of the German air and earth' (Gary 1967: 15), through a process aptly described in the Yiddish phrase, 'the dead grasp the living'. In this 'assimilation' (ibid.: 82) of cultures, the police chief, who when he is drunk speaks of settling in Israel, is forced amongst other things to recite kaddish for the dead. A series of murders perpetrated in the area under the police chief's jurisdiction are found to have been committed by a couple – a noblewoman and her gamekeeper – who allegorically represents Humanity in her marriage with Death. Death preys on the lovers of Humanity, who is never satisfied by such sacrificial loves, because what she is seeking, namely, true love, does not exist. The crimes take place in the Forest of the Spirit (Geist). Gengis Cohn repeatedly attacks art and culture, which swallow anything. The state of Israel signs a cultural agreement with Germany and the police chief offers brotherhood to his dybbuk, who flees in terror before the new Nazis who are no longer anti-Semitic. In his flight, he encounters someone else exactly like him; none other than Jesus, come back to the earth after two thousand years to discover that 'it was not worth getting himself crucified' (ibid.: 309). Immediately afterwards, Gengis Cohn finds himself dressed in a camouflage suit with his police chief, now American, who has just bombed a South Vietnamese village by mistake. In his final transformation, however, Cohn follows Humanity 'dragging Her enormous cross' in the place where the Warsaw ghetto stood (ibid.: 353).

Faithful to his traditional task, the dybbuk Gengis Cohn has brought two cultures into contact, but love no longer exists: the hybridisation between cultures is seen in its sinister aspects, as an assimilation devoid of memory, shared by tall, blond, young Germans heading for the Olympic Games, very similar to the Israeli *sabras*, who have never known the ghetto (ibid.: 28–30). However, a reconciliation takes place: the contamination between the dybbuk and Christ, both Jews, represents the persistence of the sacrifice made by the 'humanists' in their pursuit of indifferent humanity. The tragedy of the age is expressed by the final sentence of the novel, spoken by Cohn as he is doubled beneath the cross, 'nobody cares'.

While the dybbuk took the form of a bitter and sarcastic memory of the Shoah in 1960s Europe, more recently in the United States the character has been politicised to meet the requirements of identity politics. The protagonist of *The Dyke and the Dibbuk* by Ellen Galford (1993)[121] is a female dybbuk named Kokos, who emerges after two hundred years from the tree in which she had been imprisoned by magic after persecuting a young woman who had betrayed her promise of loyalty to her woman friend by marrying a student of the Torah. Kokos tracks down a descendant of the woman through the Central Dybbuk Office: Rainbow Rosenbloom, a taxi driver in London, lesbian, film critic and niece to a set of aunts who are intent on getting her back on the straight and narrow. Kokos also adopts the same course of action, to overcome Rainbow's 'strangeness' and eventually force her into marriage in order to ensure a descendant to persecute. However, Rainbow meets the daughter of a Rabbi who has studied the holy books in secret and learned the spells for casting out dybbuks. Once Kokos has been exorcised by her, she joins other dybbuks to work in the cinema, while Rainbow and her lover dine happily with the maiden aunts.

This feminist, lesbian treatment stands alongside Tony Kushner's interpretation of the *Dybbuk*, which tempers the theological setting with a note of protest. Kushner's world-famous piece *Angels in America* describes the life and death of some gay men and harshly condemns US society at the time of Ronald Reagan. He then adapted Ansky's *Dybbuk* (Anski, Kushner and Neugroschel 1998) and staged it in 1995 and 1997. True to his inspiration, Kushner interprets the final exorcism as a symbolic disaster representing the end of tradition. At the end of the play, after driving Hanan from Leah's body, the Miropol Rabbi asks the scribe to read a page that has miraculously appeared in his book: this announces that 'the wonders of the coming age' – the Holocaust according to Kushner (Bloom 1998: 109–112) – will sweep away all his magic, the martyred dead will build up and the history books will speak of piles of bodies. The Rabbi then entrusts the Messenger with a message for God: even though his love has become only abrasion, derision and excoriation, 'we will find Him, however few we are, tell him we will find Him to present our lament' (ibid.: 101, 106).

The figure of the dybbuk takes on specific meanings throughout European history, when the Jews were alteratively treated as invaders or cruelly invaded. Attributing a fantastic and other-worldly dimension to the invasion means that 'horror' is deemed to be the play's dominant genre. Although this seems to me a reductive assumption, I recognise its value if we accept the viewpoint of a 'horrific European space, full of preconceptions about Europeans, which is invaded by the long-awaited Jewish *Dybbuk*'.[122] The strength of this interpretation is that the invaded side speaks with a free voice, the only possible voice in a besieged community. From this viewpoint, the entire work in all its various versions can be seen as a dybbuk that is attempting to invade Europe – Fortress Europe – bearing its message of communication between worlds that appear far from one another although they are adjacent in space.

Versions of the *Dybbuk* updated to the second post-war period emphasise this message and help place the character at the centre of deep-seated problems in contemporary society while relegating the theme of love to the background. This also happens in the version of the *Dybbuk* created by Abraham Yehoshua in his novel *The Liberated Bride* (2003). The novelist imagines a festival organised by 'partially liberated' Palestinians in Ramallah, in which a female student who is a pupil of the protagonist performs a scene from the *Dybbuk* as an act of peace and love. The scene is that of the exorcism, in which the young woman herself portrays the Rabbi, and the *Dybbuk*, with its focus on the female 'Arab Rabbi', is performed with a simultaneous translation into Arabic. On this occasion, the contamination expresses hopes of an opportunity for communication between two bloodily divided communities. While Yehoshua's version is moving because of its utopian content, it can only confirm the growing difficulty that our contemporary society, so deeply troubled by conflict between cultures and religions, finds in imagining the relationship between public and private. Our society is no longer able to place the love that the couple feel for one another in a public context, while the original play draws regenerative strength from this inclusion.

Notes

1. Baldur von Schirach, leader of the youth wing of the German National Socialist Party and *Gauleiter* of Vienna; cited in Lipgens (1982: 103).
2. Similar claims are also made by R. Patai (1959).
3. *Encyclopaedia Judaica* (1980–81; entry 'Love': 523–30). The first part of the entry is signed by 'E.Li.', Edward Lipinski, a lecturer at the Catholic University of Louvain.
4. Ibid.; second part of the entry 'Love', 527, signed 'E.B.B.', Eugene B. Borowitz, Rabbi, lecturer at the Hebrew Union College – Jewish Institute of Religion, New York.
5. Hasidism arose during the second half of the eighteenth century between Poland and Lithuania and spread throughout the Pale of Settlement. Its features were ecstasy, mass fervour and charismatic leadership: optimism and joy came from the conviction that everything is contained within God, adored through the bodily and worldly dimensions of existence. One of the great figures of the movement was Israel ben Eliezer Ba'al Shem Tov (1700–1760). Hasidism facilitated the spread of the Haskalah movement, a form of Jewish Enlightenment that arose in the eighteenth century and represented a significant challenge to rabbinic authority. The Hasidic tradition is very important in music, song and dance, which are considered a higher form of prayer. On Hasidic and Kabbalistic music, see Idelsohn (1929: 321 et seq.). Forms of neo-Hasidism occur in the twentieth century in Europe (for example in Martin Buber) and in the United States; see *Encyclopaedia Judaica* (*Enc. Jud.*), *S.V.*, Vol. 7, 1390–1432.

6. According to Biale, the metaphor of unhappy love is used in the literature produced by the Maskilim at the beginning of the twentieth century to indicate political impotence; see Biale (2002: 833).

7. Yiddish is the vernacular language of the Ashkenazi Jews, spoken in the Middle Ages by the German, Bohemian, Moravian, Polish, Lithuanian, Ukrainian and Byelorussian communities, but also extending to Alsace, Holland and northern Italy up to the seventeenth century. Written using Hebrew characters, it gave rise to a wealth of literature, first religious and then profane. Since the time when the Jews left the ghettos, Yiddish was defined as slang or dialect. Since the end of the nineteenth century, however, its rehabilitation was started by pioneering intellectuals. It is estimated that in 1935 it was spoken by ten to eleven million people, a number now fallen to one to two million. The Yiddish language was ruthlessly suppressed by Nazism and Stalinism; see Baumgarten (2002).

8. Biale (2002: xix) prefers the term 'acculturation' to that of 'assimilation', which is often used for such processes. The term 'integration' further underscores the process of fusion. These terms vary according to their period and also the social and political actors involved. In this chapter, I use 'assimilation' with reference to the 'Israelites of France'. Integration has been defined as 'cultural neosyncretism', which does not rule out an element of integration in the state, and assimilation as an extinguishing of diversity; see Molinari (1991: 40–42; 119). This terminological question refers back to conceptual problems. Scholars differ over the question of whether it is possible to apply the category of colonialism to the condition of Jews as a minority: Biale sees only some analogies (ibid.: xxii), while J. Boyarin (1994: 424–52) considers that the situation of the Jews after the Second World War reveals strong similarities with the post-colonial situation.

9. Although many forms of the term exist, namely *dybuk*, *dybbuk*, *dybuq* (in Yiddish *dibek*), the Anglicised form *Dybbuk* has been used (in italics starting with a capital letter to indicate the play in general, over and above its various versions, and in lower-case roman type to indicate the spirit), except when referring to the title of specific productions, such as Baty's *Dibouk*.

10. Yiddish narrative and poetry contains numerous references to the fantastic and the supernatural, but fewer appear in the theatre. Two important exceptions are Ansky's *Dybbuk* and H. Leivick's *Golem* (1921).

11. See the stories contained in the anthology of Yiddish literature by J. Neugroschel (ed.) (2000: 59, 61, 73, 129, 365, 368).

12. According to the teachings of Ba'al Shem Tov, 'a man should desire a woman so much that he purifies his material existence through the strength of his desire', *Enc. Jud.*, Vol. 7, 1410.

13. The collection was donated firstly to the ethnographic museum in St Petersburg, then part was transferred to the Museum of Odessa, which was raided by the Nazis during the Second World War. The fate of most of the collection is uncertain; see Krupnik (1992–94: 16–23). The St Petersburg State Ethnographic Museum's current core is partly made up of Ansky's material; see Uritzkaya (1994: xvi, n. 37).

14. The legend illustrates the spiritual unity of the universe; see Safran (2000: 761–81).

15. Shlomo/Solomon Seinvel/Zanvil/Zainwill Rappoport/Rapaport/Rapapport (1863–1920) was born in the village of Tchaschniki/Chashnik near Vitebsk, Chagall's birthplace, in Belarus, where his father worked as the agent of a land owner and his mother kept a tavern. There are two hypotheses about the pseudonym: according to one, he based it on the name of his mother, Anna, abbreviated to Ansky; according to another hypothesis, it was suggested by the writer Gleb Uspensky; see Roskies (1992a: xvi). Vitebsk was a stronghold of orthodox Judaism with Hasidic influences, but it also had a significant Haskalah presence. Vitebsk formed part of the area known as Pale of Settlement, the only land where Jews were legally authorised to reside within the Russian empire. In 1897, nearly five million Jews lived there, some 94 per cent of the Jewish population of Russia. The area, which became increasingly overpopulated and fed an incessant wave of emigration towards the United States, was abolished by the Russian Revolution of 1917. See *Enc. Jud.*, entries on 'Ansky' and 'Pale of Settlement'.

16. The expedition was financed by Baron Naftali Horace Günzburg, banker and philanthropist. It collected a huge amount of art works and artefacts from seventy shtetls, and also magnetophonic recordings of music, songs and interviews: 2,000 photographs, 1,800 legends, 1,500 Purim songs and mysteries, 500 rolls of folk music, 1,000 tunes without words, innumerable proverbs and beliefs, 100 historical documents, 500 manuscripts and 700 objects.

17. It has been found in the library of the St Petersburg Theatre; see a translation by C. Stevens and G. Safran in Safran and Zipperstein (2006: 374–435).

18. Konstantin Sergeyevich Stanislavsky (1863–1938), theatre director and theoretician, founded the Moscow Arts Theatre. Werses suggested that an initial version of the *Dybbuk*, in 1912, was in the rationalist mould, because it did not contain the character of the Messenger or Meshulah; see Werses (1986: 115).

19. Bialik (1873–1934), the poet of the Jewish nationalist renaissance.

20. Werses is the main opposer of this tradition: it was impossible, he maintained, to rewrite the entire text in one week. Ansky must therefore have worked on the old manuscript and the changes must have been due only to his incessant desire to improve the text. The comparison carried out by Werses between the Hebrew and the Yiddish texts reveals that the second one is closer to the original folk tale. While Yiddish is more expressive and emotional, using diminutive and pejorative terms, Hebrew is more linear and neutral, but restores the spirit of the original Talmudic expressions.

21. In 1909, he gave a speech on the difficult fate of the writer, particularly the Jewish writer, 'whose soul is torn. He lives on two streets where three languages are being spoken'; see Werses (1986: 122).

22. According to Werses, the Yiddish in the *Dybbuk* consists of at least two layers: the language imbued with Hebrew spoken by the *batlanim*, the Rabbi and the Messenger, and the Volhynian dialect full of Slavic expressions spoken by the common people. Both languages are juxtaposed to comic effect, something that is lost in translation.

23. Neugroschel observed that translating Yiddish into English involves a risk of assimilation and both the translations and the adaptations may be imperialistic in nature (Neugroschel 2000: xii).

24. The questionnaire on the ethnographic expedition included 2,657 questions, including many relating to death, for example 'Do bodies leave their tombs at night?' A sequence reveals its accuracy:

2034. Do you know stories about the soul of a dead person who cannot find peace and changes into a dybbuk and enters a living person?

2035. What does a dybbuk normally say or shout?

2037. Does a male dybbuk enter a woman and vice versa?

2038. Do most of the dybbuks enter a man, a woman, a young person, or an old person?

2039. What antidotes or remedies may be effective in this case?

2040. Does a dybbuk hurt people [apart from the person it enters]?

2041. Which *zaddikim* were famous for their ability to exorcise dybbuks? (ibid.: 55–56)

25. All the *zaddikim* quoted by Ansky in the *Dybbuk* really existed; see Aslan (1979: 156–241, 162n.).

26. Bogdan Chmielnicki/Khmelnitski (1595–1657), head of the Cossacks during the insurrection against Polish rule in 1648 that led to the destruction of at least 300 Jewish communities. Other pogroms occurred in 1654, 1881, 1903 and 1905–6, during the First World War, and the Russian Civil War.

27. In a groundbreaking essay of 1914, Ansky defined the oral tradition of Jewish folklore as a product of the Jewish spirit, exactly like the Bible (Biale 2002: 843).

28. The first expression of Yiddish theatre can be found in the tradition of the Purimshpil, performed from the sixteenth to the twentieth centuries.

29. According to Sandrow (1977: 17), Jewish law prohibited portraits, sculptures and even masks. Biale (2002: xix–xx) expresses a doubt that this ban ever really existed.

30. The choice of Sephardite pronunciation corresponded to the belief that this was closest to the ancient pronunciation; see Luzzatto (1992: 120).

31. This part of the accusation is understandable due to the Messianic and other-worldly nature of the Messenger.

32. The theme of the grotesque was present in the carnival-like tradition of Purim theatrical performances, featuring big noses, protruding eyes and open mouths; see Belkin (2003: 29–43). The first version of the set design incorporated a mixture of cubist–futurist elements and traditional Jewish folk motifs into the set; see Kampf (1984: 38–39, 207n.).

33. Tadeusz Kantor (1915–90), Polish set designer and director.

34. Habima, by now the national Jewish theatre of Palestine, returned to London in 1937; see Eric (1937: 581).

35. If we accept the distinction proposed by P. Stefani (2004: 15 et seq.), the 1928 pamphlet expressed anti-Judaism towards the Jews on the basis of religion, while the Nazi pickets expressed anti-Semitism informed by a racist ideology.

36. This was a production staged at the Neighborhood Playhouse, described in *Theatre Arts Monthly*, New York, 1925 (vol. 9, 8 August 1925) and again in 1926 (vol. 10, 1 January, 2 February, 11 November). The production was resumed in 1937 (*Theatre Arts Monthly*, vol. 21, 2 February 1937). In 1932, the Dallas Little Theatre also produced a *Dybbuk* (*Theatre Arts Monthly*, vol. 16, 7 July 1932).

37. B. Terracini (1886–1968), a prominent comparative philologist and linguist.

38. Gualino was surrounded by intellectuals such as the art historian Lionello Venturi and the painters known as 'the Turin Six', including Felice Casorati.
39. 'La Compagnia Ebraica "Habima". *Dybuk* Leggenda di Ansky', in *Gazzetta del Popolo*, 9 October 1929.
40. Drama critic of the newspaper from 1928, author of 'thousands of theatre reviews'; see Damerini (1965) and Calcagno (1970). 'Al Teatro di Torino: Habima' appeared on 9 October 1929.
41. Paolo Milano (1904–88), critic and essayist, migrated to the United States after the introduction of the race laws; see Treves (1981: 63) and Gonsalez (1991). Dante Lattes (1876–1965) was one of the first Italian Zionists, Rabbi in Trieste and author of numerous writings. On Lattes, see Bidussa, Luzzatto and Luzzatto Voghera (1992) and Marzano (2003).
42. Teatro di Torino, Società degli Amici di Torino, *Ottobre 1929. Rappresentazioni Straordinarie del Teatro Ebraico Habima.*
43. In the French translation by Marie-Thérèse Koerner, produced by André Boll, with music by Léon Algazi and set by Baty; see Brillant (1928: 618–30). The *Dibbouk* was revived in a new theatre in 1929 and a longer revival was held at the Théâtre de Montparnasse in 1930–31 (Blanchart 1952: 74).
44. Baty (1885–1952) studied with the Dominicans, then at the University of Lyon and subsequently in Munich. In 1910, he visited Russia and, in particular, Stanislavsky's theatre and the Meyerhold Studio. February 1922 saw his first production for the Chimère, one of the first alternative theatres, which lasted until 1924. He created some one hundred productions, including many staged with marionettes; see Blanchart (1939) and Simon (1972).
45. La Chimère was the theatre that Leo Ferrero tried in vain to copy in Italy. Ferrero gave the show *Têtes de Rechange* by J.-V. Pellerin a positive review in the 1925–26 season; see Ferrero (1927c: 55).
46. According to Baty, 'everything that can be expressed by lighting, gesture, colour, movement, sound or silence I need not describe in words'; quoted by Cogniat (1953: 25).
47. Yiddish theatre in Paris, which dates back to 1889, represented for the immigrants a kind of homecoming, but also a focus for hopes and dreams. There were sometimes as many as four Yiddish shows running concurrently in various theatres throughout the city between the 1920s and 1940s; see Frydman (n.d.). According to some estimates, in the 1930s 65 per cent of Parisian Jews spoke Yiddish; see Legris (2000).
48. According to J.-L. Amselle (1996), the process of Jewish integration since the French Revolution gave rise simultaneously to emancipation and the attribution of a common religion to French Jews from different countries. At the end of the 1930s, the French Jewish community was the largest in Western Europe, with more than 300,000 people, of whom 100,000 were originally Yiddish speakers; see Becker and Wieviorka (1998: 108) and Weil (1998: 11).
49. The French Jews often believed they were culturally above immigrants who spoke Yiddish, an idea that was reinforced by class differences; see Weil (1998: 134).
50. J.-C. Kuperminc (1998: 141) states that the journal was inspired by the Consistoire, the institution responsible for religious public records and matters of worship. *L'Univers Israélite*, 1844–1940, and *Les Archives Israélites*

de France, 1840–1935, were the two main journals among a host of French Jewish publications.

51. Tristan Bernard (1866–1947), novelist and playwright.

52. Fleg (1874–1963), a pseudonym of Flegenheimer, was a supporter of Zionism since the end of the First World War, during which he was in the Foreign Legion. In 1921, he took French citizenship and was awarded the Legion of Honour. In the period between the two wars, he edited the series *Judaïsme* for Rieder (which included an anthology of Yiddish stories in addition to the *Dibbouk*).

53. On the Yiddish press in Paris, see Weil (1998: 124 et seq.) and Kuperminc (1998: 140–42). On Zionism's lack of popularity in France up to the Second World War, see Nicault (1998: 130–35).

54. 'A spectator, *The Dybbuk* on the French Stage', in *Der Parizer Haynt*, 15 December 1930.

55. Maurice Courtois-Suffit gave a description of these 'obscure theatres specialising in Yiddish art' (article published in *Temps*, 8 August 1927, then in *Masques*, 11). Biélinky takes issue with Courtois-Suffit, without naming him (Biélinky 1928b: 651).

56. Written by G. de Pawlousky in *Journal*, quoted in Biélinky (1928b: 651).

57. See also the theatrical notices in *L'Univers Israélite* (93, 6, 8 October 1937: 83), and Schnéour (1937).

58. Yoel Engel (1868–1927), originally from the Crimea, critic, lexicographer and folklorist, published Jewish folk songs and founded the Society for Jewish Folk Music in 1908; see Idelsohn (1929).

59. Rocca (1895–1986) studied law and, at the same time, devoted himself to musical studies. He took part in the First World War, when he was awarded the Military Cross. He was director of the Turin conservatory from 1940 to 1966. Rocca's compositions for small orchestras include *The Proverbs of Solomon* (1933); his operas include *La Morte di Frine* (1920) and *Monte Ivnor* (1936–7), inspired by *The Forty Days of Mussa Dagh* by F. Werfel. *Dybbuk*, composed in 1928–30, is his best-known opera.

60. Alban Berg (1885–1935) applied for the rights to the *Dybbuk* between composing *Wozzeck* (1921) and *Lulu* (1928); see Bardi (2002–3). Habima had come to Vienna in May–June 1926, arousing much excitement; see Dalinger (1998: 148–49).

61. Approximately two million between 1881 and 1914, and the migration continued at a rate of approximately 4,000 per year. In 1924, another 1,250,000 arrived, almost all orthodox Jews driven out by pogroms and the new anti-Jewish laws following the assassination of Tsar Alexander II. Several found work in the New York Lower East Side factories, the area where the Yiddish concert halls and theatres were located.

62. For example Levi (1982: 210–14). See also Pugliaro (1978–79: 87).

63. For example in Trieste, in 1938; see 'Il Maestro Lodovico Rocca Parla del Suo Dibuk', in *Il Piccolo delle Ore Diciotto*, 8 February 1938. The Rocca archive contains a cutting from *La Stampa*, 23 May 1927, and a list of 'Books received' which includes De Benedetti's and Goldfischer's translation, which are evidence of Rocca's interest from this early stage.

64. This must evidently have been the first Italian translation, *Il Dijbuch (Tra i Due Mondi)* (1926).

65. Letter from Rocca to Grünbaum, 9 July 1931.

66. Letters from the Italian Society of Authors and Publishers (SIAE) to Rocca dated 22 April 1930, 7 October 1930, 23 June 1931; SIAE receipt for 60 lira paid by Rocca on 12 June 1931.
67. Letter of 7 January 1928.
68. *Il Dibuk*, Leggenda Drammatica in un Prologo e Tre Atti di Scialom Ansky, adapted by Renato Simoni (Ansky 1957). Simoni (1875–1952) was an author, drama critic, theatre director, cinematographer and librettist.
69. Simoni's libretto was also praised by 'g.c.' (1934).
70. Ferro (1998–99: 54 et seq.) observes that Simoni plays up the human and sentimental aspect, to the detriment of the character of the Rabbi and the religious aspect.
71. The cast included Leone Paci (Reb Sender), Augusta Oltrabella (Leah), Silvio Costa Lo Giudice (Hanan) and Alessandro Vesselovsky ('the Messenger'). The conductor was Franco Ghione. During the period 1934–38, the La Scala production was staged in Rome, Turin, Genoa, Trieste, Warsaw, Cracow, Zegreb, Chicago, New York and Detroit.
72. For example in Turin in January 1935, where Bruni reported that the work was greeted with enthusiasm.
73. Note of 24 March 1934, Milan; see Ferro (1998–99: 191).
74. Note by Giorgio Federico Ghedini of 25 January 1935, declaring his enthusiasm 'for the magnificent *Dybbuk*' (Ferro 1998–99: 197). G. Francesco Malipiero wrote from Asolo on 14 March 1936: 'I find your *Dybbuk* truly remarkable for all the expression you maintain and obtain using your own resources' (ibid.: 203–4).
75. '*Il Dibuk* di Ludovico Rocca Stasera al Carlo Felice', in *Il Secolo XIX*, 9 March 1937.
76. 'Il Maestro Lodovico Rocca Parla del Suo *Dibuk*', in *Il Piccolo delle Ore Diciotto*, 8 February 1938.
77. R. Maucci, in *Il Popolo di Trieste*, 11 February 1938.
78. According to E. Collotti, during 1937 Mussolini and his regime decided to introduce state anti-Semitism, but the press campaign of that year did not yet have a clear operational outlet. Mussolini's first statement on 16 February 1938 prolonged the debate, 'by simultaneously denying and affirming the will to embark on a new policy toward the Jews' (Collotti 2003: 58). As far as anti-Semitic cultural persecution was concerned, Fabre observes that until halfway through 1936 no distinct action was taken but acts of hostility were apparent (Fabre 1998: 42–43).
79. *Il Piccolo di Trieste*, 15, 16, 19 February 1938.
80. Ibid., 20 February 1938.
81. For example G.M. Ciampelli (1934: 135–38): the round dance scene is 'authentically Jewish'; the laments in the synagogue transport us to an 'authentically Jewish' world.
82. In *Israel*, XIX-24–25, 28 Adar–6 Nissan 5694/15–22 March 1934, 5. The weekly magazine *Israel* was set up in Florence in 1916 with the aim of providing information on Jewish community life and promoting a revitalisation of the Jewish cultural world; see Bidussa (1992: 155–279). *Israel* operated up to 1938 (when it was banned by the fascists) and started up again after the Second World War.

83. Bloch (1880–1959), a US composer of Swiss origin.
84. This is a deduction based on the fact that no documentary evidence exists to support the existence of one or more distinctly Jewish folk corpuses; see Acanfora Torrefranca (1996: 477–93).
85. The letter is dated 29 January 1934, but this is probably a typical New Year mistake and the actual date is 1935.
86. As well as 'all the pleasure of listening to your *Dybbuk* and reading in the eyes of other spectators the same emotion', 31 January 1935 (Ferro 1998–99: 198). Mario De Benedetti (1894–1963) was included on the list of Jews resident in the province of Cuneo at midnight on 22 August 1938, reported by A. Muncinelli (1994: 35n.). The Cuneo Public Records Office contains records of a Mario De Benedetti born in Turin in 1894, a post and telegraph inspector, who moved from Cuneo to Genoa in 1939. In March 1939, he was temporarily excluded from the persecutions.
87. Letter of 27 March 1934. Goldfischer, who had heard the broadcast from La Scala, signed himself a 'former student at the University of Turin'.
88. Letter signed Gino, 4 February 1935 (Ferro 1998–99: 200). The opera was broadcast several times on the radio. Another letter from Gino, dated 28 March 1934 from Casale notes, 'yesterday evening, with the libretto at hand, I followed your entire work on the radio more calmly and with less anxiety' (ibid.: 193).
89. Ettinger was forced to emigrate to Switzerland in 1933, where he composed music banned by the Reich, such as oratorios and cantatas on Jewish themes. From a letter of G.L. Brezzo to Rocca from Switzerland dated 2 February 1937; see Ferro (1998–99: 37).
90. '*Il Dibuk* alla Scala di Milano', in *Israel*, XIX-24–25, 28 Adar–6 Nissan 5694/15–22 March 1934, 5.
91. 'Il Libretto di Renato Simoni', in *Israel*, XIX-26, 13 Nissan 5694–29 March 1934, 5–6.
92. For example *Il Messaggero* of 28 December 1935 published a detailed plot of the opera '*Dibuk* di Lodovico Rocca che Andrà in Scena Stasera'. Similarly in '*Il Dibuk* di Ludovico Rocca Stasera al Carlo Felice', in *Il Secolo XIX*, 9 March 1937. The same practice was followed by *Il Piccolo di Trieste*, 9 and 10 February 1938. A large spread on Rocca and the opera could also be found in the official newspaper of the Trieste Fascist Party, *Il Popolo di Trieste*, 10 February 1938.
93. '[N]ot a Jewish drama, not a Hasidic drama, but a human drama' because it centres on love.
94. The letters testify that *Dibuk* was broadcast on the radio on 27 March 1934. Several telegrams dated January 1936 were sent after another radio broadcast of the work. These include a letter from Salomea Handwerger dated 4 April 1934 from Tomaszow-Maz, Poland, which reports the success of the work heard on the radio by 'thousands of Jews in Poland'.
95. Article preceded in *La Stampa* of 22 January 1935 by an unsigned article, 'Stasera al Regio *Il Dibuk*', which explained the plot and features of the *Dybbuk*.
96. Alberto Basso maintains that *Il Dibuk* was performed at the Regio theatre in Turin only for local reasons, due to the 'blindness to the new European musical output' demonstrated by the theatre management (see this chapter, Part II), and that it constituted one of the very few 'modern productions' performed during the period; see Basso (1976: 578, 609).

97. Malipiero, from Asolo, 14 March 1936, quoted in Ferro (1998–99: 203).
98. Amongst these, Alfredo Casella and Gian Francesco Malipiero were musically the most radical while Ildebrando Pizzetti, Ottorino Respighi, Franco Alfano and Riccardo Zandonai were more conservative. Politically 'more or less all of them were followers' of fascism, according to Goffredo Petrassi, interviewed by Sachs (1987: 188). 'The music-loving tyrant', as Nicolodi (1984: 293) described Mussolini, exercised constant control over Italian music and musicians, combining censure with commissions.
99. Letter from Rocca dated 13 April 1927, in Nicolodi (1984: 457).
100. Letter from Rocca to Guido (probably Guerrini) dated 10 August 1946. In a letter to Pietro Montani dated 1952, Ferro, 'Il Teatro Musicale di Ludovico Rocca', 58, Rocca emphasised, '[I]f anyone really wants to know, I descend on my father's and mother's side from Catholic families that go back a very long way'.
101. According to Basso (1971: 83), Rocca's inclusion among Jewish composers was the result of an error 'by a zealous bureaucrat'. The list included some 900 authors with names presumed to be Jewish (approximately 90 were 'Aryan'; see Fabre (1998: 362, 370–71).
102. Other works on Jewish subjects included *Salmodia* of 1934 and *I Proverbi di Salamone*, which were also banned.
103. Begründet von (established by) H. Brückner, C.M. Rock, *3. Auflage, Bearbeitet und Erweitert von H. Brückner*, Munich: H. Brückner-Verlag, 1938.
104. I thank Annalisa Capristo for her courtesy in allowing me to consult this file.
105. The National Ministry of Education survey form was completed by musicians such as Casella and Dallapiccola (who had Jewish wives), Cilea, Petrassi, Pizzetti and Zandonai; see Capristo (2002: 34). Toscanini and Croce were amongst those who refused to complete the form.
106. Letter from Rocca dated 27 October 1946, from Turin, reported in Ferro (1998–99: 220).
107. With only three performances and little public success. Massimo Mila wrote a positive review in *L'Unità*, 26 April 1949.
108. According to Bardi (2002–3), several films on the subject of the *Dybbuk* were shot in Poland in the 1930s but were destroyed during the anti-Semitic persecutions. After the Second World War, in the United States, a TV film was produced in 1949 and a TV adaptation in 1961. In Israel, versions included a documentary and a film in the 1970s. Recently, Agnieszka Holland, who had seen Wasynsky's film in Poland in the 1950s, made her own *Dybbuk*, presented in 2003 at the Zeitgeist International Film Festival, San Francisco.
109. On 21 May 1938, *Parizer Haynt* carried an advert for the film, which was shown in two Parisian cinemas: Studio Parnasse and Studio Monceau. The former was a cinema that specialised in avant-garde films in the cosmopolitan quarter of Montparnasse.
110. Born in 1904 in Volhynia, he studied theatre first and then became assistant to Friedrich Murnau; from 1929 he made about forty films. Between 1949 and 1952, he was Orson Welles' assistant on *Othello* and the artistic director for US productions such as *Quo Vadis* (1951) and *Roman Holiday* (1953).

After 1960 he moved to Spain, where he died in 1965. See Hoberman (1991); C. Singer (1998: 49–58).

111. The screenplay for *Der Dibek* was written by Alter Kacyzne and Andrzej Marek, with advice from the Jewish historian Meyer Balaban. The production hired the best Yiddish actors, who were also skilful musicians. The part of the Miropol Rabbi was played by Avrom Marevsky, who had played in the Vilna Troupe. Some of the other actors were also veterans of various theatre productions, such as Dina Halpern, who played the part of Leah's aunt. The roles of the two lovers were played by Leon Liebgold and Lili Liliana (who learnt Yiddish for this film).

112. In the 1930s, the use of Yiddish in cinema was forced out by the majority languages. Therefore, the use of Yiddish in a film suggests a degree of intimacy; see Singer (1998: 54–55).

113. According to Joseph F. Coughlin (1938: 47), the film, which was shown at the Continental Theatre in New York, in Yiddish with subtitles in English, aroused 'evident public appreciation'. On the other hand, *Variety* (2 February 1938, 17), found that the film, based on 'medieval superstitions' was 'very tedious in parts' and 'somewhat absurd'.

114. Safran (2000) interprets this scene, and a similar scene in the film *Austeria*, to be symbolic of the future disintegration of the community.

115. 'Dr. Goebbels at the Cinema', in *Sight and Sound*, 19 (NS), 6, August 1950, 235.

116. Professor Avrom Udovitch of Princetown University, whom I thank for his reminiscences.

117. According to Safran, Stryjkowsky (who spent his childhood in Galicia) had seen the dancing Hasidim in the Habima production in Lvov in 1927, and half a century later paid his debt of gratitude by including the dance scene described in the short story.

118. Twenty-five years after the theatrical production, the operetta composer Joseph Rumshinsky still remembered the dance of death, 'they were more than actors ... it was something I had never seen or heard before'. Sandrow, *Vagabond Stars*, 219.

119. The film was classified as 'one of the greatest horror and fantasy films of the 1930s' by D.M. Kimmel (1990: 44–45). Others speak of a 'romantic ghost story', the final message from a condemned community 'that has an obsessive potential', see *Hollywood Reporter*, 315, 1, 8 November 1990.

120. Romain Kacev or Kacew was born in Vilnius in 1914 of a French mother and a Russian father and moved to France when he was thirteen years old. He was a pilot during the Second World War and fought with the Resistance. He married the American actress Jean Seberg, who committed suicide in 1979. Gary also killed himself, in 1980.

121. The book won the Lamda Literary Award.

122. Giuseppe Lauricella, unpublished communication, which I thank the author for granting me permission to quote.

Chapter 6

'Notre Mère l'Europe':
Giorgina Levi and Heinz Arian

In La Paz I watched amazing coloured sunsets over Mount Illimani, which is nearly seven thousand metres high. The sky in winter is a really bright blue when the weather is fine on that side of the world. At night I used to gaze at constellations like the Southern Cross, so different from our own. We loved to watch the stars, galaxies that were easier to see and brighter than our own Milky Way. I loved that great sense of space, that solitude, that immensity. In Europe we have no such great spaces. Everything is larger than life, everything is impressive, everything is infinite, very beautiful. It is a new feeling ...

At time went by, the nature of my homesickness changed. At first I was homesick for my own road, my own neighbourhood. I listed all the streets that crossed via Cibrario so that I did not forget their names, the neighbourhoods. Then I felt homesick for the whole city, and in the end I felt homesick for all Italy. I longed to go back to that country at all costs. Then by the end, I yearned for Europe. From my home to the whole continent, which represented a culture, a civilisation, a way of living.[1]

Giorgina Levi was born in Turin on 15 August 1910 into a family of socialist and communist tradition. Her mother, Gemma Montagnana, married Marco Amadio Levi, who started his career as an office messenger but ended up as a bank attorney. A man of varied cultural interests and a fine photographer of urban and rural landscapes in Piedmont,[2] he survived fascism and Nazism, but lost a brother and many relatives in the extermination camps. Giorgina's maternal aunts and uncles included militants such as Clelia, Elena, Mario and Rita Montagnana, who was married to Palmiro Togliatti for many years. Mario, whom Giorgina considered her political mentor, was one of the most important labour leaders in Turin, first

Figure 6 Giorgina Levi in Bolivia (courtesy of the Fondazione Istituto Antonio Gramsci in Turin)

Figure 7 Heinz Arian in Bolivia (courtesy of the Fondazione Istituto Antonio Gramsci in Turin)

for the Italian Socialist Party (PSI) and then for the Italian
Communist Party (PCI). He was a prime mover in the Peace and
Bread movement of August 1917, then one of Gramsci's colleagues
in the 'New Order' (G. Levi 1979: 481–550). He was repeatedly
imprisoned by the fascist regime and later forced into exile in Paris,
Brussels and Moscow, where he continued his activities as a
communist organiser.[3] The history of the Montagnana family is an
outstanding example of the ability to wed Jewish tradition with
involvement in the antifascist struggle and the Resistance (G. Levi
and Montagnana 2000). With the exception of Giorgina's
grandmother, the family's Jewishness was generally a lay form
separate from religious practice but loyal to cultural practices; a
form which has been termed 'humanistic European Jewishness'.[4]

Giorgina Levi graduated in June 1933 with a thesis on 'The
Social and Political Evolution of Jews in Piedmont from the French
Revolution to Emancipation (1789–1848)', which included
references to the condition of Jews in Europe. Her supervisor was
Professor Francesco Lemmi, lecturer in modern and Risorgimento
history in the Turin University Arts Faculty. According to
Giorgina, the janitor Mangiarotti – a legendary figure in the Arts
Faculty – heard the medievalist Giorgio Falco declare in the closed-
door session that the thesis should not be awarded a First under any
circumstances. According to her, Falco acted in that way because he
was a Jew himself and 'he was already scared … And then he went
and got himself christened when the race laws were introduced'.
Lemmi harboured anti-Semitic prejudices of his own but, aware of
the cleverness of his student (who retains fond memories of him
despite her shabby treatment, 'my much-loved history professor',
'my great teacher' [Filippa 1990: 20]) replied tartly, 'if I had three
Firsts, I would award all three to this thesis'.[5] Various articles taken
from the thesis were published (G. Levi 1935, 1937, 1952), and a
book came out many years later (G. Levi Arian and G. Disegni
1998). After the Second World War, the author, who had become a
Marxist in the meantime, felt some embarrassment about the
conclusion of her thesis, which she judged a 'Zionist rant'.[6] In
actual fact, it was a discreet allusion – at the end of a long quotation
on the risks of assimilation following the emancipation of the Jews
– to the movement that aimed to rebuild the Jewish nation in the
land of Israel (G. Levi 1933 and interview GL2).

The young graduate did a little supply teaching in high schools.
From 1934 to 1935, she was given a steady post at the Liceo
Lagrange high school in Vercelli, at that time known by its

Italianised name of Lagrangia. The following year, when she was successful in the state examinations, she held a teaching post in Grosseto for a short time but was soon called back to the same *liceo* in Vercelli, where she taught Italian, Greek, Latin, history and geography. Finally, she transferred to the Liceo Alfieri in Turin, where she stayed from 15 November 1936 to 16 October 1938, the date 'on which she was suspended from teaching following measures issued by the fascist government in defence of the Italian race'.[7]

The figure of Giorgina Levi finds its context in the history of the emancipation of Jewish women in Italy, which swung between claims based on gender and the claims of the community from the mid-nineteenth century onward. From the end of that century, when all Italian Jews finally gained civil and legal equality, Jewish women were affected both by this process and the general emancipation of Italian women. The 'matter of Jewish women' cropped up particularly in the fields of education and charity (Miniati 2003: 96–97). Because the family remained the centre of gravity during the process of Jewish emancipation in Italy, Jewish women were burdened with a dual identity: Jewish mother and Italian mother. The cultural interaction between the Jewish community and Italian society meant that many Jewish women were active in organisations such as the Unione Femminile, at least until the Associazione Donne Ebree d'Italia (ADEI) was founded in 1927. The drive towards education and better career prospects for women came mainly from the upper echelons of Jewish society, but also filtered down to young upper- and lower-middle-class Jewish women, who turned to the state education system to achieve their goals (ibid.: 266–67). Giorgina Levi may be considered an example of this process, in which her social origin and lively intelligence prompted her to take into account the ideological movements of the period – Marxism and Zionism – and to put motherhood on hold to pursue her professional and, later, her political career. She has always protested, even in her recent book (G. Levi 2005), her 'proletarian' roots, recalling that some men did not invite her to dance at the Purim dances in the 1920s 'because you had to have the amount of your dowry written on your dress'.[8]

Despite her secular habits, the Jewish community gave her the opportunity to meet her future husband. Giorgina Levi remembers that she saw Heinz Arian for the first time in January 1934 at a meeting of the Jewish Youth Organisation of Turin. Later she met him at a religious social event, when they danced together. Heinz Simon-Saul David Arian was born on 17 June 1912 in Berlin, where his father ran a chemist's shop, a popular career for Jews in Austria and Germany (Leimkugel 1999). In 1931, after graduating from high school, he registered with the Berlin University medical faculty. He was expelled in July 1933, after being mistreated – when closed numbers were introduced in German universities limiting the proportion of Jewish students to 1.5 per cent – because he was a Jew and also suspected of being a Marxist (he had been active in the League of Human Rights, but he was not yet a communist). He would have liked to have continued his studies in France, but if he had done so he would have been forced to resit his high-school graduation exam, whereas in Italy he was let off one year of university studies. He visited various universities and decided to stay in Turin, partly due to the welcome he was given by Professor Giuseppe Levi, to whom he was sent by his teacher in Berlin, the psychiatrist Hertzberg (an example of the way the international academic networks operated throughout the history of Jewish emigration). Arian was registered as a member of the permanent population in the city of Turin Registry Office from 14 November 1933.[10]

He was, therefore, one of the first of the many Jewish exiles who were forced to leave German-speaking countries from 1933. Many of them moved to fascist Italy, because in April 1933 the Italian Minister of Foreign Affairs declared his willingness to accept German Jews provided they did not play a militant role in antifascist political parties (Voigt 1995: 25–32). No distinction was drawn between Jews and other foreigners, no visa was required and a residence permit was relatively easy to obtain. Although anti-Semitic rumblings became louder in Italy during the period from 1933 to 1938, it was not until 1938 – coinciding with Hitler's visit in May – that exiles began to be stopped and detained in any number. As a general rule, the living conditions in Italy were relatively good for Jewish exiles compared with other countries (Voigt 1989). A census of foreign Jews (which Arian was obliged to complete) taken in September 1938 counted 2,803 German citizens. Much greater numbers (tens of thousands) passed through Italian ports on their way to the Americas or Palestine. Their choice of Italy was partly determined by the traditional appeal of the country, which made it the most popular destination for cultural tours from Germany, and also the fact that Italy represented a staging post on the way to other destinations. Some of the intellectuals and artists involved found the time they spent in Italy very stimulating, and it often inspired them to produce pioneering works in their own respective academic areas (Hausmann 1995: 175 et seq.). In this way, fascist

Italy 'with its mild and tolerant face' represented a 'good refuge' for some years and granted the exiles a calm breathing space, only to betray them and show its true face of 'shameful cowardice and complicity' (Bevilacqua 1995: 246).

Heinz Arian is not listed in the registers of German intellectual émigrés (*Biographisches Handbuch* 1980), which include some 8,600 scientists, artists, politicians and writers forced into exile after 1933, because he was a student at that time and not as well known as others who were a few years older. The exodus of intellectuals, which totalled approximately 25,000 people, represented only a small part of the overall exodus, which is calculated to have amounted to some 330,000 people from Germany, 150,000 from Austria and 25,000 from Sudetenland (Möller 1984: 38). Among the 1,851 foreign university students present in Italy in 1933, the students registered with faculties of medicine accounted for no less than 64.9 per cent, made up of Polish, Hungarian and Rumanian Jews who resolved the problem of the anti-Semitic 'closed number' rules in their own countries in this way (Voigt 1989: 220). The figures for 1934 were 1,124 German Jews in Italy, mostly in Milan (500), Trieste (204) and Rome (73), with only 17 in Turin (ibid.: 518–19).

Once a certain amount of initial mistrust, with which young foreign exiles often had to contend, had been overcome, Heinz Arian soon assumed an important role in the Turinese Jewish community. He regularly attended Oneg Shabbath, an occasion when young Jewish people met on Friday evenings to discuss topics of Jewishness and Zionism.[11] He worked at a clinic in Torre Pellice as he went on with his studies. A correspondence immediately sprang up between himself and Giorgina that was to last many years. A note dating from February 1934, stamped 'Stud. Med. Heinz-D. Arian', reveals that the young exile still had an uncertain knowledge of the Italian language: '[I]f you would allow me to spend an evening in your company (or – when you prefer – an hour or so some afternoon); if so, tell me a day and a time on which you will be free. Please accept the expression of my most sincere respect and also a friendly poignée de main.'[12] Their relationship was on a formal footing but the young man obviously already had more seductive intentions. He used French to draw attention to his cosmopolitan side. He continued to address her using the formal 'Lei' during the coming months even as the relationship became closer. 'We went for walks, we went to concerts, he gave me books, flowers', thus Giorgina remembers this first stage of their relationship (Filippa 1990: 11). Arian (who soon Italianised his first name to Enzo, as a first sign of his changing identity and broader sense of belonging) always signed his letters using only his surname, even as the years went by (this is why I often refer to him only by his surname). At the beginning of April, the young man had to go to Nervi to see a relative: 'I would really like to see you once more before I leave. Would you like to come to the concert at the Liceo Musicale tomorrow evening?'[13] Arian took advantage of his trip to visit Genoa, which he found 'marvellous after the terrible rectangularity of Turin', and the Ligurian coast. He continued to write to Giorgina from there, still addressing her using the formal Lei, but in a more confidential manner, 'Chère Giorginette', quoting Rilke and deploying a typical array of weapons from his seductive armoury (he was a very cultured man and this meant he could easily slip from one language to another and from one quotation to another), but also displaying an extreme, almost boyish desire to be consoled, supported and looked after. Arian described the natural beauties interspersed with literary reminiscences, but soon admitted:

> But despite all this I am alone, alone, alone. I am (for the first time in my life) absolutely overtaken by a primitive and weak desire to talk to somebody about beauty and sadness – someone who knows how to understand and respond. – Try to come Giorgina. For ten hours or for twelve – 'gute' ['good'] hours. Try to forget those who could stop you living your life 'das leben, wie wir es begreifen, und wie sie's nicht verstehen'[14] (do you remember these words of Rilke?). Try to forget also that terrible (but so useful and necessary) 'sois considérée!' ['have a good reputation'] of Beaumarchais. ... I hope you are not cross with me for having asked you once again – I am well aware you won't come. ... At least write me a few nice words. Will you? Farewell Giorgina.[15]

His correspondent evidently did not accept the invitation because a few days later Arian continued in the same vein, trying to persuade her that a trip to Genoa 'would not harm your good name in the least'. In the same letter, he quoted a great European whose fate was to be somewhat similar to their own: Stefan Zweig, who had to emigrate first to England and then to Latin America (where he committed suicide with his wife in 1942) to escape Nazi persecution. Something Giorgina had said made him remember 'some words by STEFAN ZWEIG [capitalised in the text], which made such a deep impression that I am repeating them here':

> – nimmst du ein einzeln Ding aus deinem Leben
> und wigst es in der hohlen Hand –
> so fuehlst du drin das grosse Dunkel beben.[16]

Giorgina jotted down the Italian translation of some words. She was learning German, encouraged by her correspondence with him. On 19 April, still writing from Genoa, Arian fell back on a tried and tested lovers' formula, 'You wouldn't really care if I killed myself – because you do not know me well enough yet'. He then immediately launched into an almost page-long explanation of the idea of *Erlebnis*, 'enhanced enjoyment – no longer an episodic event', which ends up being a lesson in its own right, 'enjoyment *ravit* [enchants, seduces]; an Erlebnis *ébranle* [shatters]. Understand?' His tone recalls an attitude common amongst educated European men that could be defined as a Pygmalion complex, in other words a tendency to instruct and educate, almost to mould his mate intellectually, a tendency not always appreciated by Giorgina. While this attitude allows Arian to enrich their relationship by falling back on his European cultural heritage, it nevertheless reinforces a hierarchical situation whereby the male is superior and turns this superiority into one of the cornerstones of their relationship. Be that as it may, *Erlebnis* was to become one of the codewords that the lovers used to express the idea of an intense experience, 'One Erlebnis with you / Are two / Erlebnisses' wrote Enzo on the back of a Teatro alla Scala ticket, 1934–35 season.[17]

Their relationship underwent a qualitative leap after this, when Giorgina, who observed the puritanical traditions of the Turinese 'Sanpaolini'[18] communists (though her family did not have any say in what she did with her time), allowed her misgivings to be overcome: 'I did not give in to him for months. I was a girl of rigid morality' (Filippa 1990: 13). This was a philosophy she shared with her sisters and was strengthened by the discipline of her studies, to which she devoted herself with passion. Used as she was to this attitude, Arian's influence led to a sort of reawakening and an explosion of feelings in the young woman. It is almost as though she herself was taken by surprise, as though she had really not expected such a great love, while at the same time it is evident that her initial caution did not arise out of narrow-mindedness. Giorgina threw herself generously into their love, though a sort of inbred restraint often kept her from the ecstatic terms so dear to her companion. She wrote to him, for example, in a dedication of 17 June 1937: 'Even if you had only taught me how to understand music, and in particular the music of J.S. Bach, just for this you would be a great friend. Thank you, Giorgina.' The appellation 'friend' is certainly a very high compliment in Giorgina's language (see, for example, the opening of a letter dated a few years later, written from Oruro on 6 June 1943, 'My dearest sweet friend'), but it does not immediately suggest passion. Enzo, on the other hand, abandons himself sometimes to orgies of words and quotations, often in Latin.

As the relationship progressed, the tone of Enzo's letters changed and hence also the salutations he used:[19]

> Geliebtes Maedel (beloved maid) (18 June)
> Ma chérie (19 June)
> mon aimeé (7 August)
> berachah mia (my blessing) (17 August)
> canzone mia (my song) (28 August)
> vas eburneum (ivory vase of my joy) (1 September)
> Mein liebes Schatzele (my little love-treasure) (3 September).

Their correspondence on language learning also took on the tones of love, for example the full male, female and neutral declinations of the expression 'mein Liebster' appeared in a table that Arian wrote on 19 June.

Very few of Giorgina's letters have remained, but some echoes of her own letters can be inferred from those of her correspondent, who on 19 June put to rest some feelings of insecurity she had about her letter writing: 'Of course you haven't written anything stupid – protested Arian – your comments about the cobbler, the market and the shoes are a charming description of the provincial atmosphere in Alessandria that – at least I hope – will not poison you.' One of the few letters that has been saved of all the many written by Giorgina dates from 20 August 1934. She had recently returned from a camp in Cortina, where she had spent a week of 'almost total Jewishness'. It was the fourth Jewish camp, in Chiave, a village near Cortina d'Ampezzo, which that she described as having a 'lovely atmosphere' due to its spiritual leader, Rabbi Castel-bolognesi (Savaldi 1988: 1121–52).[20] The Jewish camps were held regularly from 1931 to 1938 and were a sort of summer holiday for young Jews of various social origins, who were able to combine recreation and sport with the study of Judaism (Della Seta and Carpi 1997: 1343). Giorgina found two long letters and the present of a book on the bedside table of her room in Turin from Arian, who was in Berlin visiting his parents: her long letter sent in reply (eleven pages) opens with the greeting 'Heinz, my dearest' and goes on to tell him gleefully about her stay in the Jewish camp where she divided her time between worship ('Shabbath celebrated in a meadow under the stars. Many hymns sung, very beautiful') and day trips, to the Luzzatti refuge or to drink water from the Mount

Sorapis glacier. She also reported that she had managed to pick out 'our constellation' in the clear mountain sky. Her new acquaintances included a student of natural sciences, who was 'ugly' (Giorgina perhaps wanted to reassure her far-off lover), 'intelligent, good, serious'. He decided to give her a book for her birthday and they went to buy it together: '*A House of Gentlefolk* by Turgenev', but she had to pay for it herself, because the student did not have any money ('I hope he gives me the money back: so far I have not seen anything'). Giorgina also noted with a certain satisfaction that at the camp 'everyone came to confide their affairs of the heart to me'. 'Heinz! I am so sorry! On Saturday at the camp you could not let yourself be seen putting pen to paper. I spent all day Sunday on the train. Even now it is late in the evening'.

Giorgina asked Enzo why he was always troubled and no longer able 'to be froh' ('happy'): 'I take your forehead and I kiss it, I stroke your hair, I kiss your hand, I place my hand on your heart.' Then she immediately gives us a glimpse of her upbeat, sunny nature, slightly miffed by compliments passed to her on the street by 'many old men – grey-haired – singes!' ('monkeys') as she walked around Turin in the morning, 'perhaps because I am very suntanned':

> I was alone, but in a really good mood, I don't know why, I was light as a bird, rested, I was thinking all the time, I had so many sweet words to say to you in my mind. I was as happy as when I was walking with you by my side in the hills, when we were sitting close to each other in Regio for the concert, and even during the 'böse Stunden' ('bad times').

The letter also showed concern about the physical condition of Enzo, who tended to neglect himself ('are you eating enough?') and did not forget to mention some news of her everyday life: '[T]his afternoon I gave two private lessons: I keep getting new students'. Lastly she apologised for the 'huge untidiness' of her letter and stressed her feelings of insecurity in the face of her correspondent's great learning:

> You write such beautiful letters that I am often, deep inside, ashamed of my own, so flat, superficial, as if written by a very average little girl. Your pages keep me company almost as if they were your hand: they are like a beautiful book, like a verse from Dante, like a gorgeous piece of music. I need to read them several times to tease everything out of them: every time I always discover something new.

The letter delighted Arian ('the best I have received'), who lost no time in replying: '[N]o – dear – I can't be froh any more – if you are not close to me. I have taken root inside you'.[21] He was still at his parents' house in Berlin, from where he went to visit his paternal grandmother in Katowice (Kattowitz in German) in Silesia. The letter he wrote from this city was headed 'Katowice Europe 9.9.1934', underlining the European nature of this Eastern area but also making implicit reference to its disputed nature: despite a referendum taken in 1921 that had expressed a preference for the city forming part of the German Reich, in 1922 it had become part of Poland. This was the reason Arian used the Polish form of the city's name and why he later preferred to say he came from his father's birthplace. During this period, it seems that as far as Arian was concerned 'Europe' was restricted to Mitteleuropa, as when he wrote, on the train from Venice to Tarvisio on 7 March 1936, 'I send you one more greeting, before I enter europe [sic]'.

During the first year of their relationship, the European nature of their correspondence was broadly implicit, although the beginning of the letter from Katowice was the first explicit reference. Its Europeanness lies above all in the multitude of languages and cultures that are woven through the dialogue of the two lovers, and that are to a great extent part and parcel of it. Giorgina declared later that Arian was 'very mitteleuropean' (Filippa 1990: 12), in reference to his vast and diverse knowledge of languages and texts and also of people. He knew Yiddish, Hebrew, Latin, English and French. He learned Russian with ease as well and dabbled in 'a little Czech' and Dutch. When in Turin, he wanted to learn Piedmontese as well as Italian and took lessons from Giorgina in the cafés. He succeeded in mastering this language, as we can see from a postcard of 1936, which mixed Italian, German and Piedmontese in a delightful jumble:

Dear Giorgia,

grazie! Ca vin'a pura, totta cara. A ssa bin: mia cà aspeta sempre chila, niun'auta, mac chila. Ca vin'a pura dal cit dottorin coi occiai: al'ha tanta veuia d'fé 'na consultassion mac per chila! … Camera affittata; sessanta. … Thanks also for my cousin's postcard; I'm the one who is entitled to be stolz of what she writes because I was smart enough to find and keep ein so herrliches Mädel, meine so liebe, kluge, grosse, reife und dennoch mädchenhafte Frau Freundin.[22]

The use of dialect has a long history in the Jewish community of Piedmont (Mayer Modena 1997: 953–54). Piedmontese Jews had an abiding passion for science, dialect and the mountains (Cavaglion 1988: 541–62). Primo Levi jokingly referred to an unexpected phonetic analogy between Hebrew and the Piedmont dialect and observed the admirable comic effect achieved by mixing Piedmontese dialect with Hebrew (P. Levi 1987: 431, 434). With his acute linguistic sensibility, Enzo Arian was well aware of this and often fell back on expressions in the Piedmont dialect ('I have eaten like a crinet').[23] Giorgina also peppered her letters with colourful Piedmontese expressions. At the end of her Bolivian period, when she became angry with some people who had insulted Enzo, she described them as 'bastards', 'filthy pigs! I wish they would all die', and added 'ch'ai tacheisa 'na cita goeba!'[24]

Arian resolved not to speak German any more because he hated the use to which the Nazis put his language, but he carried on including many German words and expressions in the everyday remarks scattered though his letters to Giorgina. In this way, he conveyed his interest in German to her (she already knew Latin, Greek and French). Later, during their Bolivian exile, both also used Spanish, which Giorgina had begun to study during her ocean voyage. The presence of many languages in their private lexicon emphasises the underlying Europeanness of their bond. In Giorgina's case, the extended sense of belonging that had entered her cultural development did not reduce her Italianness. Enzo, on the other hand, allowed first Poland, then, and above all, Italy to replace Germany in his affections.

Europe was also the space within which this couple moved in idealistic and practical terms: their letters are full of references to European literature, poetry and art, together with readings from Dante to Rilke, Goethe to Kollwitz, and also Zweig, Schnitzler, Turgenev, Beaumarchais, Lamartine, Molière, Verlaine, Nietzsche, Heine, Bach and Beethoven. The books that the pair took on their Bolivian exile included volumes by Schnitzler, Fontane, Werfel, Feuchtwanger, Romain Rolland, Dos Passos and even *I Promessi Sposi*, Dante and all the classics (Filippa 1990: 27). Giorgina herself claimed that she had read 'very much and about everything' (FIPAGT, *Autobiografia*, b. 85, f. 11), and kept lists of the books she had read, which confirm her voracious appetite. One list from 3 January 1925 includes works by D'Annunzio, Pirandello and Deledda, and also Malaparte, Annie Vivanti, Jack London and Thomas Mann. She drifted from Shakespeare to Zweig, from Alcott to Carola Prosperi. The very long list of books she read in Bolivia includes Marx, Engels, Lenin, Krupskaya, Stalin in Spanish, but also Steinbeck, Malraux, Duhamel, Croce and Romain Rolland (FIPAGT, b. 54, f. 5).

The first year of their relationship, 1934, was a period of short and long journeys that punctuate the rhythm of their letters. Arian wrote to Giorgina from Berlin in August, and from Vienna in September. Giorgina, in turn, wrote to him in Berlin from Cortina. In effect, the pair perpetuated the European tradition of travel as education – and their relationship breathed new life into it. Together they made trips to Venice, Paris and Dubrovnik, classic destinations for European lovers, though a political interest is apparent in the fact that their reason for visiting Paris was to see the Soviet Union Pavilion at the International Exhibition of 1937. In 1935, they went to Verona to meet Arian's parents. They also made trips organised for public entertainment, the new holidays that the fascist regime made possible by issuing cut-price train tickets, for example to Moncenisio or Domodossola, but always with the intent of 'going one step further' beyond those popular, crowded destinations, on the way to France and Switzerland. Their experience seems to confirm the idea that travel is a dimension of love in a metaphorical sense, that is, love as a journey outside and inside oneself – and also in a literal sense, because it drives you to move in different directions. Giorgina travelled such a lot on her own during that period that Enzo called her 'my sweet vagabond'[25] at one point. She visited Berlin and Frankfurt, Nuremberg and Munich, taking advantage of the special discounts for the 1936 Olympics to buy a half-price round-trip ticket. She also visited Rome, while Enzo went to Florence, Rome and Naples for his state examination and other business matters.

The sense of moving through a common European territory was certainly strong in Enzo Arian, '[H]ow much sweetness – how much love – how much froheit [happiness] you have sent me through Europe!'[26] During the first year of his time in Italy, Enzo went to meet his parents in Berlin, but later he no longer wished to set foot in Germany, and in 1936 he met his parents in Poland, almost as though his own emotional geography of Europe no longer included Nazi Germany. Albeit in a perverse and contradictory way of theirs, the Nazis made claims for a 'Europe of the future' and boasted that the division between nations would be done away with under their rule to allow the creation of a single continent.

If we examine their combined reading, the Europe of the two lovers was the Europe of the novel, a Europe of which the centre and east are distinctive features – as Milan Kundera put it. Yet it was also a Europe where Jewishness and Europeanness were strongly intertwined. In a letter of 15 August from Berlin, Arian responded to a light-hearted comment of Giorgina's with the following: 'you do me a great honour, telling me that I am the only

Jew you appreciate; but what about Spinoza – Hillel – Cohen – Pitigrilli – you have left out Heine, Boerne, Lombroso, Bergson, Freud ...?' The conversation between the couple is shot through with reflections on the Jewish culture and images of Jews. The greeting 'good sciabbat' is never left off at the end of their letters. In Katowice, Arian noted that 'many Jewish brains make this region buzz', but also that many of them, including his own family, are 'people who live by sucking blood directly or indirectly from others – capitalists in the true sense of the word. They are not at all bad people, but were the dinosaurs bad?' As he strolled through the Crakow ghetto, Enzo observed 'the most fantastic and marvellous types of jiden',[27] 'fat mammas with their innumerable offspring and grubby aprons', 'beggars or near-beggars with magnificent beards and the gestures we love', and he listened to the voices of the pupils floating from the open windows of the yeshiva 'who were singing the melodies of our heart, hiedlach and tehillim, debate and talmud'.[28] He describes:

> The women of Crakow: the strong healthy (yet not bombastic[29]) blonde Polish women with their steely teeth and velvet lips and small sparkling eyes – and the Jewish women – very stylish – with their smoothly curved porcelain brows, with mouths like Titian girls ... under the heavy soft frames of the Russian fur hats that they are wearing here at the moment – and – with their little hands t-t-t-t- and their little feet oj-oj-oj-oj- DAS MACHT UNS KEIN GOI NACH.[30]

The two lovers shared a lay and light-hearted way of being Jewish, in keeping with the traditions of the Jews of Piedmont (Cavaglion 1988). They often poked fun at their own Jewishness and the associated stereotypes, 'I hope at least he doesn't ask for too much money!' Giorgina wrote in 1943 about the doctor who failed to save the baby she lost in a difficult birth, and immediately added '(what a loathsome Jew I am!)'.

Our protagonists show no trace of that Jewish persecution complex that has been interpreted as an identification with the dominant society and sometimes with the perpetrators, a type of identification that may give rise to a persecution complex and also a form of imprecation. Neither do they show any signs that they had interiorised the claim that the Jews occupied a marginal position in relation to a European cultural heritage.[31] Enzo and Giorgina felt fully part of Europe. They felt that they occupied a central position in Europe and that they were engaged in experiencing and broadcasting its culture. Even after they had been expelled from their continent and had opened up to other cultures, this feeling of centrality did not change. It is, nevertheless, worth considering that the feeling of Europe as an *elsewhere*, widespread in certain countries that are considered by others and themselves to be peripheral to Europe, such as England and Spain, also constitutes a form of European identity (Passerini 1999: 10–11, 222 ff.).

The couple's love was strengthened and enhanced by their common sense of Jewish belonging, as is also apparent from the pet names they called one another that refer to their shared tradition as part of a cultural heritage that went beyond mere religion. Their common origins and also the appeal of a different culture are factors at play in their loving interaction. This second factor is certainly at work in the so-called mixed couples, which were common between Jews and non-Jews.[32] Part of the Italian population of Jewish origin, nevertheless, still followed the custom of endogamy or internal marriage,[33] although they were allowed a certain amount of freedom to indulge in relationships before marriage. One significant example from the interwar period is a memoir by Davide Jona, who recounts the great love that attached him for five or six years to a young girl of great beauty and sweetness, but 'Catholic and from a Catholic family with particularly strict views' (Jona and Foa 1997: 106–7). Davide's mother – a defender of the Jewish cultural heritage, who always feared that her sons would marry non-Jewish girls, who were supposed to be after them for their money and maybe would even force them to Catholicism – repeatedly reminded him of his responsibilities. Because he had taken such responsibilities to heart to the point that he could not even imagine marrying the girl, the love story ended 'in a very painful manner', in 'a pile of ashes'. Later on, he said he had been 'lucky' to have gone through that 'disastrous experience', because the subsequent political and racial developments 'would have made a family and sentimental union between ourselves intolerable' (ibid.: 128–29). The practice of keeping feelings separate seems to prolong the tendency that had arisen amongst Italian Jews after emancipation to keep national public spaces separate from their private spaces, which remained Jewish (Cavaglion 1997: 1297), and in particular to perpetuate an age-old tradition of Italian Jewish families, whereby it was 'taken for granted that love and marriage ran along parallel tracks and that there was often no relationship whatsoever between them' (Toaff 1996: 241). This approach, which held true during previous centuries, was no longer applicable in the new age, as the fate of

Davide Jona revealed. In the end, he entered into a marriage based on love with Anna Foa, but he is the first to admit that, when they married in 1932, he could never have even imagined how brave and proud his partner would prove, or her ability to love, implying that personal feelings did not figure largely in his decision to marry.

In the case of the relationship between Giorgina and Enzo, love in all its traditional guises was always to the fore. One quintessentially loving aspect was that of their mutual care for each other, which is implicit in the phrases that formed part of the secret code between the lovers, as occurs in any loving correspondence, great or small, a code that we are not always allowed to decipher. Time-honoured lovers' gestures reappear, such as the kissing of letters or gloves: 'in a great moment of light-hearted exuberance', he cuts a lock of her hair, which she then gives to him 'in an envelope sealed with a kiss and our sign – '–', from which he breathes in her scent when she is not present.

A few disagreements are apparent, in those mutually spiteful exchanges that are typical of intense relationships between lovers. We can detect a trace of this in a letter from Enzo dated 4 June 1935:

> Dearest –
>
> I am writing you this to say sorry. It is difficult to say exactly: sorry for what; because I have hurt you in a very subtle way ... yesterday you treated me badly. I don't know why I had to wait two hours after lunch before I could speak to you ... in the evening you made me wait twenty minutes. I didn't deserve this treatment at all. I wasted two hours and twenty minutes. a nice total. arian is an idiot. you said sorry. i'm not excusing you anything ... I have simply decided not to see you this week and to phone you only at agreed times.

These resolutions last for a page and then soon give way to a confession: 'I am not sane. I am ill. I miss your love. I am not alive: you are my life. I can't work: you are my strength. my throat is dry and my heart is shrivelled and my brain is dark with depression.' In two lines added on the back beside the heading, Arian nevertheless wonders if he has not mistaken a fleeting sadness on the part of Giorgina for a crisis in their relationship: '[R]ereading this letter, the thought came to me, that perhaps you don't understand me. that perhaps I am exaggerating, that perhaps you are just a little sad.' Enzo makes reference to a slight shadow over their relationship again on 18 June: 'Geliebtes Maedel, thank you for everything that you have given me – and particularly for yesterday. Excuse me if, due to my indiscipline, I wasted a part of it.' In general, though, the relationship seemed to be characterised by harmony and the ability to create and inhabit a separate world. As they breathed new life into old traditions, the pair also created new traditions, as the ever-attentive Enzo observed (on 7 March 1936), 'Mon aimée – traditionis causa (now already traditionis causa) I send you another greeting'. A letter of 28 August 1936, typewritten, on a Sciabbat Gadol day, Great Sciabbat, harks back to 'the night of Our Christmas ... when our Great Love was born'. This letter is written in the style of a litany, repeating short verses with a rhythm that suggests the sacredness of their loving relationship. Enzo applies his light-hearted tone to liturgical memories, '[E]yes – breast – forehead – all my Holy Trinity', and is tireless in his constant inventing of new terms of endearment:

> Giorginetta dolce cara.
> Giorgi mia adorata [reminiscent of Mozart's and Da Ponte's *Don Giovanni*: 'Zerbinetta mia adorata?']
> Giorginerle.
> Schnupperle.
> Schlumpfele.
> Giorginetterle Liebelieb.[34]

One tradition that the couple started was to create a mixed European language made up of amorous epithets spoken only by the pair:

> je voudrai [sic] me plonger dans ta bonté – dans ton buono sguardo – dans la douceur de ton corps (Enzo, 11 March 1936).
> je t'embrasse de tout mon cœur – all of you – your eyes – your joues – your beloved mouth – your neck – your nape – now your magnificent breasts and the sweet vale warm and herrlich, between them (12 March 1936).
> giorginerle – dear – sweet – herrliche frau – je t'aime (15 March 1936).
> my only relative – blood of my blood (11 March 1936).
> my homeland, my anchor, my roo (17 March 1936).[35]

Though he was indubitably in earnest, Heinz Arian occasionally yearned for freedom, the ability to wander, solitude. For example, in a letter from Vienna, he describes the feelings he felt when travelling by train, which revealed his 'almost pathological tendency toward independence': this aroused in him 'serious doubts' over the advisability of 'our permanent union'.[36] He then advised Giorgina to take some trips on her own so that she could enjoy the same pleasures 'experimenti causa'. She also experienced a similar desire for independence and in the end agreed to marriage only because of the situation of persecution that arose on the eve of their exile. In Heinz's melding with his beloved and her land, there lay a passion for Jewishness[37] and also a passion for the South: 'I think of you as a beloved country that only I know – a country full of sun, of marvels, of things to discover and rediscover, of infinite Froheit'.[38]

The relationship between the pair formed part of a cross-European exchange with Enzo's family, as we can see from the many postcards that Else and Siegfried Arian sent to Giorgina, who went to visit them in 1936. Sometimes Eva, Enzo's sister, who would marry a man from Trieste, also added a few lines. The postcards are addressed to 'Sign. Giorgina Levi, BA'. This title aroused the admiration and the esteem of Enzo and also of his parents, who rightly saw it as a sign of Giorgina's emancipation and intelligence, all the more so because her thesis was concerned with Jewish history. In their eyes, the young Italian woman held the fascination of a culture that was both Jewish and Italian and also generally Mediterranean, in which radical change was combined with tradition. Although we are entering a very private area, we may be led to believe by analogy that in this area, too, Italians represented an 'original blend' of the various strands of Jewishness and more precisely between the past and the tendency to emancipation (Cavaglion 1997). We are therefore seeing, under the banner of Europeanness, a reciprocal extension of their sense of belonging (in terms of their identities) made possible by their loving interaction. The circumstances helped to create institutional contexts of identity, but the process was strongly emotional by nature: when you identify yourself with another person, you marry their sense of belonging, and the boundaries of 'identity' and 'otherness' shift during this process, while the two states of 'sameness' and 'otherness' mix and re-form.

In 1935, Arian applied for Italian citizenship. In 1937, he graduated with a thesis 'On Psychic Disturbances in Lethargic Encephalitis', which was granted the honour of publication. He completed a six-month practical hospital training period in Turin and in February 1938 he passed the state examination. He finally found permanent employment in San Maurizio Canavese, in a clinic for mental illnesses. During those years, Giorgina went to Rome to pursue Arian's application for citizenship, obtaining a hearing with the private secretary to Bocchini, head of the police, through a letter from her teaching colleague Marchesini Gliozzi to the head of the General Educational Inspectorate:

> This Emilio Manganiello suddenly embraced me and put his hand on my bottom. I stiffened, he realised that I wasn't going along with it, that I wasn't about to sell myself for a citizenship and so he went cold again and I left. I subsequently found out that Manganiello was one of the people shot by the partisans.[39]

A letter from Manganiello to the head of the Inspectorate, dated 17 July 1937, states that the difficulties of granting Italian citizenship (to her fiancé) are 'almost insurmountable, partly because they are both of the Israelite religion'. He also wrote that he had 'suggested and advised the person you had recommended to him' to turn to the head of the government, the only person with 'the power to rule favourably on the matter as a completely exceptional action' (CDEC, series 5).

Enzo completed the various bureaucratic stages in order not to leave any stone unturned, with a lack of conviction justified by events. For example, in March 1938, he was in Rome for a competition and tried in vain for an audience with the Minister. His reaction reveals an aspect of the traditional rivalry between Rome and Turin:

> My Pucci: you are right to be disgusted by this city. ... I really feel like sending the whole matter to the Devil and coming back to you: near to you on the Platti bar's sofa, near to you at your front door, near to you in some two-bit restaurant, and above all near to you in meinem Bettele [little bed].[40]

A postcard of '19 August 1939 – XVI' recounts: 'I have wasted the entire afternoon drawing up the application to his Excellency with reference to qualifications etc. You are a fine little romantic if you think that an application from a J. will still be accepted these days.'

Then came the ill-fated year of 1938. At the beginning of the year, Arian wrote to Giorgina from Nice (22 January), from Florence (17 February), from Rome (19 February), from Naples (20 February), always on paper headed 'Dr. Enzo Arian – Doctor'. He told her he had strolled along the Lungarno whistling the 'Trout Quintet – as we used to do together' and that he admired 'the eternal flower of Italy' more every day. Halfway through the year, however, their anxieties began to gather force, some due specifically to separation imposed by travel and others much more threatening. Giorgina was awarded a grant from the 'Dante Alighieri' postgraduate institute that took her to Rhodes for the summer. The grant was for two years but Giorgina would not receive anything the second year because to reconfirm she needed a declaration proving that she did not belong to the 'Semitic race'[41] and in any case during that period the two were already about to go into exile. During her journey to Rhodes, Giorgina stopped over in Naples, from where she sent two letters to Enzo. He, in turn, sent her letters that were waiting for her when she got to Piraeus and Rhodes, but he was gripped by an attack of acute loss and complained touchingly about it in a passage that, for once, is not burdened by too much literature:

> Pardon me if I am small and mean-spirited. I've been engaged in an endless struggle between myself and the world throughout this horrible night. I do not want to be sentimental. Now I see, how sentimental I have been, when I gave you the proud and poorly thought-out advice to go to Rhodes – the greatest foolishness of my life so full of foolishnesses. I did not have the right to deprive myself of you for so long, an interminable time (or so it seems to me) made intolerable by the enormous weight of the immense distance. And I'm cross with you: because you had no right to go so enormously far away ... The books and the chairs that you touched are still here. I have still got the same beard as the last time we saw each other.[42]

The letter concludes by asking her not to take any notice of his 'jérémiades' and to enjoy to the full 'your trip, your trip, that you alone have deserved and won'. Two days later, Arian was again absolutely desperate, but lucidly aware: 'No letter from you! I can't stand it any more. I feel like going to bed and dying until you come back – just as hysterics do'.[43] He wrote that he hated himself because he was 'so weak and lost in his attachment', then he excuses himself, makes amends and concludes with a blistering finale: 'Yes: I will hesitate no longer over base revenge: if you do not come back soon, Pucci, I will be ill. I mean it. Je t'adore. I cover you with kisses. I hide my eyes between your thighs and cry and laugh and I am mad and shout. Je t'aime. A.'

On 5 August 1938, a series of letters began in which Arian expresses increasingly serious concerns over the situation in Italy, due to the measures against foreign Jewish intellectuals expelled from the universities, 'all sorts of horrors could happen to me', including the possibility of being forced to leave Italy. He challenges Giorgina to consider seriously whether she wishes to ally herself with him under such circumstances, 'I beg you, herrliche Frau, not to ruin your life'. The next day (6 August) he explains to her that his 'uncertainty tortured him even more' than that which he had experienced five years previously in Germany: 'Because now I have you to lose, the only thing that is mine. You are my only heritage. You are my only punctum fixum. You are, now more than ever, my Earth: my roots are in you. And if I must leave you, I am lost.' This pattern in the relationship was not only imposed by the state of emergency in which Enzo found himself. On the contrary, it seems to have been the default form of the relationship, or so it appears from the correspondence taken as a whole. Between the pair of them, it was she who constituted the stronger, more stable and positive part. Despite her sense of inferiority on a cultural level, it was she who represented the basis of the identity investment. Aptly enough, one of the quotations that Giorgina remembers Enzo liked to dedicate to her was a verse by Rilke, 'Ich bin das Beginnende, / Du aber bist der Baum'.[44]

Painful news is interwoven in their subsequent letters. Giorgina suggests Rhodesia, but Enzo found out that this country also forbade the immigration of Jewish foreigners (8 August). She suggests Rhodes, where she was staying at that time, but he does not believe in this option: '[U]nfortunately, my joy, even though it might give you a glimmer of hope *now*, in a short while there will no longer be anything we can do'. He was absolutely right: the Jews of Rhodes were subsequently forced to emigrate to Argentina or deported to Auschwitz and Dachau (Fanesi 1994: 23–36). Enzo read all the newspapers, from the ordinary dailies to the political press and the Catholic press and was able to see 'the development of events without the rose-tinted spectacles of Rhodes'. However, many Jews in Italy still did not want to believe in anti-Semitic persecution, either due to conformism or because they were settled in the country, and 'even when the persecution started, they convinced themselves that they could hope for mitigating circumstances or postponement' (P. Treves 2002: 7) or they received the news with 'horrified incredulity' (Zuccotti 1995: 66). Enzo had no doubts over their fate: 'We are terribly alone, expelled from our environment, thrown into the uncertainty and anguish of the stateless ... we are alone as only two Jews can be alone'.[45] From the tone of Enzo's subsequent letters we may infer that Giorgina strongly rejected any sort of separation. We could never have doubted otherwise, given her rectitude and the strength of her feelings. Enzo then appeared calmer, although he was just as lucid and realistic:

> We will always be together – and as far as the rest is concerned we will see. We will see, we will have to make sure, first of all, that your attitude does not cause you to sink into a miserable heap of suffering and absurdity when you are forced to face the reality of emigration: because experience teaches that the lack of a big enough monthly income can easily change the way one feels ... But, with you by my side, always by my side, I feel as if I can face anything ...[46]

A few days later, though, his tones were gloomy and rightly prophetic: 'This afternoon I filled in the form for the census of Jews in Italy. Today they carried out a census of the livestock; when will they slaughter them?'[47]

In September 1938, just returned from Rhodes, Giorgina lost her job due to the Decree Law for the Defence of the Race (which became law in January 1939), the first legal measure adopted by the fascist government against the Jews. This measure hit some 104 university lecturers (196 qualified lecturers lost their jobs) and 174 upper-middle school teachers (Luzzatto 1997: 1831–900), in addition to thousands of civil servants, professionals, office workers and students (De Felice 1972: 328). A novel by Lia Levi effectively describes the pain and the bewilderment of her Jewish hero who suddenly had to leave the school where he taught Greek and Latin. His fate was made particularly dramatic by the fact that he was married, in a mutually loving relationship, to a Catholic woman from a fascist family (Levi 2001).

The various reactions of the Italian Jews were understandable in the light of the ambivalence and the hot-and-cold attitude of the Mussolini regime to Zionism and anti-Semitism (Michaelis 1978: 411). There is no doubt that De Felice's claim – that 'the anti-Zionist and anti-Jewish debates in general in Italy in 1933 and above all in 1934 took place outside Mussolini's inner circle' (De Felice 1972: 160), and all the Duce did was not deny it – is astounding to say the least.[48] The decisive turn in the policy of the fascist regime towards anti-Semitism and racism took place, however, between the end of 1936 and the first half of 1937, for a whole set of reasons. These included racial policy in Ethiopia, an increasingly sympathetic attitude to the Arabs within Italian politics and, naturally, the fact that Italy was coming closer to Germany. Though even in 1937 the government was still issuing numerous reassurances that the official attitude towards the Jews was not about to change for the worse (Della Seta and Carpi 1997), the census of the Jews in August 1938 demonstrated not only the harshness of the directives from on high but also a willingness to put them quickly into practice from below (F. Levi 1991).[49]

From September 1938, the persecution of Jews in Italy gathered pace; various legal and practical measures meant that things got worse every day. The Decree Law of 7 September 1938 established that Jews who had entered the country after 1918 had to leave the country within six months (even though an extension was granted the following March). 'Marriage between Italian men and women and members of the Camite, Semite and other non-Aryan races' was forbidden, while 'marriage between Italian men and women and foreigners even from Aryan races' required the prior consent of the Ministry of the Interior.[50] Apart from the legal measures, violent persecution grew. On 27 October, twenty-seven Turinese Jews were arrested, and numerous other arrests followed in Rome and Milan (Zuccotti 1995: 174).

On 3 December 1938, the Female Fascist Federation of Turin, part of the National Fascist Party (PNF), which Giorgina had been forced to join so that she could enter state competitions for teaching jobs, sent her a letter signed by the federal secretary Piero Gazzotti: 'This is to inform you that your membership of the PNF will cease as of today because you are of the Jewish race. Return the PNF card and badge in your possession to the Card Office of this Federation as soon as possible' (FIPAGT, b. 76, f. 4). In view of the worsening situation, Enzo and Giorgina decided to emigrate and, after considering Ecuador, opted for Bolivia following an appeal from that country for Jewish doctors and after learning that it would be possible for a woman graduate to teach.[51] To prevent the white slave trade, however, Bolivia would not grant visas to women under fifty unless they were accompanied by their husband or father or brother. Marriage to foreigners was also only possible with a permit from the fascist government, which took a long time and would have cost Giorgina her Italian citizenship – a price she refused to pay. The couple therefore decided to undergo a religious ceremony alone. The Turinese Rabbi refused to perform the ceremony, however, because he would have had to report it to the registry office under the terms of the Concordat. In the end, the brave Rabbi who led the Genoese community, Riccardo Pacifici,[52] agreed to perform the religious ceremony, against the wishes of the president of his community 'who was scared' (Filippa 1990: 8). These events reveal the variety of reactions to the persecutory measures displayed by the Jewish community and their official representatives. Enzo and Giorgina married in Genoa on 9 February. They should have left Italy by March 1939, but by that date only half of the 9,000 affected people had managed to obtain a visa and the deadline was extended by six months (Voigt 1995: 28); they eventually left in June from the port of Genoa on the cruise ship *Virgilio*.

The boat was full of Jews who were escaping from all over Europe (Filippa 1990: 31) – Germans, Poles, Rumanians and Czechs. They stopped in Barcelona, from where Giorgina and Heinz sent two significant letters, which reveal how their common awareness as Europeans was accentuated by the prospect of separation (and perhaps echoes an exchange of views between themselves on this subject). Enzo wrote to French friends, 'C'est la dernière poignée de mains à notre mère l'Europe' ('It is the last handshake with our mother Europe'), and Giorgina to her relatives in Turin, 'there only remains the great pain of saying farewell to the

European homeland, against the poignant backdrop of Barcelona', which had been severely bombed. Barcelona was the last European port after Marseilles and their pain was even more keenly felt at this stage: the two newly-weds suffered not only from leaving Italy but also from leaving Europe. When they arrived at Arica in Chile, they felt the entire weight of their dispossession, '[W]e really felt we were in a foreign land' (ibid.: 42). From there, they continued by train across the Andes. Giorgina found that she was the only Italian woman amongst a hundred Germans – and for a long time she remained the only Italian woman in a Central European Jewish world. The main destinations of Italian Jews emigrating to Latin America were Argentina and Brazil. These two countries, albeit to a lesser extent than the United States, attracted Jewish intellectuals whose presence 'contributed to the intellectual prestige of anti-fascist émigrés' (Garosci 1953: 192–93). Countries such as Peru and Bolivia were considered more 'difficult' (Toscano 1988: 1287–314). At the beginning of the 1940s, more than one thousand Jews were counted in Argentina, two hundred in Cuba, approximately one hundred families in Brazil, and groups of exiles in Bolivia, Uruguay, Peru, Ecuador and Mexico (Fanesi 1994).[53] Many exiled Jews took part in the organisation of antifascist groups in Latin America, such as Italia Libera, 'Garibaldi, Mazzini Society, Unione Patriottica Italiana, whose history has not yet been written.[54]

In Bolivia, Enzo did various jobs as a doctor in different places that were often very deprived, accepting posts that many Bolivian doctors refused: in the village of Zudanez, in the towns of Sucre and Oruro, in the mines of Villa Apacheta, Santa Fé, and in the subtropical area of Yungas. Giorgina taught in all levels of school, from primary schools in Zudanez and Villa Apacheta (where her pupils were the children of *indio* miners) to secondary schools and, finally, at the universities of Sucre and La Paz. At a certain point, the Jewish community in Oruro founded a Jewish school that they proudly called Colegio Europeo, where Giorgina agreed to teach German, Austrian and Polish children from six to thirteen years of age. Their different jobs forced the couple to accept periods of separation, during which they experienced severe difficulties with communication and transport. Their life was often extremely harsh with very few material comforts and it was a tough job to live from day to day. Renato Treves, who met Giorgina, with whom he was in correspondence, at the La Paz station in December 1941, remembers that 'she was leading a hard and difficult life' (R. Treves 1985: 99). In Bolivia, too, Giorgina and her husband experienced forms of anti-Semitism and did not find a true united community. They tended to mix mainly with 'the European Jews', including those of the left, and some Italian traders. Both worked in antifascist organisations and formed links with groups (such as Freies Deutschland – Enzo's correspondence reveals a strong commitment to build up this network – and the Associazione Garibaldi) and also with German, Yugoslav, Austrian, Czech and Italian individuals in the United States, in Mexico, in Chile and in Argentina.[55] They repeatedly attempted to join the militant movement in Europe, writing numerous letters to offer themselves as volunteers in the Red Army in the Soviet Union, in 1941, and in the UNRRA (United Nations Relief and Rehabilitation Administration), in 1944, but always received polite rejections.[56]

During their Bolivian exile, Giorgina devoted herself with passion to a study of Marxism. Despite the family tradition and her knowledge of many senior teaching staff who were initially socialists but later became communists, she had had no teachers in fascist Italy or occasions to explore the subject. Her contact with Enzo gave her the stimulus to do so, as she herself declared in her *Autobiografia* written in 1954 for the Turinese Federal Committee of the Communist Party of which she was a member. This confirms Enzo's tendency to act as her Pygmalion. It was he who lent her the *Communist Party Manifesto* and allowed her to experience 'her first frank and open discussions' (FIPAGT, b. 85, f. 11). Both joined the Italian Communist Party when they returned to Italy.

In Bolivia, the correspondence between Enzo and Giorgina continued due to their frequent separations, and we are lucky enough to have her letters as well as his for this period. In many ways, the exile reinforced their bond, although sometimes it tested it to the limits. Enzo wrote to Giorgina: 'But in my darkest hours – sorry for the triteness – I have been able to appreciate what it means to have a friend, a wife in the world. You are very, but very Mutti[57] for me … You are my friend. You are my woman.'[58] Giorgina, as usual, recounted the various aspects of her everyday life to Enzo, providing us with an important record of life in exile. She also showed him a constant and tender love, now tried and tested by time and events that had brought them closer together (cemented by the loss of the child who died during birth but could have been saved by proper medical care). The letters from exile contain a wealth of loving expressions that show their usual level of understanding and exchange of feelings. The language used between the pair includes the terms they used amongst themselves, the oral tradition of their relationship, and also the childlike, dialectal and multilingual phrases or terms that they had built up over the years. Giorgina:

> Darling Pucci ... I am practically dead with longing for you, my only friend, sweetest darling – Je t'aime. Je t'adore, je te remercie, vuelte prontito prontito [Come back as soon as possibile]. Je t'aime. Infinite kisses (5 Dec. 1939).
> Sucre 29 Jan. 1940: I kiss you all over.
> Sucre 30 Jan. 1940: Dearest beautiful darling my sweet little husband.
> Sucre 11 Feb. 1940: I have a *magone* [Piedmontese dialect: I've got a lump in my throat] because I am separated from you! ... We are so lucky to love each other so much ... I feel like a queen ... . Feel me because I am close, so close, with my head resting on your beautiful white neck, and I sleep with my hand on your beloved leg. I really adore you, you are my God! I am always scared I've been naughty and that you will have to scold me for something, for not doing everything really really well, like a big kluge [clever] Frau! ... Holy darling, infinite one!
> 12 Feb. 1940: Up with Pucci and life with him!
> Sucre 14 Feb. 1940: je t'aime all, all, and *I want only you*, do you understand, crapotto d'oro [Piedmontese expression meaning 'golden head' or 'Goldilocks']. ... Sweet pink and gold love.
> Sucre 19 Feb. 1940: Always, always I am left in awe, after so many years, of the marvellous balance of our life, of our love!
> Sucre 20 Feb. 1940: I feel the need to give everything up lock, stock and barrel and run away and hide in the beloved heat of your real botiquin, to kiss my pêcheur d'Islande, cuddle you, taste you and let the hours slip away so fine and sweet like Saturday – Sunday.
> Sucre 27 Feb. 1940: I hide away in the sweet love of our intimate eternal puesseria to talk a little with you. ... I am sending you 5 oranges so that you will sweeten up a bit. I would like to put the juice into your beloved mouth myself! How are the mattresses, on which we will hold our nightly or morning celebrations? Make sure they are thick enough, don't let yourself be cheated.
> 6 Mar. 1940: companion of my life.
> Oruro 3 Mar. 1942: animae dimidium meae [half of my soul].
> Oruro 11 Mar. 1942: Sometimes I am almost afraid of our wondrous love. I am no longer able to be truly and entirely myself if I am alone: everything is infinitesimally related to you and you alone.
> Oruro 6 Jun. 1943: I am all yours, more than ever. Save yourself for me.
> Je t'adore tutto, je t'aime, I think always of you, I speak only of you, I live only of [or for] you [date and place are missing, but this was towards the end of their stay in Bolivia].

Giorgina always showed a sense of humour, even when asking dramatic questions, 'because our love is the only thing in which we believe, solo uniti torneremo!' ('only together will we return!' – taken from the aria in *La Traviata*!) (La Paz, 8 August 1944). The letters reveal and convey the secret language of the lovers and their intimacy, testifying above all to their level of agreement. However, the couple's shared experiences also included other tones and other experiences, with times of separation and divergence that it is not possible to document. Suffice it to say that not everything was rosy and happy, and the relationship between the pair went through various difficult patches.

The pair remained in Bolivia for no less than seven years before they could return to Europe. During those years, Giorgina learnt to appreciate the wonder of the new emotions aroused by the vast landscapes, as the quotation at the beginning of the chapter shows. Not only did she reflect on colonialism and the exploitation of the *indios*, but also recognised her own Eurocentric prejudices and succeeded in altering them, as she noted on the subject of the half-castes: 'I was wrong to view them from my European viewpoint and I didn't try to see things from their point of view, when I would have been able to understand their lying, unpunctuality and laziness' (Filippa 1990: 57). She felt particular sympathy for the Polish Jews, the most despised, and the *indios*, 'that the other Bolivians treat like animals' (ibid.: 68).

Her constant concerns were for the families left in Europe. During the months of September and December 1939, Giorgina's letters contained good news of Enzo's parents, who were in contact with her parents and hoped to be able to leave Germany soon. In actual fact, they never did succeed. They survived for some time in great difficulty and humiliation,[59] then they disappeared. The last certain news that we can trace, with the aid of the Centrum Judaicum archive in Berlin, is that Siegfried and Else Arian, born in Silesia in 1883 and 1882 respectively, were deported in the twenty-first transport heading for Riga on 19 October 1942; 'we know nothing of their next destination'.[60]

The letters from the Bolivian exile often contained references to the continent that the couple was forced to leave. Giorgina to her parents, 'I think more than ever before of beautiful Europe and Turin' (2 November 1939); to Professor Lemmi, 'When will we be able to see our dear Europe again?' (11 August 1941); to Eva Terracini, '[W]hen we go back to Europe, how much we will have to tell everyone!' (4 November 1942). Enzo to Giorgina, probably in June 1942: 'Let us leave quickly. Let us try to get back soon to our dear Europe with her immediate hopes, with her immediate possibilities, with her innumerable possibilities that are achievable within our own lifetimes.' In an article published in *Unità* on 23 May 1952, Giorgina conjured up the questions of the children she taught, children of the miners: 'Where is Europe? Where do you come from? Why did you come here? What do you think of us?' (G. Levi 1952b: 3).

The bond with Europe, so paradoxically reaffirmed during the period of the persecutions, is of great significance. It is important to remember that some put up deliberate opposition to the attempt to expel the Jews not only from the land itself but also from European history and culture. At the very beginning of that terrible year 1938, in January, the Jewish Historical Society of London (founded in 1893 by Lucien Wolf and Alfred Newman) had organised a lecture by the historian Cecil Roth[61] on the topic 'The Jew as a European' (Roth 1938).[62] A few years previously a book with a similar title, *Jude oder Europäer: Porträt von Georg Brandes*, by Henri Nathansen (1931), had been published.[63] The text was reviewed in Italy by Guido Lodovico Luzzatto who treated it highly critically, defining it as 'defective and inept', but emphasising that 'Jew or European' was not the central dilemma since Brandes was, 'in his small Denmark, a European because he was a Jew'. Luzzatto connects in a single sequence the sense of belonging to a nation and to Europe and to the 'cause of humanity', according to his conception of a humanistic Europeanness.[64]

In his pamphlet, Roth claimed that it was no longer enough to vindicate Jews by giving them the character of Englishness ('the vindication of the Jew as an Englishman'). Quite the contrary; this was secondary to the urgency of stressing their Europeanness, because the wave of anti-Semitism coming from Nazi Germany was undermining the basis of European life and even interpersonal relationships. The idea of an 'international' enemy took xenophobia to a whole new level; now it was claimed that the entire Jewish community constituted an alien 'Asiatic' race that threatened the purity and cohesion of European life as a whole. Roth went on to consider the contributions of Jews to European civilisation, from the first dawn of civilisation in Palestine, when Greek history was still in its infancy and the rest of Europe was in a state of barbarism. Roth was setting out a thesis that we have encountered in the *Cahiers du Sud*, that the eastern Mediterranean basin was a focal point for the history of civilisation because it represented the meeting of Asia, Africa and Europe. His long list of Jewish contributions to European civilisation extends through all historical periods. Roth includes in his argument the participation of Jews in imperial colonisation and expansion, notably their contribution to the setting up of the British empire in India, Canada, South Africa and New Zealand. He then lays claim to their European heritage in its entirety – the good parts and the bad parts. As far as he was concerned, 'the Jews, then, are a European people – more truly than are more than one of the peoples of the Western world'. They are in fact 'more European' than many of the peoples of Western Europe since they acted as pioneers of European civilisation in the extreme northern and eastern outposts of the continent (Roth 1938: 11).[65]

One interesting aspect of Roth's argument is the importance he allocates to the fact that Jews chose to speak European languages even when exiled due to intolerance, for example in Eastern Europe (the figure of the Wandering Jew typically knew the languages of all the European countries he passed through). At the same time, he observed that the ethnic differentiation had been grossly exaggerated, while through the course of the centuries the exchanges between peoples had been very numerous and not only 'the Jewish strain in the German people is necessarily stronger than what the most fanatical Nazis would like to believe', but quite the contrary is true as well (ibid.: 14).

Roth's discussion contains essentialistic undertones, more with regard to the idea of Europe and being European than of being Jewish, in the sense that some people seemed to him to be more authentically European than others. This was not at all strange for the period when the argument was written: the same thing may be said of his acceptance of the imperialist nature of European civilisation and particularly that of Britain. It may be that his essentialistic viewpoints were also prompted by a need to oppose the Nazi idea of Europe. Roth's argument actually goes as far as to consider Europe a battlefield in terms of the political struggle and to champion the cause of 'the true Europe' against that of Nazism:

> In maintaining as I do that the Jew is essentially a child of the Western world and Western civilisation, I am thinking of the civilisation that our fathers knew and cherished – the civilisation represented by Dante and Shakespeare, by Gladstone and Lincoln, by Leonardo da Vinci and Rembrandt, van Rijn, by John Wycliffe and St Francis of Assisi.

This is the civilisation that Roth sets in contrast to that claimed by the 'voice':

> [W]hich claims that it expresses that which is noble, and which is essential, in European life; a voice that glorifies war, which derides the rights of the weak, and which has elevated race into a religious principle demanding sacrifices yet more harrowing than those offered up before Moloch of old.'

If this were the real Europe, he continues, he would be left with no alternative but to withdraw his claims for the Europeanness of the Jews. He therefore concludes his exhortation, 'If this is the true Europe, it is for us to take our stand four-square, now as never before, on Sinai', a conclusion that echoes his Zionist beliefs (ibid.: 16). Cecil Roth resigned his membership of all the Italian academic societies of which he was a member in 1939 as a protest against the anti-Semitic laws of the fascist regime.

Roth had a direct link with Giorgina, who had written to him in 1932 to ask him for advice on her thesis. He answered her in good Italian with some slightly Anglicised turns of phrase and provided her with some bibliographic references, while asking her in turn for information on seventeenth- and eighteenth-century tax regulations, which he told her he collected. Lastly, he sent 'his warmest regards to Profs Castelbolognesi and Terracini'.[66] By contrast, the same archive source[67] preserves a cutting from *La Stampa* of July 1940 (perhaps sent to Giorgina by friends or family): an article by Alfredo Signoretti[68] on 'La Nuova Europa Senza Ebrei', in which he claims that Europe will be reborn in the spirit of the Italian and German national revolutions, to found a civilisation based on labour as opposed to one based on gold, inspired by the Judaism that had led to European decadence. Signoretti called for 'Europe to be rid of the Jews once and for all', emphasising the urgency of 'clearing' the Jews from the continent and forcing them to migrate to Madagascar, as a necessary condition for the creation of a new Europe. During May of the same year, a book by G. de' Rossi dell'Arno, editor of *Italia e Fede*, had been published in Italy. *L'Ebraismo contro l'Europa*,[69] considered the war in progress to be a 'duel between Europe and Judaism'. Anyone whose sympathies lay with the Allies was 'hebraised', and 'European civilisation' meant the Roman and Christian spirit in that context. A global anti-Semitic movement grew up around this restricted and autarchical idea. The claim of a link between Jewishness and Europeanness was, on the other hand, associated with a wide-ranging and open idea of Europe and its cultural heritage.[70]

By stating the close connection between Europeanness and Jewishness in the context of the history of identities and feelings, I intend to explore an aspect of the phrase written by Cioran, according to which a dead city is a city without Jews (Cioran 1968). My intention is not to ally myself with his pro-Semitism, but to rethink the stage in history when fascist systems set out to break the link between being Jewish and being European in a bloody and final manner: a Europe without Jews would be unthinkable or 'unbreathable', as was the imaginary Vienna purged by anti-Semitism in Bettauer's novel *Die Stadt ohne Juden* (*The City without Jews*) (Bettauer 1922). It is not, however, my intention to support a single form of Jewishness nor a monolithic Europeanness and still less an exclusive relationship between the one and the other, being entirely aware that there have always been many ways of being Jewish, and, at the same time, the presence of Jews in many world cultures makes it impossible to identify them with Europe alone. It is conversely not possible for us to ignore the ambiguous nature of the identification between Europeanness and Jewishness, as we saw with Roth. This identification cannot have been other than conflicting in the 1930s and 1940s. Even Giorgina Levi and Heinz Arian – who were critical, unlike Roth, of the colonial and imperialist legacy of Europe – would have found it impossible not to be aware of these contradictions if they had thought at all about the anti-European stance of the Stalinist regime in the Soviet Union. Nowadays, any claim of the link between being Jewish and being European is bound to include an implicit criticism of the way of understanding Europeanness on the one hand (Passerini 2003, Part 2) and on the other the forms of Jewish identity recognised in all their multiplicity (Pinto 2002: 3–36).

There are consequences to acknowledging the intimate link between being European and being Jewish even for people who are not Jewish by birth or by faith. This recognition invites us to underscore the flexibility and plurality of the relationships between senses of belonging: a feeling may prevail in many Jews, alongside their Jewish identity, of belonging to nations such as Israel or the United States and this makes the loyalty relative, at least in a historical sense, and not necessarily in specific individuals. Those Jews who are still willing to acknowledge their loyalty to the European heritage are faced with a great task of redefinition, which involves an effort similar to that of redefining their European identity. For this reason we, in the present day, are inspired by the example of those who, like Giorgina Levi and Heinz Arian, experienced a dual identification during the period when Jews endured the 'persecuting of lives', to use a term coined by Michele Sarfatti (Sarfatti 2006) to describe the events when legal persecution gave way to physical persecution.

The protagonists of the love story we have followed during this chapter felt themselves to be profoundly European and they felt their belonging to Europe as an integral part and continuation of their being Italian by birth or by adoption. It was a bond as emotional as it was fed by intellectualism: the books Giorgina read during her Bolivian period include works like *Los Constructores de la Europa Actual* by Sforza and *La Rebelion de las Masas* by Ortega y Gasset (FIPAGT, b. 54, f. 5). Their generosity in calling Europe

'our mother' and 'homeland' even as they were expelled is moving
and significant. The pianist and composer Artur Schnabel, who was
forced to leave Berlin for Tremezzo on Lake Como, also used
similar words in 1935: 'Poor very sick old mother Europe! Her
death throes will begin when Germany has achieved its aims in its
own land' (Oehlmann 1995: 229). Similarly, later, Stefan Zweig
recalls the exodus of the Jews from Vienna 'in order to escape from
Europe', because 'Europe, our homeland for which we had lived,
was destroyed' (Zweig 1964).

Léon Poliakov maintained that in other continents, such as Asia,
the Jews did not become the subjects of hatred and massacres
(Poliakov 1974 [Eng. tr.] vol. 1), although this did happen in Africa,
as the example of Sudan shows. It is not, therefore, possible to infer
from the spread of anti-Semitism through Europe the existence of a
privileged link, in the sense of a special albeit pejorative relationship
between Jews and Europe. It is, nevertheless, true to say that the
Jews were persecuted by the Europeans in the name of the supreme
values of Western society (ibid., vol. 2: ix). One of Poliakov's
arguments certainly suggests this, when he maintains that the anti-
Semitism experienced from the end of the First World War 'turned
out to be a symbol and at the same time an agent of European
disorder or decadence', even a sign of its tendency to self-
destruction, in short a sign of the decline of the West (ibid., vol. 4:
8 *passim*). Since anti-Semitism has been a feature of all the ages of
European history, it cannot in itself be assumed as a sign of decline.
The matter cannot be decided, however, if we ignore the fact that
during the third decade of the twentieth century, the idea of Europe
was contested and torn apart by opposing factions and no single
argument was dominant. The Europe to which we refer in this
context is that of the Rossellis and of Colorni, who were
determined Europeanists and antifascists of Jewish origin (Zuccotti
1995: Ch. 12). My aim in postulating a bond between Europeanness
and Jewishness is, therefore, not to highlight a link between two
essences but a series of historical links, particularly as far as
investments in identity and feelings are concerned.[71]

During the course of their Bolivian exile, both Giorgina and
Heinz underwent an extension of their investment in identity. For
Enzo, the process began with his Italian stay and, above all, through
the relationship with his partner. The starting point for him was an
identification with Italy through Giorgina, which meant that as
time went by Europe was more than just Central Europe as far as he
was concerned. Enzo still felt and wanted to be in some way

cosmopolitan and stateless, although he suffered from the injury inflicted by Nazism in denying his belonging to Germany (he no longer wished to apply for German citizenship, even when it was possible for him to have it back). Yet the connotations of a nomadic identity are not off-key if they are considered as part and parcel of being European. The figure of the Wandering Jew has been reinterpreted as symbolic not merely of internal colonialism by the Europeans of those they define as 'foreigners', but also as an indication of the fusion between identity and otherness with regard to Europe by the Jews (Hasan-Rokem 2001–2002). A compelling link exists between this nomadic figure and Nietzsche's Shadow, which may be seen as the 'good European', always critical, always in flux, adverse to any ideas of nationalism, ironical and self-ironical (Passerini 2007a). This identification with Europe is often linked with a feeling of universal solidarity. Giorgina remembers that one of the quotations dear to Enzo and herself came from the 'Marseillaise of Peace' composed in 1841 by Lamartine, 'Je suis concitoyen de toute âme qui pense: / La vérité, c'est mon pays' ('I am the fellow citizen of every thinking soul: / truth is my country').

For her part, Giorgina gives us an accurate description of the process of extending her identity investment, which must have been similar for many exiles and migrants. Examples include those who migrated for work to continents such as America, Australia and Africa, where they developed more or less knowingly a sense of belonging not only to a nation but had the experience of being lumped together with 'whites' of other nationalities. For a long time, 'white' was a synonym for 'European' in Africa, with racist overtones. In the case of our protagonists, the extension was progressive, despite their initial Eurocentrism,[72] which gives tangible expression to the limits of Europeanness and of its intrinsic empathy. Giorgina expresses this extension in the terms of a 'growing homesickness', recalled in the quotation at the beginning of this chapter, which continues thus:

> I used to say: 'better polida cess [clean toilets] in the last village of Europe than to be rich and loaded with money and prestige in a Latin American country'. … It was a set of conflicting emotions: idealising life in Europe and at the same time getting used to, accepting the Latin American lifestyle (Filippa 1990: 80).

Europe became a subject of idealisation and distance as in courtly love (see Part II, Chapter 4); it increasingly appeared as 'beautiful Europe',[73] despite the atrocities that were being committed there against the Jews.

Giorgina Levi later maintained that she had reached the point where she envied those who had been exiled to Switzerland or England or France. Paradoxically, people's feelings during exile sometimes included the 'very strange envy' felt towards those who had remained in Europe at risk of mortal peril.[74] Giorgina also expressed feelings of this type, although it was painful for her to leave Latin America. Yet if she and Enzo had remained in Italy, it is easy to imagine the extreme dangers to which they would have been exposed: on 10 June 1940, a few days after Italy entered the war, the internment of foreign Jews began – 6,300 during the spring of 1943 (Voigt 1995). In Italy, approximately 7,700 to 7,900 Jews fell victim to the Shoah (Sarfatti 2000: 271), and the population of approximately 45,000 people of Jewish faith in 1938 fell to some 28,000 in 1945 (Della Pergola 1997: 929).

Giorgina Levi and Heinz Arian went back to Italy in 1946.[75] They went back to a Europe split into West and East between two blocs of influence, the Soviet Union on one side and the United States and Great Britain on the other. A Europe whose value of emancipation had been diverted and overshadowed, the utopian charge it had enjoyed between the two wars having disappeared. The identity investment of our protagonists was mainly cultural and this took on a secondary importance and again became implicit in the new context. Their political investment in communism emerged, instead, as a main driving force. Once she returned from Bolivia, Giorgina Levi went back to her teaching in secondary schools, but also played an active role in politics within the Italian Communist Party. She became a town councillor in Turin (1957–64) and a member of parliament (1963–72). Her *Autobiografia*, written in 1954 for the party (FIPAGT, b. 85, f. 11), describes her progressive politicisation, due to her reading in exile and also to contact with comrades such as Mario Montagnana and Camilla Ravera. Later, she was to recognise the presence of forms of anti-Semitism even in the Italian Communist Party.[76]

In her years of political activity as a parliamentarian, Giorgina Levi was concerned with the topics of pensions and culture and also schools and universities. She was involved in international cultural links with Latin America, and with the Soviet Union as secretary and vice-president of the Associazione Italia–URSS (FIPAGT, Inventory: biographical data). She wrote on these topics and co-wrote a pioneering study on student workers that raised the matter of free evening classes (G. Levi Arian et al. 1969). She collaborated with Ada Gobetti on the journal *Scuola Democratica*, and contributed to many publications such as *Riforma della Scuola, Nuova Società* and *Rinascita*.

Heinz registered in the postgraduate School of Psychiatry and Neuropathology at the University of Turin, where he obtained a postgraduate degree in neuropsychiatry in 1947 with a thesis entitled 'The Application of Gestalt Psychology to Neuropsychiatry'. He gained official recognition as a 'stateless person' (he had been declared as such by the Nazi government in 1941) and was then able to marry Giorgina in a civil ceremony in 1948.[77] He was later active as a psychiatrist and he, too, produced many publications (approximately seventy between 1948 and 1965) in his specialist field. One piece, of particular interest because it reveals his many scientific, professional and humanistic interests, was a long review of Volponi's novel *Memoriale*, from a medical, psychiatric and socio-medical point of view. With great finesse, Arian analyses the extent to which the novel's hero represents a clinically accurate reconstruction of the hero's psychosis, but also shows that *Memoriale* paints an accurate picture of health and social care procedures and of the organisational and psychological relationships between patients and care organisations in Italy at the beginning of the 1960s. His clinical and social analysis was supported by an active political commitment that prompted him to contrast the industrial civilisation of the day with a future world of new factory-based relationships and values (Arian 1963: 176).[78]

Arian wrote of factories and occupational diseases from first-hand experience because he was employed for a long time by the Fiat company health insurance scheme and offered his clinical and scientific services at the University of Turin clinic for nervous and mental diseases. From 1946, he renewed his application for Italian citizenship every year, couching his choice of Italy in moving terms, though to no avail. For example, on 6 January 1948, he wrote to Count Zoppi of the Political Affairs Department of the Ministry of Foreign Affairs:

> Many reasons prompt me to persist with my appeal for naturalisation: reasons of a sentimental nature play a leading role. When I arrived in Italy as a young man in my twenties, I spent my formative years in the Italian cultural and social environment. I studied in Turin, I graduated in Turin, I have worked in Piedmontese clinics and hospitals … . When I returned to this homeland after seven years of painful exile, I resumed my work amongst my colleagues in the Turin Medical Corp … . I have 'married' (only in a religious ceremony, because the race laws of 1938 prohibited a civil marriage) an Italian woman … . What remains of my family (my parents disappeared in Germany in about 1943, probably deported to one of the Nazi 'extermination camps') is Italian or intimately linked to Italy: my wife's family is of ancient Piedmontese Jewish stock; my sister is married to an Italian doctor; my brother, who was granted British citizenship a few months ago, fought for Italian freedom with the British Army throughout the Italian campaign. (CDEC, series 5)

His application was not granted even by the new Italian regime, probably due to Arian's membership of the Communist Party (CDEC, series 6).[79] Enzo Arian finally obtained Italian citizenship at the end of 1962, no less than twenty-six years after applying for it, as a result of a forceful intervention by Senator Umberto Terracini, and less than three years before his death, which was due to heart failure in October 1965, at the age of just fifty-three. Numerous obituaries and commemorations in Turin reveal the important role that the two one-time exiles had assumed in city life.

Giorgina Levi kept up her interest in Latin America, as her many activities in this field reveal. For a long time (1975–87), she edited the Jewish cultural review *Ha Keillah* ('The Community') and she has written many historical works based on oral sources about the movement and the Turinese working class (G. Levi 1999, 1985) and the history of the Jews in Turin (G. Levi Arian and E. Viterbo 1999; G. Levi 1995). Even today, she retains her fighting spirit and calls for a progressive form of Jewishness, sympathising with the oppressed peoples of the world and critically recalling the long and hard-fought debates on the creation of a state of Israel in Palestine.

Notes

1. Thus Giorgina Levi remembers the Bolivian landscape during the late 1930s to early 1940s; see Filippa (1990: 77–79).
2. As we can see from a collection of his photographs (M.A. Levi 1994); see G. Levi (2005) for information on him and her childhood.
3. Interned in a concentration camp in the French Pyrenees and released following the intervention of the League of North American writers, Mario Montagnana emigrated to Mexico with his wife and there wrote a book of memoirs (Montagnana 1944).
4. See my interview GL2, 3 December 2002, in which Giorgina Levi recalls that the only person who was happy when she chose a Jew as her life's partner was her grandmother Montagnana, because 'by then, everyone was marrying Catholics'. The term 'humanism' is used by Pinto (2000).
5. See interview GL1, 21 April 1996.
6. See interview GL1.
7. Statement by the Liceo Ginnasio 'V. Alfieri' in Turin, 25 October 1938, preserved at the CDEC, series 1–2.
8. Interview dated 3 December 2002.
9. Curriculum vitae of Heinz Arian, OPSS.
10. Statement of 8 September 1937 issued by the *podestà* 'for the purpose of acquiring Italian citizenship', CDEC, series 3–4.
11. Leo Levi hit out at people's attitudes to this type of meeting in Turin ('chatting and superficiality') in *Israel* in December 1933; see Marzano (2003:

104–5). According to Marzano, this lack of commitment was connected with the typically Turinese tension between Zionism and a radical antifascism, 'two adjacent worlds, overlapping and communicating in certain senses, but alternatives to one another' (ibid.: 108). In the case of Giorgina Levi, there was a third world, communicating with both the others, closer to the proletarian area and communist inspiration.

12. Note of 20 February 1934; unless otherwise indicated, the quoted correspondence is filed in the ADNPSS.

13. Note of 6 April 1934.

14. The verses he refers to here are taken from 'Im Saal' ('In the Drawing Room') in *Neue Gedichte*: 'Sie lassen, voller Takt, uns ungestört / das Leben leben wie wir es begreifen / und wie sie's nicht verstehen' ('Considerate, they let us live as we / conceive a life – so different from their own') which must mean beauty – the subject is 'all those gentlemen' who follow the honour of the world in limited fashion; in Rilke (1992: 87).

15. Letter of 11 April 1934.

16. Letter of 16 April 1934. The original is the following, taken from the poem 'Die Frage' ('The Question'):
Nimmst du ein einzeln Ding aus deinem Leben
Und wiegst es pruefend in der hohlen Hand,
Du fuehlst darin das grosse Dunkel beben.
(Take one thing from your life / and weigh it in your hand / you will feel the great darkness tremble) (Zweig 1966: 88–89).

17. In ADNPSS.

18. From the San Paolo quarter, where many of them lived.

19. On the significance of salutations, see Lyons (1999: 232–39).

20. The fourth camp was organised with particular care by a group of youngsters because the third had not gone so well; it was a time of 'Jewishness in action, a Jewish life, for every day, for every hour, for every action' (quotation from Marcello Savaldi, reported by Marzano 2003: 53). The camps were attended by people with two extremes of attitude, those who saw the camp as a stepping stone to a trip to Palestine and the 'bourgeois' who saw it as a holiday, but there were intermediate positions in between. Giorgina Levi was one of those who fell in between, due to her family's political traditions.

21. Letter of 23 August 1934.

22. Postcard of 30 July 1936, from the Torre Pellice Clinic. 'Do come, dearest signorina. I don't have to tell you: my home always awaits you, no other, only you. Do come and see the bespectacled doctor: I really want to make an appointment just for you!'. The German part says: '... proud ... such a splendid young woman, my dearest, clever, grown-up, mature and still virginal lady friend'.

23. 'I have eaten like a little pig', letter of 16 February 1940.

24. 'I hope you get a little hunchback', letter datable to 1945.

25. Letter of 13 July 1936.

26. Letter from Katowice dated 11 March 1936.

27. I owe the following explanation to the kindness of Sigrid Sohn: the correct wording is 'yidn', but the German transcription replaces the 'y' with a 'j' and also adds the 'e' in the ending, as with German verbs; 'jiden' is an old

transcription in use before the standard YIVO (Yivo Institute for Jewish Research, New York) term came into use and means 'Juden' or Jews.

28. Letter from Crakow, 15 March 1936. 'Tehillim' means psalms and sometimes this term is used for the Book of Psalms. As far as 'Hiedlach' is concerned, no specific corresponding term can be found. I am again indebted to Sigrid Sohn for the following suggestion: the only word that comes close to it is 'hitl' ('hitlekh' or even 'hitlakh' in the plural), which is the diminutive of 'hut' and means hat, beret. The diminutive is often used for the traditional male headgear. In such a case, this utterance means: 'traditional hats and psalms, debate and talmud'.

29. Germanism coined by Heinz based on 'bombastisch', meaning self-important.

30. This sudden switch to German allows Heinz to use an idiomatic phrase that means: 'no goy could do this' or rather, 'I challenge any goy to do the same'.

31. This interiorisation is mentioned by Poliakov (1961: vol. 2, ix–x), who claims that the situation of the Jews was marginal, because they formed part of European society without, however, wholly belonging to it.

32. According to the Interior Ministry, the number of 'mixed families' amounted to 'no fewer than 6,820' in 1940; see Cavaglion and Romagnani (2002: 98).

33. Luciano Allegra (2003: 125) speaks of 'strict endogamy amongst the Jewish community, which lasted at least until the first decades of the nineteenth century'.

34. Sweet dear; my adored; followed by a series of invented words based on puns with verbs, which can be translated freely as: little nose, doll, sweetheart. Giorginerle and Giorginetterle are diminutives of Giorgina with the prefix used in southern Germany.

35. 'I would like to dive into your good gaze, in the sweetness of your body; I kiss you with all my heart.'

36. Letter of 17 March 1936.

37. G. Levi: 'In Me Vedeva l'Ebrea', interview with L.P. GL1.

38. Letter of 7 June 1938.

39. Interview GL1.

40. Letter of 1 March 1938.

41. Letter to G. Levi from *Dante Alighieri* of 7 February 1939 (CDEC, series 1–2).

42. Letter of 20 July 1938.

43. Letter of 22 July 1938.

44. From the poem Verkündigung, Die Worte des Engels, in *Das Buch der Bilder*. 'I'm whatever is beginning, you though are the tree' ('Annunciation, The Words of the Angels') (Rilke 1991: 109).

45. Letter of 12 August 1938.

46. Letter of 17 August 1938.

47. Letter of 22 August 1938.

48. As Michaelis argues convincingly (1978: 415).

49. This belies the conviction expressed by Guido Lodovico Luzzatto in 1938–1939 that there was not 'even a shadow of hate against the Jews in Italy', which in his opinion made the 'wicked betrayal' by the fascist regime even more serious; see G.L. Luzzatto (1996: 83–91).

50. Declaration on Race by the Great Council of Fascism of 6–7 October 1938, in Cavaglion and Romagnani (2002: 80).
51. They apparently did not consider the possibility of going to Palestine. Emigration from Turin to Palestine was very low in the 1930s due to the 'specific nature of the Piedmontese Jews, who had been the first to achieve emancipation and equal rights in 1848'. This led them to feel a strong sense of belonging to Italy and a somewhat closed attitude to Zionism; see Marzano (2003: 103 et seq.).
52. See the certificate signed by him dated 9 February 1939 (FIPAGT, b. 76, f. 4).
53. One of the few Bolivian statistics gives a figure of 6,898 immigrants for the first half of 1939, including 3,086 from Germany, 180 from Austria, 498 from Czechoslovakia, 7 from Danzig, 737 from Poland and 84 from Rumania. These numbers were considered too low by the German legation of La Paz, particularly the German figure; see Seelisch (1989: 77–101, 86).
54. On the political commitment of Jews exiled from Germany in Latin America, see Bankier (1989: 213–25) and Mühlen (1989: 242–49).
55. See the CDEC, series 12. The correspondence testifies to the continental scope of Heinz Arian's activities as part of the Freies Deutschland movement. The Nationalkomitee Freies Deutschland (NKFD) was founded in 1943 in the Soviet Union by German officials and soldiers who were prisoners of war and communist German exiles, as a means of aiding the struggle against Nazism. We have already discussed (Chapter 4) the role of Karl Barth and Charlotte von Kirschbaum in the section of the movement set up in Switzerland, which, unlike the Russian movement, was not communist.
56. Documentation in CDEC, series 7 and series 17.
57. Affectionate term for 'Mutter' ('mother').
58. Letter of 31 August 1941.
59. In 1938, anti-Semitic writings appeared on their chemist's shop (Berlin Tegel, Ernstrasse 29) and their walls were plastered with *Der Stürmer*, the violent anti-Semitic satirical newspaper directed by Julius Streicher during the period 1923–1945. See the photo relating to the event kept at the CDEC, Fondo Giorgina Levi Arian, series 3–4.
60. Letter from the Centrum Judaicum in Berlin, 21 July 2003. I give my thanks to Sabine Hank of the Centrum for this information.
61. Cecil Roth (1899–1970) was a Reader in Jewish studies at Oxford from 1939 to 1964. He then taught at the Bar-Ilan University in Jerusalem and at the City University of New York. He was the chief editor of *Encyclopaedia Judaica* from 1966 to his death, and the author of more than 600 articles, including histories of Jews in Great Britain and in Italy. A. Luzzatto (1992: 119) remembers that Roth belonged to the Ashkenazi jewry, which was hegemonic in Zionism during that period, but he was 'an enthusiast for the Mediterranean Jewish culture, the Italian culture and the Sephardic culture'. His first major work was, in fact, *The Last Florentine Republic* (1925).
62. The essay was translated into Italian under the title 'Gli Ebrei Quali Europei', in *Rassegna Mensile di Israel*, 12, 10–11–12 5698 (July–August–September 1938), 308–17. It must have been circulated outside Great Britain because a copy of the leaflet was found at the Alliance Israélite in Paris.

63. Nathansen combined the genres of biography and portraiture by documenting the many conversations he had with his friend Brandes (1824–1927), the Danish critic and student of aesthetics. He described Brandes as a cosmopolitan, progressive person who believed in freedom and individuality, but he deplored his attitude to Jewishness, because Brandes denied that this was his identity. Brandes' letters declared himself to be European, even a 'good European' in a Nietzschian sense, against all nationalism, including Jewishness, which he did not wish to consider a nationality.

64. G.L. Luzzatto, 'Ebreo o Europeo', in *Israel*, 17.7.1931, now in Luzzato (1996: 51–53). Luzzatto (1903–1990) was an intellectual, political commentator with socialist views and an art critic; see A. Cavaglion, Introduction to Guido Lodovico Luzzatto, *Scritti Politici*.

65. Amos Oz, in *A Tale of Love and Darkness* (2004), reminds us that many Jews throughout Europe between the two wars were 'enthusiastic Europhiles who were familiar with the entire range of languages spoken in the Old Continent', indeed 'the only Europeans of all Europe, during the Twenties and Thirties, were the Jews'. Half a century later, the 39th ordinary session of the Parliament of the Council of Europe on 5 October 1987 passed Resolution 885 on 'The Jewish Contribution to European culture' (Doc. 5587 – F).

66. CDEC, *Giorgina Levi Arian*, series 1–2.

67. CDEC, *Giorgina Levi Arian*, series 6.

68. Signoretti (1901–1971) had a long career as a journalist and writer, from *Popolo d'Italia* to *La Stampa*, of which he was editor from 1932 to 1943.

69. In Rome, by the publisher 'Prof. P. Maglione'.

70. A tangible basis for this claim existed in the 1930s: Arthur Ruppin in his classic work *The Jews in the Modern World* (1934: 26–27) gave the following figures: 9,690,000 Jews in Europe, 5,000,000 in the Americas, 618,000 in Asia and 33,000 in Africa.

71. I am aware of the risk I run by using terms such as 'Europeanness' and 'Jewishness' in connection, which could make the process of identification in coded mentalities more inflexible. However, I adopt them as shortcuts to indicate these processes. Poliakov uses 'judéité' (vol. 3: 481), and also speaks of the formation 'd'une mentalité juive' in the twelfth and thirteenth centuries, from the First Crusade (vol. 1: 100 et seq.). The thing that matters is the ability to maintain a balance between acknowledgement of the processes of investment in identity that lead individuals and groups to value their traditions, on the one hand, and the refusal to allow these attitudes to become over-rigid on the other; see Hertzberg (1972). On a Jewish sense of belonging devoid of the inflexible sense of 'judéité', the text by A. Memmi, *Portrait d'un Juif* (2003) is fundamental. The same approach is adopted by Cavaglion (2006).

72. Eurocentrism evident in Giorgina's statements such as: 'in the end, the *indios* too were part of the nature of that country' (Filippa 1990: 77), coupled, however, with her self-critical attitude to her own Eurocentric prejudices.

73. Letter from Giorgina Levi to her parents, from Zudanez, 2 November 1939.
74. A. Zargani, Introduction in Jona and Foa (1997: xii).
75. The desire to 'return' had been constant, even though they had been willing to join the Red Army or the UNRRA, which meant that their desire was not aimed directly and exclusively at Italy. This country was, however, crucial in kindling their hopes of return, a role that could not have been played by Germany.
76. Interview GL1.
77. See civil marriage certificate, Turin, 6 December 1948, kept in CDEC, Fondo Giorgina Levi Arian.
78. Volponi's novel dates from 1962.
79. The CDEC file holds all his PCI membership cards from 1946 to 1965, in addition to many other cards that bear witness to his antifascist and progressive commitment, such as a card showing his membership the Algerian Revolution Solidarity Front, the Resistance Club chaired by Franco Antonicelli and the Italian Federation for Cremation.

Primary Sources and Archives

1) Works by Giorgio Quartara

Books

1911. *I Diritti della Donna e della Prole*, Rome: Loescher.
1917. *Dalla Guerra Mondiale alla Civiltà Internazionale*, with a letter from Minister Scialoja, Milan: Treves.
1919. *Per l'Umanità*, Milan: Treves.
1928. *Le Leggi del Libero Amore*, Milan: Bocca.
1930. *Gli Stati Uniti d'Europa e del Mondo*, Turin: Bocca.
1934. *I Quattro Errori di Kerenski*, Turin: Bocca.
1938. *La Riforma del Codice Civile, i Libri I e III: La Famiglia*, Milan: Bocca.
1939. *Un Viaggio nel Sud-America*, Milan: Bocca.
1941. *L'Italia Tradita*, Milan: Bocca.
1942. *La Futura Pace*, Milan: Bocca.
1944. *La Donna e Dio*, Turin: Bocca.
1945. *Del Risorgimento Legislativo*, Milan: Bocca.
1949. *Viva il Papa? O Viva il Re?*, Milan: Bocca.

Reviews and Articles

1910. 'Storia e Critica dell'Art. 57 C. C.', *Rivista Italiana per le Scienze Giuridiche*, 48, issue 1–2, pp. 73–88, republished in *Le Leggi del Libero Amore* and reprinted as a separate work with a preface and note on the USSR: 1945. *Storia e Critica dell'Art. 57 C.C. 1865. Una tra le Leggi del Libero Amore*, Milan: Bocca.
1915. 'Dalla Guerra alla Confederazione Europea per Mezzo dell'Arbitrato', *Critica Sociale*, 25, 23, 1–15 December, pp. 359–61.

1933.   'Vittorio Scialoja Proposto per il Premio Nobel', *Il Lavoro*,
        8 April 1933, p. 3: review of Vittorio Scialoja. *Discorsi alla
        Società delle Nazioni*, with a preface by D. Grandi, Rome:
        A.R.E.
1934a. 'Inghilterra e Unione Europea', *Il Lavoro*, 24 March 1934,
        p. 1: review of Sir Arthur Salter. 1933. *The United States of
        Europe*, London: George Allen and Unwin.
1934b. 'Italia e Francia', *Il Lavoro*, 5 April 1934, p. 1.

Conference Reports

1931.   'Programme Féministe International et National', *Congrès
        International de Belgrade*, May 1931. Milan: Macciachini.
1932.   'Organisation de la Paix Européenne par la Fédération,
        Exposé du Marquis Giorgio Quartara, Avocat, Membre
        Italien de l'Union Paneuropéenne', *Congrès Européen*,
        Basilea, 1932. Milan: Macciachini.
1933a. 'L'Illégitimité des Amantes, des Mères, des Enfants. Exposé
        par le Marquis Giorgio Quartara, Avocat, Membre Italien
        de l'International Alliance of Women', *Congrès Féministe*,
        Marseilles 1933. Milan: Macciachini.
1933b. 'L'Esclavage de la Femme Mariée. Deuxième Exposé par le
        Marquis Giorgio Quartara, Avocat, Membre Italien de
        l'International Alliance of Women', *Congrès Féministe*,
        Marseilles 1933.

        'Memoriale. A S. E. il Ministro della Giustizia, Osservazioni
        sul Progetto del Nuovo Codice Penale, Milano, 30 gennaio
        1930 VIII', typewritten copy sent to Beatrice Sacchi on the
        same date, and held by the Unione Femminile Nazionale,
        Milan.

Translations

The following French translations exist:

1929.   *Les Lois du Libre Amour*, Paris: Alcan.
1931.   *Les Etats Unis d'Europe et du Monde*, Paris: Les Œuvres
        Représentatives.
1935.   *La Femme et Dieu*, Paris: Alcan.

1936. *L'Italie Déçue*, Paris: Alcan.

According to Quartara, a translation of *Gli Stati Uniti d'Europa e del Mondo* in Spanish published by Editorial Colon, Madrid, existed but it has not proved possible to trace it.

Interviews

ET 1   With Ernesto Treccani and Lydia De Grada, recorded by Marina Nordera, Milan, 7 June 1996.

ET 2   With Ernesto Treccani, recorded by Luisa Passerini, Milan, 28 March 2000.

P1   With Gianni and Marilena Puecher Passavalli, recorded by Luisa Passerini, Milan, 17 April 2000.

ETL   Letter from Ernesto Treccani to his mother Giulia Quartara, dated 4 December 1951.

Reports of the IWSA International Congresses (IWA Archive)

Third IWSA Congress Report, Copenhagen 1906.

Eighth IWSA Congress Report, Geneva 1920.

Ninth IWSA Congress Report, Rome 1923.

Eleventh Congress Report of the International Alliance of Women for Suffrage and Equal Citizenship, Berlin 1929.

Third International Suffrage Conference, Copenhagen 1906.

Documents regarding the national activities of Ada and Beatrice Sacchi are held in the archives of the Unione Femminile Nazionale in Milan; those concerning their international activities are held in the archives of the International Association of Women.

2) Works by Leo Ferrero

Essays

1929.   *Léonard de Vinci ou l'Œuvre d'Art*, prefaced by a study *Léonard et les Philosophes de Paul Valéry*, Paris: Kra (It. edn 1929. *Leonardo o dell'Arte*, Turin: Buratti).

1932.   *Paris Dernier Modèle de l'Occident*, Paris: Rieder.

1939a. *Amérique, Miroir Grossissant de l'Europe*, Paris: Rieder.

1939c. *Meditazioni sull'Italia. Letteratura e Politica*, with a preface by Count Carlo Sforza, Lugano: Nuove Edizioni Capolago.

1940.   *Appunti sul Metodo della Divina Commedia, del Dramma, dell'Arte Classica e Decadente*, Lugano–Geneva: Nuove Edizioni Capolago.

1941a. *Le Secret de l'Angleterre*, Geneva: Editions de Présence.

1993.   *Diario di un Privilegiato sotto il Fascismo*, Milan: Claudio Lombardi. Other editions also exist, such as that of Chiantore (1946) and that with a preface by S. Romano, Florence: Passigli (1993).

1999.   *Lettere Europee. Le Lettere Familiari di Leo Ferrero dal 1919–1933*, A. Kornfeld (ed.), Rome: Bulzoni.

Literary and Theatrical Works

1919.   *La Favola dei Sette Colori*.

1921.   *Il Ritorno di Ulisse*.

1923.   *La Chevelure de Bérénice*, in *Trois Drames*.

1924.   *Les Campagnes sans Madones*, in *Trois Drames*.

1924–28. *Poids d'Or*, in *Trois Drames*.

1929.   [1934]. *Angelica* (Fr. edn), Paris: Rieder; 1937. *Angelica* (It. edn), Lugano: Capolago.

1935.   *Espoirs. Comédie Italienne*, Preface by G. Ferrero, Paris: Rieder.

1937.   *Désespoirs. Poèmes en Prose – Prières – Pensées*, Preface by G. Lombroso, Paris: Rieder.

1939b. *La Catena degli Anni. Poesie e Pensieri fra i Venti e Ventinove Anni*, Lugano–Geneva: Edizioni di Capolago.

1941b. 'Chassé-croisé', short story, *L'Illustré*, 6, pp. 158–59. Combined in *Il Ritorno di Ulisse. La Favola dei Sette Colori*, Lugano: Nuove Edizioni Capolago, n.d.

1942. *Trois Drames*, Preface by R. de Traz, Geneva: Editions de Présence. It. edn: n.d. but 1924. *La Chioma di Berenice. Le Campagne senza Madonna*, Preface by A. Tilgher, Milan: Atena.

Collections Containing Works on and by Leo Ferrero

1936. *Angelica à travers le Monde. Jugements sur la Pièce avant sa Représentation*, Paris: Rieder.

1943. G. Lombroso-Ferrero. *L'Œuvre de LF à travers la Critique*, Geneva: Grivet.

1984. *Il Muro Trasparente. Scritti di Poesia, di Prosa e di Teatro*, M. Scotti (ed.), Quaderni della Fondazione Primo Conti, Milan: Scheiwiller.

Most letters and documents by and on Leo Ferrero are held at the Fondazione Primo Conti di Fiesole, and a small part at the Centro Studi Piero Gobetti in Turin.

Articles in Italian

1926a. 'Appunti su Umberto Saba', *Solaria*, July–August, 7–8, pp. 42–46.

1926b. 'Guido Lud. Luzzatto – Brunelleschi', *Solaria*, December, 12, pp. 50–51.

1927a. 'Italo Svevo: *Senilità*', *Solaria*, October, 7–10, pp. 56–59.

1927b. 'Corrado Alvaro – *L'Uomo nel Labirinto*; Louis Martin-Chauffier – *Jeux de l'Ame*; Luigi Pirandello – *Diana e la Tuda*', *Solaria*, June, 6, pp. 49–54.

1927c. 'Jean Pellerin: *Têtes de Rechange*', *Solaria*, June, 6, pp. 55–56.

1927d. 'Il Valore del Silenzio', *Solaria*, June, 6, pp. 56–61.

1929a. 'Visita a Svevo', *Solaria*, March, pp. 3–4.

1929b. 'Il Destino delle Donne Inglesi', *Il Piccolo della Sera*, Trieste, 24 May.

1932. 'Drieu la Rochelle – L'Europe contre les Patries', *Solaria*, May, p. 59.

1939d.   'Il Compito degli Scrittori e il Coraggio', *Giustizia e Libertà*, 14 January; now in *MT*, pp. 100–101.

Articles in French

1928.   'La Faillite des Femmes Anglaises', *Notre Temps*, December, pp. 76–78.

1930a.   'Forces Conservatrices et Esprit Révolutionnaire (Réponse au Comte de Keyserling)', *L'Europe Nouvelle*, 5 July, pp. 1009–10.

1930b.   'Poésie Maigre: Montale et Quasimodo', *Notre Temps*, 20 July, p. 239.

1930c.   'José Ortega à Paris: Un Jugement sur la France', *L'Europe Nouvelle*, 22 March, pp. 470–71.

1932.   'Loria et l'Obsession du Bonheur', *L'Européen*, 9 September.

1933.   'Contemplation de New York', *Nouvelles Littéraires*, 9 September.

3) Works by Denis de Rougemont

1933.   Review of K. Barth, *Parole de Dieu et Parole Humaine, Les Nouvelles Littéraires*, 30 December, p. 4.

1934.   *Politique de la Personne*, Paris: Editions Je sers.

1941.   and C. Muret. *The Heart of Europe*, New York: Duell, Sloan and Pearce.

1972.   [1936]. *Penser avec les Mains*, Paris: Gallimard.

1937.   *Journal d'un Intellectuel en Chômage*, Paris: Albin Michel.

1938.   *Journal d'Allemagne*, Paris: Gallimard.

1939.   *L'Amour et l'Occident*, Paris: Plon.

1945.   *La Part du Diable*, Neuchâtel: A la Baconnière (first edn New York: 1942).

1947.   *Doctrine Fabuleuse*, Neuchâtel–Paris: Ides et Calendes.

1956.   *L'Amour et l'Occident*, Edition remaniée et augmentée, Paris: Plon.

1961.   *Comme Toi-Même. Essais sur les Mythes de l'Amour*, Paris: Albin Michel. (Republished 1996 as *Les Mythes de l'Amour*, Paris: Albin Michel.)

1968.   *Journal d'une Epoque (1926–1946)*, Paris: Gallimard.

1971.   'L'Amour et l'Europe', Interview in *L' Express*, 12 April, pp. 124 ff.
1972a.   *L'Amour et l'Occident*, Edition définitive, Paris: Plon.
1972b.   [1936]. *Penser avec les Mains*, Paris: Gallimard.
1977.   [1926]. 'Adieu, Beau Désordre ... (Notes sur la Littérature et la Morale)', *Revue de Genève*, March; now in *Bulletin du Centre Européen de la Culture*: 'L'Itinéraire d'un Penseur Engagé. Les 70 ans de Denis de Rougemont', 16, 3, pp. 19–26.
1982.   [1932]. *Le Paysan du Danube et Autres Textes*, Clamecy: L'Age d'Homme.
1983.   [1940, 1956]. *Love in the Western World* (*L'Amour et l'Occident*), tr. Montgomery Belgion, Princeton, NJ: Princeton University Press (UK title 1956. *Passion and Society*, London: Faber and Faber).
1989.   *La Suisse ou l'Histoire d'un Peuple Heureux*, Lausanne: L'Age d'Homme.
1995.   *Ecrits sur l'Europe*, Œuvres Complètes, 3 vols, C. Calame (ed.), Paris: La Différence.

An anthology of Denis de Rougement's works written in Italian has been published by S. Locatelli and G. Huen de Florentiis (eds). 1965. *Denis de Rougemont. La Vita e il Pensiero*, Milan: Ferro.

Denis de Rougemont's letters, works, reviews and several volumes from his library are held in the Fonds Rougemont at the Bibliothèque Publique et Universitaire de Neuchâtel.

Interviews

SVS 1 with Simonne Vion Sinclair.
LS 1 with Luigi Santucci.

4) Giorgina Levi and Heinz Arian

The correspondence between Giorgina Levi and Enzo Arian is preserved in the Archivio Diaristico Nazionale di Pieve Santo Stefano (ADNPSS); the collection also contains telegrams from Enzo and some of his sketches and postcards. Information on Enzo's life comes from the Fondo Arian at the Archivio della

Biblioteca 'Vincenzo Chiarugi' of the homonymous Ospedale Psichiatrico di San Salvi (OPSS), Florence.

Other archives consulted are those of the Centro di Documentazione Ebraica Contemporanea in Milan, Fondo Giorgina Levi Arian, indicated in the text as CDEC; that of the Fondazione Istituto Piemontese Antonio Gramsci in Turin (FIPAGT), Fondo Giorgina Levi: seventy-eight envelopes, as well as numerous certificates and cards.

The interviews with Giorgina Levi were recorded on the following dates:

GL1 21 April 1996

GL2 3 December 2002.

The list of works by Giorgina Levi is limited to those relevant to the chapter, but there are many more. Several may be consulted at the Biblioteca della Fondazione Istituto Gramsci Piemontese, which also holds lists of her articles. Two typewritten documents are also held together with the inventory of the Fondo Giorgina Levi: biographical data compiled by the person who catalogued the material, and a biography entitled 'Giorgina Levi ved. Arian' dated 1 July 1998, with a note by the author.

References

Acanfora Torrefranca, M. 1996. 'Sulle Musiche degli Ebrei in Italia', in C. Vivanti (1996), op. cit., pp. 477–93.

Ackermann, B. 1996. *Denis de Rougemont. Une Biographie Intellectuelle*, 2 vols, Geneva: Labor et Fides.

———. 2000. *Denis de Rougemont. De la Personne à l'Europe*, Lausanne: L'Age d'Homme.

'a.d.c.' [initials of Andrea Della Corte]. 1935. '*Il Dibuk* di L. Rocca', *La Stampa*, 23 January.

Agnelli, G. and A. Cabiati. 1918. *Federazione Europea o Lega delle Nazioni?*, Turin: Bocca.

Akademie der Künste. 1995. *Rifugio Precario. Zuflucht auf Widerruf. Artisti e Intellettuali Tedeschi in Italia 1933–1945. Deutsche Künstler und Wissenschaftler in Italien*, Milan, Palazzo della Ragione, 9 March–30 April 1995, Berlin, Akademie der Künste, 29 August–22 October 1995, Milan: Mazzotta.

Albasio, F.A. 1917. Review of 'Giorgio Quartara, *Dalla Guerra Mondiale alla Civiltà Internazionale*', *Nosotros*, 11, 102 (December), pp. 536–38.

Albert, C. 1921. *L'Amore Libero*, Foreword by L. Rafanelli, Milan: Casa Editrice Sociale.

Alessandrone, P.E. 1985. 'La Cultura Francese nelle Riviste e nelle Iniziative Editoriali di Piero Gobetti', in Centro Studi Piero Gobetti, *Piero Gobetti e la Francia*, Proceedings of the Colloquio Italo-Francese, 25–27 February 1983, Milan: Angeli, pp. 111–36.

Alibert, L. 1942. 'Origine et Destin de la Langue d'Oc', *Le Génie d'Oc et l'Homme Méditerranéen*, *Cahiers du Sud*, 249, August–September–October, pp. 17–25.

Allegra, L. 2003. 'Né Machos, né Mammolette. La Mascolinità degli Ebrei Italiani', *Genesis*, 2, 2, pp. 125–55n.

Allegri, R. 1982. 'Cinquant'Anni fa Dicevano Che Ero un Genio', *Gente*, 23 April.

Alvaro, C. 1994. *Opere. Romanzi Brevi e Racconti*, G. Pampaloni (ed.), Milan: Bompiani.

Amengual, B. 1952. *Le Mythe de Tristan et Yseult au Cinéma*, Algiers: Travail et Culture.

Amselle, J.-L. 1996. *Vers un Multiculturalisme Français. L'Empire de la Coutume*, Paris: Aubier.

'Angoli Bui'. 1930. *L'Osservatore Romano*, 25 May, p. 1; 'Una Ipotesi', *L'Osservatore Romano*, 1 June, p. 1.

Ansky, S. 1926. *Il Dijbuch (Tra i Due Mondi)*, Leggenda drammatica in 4 atti di Scialom Ansky, It. tr. M. De Benedetti and L. Goldfischer, Preface by B. Terracini, Turin: Istituto Editoriale di Propaganda.

———. [S. An-Ski]. 1927a. *Le Dibbouk*, Fr. tr. M.-T. Koerner, Paris: Rieder.

———. 1927b. *The Dybbuk*, Eng. tr. H.G. Alsberg and W. Katzin, Introduction by

———. G.W. Gabriel and Note on Hasidism by C. Zhitlowsky, London: Ernest Benn.

──────. 1957 [1934]. *Il Dibuk*, Leggenda Drammatica in un Prologo e Tre Atti di Scialom Ansky, Adapted by Renato Simoni, Milan: Ricordi.

──────. 1997 [1992]. *Il Dibbuk*, It. tr. S. Avisar, Rome: Edizioni e/o.

──────. 2000. *The Dybbuk*, in J. Neugroschel (ed.), *The Dybbuk and the Yiddish Imagination. A Haunted Reader*, Syracuse: Syracuse University Press, pp. 3–52.

Ansky, S., T. Kushner and J. Neugroschel. 1998. *A Dybbuk*, New York: Theatre Communications Group.

Arian, E. 1963. 'Recensione di Paolo Volponi, *Memoriale*', *Rivista di Sicurezza Sociale*, January–March, pp. 173–80.

Arni, C. 2004. 'Simultaneous Love: An Argument on Love, Modernity and the Feminist Subject at the Beginning of the Twentieth Century', *European Review of History*, 11, 2, Summer, pp. 185–205.

Aron, R. and A. Dandieu. 1931a. *Décadence de la Nation Française*, Paris: Rieder.

──────. 1931b. *Le Cancer Américain*, Paris: Rieder.

Artaud, A. 1980. *Œuvres Complètes*, Paris: Gallimard.

Aslan, O. 1979. '*Le Dibbouk*', in D. Bablet (ed.), *Les Voies de la Création Théatrale. Mises en Scène Années 20 et 30*, Paris: CNRS, pp. 156–241.

Aubray, T. 1940. 'Battements', *Cahiers du Sud*, 229, November, pp. 520–26.

Audard, J. 1932. Review of '*Le Déclin de l'Occident* par Oswald Spengler', *Cahiers du Sud*, December, pp. 804–8.

Auden, W.H. 1941. 'Eros and Agape', *The Nation*, 28 June, pp. 756–58.

Audisio, G. 1933. 'La Patrie Méditerranéenne', *Cahiers du Sud*, 155, October, pp. 601–9.

──────. 1935. *Jeunesse de la Méditerranée*, Paris: Gallimard.

──────. 1936a. *Sel de la Mer*, Paris: NRF.

──────. 1936b. 'Documents sur l'Esprit Méditerranéen', *Cahiers du Sud*, 181, March, pp. 273–76.

──────. 1936c. Ibid., 183, pp. 427–29.

──────. 1936d. Ibid., 184, pp. 519–20.

──────. 1937a. 'Sur Quelques Livres d'Esprit Méditerranéen', *Cahiers du Sud*, 191, February, pp. 133–36.

──────. 1937b. 'Culture Méditerranéenne', *Cahiers du Sud*, 195, July, pp. 457–60.

──────. 1938. 'Conférence La Méditerranée Vivante', *Cahiers du Sud*, 208, August, pp. 574–75.

──────. 1942. 'Vues sur Ulysse ou l'Ambivalence des Méditerranéens', *Cahiers du Sud*, 249, August–September–October, pp. 271–82.

Avisar, S. 1957. *Teatro Ebraico*, Milan: Nuova Accademia.

Babini V.P., F. Minuz and A. Tagliavini. 1989. *La Donna nelle Scienze dell'Uomo*, Milan: Franco Angeli.

Bagnoli, P. 1986. 'Leo Ferrero e Firenze', *Nuova Antologia*, vol. 555, issue 2158, April–June, pp. 329–38.

──────. 1993. 'Piero Gobetti e la Francia', in M.C. Chiesi (ed.), *Il Mito della Francia nella Cultura Italiana del Novecento. L'Immigrazione Letteraria e Politica in Francia dagli Inizi del '900 al Fascismo*, Proceedings of the Conference in Florence, 13–14 May 1993, pp. 55–64.

Baldi, S. 1998. *Musica e Musicisti a Torino: 1911–1946*, Provincia di Torino: Ordine Mauriziano.

Ballard, J. 1935. Presentation to André Rolland de Renéville, *Les Poètes et la Société*, *Cahiers du Sud*, 178, December, p. 852.

————. 1938. 'Propos de Nos Vingt-cinq Ans', *Cahiers du Sud*, 201, January, pp. 61–64.

————. 1940. 'Mission de l'Esprit', *Cahiers du Sud*, 225, June, pp. 353–56.

————. 1942. 'Soirée Languedocienne – Entretiens dans la Cité', *Cahiers du Sud*, 249, August–September–October, pp. 390–405.

————. 1993. 'Coup d'Œil sur Notre Demi-siècle', in *Jean Ballard et les* Cahiers du Sud, Catalogue de la Ville de Marseille, pp. 255–67.

Bankier, D. 1989. *Die Beziehungen zwischen Deutschen Jüdischen Flüchtlingen und Deutschen Politischen Exilierten in Südamerica*, in A. Schrader and K.H. Rengstorf (eds), *Europäische Juden in Lateinamerika*, St Ingbert: Röhrig, pp. 213–25.

Barbieri, M. 1937. 'Il Dibuk di Ludovico Rocca Eseguito con Successo al Carlo Felice', *Il Secolo XIX*, 10 March.

Bardi, A. 2002–3. '"Tra due mondi". *Il Dibuk* come Spettacolo e sua Penetrazione nel Mondo non Ebraico', *Bollettino dell'Amicizia Ebraico-Cristiana*, Autumn–Winter.

Barth, K. 1953. *Dogmatique*, vol. 1, *La Doctrine de la Parole de Dieu. Prolégomènes à la Dogmatique*, 1*, Geneva: Labor et Fides.

————. 1963. *Church Dogmatics*, vol. 1, *The Doctrine of the Word of God (Prolegomena to Church Dogmatics)*, tr. G.W. Bromiley, Edinburgh: T. and T. Clark.

————. 1964. *Dogmatique*, vol. 3, *La Doctrine de la Création*, 4, Geneva: Labor et Fides.

————. 1981. *Ethics*, tr. G.W. Bromiley, Edinburgh: Dietrich Braun.

————. 1983. *Antologia*, tr. and ed. E. Riverso, Milan: Bompiani.

————. 1986. *Volontà di Dio e Desideri Umani. L'Iniziativa Teologica di K. Barth nella Germania Hitleriana*, Introduction by E. Genre, Turin: Claudiana.

Barthes, R. 1990. *A Lover's Discourse. Fragments*, tr. R. Howard, Harmondsworth: Penguin. (Original version 1977. *Fragments d'un Discours Amoureux*, Paris: Seuil.)

————. 2002. *Le Neutre. Notes de Cours au Collège de France*, Paris: Seuil.

Bartov, O. 2005. *The 'Jew' in Cinema. From The Golem to Don't Touch My Holocaust*, Bloomington–Indianapolis: Indiana University Press.

Basso, A. 1971. *Il Conservatorio di Musica 'Giuseppe Verdi' di Torino. Storia e Documenti dalle Origini al 1970*, Turin: UTET.

————. 1976. *Il Teatro della Città dal 1788 al 1936*, vol. 2, Turin: Cassa di Risparmio di Torino.

Baty, G. n.d. Article in *Masques. Cahiers d'Art Dramatique*, 9, *Le Théatre Yiddisch. Etude et Documents*, Paris, 5.

Baumgarten, J. 2002. *Le Yiddish. Histoire d'une Langue Errante*, Paris: Albin Michel.

Beaurepaire, P.-Y. 2002. *L'Europe des Francs-maçons. XVIII–XXI Siècles*, Paris: Belin.

Bechtel, D. 2002. *La Renaissance Culturelle Juive en Europe Centrale et Orientale 1897–1930: Langue, Littérature et Construction Nationale*, Paris: Belin.

Becker, J.-J. and A. Wieviorka (eds). 1998. *Les Juifs de France. De la Révolution Française à Nos Jours*, Paris: Liana Levi.

Beer, M. 1982. 'L'Anima della Donna. A Proposito del Libro di Gina Lombroso', *Memoria. Rivista di Storia delle Donne*, 4 June, pp. 155–60.

Béguin, A. 1939. 'L'Amour et l'Occident', *Journal de Genève*, 26 May.

Belgion, M. 1939. 'Courtly Love', *The Tablet*, 18 February, 205 et seq.

Belkin, A. 2003. 'The "Low" Culture of the Purimshpil', in J. Berkowitz (ed.), *Yiddish Theatre. New Approaches*, Oxford–Portland, Or.: The Littman Library of Jewish Civilization.

Belperron, P. 1948. *La 'Joie d'Amour'. Contribution à l'Etude des Troubadours et de l'Amour Courtois*, Paris: Plon.

Belsey, C. 1994. *Desire. Love Stories in Western Culture*, Oxford, UK–Cambridge, Mass.: Blackwell.

Benabed, H.H. 1947. 'La Condition de la Femme Musulmane', reissue of special edition of *Cahiers du Sud* on 'L'Islam et l'Occident', pp. 211–19.

Bénac, H. 1937. Review of '*Synthèse de l'Europe* par Count Carlo Sforza', *Cahiers du Sud*, 195, July, pp. 446–47.

Benetti Brunelli, V. 1933. *La Donna nella Civiltà Moderna*, Turin: Bocca.

Ben-Lazare. 1930. 'Comment Partit, Prit Forme et Grandit le Théatre Juif', in *Le Théâtre Juif dans le Monde*, Paris.

Benoit, F. 1942. 'L'Unité Méditerranéenne. Quelques Points de Contacts entre l'Orient et l'Occident', *Le Génie d'Oc et l'Homme Méditerranéen, Cahiers du Sud*, 249, August–September–October, pp. 312–23.

Ben-Sasson, H.H. 1976. 'The Middle Ages. Social Life and Cultural Achievement', in idem (ed.), *A History of the Jewish People*, London: Weidenfeld and Nicolson, pp. 517–60.

Berl, E. 1931a. *Le Bourgeois et l'Amour*, Paris: Gallimard.

———. 1931b. *Recherches sur la Nature de l'Amour*, Paris: Plon.

Bernardi, M. 1970. *Riccardo Gualino e la Cultura Torinese*, Turin: Centro Studi Piemontesi.

Bernhard, E. 1977. *Mitobiografia*, Milan: Bompiani.

Bertin, G. 1930. Review of '*Scènes de la Vie Future* par Georges Duhamel', *Cahiers du Sud*, 125, September, pp. 629–31.

Bertolone, P. 1996. 'Dialoghi e Riflessi dagli Stati Uniti all'Italia', *La Rassegna Mensile di Israel*, 62, 1–2, January–August, pp. 331–45.

Berton, C. 1928. 'Les Visages de la Comédie. Le Cartel des Quatre', *Nouvelles Littéraires*, 18 February.

Bettauer, H. 1922. *Die Stadt ohne Juden. Ein Roman von übermorgen*, Vienna (Eng. tr. 1926. *The City without Jews, A Novel of Our Time*, New York: Bloch Publishing).

Beukers, M. and R. Waale (eds). 1992–94. *Tracing An-sky. Jewish Collections from the State Ethnographic Museum in St. Petersburg*, Zwolle: Waanders Uitgevers.

Bevilacqua, G. 1995. 'Considerazioni Conclusive', in *Akademie*, op. cit., pp. 245–46.

Biale, D. 1983. 'Love, Marriage and the Modernization of the Jews', in *Approaches to Modern Judaism*, Chico, Ca.: Scholars Press, pp. 1–17.

———. 1997. *Eros and the Jews*, Berkeley–Los Angeles–London: University of California Press (It. tr. 2003. *L'Eros nell'Ebraismo. Dai Tempi Biblici ai Tempi Nostri*, Florence: Giuntina).

Biale, D. (ed.). 2002. *Cultures of the Jews. A New History*, New York: Schocken.

Bidussa, D. 1992. 'Tra Avanguardia e Rivolta. Il Sionismo in Italia nel Primo Quarto del Novecento', in D. Bidussa, A. Luzzatto and G. Luzzatto Voghera (1992), op. cit., pp. 155–279.

Bidussa, D., A. Luzzatto and G. Luzzatto Voghera. 1992. *Oltre il Ghetto. Momenti e Figure della Cultura Ebraica in Italia tra l'Unità e il Fascismo*, Brescia: Morcelliana.

Biélinky J. 1928a. 'Le "Dibbouk" au Studio des Champs-Elysées', *L'Univers Israélite*, 83, 19, 27 January, pp. 591–92.

———. 1928b. 'Autour de la Première', *L'Univers Israélite*, 83, 21, 10 February, 651.

Bignardi, I. 1983. 'Cominciò con l'Amore', *La Repubblica*, 19 May.

Biographisches Handbuch der Deutschsprachigen Emigration nach 1933. 1980. Munich–New York–London–Paris: Saur (Eng. tr. 1980. *International Biographical Dictionary of Central European Emigrés 1933–1945*. Munich–New York–London–Paris: Saur).

Bisi. C. 1930. 'Il Martirio della Donna', review of Giorgio Quartara, *Le Leggi del Libero Amore*, *Il Lavoro*, 12 July, p. 3.

Blanchart, P. 1939. *Gaston Baty*, Paris: Editions de la Nouvelle Revue Critique.

———. 1952. *Gaston Baty. Notes et Documents*, *Revue d'Histoire du Théâtre*, pp. 1–2.

Blanchot, M. 1969. *L'Entretien Infini*, Paris: Gallimard (It. tr. 1977. *L'Infinito Intrattenimento*, Turin: Einaudi).

———. 1983. *La Communauté Inavouable*, Paris: Minuit (Eng. tr. 1988. *The Unavowable Community*, New York: Station Hill Press).

Blin, G. 1935. Review of '*La Créole du Central Garage* par Jean Pallu', *Cahiers du Sud*, 176, October, pp. 691–92.

Bloom, H. 1998. *Afterword*, in S. Ansky, T. Kushner and J. Neugroschel (1998), op. cit., pp. 109–12.

Bobbio, N. 1977. *Trent'Anni di Storia della Cultura a Torino (1920–1950)*, Turin: Cassa di Risparmio di Torino.

Boella, L. 2001. *Cuori Pensanti. Hannah Arendt Simone Weil Edith Stein Maria Zambrano*, Mantua: Tre Lune.

Bois, P. 1991. 'L'Orient de Debussy à Boulez. Quelques Réflexions Concernant l'Influence des Musiques Orientales sur la Musique Moderne et Contemporaine', in *D'un Orient l'autre. Les Métamorphoses Successives des Perceptions et des Connaissances*, vol. 1, *Configurations*, Centre d'Etudes et de Documentation Economique Juridique et Sociale Le Caire, Paris: CNRS, pp. 437–55.

Bonjean, F. 1935. 'Quelques Causes d'Incompréhension entre l'Islam et l'Occident', *Cahiers du Sud*, 175, August–September, pp. 5–27.

———. 1942. 'Eurafrique, Méditerranée et Humanisme', *Le Génie d'Oc et l'Homme Méditerranéen*, *Cahiers du Sud*, 249, August–September–October, pp. 326–31.

Borrel, E. 1935. 'La Musique Orientale', *Cahiers du Sud*, 175, August–September, pp. 98–100.

Bosc, J. 1939. Review of Denis de Rougemont. '*L'Amour et l'Occident*', *Le Semeur*, May, pp. 471–73.

Bosch, M. and A. Kloosterman (eds). 1990. *Politics and Friendship. Letters from the International Woman Suffrage Alliance, 1902–1942*, Columbus: Ohio State University Press.

Bosetti, G. 1993. 'Leo Ferrero e il Mito di Parigi', in M.C. Chiesi (ed.), *Il Mito della Francia nella Cultura Italiana del Novecento. L'Immigrazione Letteraria e Politica in Francia dagli Inizi del '900 al Fascismo*, Proceedings of the Conference in Florence, 13–14 May 1993, pp. 73–81.

Bousquet, J. 1933. 'Amour qui Parle en ma Pensée', *Cahiers du Sud*, 151, May, pp. 340–49.

_____. 1935. Review of *Politique de la Personne*, *Cahiers du Sud*, December, 178, p. 875.

_____. 1937. Review of *Journal d'un Intellectuel en Chômage*, *Cahiers du Sud*, December, 200, pp. 741–43.

_____. 1939. Review of *L'Amour et Occident*, *Cahiers du Sud*, June, 217, pp. 529–32.

_____. 1942. 'Présentation de l'Homme d'Oc', *Le Génie d'Oc et l'Homme Méditerranéen*, *Cahiers du Sud*, 249, August–September, pp. 9–13.

Bouwsma, W.J. 1992. *Giovanni Calvino*, Rome: Laterza (original version 1998. *John Calvin: A Sixteenth-century Portrait*, New York: Oxford University Press).

Boyarin, J. 1994. 'The Other Within and the Other Without', in L.J. Silberstein and R.L. Cohn (1994), op. cit., pp. 424–52.

_____. 1996. 'From Derrida to Fichte? The New Europe, the Same Europe, and the Place of the Jews', in idem, *Thinking in Jewish*, Chicago–London: University of Chicago Press, pp. 108–39.

Brenon, A. 2000. *Les Archipels Cathares. Dissidence Chrétienne dans l'Europe Médiévale*, Cahors: Dire.

Breuil, R. 1937. Review of *Penser avec les Mains*, *Cahiers du Sud*, 191, February, pp. 218–22.

_____. 1946. Review of *L'Amour et l'Occident*, *Cahiers du Sud*, 222, March, pp. 209–10.

Brillant, M. 1928. Review of '*Dibbouk*', *Le Correspondant*, 25 February, pp. 618–30.

Brion, M. 1930. Review of '*Analyse Spectrale de l'Europe* par Count Hermann de Keyserling', *Cahiers du Sud*, 124, September, pp. 559–60.

_____. 1933a. Review of '*Le Secret de Mistral* par Gabriel Boissy', *Cahiers du Sud*, 155, October, pp. 631–34.

_____. 1933b. Review of '*Absence* par Marc Chadourne', *Cahiers du Sud*, 156, November, pp. 726–30.

_____. 1935. 'Sur un Concept Moderne de la Culture', *Cahiers du Sud*, 174, July, pp. 549–75.

Brisson, P. 1928. Review of *Dibbouk*, *Le Temps*, 6 February.

Brugmans, H. 1988. 'Denis de Rougemont du Personnalisme au Fédéralisme Européen', in *Du Personnalisme au Fédéralisme Européen. En Hommage à Denis de Rougemont*, Geneva: Editions du Centre Européen de la Culture.

Bruneteau, B. 2003. 'L'Europe Nouvelle' de Hitler. Une Illusion des Intellectuels de la France de Vichy, Monaco: Rocher.

Bruni, M. 1935. 'Il Dibuk di Ludovico Rocca', Torino. Rassegna Mensile Municipale, 7 July, pp. 1–12.

Burko-Falcman, B. 1967–68. Une Pièce du Théatre Yiddish: 'Le Dibbuk' de S. An-Ski, Mémoire présenté à la Faculté de Lettres de l'Université de Paris.

Buttafuoco, A. 1988. Cronache Femminili. Temi e Momenti della Stampa Emancipazionista in Italia dall'Unità al Fascismo, Dipartimento di Studi Storico–Sociali e Filosofici, Siena: Università degli Studi.

———. 1992. 'Vie per la Cittadinanza. Associazionismo Politico Femminile in Lombardia fra Otto e Novecento', in A. Gigli Marchetti and N. Torcellan (eds), Donna Lombarda 1860–1945, Milan: Franco Angeli, pp. 21–45.

Cabella, A. 1985. Piero Gobetti e le Riviste Italo-Francesi 'Vita Latina – Les Jeunes Auteurs' e 'Vita' di Jean Luchaire, in Centro Studi Piero Gobetti. Piero Gobetti e la Francia, Proceedings of the Colloquio Italo-Francese, 25–27 February 1983, Milan: Angeli, pp. 101–10.

Cadmos, 11, 44, Winter, 1988–89: 'L'Amour et l'Occident. Réflexions sur l'Homme et la Femme'.

Cahen, R. 1928. 'Courrier Théatral', Archives Israélites, 89, 6, 9 February, p. 23.

Caillois, R. 1937. 'Le Mythe et l'Art: Nature de Leur Opposition', in II Congrès International d'Esthétique et de Science de l'Art, Paris: Alcan, pp. 280–82.

———. 1938. Le Mythe et l'Homme, Paris: Gallimard (It. tr. 1998. Il Mito e l'Uomo, Turin: Bollati Boringhieri).

Caillois, R. and V. Ocampo. 2003. Corrispondenza 1939–1978, Palermo: Sellerio.

Calcagno, G. 1970. 'Francesco Bernardelli un Maestro e un Amico', Nostro Tempo, 19 May.

Calloni, M. and L. Cedroni (eds). 1997. Politica e Affetti Familiari. Lettere dei Rosselli ai Ferrero (1917–1943), Milan: Feltrinelli.

———. 1998. Gina Lombroso tra Scienza, Impegno Civile e Vita Familiare (Pavia 1872–Ginevra 1944), in L. Cedroni (ed.), Nuovi Studi su Guglielmo Ferrero, Rome: Aracne, pp. 273–94.

Camatti, P. 1994. 'Una Donna Dimenticata: Ada Sacchi', Padania. Storia Cultura Istituzioni, 8, 15, pp. 203–18.

Canciani, D. 1996. Simone Weil. Il Coraggio di Pensare. Impegno e Riflessione Politica tra le Due Guerre, Rome: Edizioni Lavoro.

———. 2002. '"Des Textes dont le Feu Brûle Encore…" Simone Weil, les Cahiers du Sud et la Civilisation Occitanienne', in Cahiers Simone Weil, 25, 2, p. 97.

Cantoni, R. 1976. La Coscienza Inquieta. Søren Kierkegaard, Milan: il Saggiatore.

Cantoni, R. and L. Cedroni. 1994. 'La Famiglia Lombroso-Ferrero. Intervista a Nora Lombroso', in L. Cedroni (ed.). Guglielmo Ferrero. Itinerari del Pensiero, Naples: Edizioni Scientifiche Italiane.

Capristo, A. 2002. L'Espulsione degli Ebrei dalle Accademie Italiane, Turin: Zamorani.

Carsin, P. 1928. Review of the Dibbouk, La Revue Hebdomadaire, 37, 11 February, pp. 242–44.

Cavaglion, A. 1988. 'Argon e la Cultura Ebraica Piemontese', Belfagor, 5 September, pp. 541–62.

_____ .1997. 'Tendenze Nazionali e Albori Sionistici', in C. Vivanti (1997), op. cit., pp. 1291–320.

_____ .2006. *Il Senso dell'Arca. Ebrei Senza Saperlo: Nuove Riflessioni*, Naples: l'ancora del mediterraneo.

Cavaglion, A. and G.P. Romagnani. 2002. *Le Interdizioni del Duce. Le Leggi Razziali in Italia*, Turin: Claudiana.

Cazzaniga, G.M. 1999. *La Religione dei Moderni*, Pisa: ETS.

Cedroni, L. (ed.). 1994. *Guglielmo Ferrero. Itinerari del Pensiero*, Naples: Edizioni Scientifiche Italiane.

_____ .1998. *Nuovi Studi su Guglielmo Ferrero*, Rome: Aracne.

Chabot, J.-L. 1978. 'L'Idée d'Europe Unie de 1919 à 1939', Ph.D. thesis, University of Grenoble, Faculty of Social Sciences.

Chambers, I. 2005. 'The Mediterranean. A Postcolonial Sea', *Third Text*, 18, 5, pp. 423–33.

Charles-Géniaux C. 1934. *L'Ame Musulmane en Tunisie*, Paris: Fasquelle.

_____ .1935. 'Les Femmes et l'Islam', *Cahiers du Sud*, 175, August–September, pp. 113–21.

_____ .1939. 'Au Centre Universitaire Méditerranéen', *Cahiers du Sud*, 213, February, pp. 185–89.

Chiaromonte, N. 1933. 'Parigi come Modello', *Solaria*, January, pp. 59–62.

Cholakian, R.C. 1990. *The Troubadour Lyric, a Psychocritical Reading*, Manchester–New York: Manchester University Press.

Ciampelli, G.M. 1934. '*Il Dibuk*', in *Musica d'Oggi*, April, pp. 135–38.

Ciferri, L. 1993. 'Nota sulla Genesi del *Diario di un Privilegiato sotto il Fascismo*', in L. Ferrero (1993), *Diario di un Privilegiato*, op. cit., pp. 115–30.

Cingria, C.-A. 1939. Review of *L'Amour et l'Occident*, *La Nouvelle Revue Française*, 27, pp. 495–58.

Cioran, E.M. 1956. *La Tentation d'Exister*, Paris: Gallimard (Eng. tr. 1968. *The Temptation to Exist*, tr. R. Howard, Chicago: Quadrangle Books).

Cirenei, M. 1934. 'Madri e Figli Illegittimi', *Il Lavoro*, 19 April, p. 5.

Cirulli, S. 2002–3. '*L'Amour et l'Occident* de Denis de Rougemont entre Succès et Contestation', Dissertation in Foreign Languages and Literature, Rome: Tor Vergata University, autumn session.

Ciuffoletti, Z. (ed.). 1979. *Nello Rosselli. Uno Storico sotto il Fascismo*, Florence: La Nuova Italia.

Cogniat, R. 1953. *Gaston Baty*, Paris: Les Presses Littéraires de France.

Cohen, R. 2004. 'Il Passato Europeo nel Presente Israeliano', *900*, 10, pp. 107–20.

Cohen, R. (ed.). 2004. *European Jews and Jewish Europeans between the Two World Wars*, Tel Aviv: The Goldstein–Goren Diaspora Research Center.

Collotti, E. 2003. *Il Fascismo e gli Ebrei. Le Leggi Razziali in Italia*, Rome–Bari: Laterza.

Comba, A. 1983. 'L'Idea di Nazione come Finalità Universale nella Pubblicistica Italiana dell'800', in Centro per la Storia della Massoneria – Collegio Circoscrizionale dei Maestri Venerabili della Sicilia, *Il Contributo della Massoneria al Progresso della Fratellanza tra i Popoli nel Corso della Storia*, Studies Conference, Palermo, 5 May 1983, Rome: Editrice Erasmo, pp. 141–51.

Combes, A. 1986. *La Massoneria in Francia*, Foggia: Bastogi.

Conti, F. 1998. 'Aspetti Culturali e Dimensione Associativa', in F. Conti, A.M. Isastia and F. Tarozzi, *La Morte Laica*. I. *Storia della Cremazione in Italia (1880–1920)*, Turin: Paravia, pp. 1–105.

———. 2003a. 'De Genève au Piave. La Franc-maçonnerie Italienne et le Pacifisme Démocratique (1867–1915)', in M. Petricioli, A. Anteghini and D. Cherubini (eds), *Les Etats-Unis d'Europe. Un Projet Pacifiste*, Brussels: Peter Lang–P.I.E. pp. 231–40.

———. 2003b. *Storia della Massoneria Italiana. Dal Risorgimento al Fascismo*, Bologna: il Mulino.

Conti, F., A.M. Isastia and F. Tarozzi. 1998. *La Morte Laica*. I. *Storia della Cremazione in Italia (1880–1920)*, Turin: Paravia.

Corbin, H. 1932–33. 'Pour l'Anthropologie Philosophique: Un Traité Persan Inédit de Suhrawardi d'Alep (†1191)', *Recherches Philosophiques*, 2, Paris: Boivin, pp. 371–96.

———. 1937. 'Pour l'Hymnologie Manichéenne', *Yggdrasil*, 25 August.

Cornille, J.-L. 2002. 'Rousseau and the Invention of the Male Love-Letter', *The Modern Language Review*, 97, 2, April.

Cotta, S. 1941. Review of 'Giorgio Quartara, *L'Italia Tradita*', *Rivista di Studi Politici Internazionali*, 8, 1, pp. 261–63.

Coudenhove-Kalergi, R.N. 1943. *Crusade for Pan-Europe. Autobiography of a Man and a Movement*, New York: Putnam.

Coughlin, J. 1938. *Motion Picture Herald*, 130, 12, 19 March, p. 47.

Coulet, M. 1993. 'A la Recherche de l'Humanisme Méditerranéen de Jean Ballard', in *Jean Ballard et les Cahiers du Sud*, Catalogue de la ville de Marseille, pp. 231–48.

Courtois-Suffit, M. 1927. Review of '*Il Dibbouk* di Baty', *Temps*, 8 August, now in 'Masques. Cahiers d'Art Dramatique', 9, *Le Théatre Yiddisch. Etudes et Documents*, Paris: n.d.

Croce, B. 1960. *Scritti Vari*, 5, *Pagine Sparse*, 2, *Schermaglie Letterarie e Filosofiche*, Bari: Laterza.

Damerini, G. 1965. 'Francesco Bernardelli', *Il Dramma*, November–December.

D'Arcy, M.C. 1947. *The Mind and Heart of Love. Lion and Unicorn, A Study in Eros and Agape*, New York: Henry Holte.

Dalinger, B. 1998. *Verloschene Sterne. Geschichte des Jüdischen Theaters in Wien*, Vienna: Picus.

Daniels, M. 1977. *The French Drama of the Unspoken*, Westport, Conn.: Greenwood.

De Antonellis, G. 1984. *Il Caso Puecher. Morire a Vent'anni Partigiano e Cristiano*, Milan: Rizzoli.

De Clementi, A. 1975. 'Canepa Giuseppe', in *Dizionario Biografico degli Italiani*, Roma: Istituto della Enciclopedia Italiana, vol. 18.

Decleva, E. 1997. 'Un Panorama in Evoluzione', in G. Turi (ed.), *Storia dell'Editoria nell'Italia Contemporanea*, Florence: Giunti, pp. 225–98.

Deering, M.J. 1991. *Combats Acharnés: Denis de Rougemont et les Fondements de l'Unité Européenne*, Lausanne: Fondation Jean Monnet pour l'Europe–Centre de Recherches Européennes.

De Felice, R. 1972. *Storia degli Ebrei Italiani sotto il Fascismo*, Turin: Einaudi.

De la Brière, Y. 1931. Review of 'Giorgio Quartara, *Les Etats Unis d'Europe et du Monde*', *Etudes*, 68, 208, pp. 761–62.

Delay, J. 1956. *La Jeunesse d'André Gide*, vol. 1, Paris: Gallimard (Eng. tr. 1963. *The Youth of Andre Gide*, tr. June Guicharnaud, Chicago University Press).

Del Bayle, L. 1969. *Les Non-conformistes des Années 30*, Paris: Editions du Seuil.

De Leo, M. and F. Taricone. 1992. *Le Donne in Italia. Diritti Civili e Politici*, Naples: Liguori.

Deleuze, G. and F. Guattari. 1980. *Mille Plateaux. Capitalisme et Schizophrénie*, Paris: Minuit (Eng. tr. 1987. *A Thousand Plateaus. Capitalism and Schizophrenia*, tr. B. Massumi, Minneapolis: University of Minnesota Press).

Della Corte, A. 1935. '*Il Dibuk* di L. Rocca', *La Stampa*, 23 January.

Della Pergola, S. 1997. 'La Popolazione Ebraica in Italia nel Contesto Ebraico Globale', in C. Vivanti (1997), op. cit., pp. 897–936.

Della Peruta, F. 1962. 'Mazzini e la Giovine Europa', *Annali Feltrinelli*, 5, pp. 11–72.

_____. 1998. Preface to F. Conti, A.M. Isastia and F. Tarozzi, *La Morte Laica. I. Storia della Cremazione in Italia (1880–1920)*, Turin: Paravia, pp. ix–xvi.

Della Seta, S. and D. Carpi. 1997. 'Il Movimento Sionistico', in C. Vivanti (1997), op. cit., pp. 1323–68.

Delpech, J. 1939. 'Non, Tristan et Iseut ne s'aimaient pas, nous dit Denis de Rougemont', *Les Nouvelles Littéraires*, 11 February.

De Luna, G. 1995. *Donne in Oggetto. L'Antifascismo nella Società Italiana 1922–1939*, Turin: Bollati Boringhieri.

_____. 1998. Introduction to F. Conti, A.M. Isastia and F. Tarozzi, *La Morte Laica. I. Storia della Cremazione in Italia (1880–1920)*, Turin: Paravia, pp. v–viii.

Demonico, A. 1993. 'Postface', in *Théâtre Yiddish*, 2, Paris: L'Arche, pp. 201–7.

Dermenghem, E. 1931. 'Le Coufisme. Mystique Musulmane et Mystique Chrétienne', *Cahiers du Sud*, 129, March, pp. 135–41.

_____. 1935. 'Conclusion: Valeurs Permanents et Problèmes Actuels de la Civilisation Musulmane', *Cahiers du Sud*, 175, August–September, pp. 141–44.

_____. 1942. 'Les Grands Thèmes de la Poésie Amoureuse chez les Arabes Précurseurs des Poètes d'Oc', *Cahiers du Sud*, 249, August–September–October, pp. 26–38.

_____. 1947. 'Témoignage de l'Islam. Notes sur les Valeurs Permanentes et Actuelles de la Civilisation Musulmane', reissue of the special edition of *Cahiers du Sud* on 'L'Islam et l'Occident', pp. 372–87.

Derrida, J. 1992. *The Other Heading: Reflections on Today's Europe*, Bloomington: Indiana University Press (original version 1991. *L'Autre Cap. La Démocratie Ajournée*, Paris: Minuit).

Deutsch, N. 2006. 'An-sky and the Ethnography of Jewish Women', in G. Safran and S.J. Zipperstein (2006), op. cit., pp. 266–80.

Deutsch, R. 1929. *The International Woman Suffrage Alliance. Its History from 1904 to 1929*, London: IWSA.

Diebold, B. 1928. *Einführung, in Habima. Hebräisches Theater*, Berlin–Wilmersdorf: Heinrich Keller.

Dolza, D. 1990. *Essere Figlie di Lombroso. Due Donne Intellettuali tra '800 e '900*, Milan: Franco Angeli.

Drieu la Rochelle, P. 1931. *L'Europe contre les Patries*, Paris: Gallimard.

———. 1939. *Gilles*, Paris: NRF.

DuBois, E.C. 1998. *Woman Suffrage and Women's Rights*, New York: New York University Press.

Dufour, P. 1936. 'Charles Géniaux', in *Revue du Tarn*, ns, issue 5, 15 March, pp. 27–31.

El Fasi, M. 1942. 'La Poésie Arabe Andalouse et Son Influence sur les Troubadours Provençaux', *Le Génie d'Oc et l'Homme Méditerranéen, Cahiers du Sud*, 249, August–September–October, pp. 39–43.

Ellena, L. 2004. 'Political Imagination, Sexuality and Love in the Eurafrican Debate', *European Review of History*, special issue *Europe and Love – L'Europe et l'Amour*, 11, 2, Summer, pp. 241–72.

Elsen, C. 1953. *Homo Eroticus. Esquisse d'une Psychologie de l'Erotisme*, Paris: Gallimard.

Enciclopedia dell'Antifascismo e della Resistenza, vol. 5. 1987. Milan: La Pietra-Walk Over.

Encyclopaedia Judaica. 1980–81. Jerusalem: Keter.

Eric, 1937. '*The Dybbuk*', *Punch, or the London Charivari*, 193, 24 November, p. 581.

Ertel, R. 1979. 'A Propos de Quelques Films Yiddish', *Potif*, 225, December, pp. 54–56.

Esposito, R.F. 1979. *La Massoneria e l'Italia dal 1800 ai Giorni Nostri*, Rome: Edizioni Paoline.

———. 1987. *Le Grandi Concordanze tra Chiesa e Massoneria*, Florence: Nardini.

L'Europa di Altiero Spinelli. Sessant'Anni di Battaglie Politiche: dall'Antifascismo all'Azione Federalista. 1994. Bologna: il Mulino.

Fabre, D. and J.-P. Pinies (eds). 1987a. *René Nelli et les Cahiers du Sud*, Carcassonne: Garae/Hésiode.

———. 1987b. Présentation, *Les Cahiers du Sud, la Génération de 1930*, Carcassonne: Garae-Hésiode/Ent'revues.

Fabre, G. 1998. *L'Elenco. Censura Fascista, Editoria e Autori Ebrei*, Turin: Zamorani.

Fanesi, P.R. 1994. 'Gli Ebrei Italiani Rifugiati in America Latina e l'Antifascismo (1938–1945)', *Storia e Problemi Contemporanei*, 14, 7, pp. 23–36.

Faraj. 1935. 'Les Médecins Musulmans d'Andalousie et le Serment d'Hippocrate', *Cahiers du Sud*, 175, August–September, pp. 95–97.

Farina, R. 1995. 'Casati Elena in Sacchi', in R. Farina (ed.), *Dizionario Biografico delle Donne Lombarde 568–1968*, Milan: Baldini and Castoldi.

Federazione Italiana per il Suffragio e i Diritti Civili e Politici delle Donne (FISEDD), affiliated to the International Alliance of Women for Suffrage and Equal Citizenship. 1932. *Relazione Morale e Finanziaria della Presidenza Centrale sul Biennio 1930–1931*, Mantua: Tipografia Barbieri.

Federazione Italiana per i Diritti della Donna (FISEDD), affiliated to the International Alliance of Women for Suffrage and Equal Citizenship and authorised by His Excellency the Head of Government by Decree of 23

April 1932. n.d. *Relazione Morale e Finanziaria sul Biennio 1932–33*, Mantua: Tipografia Barbieri.

Feraud, H. 1942. 'Quelques Aspects de la Pensée Manichéenne à l'Epoque Contemporaine', *Le Génie d'Oc et l'Homme Méditerranéen, Cahiers du Sud*, 249, pp. 343–69.

Ferrario, P. 1939. Review of 'Giorgio Quartara, *Un Viaggio nel Sud-America*', *Geopolitica*, I, 2, 30 November.

Ferrer Benimeli J.A., M.A. de Paz Sanchez. 1991. *Masoneria y Pacifismo en la España Contemporanea*, Zaragoza: Prensas Universitarias de Zaragoza.

Ferrero, G. 1918. *La Vecchia Europa e la Nuova. Saggi e Discorsi*, Milan: Treves.

———. 1946 (new edition) [1897]. *L'Europa Giovane. Studi e Viaggi nei Paesi del Nord*, Preface by M. Borsa, Milan: Garzanti (1946), Milan: Treves (1897).

Ferrero Raditsa, N. 1984. 'Gli Anni di Leo', in L. Ferrero, *MT*, pp. 9–17.

Ferri-Pisani, C.-A.-A. 1927. *Au Pays des Amazones. L'Amour en Amérique*, Paris: Les Editions de France.

Ferro, G. 1998–99. 'Il Teatro Musicale di Ludovico Rocca', Thesis for degree in the history of music, supervisor Prof. G. Pestelli, Faculty of Literature and Philosophy, University of Turin.

Fersen, A. 1980. *Il Teatro, Dopo*, Bari–Rome: Laterza.

Filippa, M. 1990. *Avrei Capovolto le Montagne. Giorgina Levi in Bolivia, 1939–1946*, Florence: Giunti-Astrea.

———. 2001. *La Morte Laica. Cremazione e Riti Funebri nell'Italia Fascista*, Turin: Paravia.

Fink, G. 1996. 'A Piedi da Wielopole: Note sul Cinema Yiddish', *Rassegna Mensile di Israel*, 62, 1–2, January–August, pp. 375–86.

Finzi, G. 1934. '*Il Dibuk* alla Scala. La Musica di Lodovico Rocca', *Israel*, XIX-26, 13 Nissan 5694–29 March, p. 5.

Fiori, G. 1981. *Simone Weil, Biografia di un Pensiero*, Milan: Garzanti (Eng. tr. *c.* 1989. *Simone Weil, an Intellectual Biography*, tr. J.R. Berrigan, Athens: University of Georgia Press).

Fishman, P. 1980. 'Vakhtangov's *The Dybbuk*', *The Drama Review*, 24, 3, September, pp. 43–59.

Fleg, E. 1927. Preface, in An-Ski (1927a), op. cit., pp. 12–13.

———. 1928. *Pourquoi je suis juif*, Paris: Les Editions de France.

———. 1930. 'Au Théâtre Montparnasse *Le Dibbouk*', *L'Univers Israélite*, ns, 86, 14, 19 December, pp. 428–29.

Fluchère, H. 1939. '*The Criterion* Cesse de Paraître', *Cahiers du Sud*, 213, February, pp. 181–84.

Fondane, B. 1936. Review of *Politique de la Personne*, *Cahiers du Sud*, 182, April, pp. 334–35.

Fourès, J. 1939. 'La Poésie Occidentale et les Troubadours. De la Capacité Révolutionnaire d'un Fait Historique', *L'Indépendant*, 2 April.

Fourny, J.-F. 1985. 'Roger Caillois au Collège de Sociologie: La Politique et Ses Masques', *The French Review*, 58, 4, March, pp. 533–39.

Francesconi, P. 2003. 'A Proposito della Mascherata Femminile', *La Psicoanalisi*, 34, pp. 101–8.

Franc-Nohain (pseudonym of M.E. Legrand). 1934. Review of *Angelica*, *L'Echo de Paris*, 17 May, now in L. Ferrero (1936, pp. 31–33).

Freixe, A. 1987. 'A Propos de la Rencontre Simone Weil – Joe Bousquet', *Cahiers Simone Weil*, 10, 4, pp. 395–405.

———. 1988. 'Simone Weil et les *Cahiers du Sud*', Part 1, *Cahiers Simone Weil*, 11, 2, pp. 165–75, and 11, 3, pp. 241–46.

Freschi, M. 1997 [1992]. '*Il Dibuk*: un'Altra Tragedia d'Amore', in S. An-Ski. *Il Dibbuk*, tr. S. Avisar, Rome: Edizioni e/o, pp. 101–124.

Frigessi, D. 2003. *Cesare Lombroso*, Turin: Einaudi.

Frydman, G. '"Les Etoiles Errantes": Le Théâtre Yiddish à Paris', Foreword in *Le Théâtre Yiddish à Paris (1889–1983), la Collection Gérard Frydman*. Inventory compiled by Laurent Héricher, Bibliothèque Nationale de France, Direction des Collections, Département des Arts du Spectacle, n.d. but probably 2001, n.p. but probably Paris.

Fubini, E. 1978. 'La Musica a Torino: tra Conservazione e Innovazione', in *Torino tra le Due Guerre*, Catalogue of the exhibition sponsored by the Assessorato per la Cultura della Città di Torino between March and June 1978, Turin: Musei Civici.

Fuzellier, E. 1939. 'Les Mythes', *Cahiers du Sud*, 219, August–September, pp. 1–11.

'g.c'. 1934. 'La Prima del *Dibuk* di Rocca e Simoni alla Scala', in *Il Corriere della Sera*, 25 March.

'G.D.' [possibly pseudonym of Gaston Derycke] 1936. Review of '*Rival et Rivale* par Joseph Breitbach', *Cahiers du Sud*, 181, March, pp. 267–79.

———. 1939. Review of *Journal d'Allemagne*, *Cahiers du Sud*, June, 217, pp. 543–44.

'g.s.' 1934. '*Il Dibuk* di Ludovico Rocca in *Il Popolo d'Italia*, 25 March.

Gaeta, G. 1982. 'Introduzione a Simone Weil', *Quaderni*, vol. 1, vol. 3, Milan: Adelphi (Eng. tr. 1956 and 1976. *Notebooks*, tr. A. Wills, London: Routledge and Kegan Paul).

Galford, E. 1993. *The Dyke and the Dibbuk*, Seattle: Seal Press.

Gallas, A. 2002. '"Jahvé ed Elohim". Gen 1–2 nell'Interpretazione di Karl Barth e di Alcuni Suoi Interpreti', *Annali di scienze religiose*, 7, pp. 299–322.

Garosci, A. 1984. 'Ricordi di un Amico Perduto e Ritrovato', in *Il Muro Trasparente* (L. Ferrero 1984), op. cit., pp. 5–8.

———. 1953. *Storia dei Fuorusciti*, Bari: Laterza.

Gary, R. 1967. *La Danse de Gengis Cohn*, Paris: Gallimard.

Gastaldi, M. 1936. *Donne Luce d'Italia. Panorama della Letteratura Femminile Contemporanea*, Milan: Casa Editrice Quaderni di Poesia.

Gatti, C. 1934. '*Il Dibuk* di L. Rocca e R. Simoni', *L'Illustrazione Italiana*, Milan: 1 April, p. 12.

Gavazzeni, G. 1934a. 'L. Rocca alla Scala', in *L'Italia Letteraria*, 1 April.

———. 1934b. 'Lettera da Milano. La Stagione alla Scala', in *Rassegna Musicale*, May–June, pp. 222–25.

———. 1954. 'Paragrafi su Ludovico Rocca', in *La Musica e il Teatro*, Pisa: Nistri-Lischi.

Gavazzi, G. 2003. *Non Solo Seta. Storia della Famiglia Gavazzi*, Milan: Caproncino.

Gavazzi, L. 1917. 'Per un'Unione Doganale dei Popoli dell'Intesa', *Critica Sociale*, 27, 7–8, 1–15 and 16–30 April, pp. 106–8.

Géniaux, C. 1909. *Les Musulmanes*, Paris: Monde Illustré.

Géniaux, C. and C. Charles-Géniaux. 1924. *Une Affranchie*, Paris: Flammarion.

Gershoni, I. 1991. 'Imagining the East: Muhammad Husayn Haykal's Changing Representations of East–West Relations, 1928–1933', *Asian and African Studies*, 25, November, pp. 209–51.

———. 1997. 'The Return of the East. Muhammad Husayn Haykal's Recantation of Positivism, 1927–1930', in M. Ma'oz and A. Pappé (eds), *Middle Eastern Politics and Ideas: A History from Within*, London–New York: Tauris, pp. 21–73.

Gibson, M. 1986. *Prostitution and the State in Italy, 1860–1915*, New Brunswick–London: Rutgers University Press.

———. 2002. *Born to Crime. Cesare Lombroso and the Origins of Biological Criminology*, Westport, Conn.–London: Praeger.

Gigli Marchetti, A. and N. Torcellan. 1992. *Donna Lombarda 1860–1945*, Milan: Franco Angeli.

Giménez Caballero, E. 1935. 'Dialoghi d'Amore tra Laura e Don Giovanni o il Fascismo e l'Amore', *Antieuropa*, 5, pp. 567–99.

Giovana, M. 1952. *Tempo d'Europa*, Turin: Tricerri.

Gleizes A. 1935. 'Arabesques', *Cahiers du Sud*, 175, August–September, pp. 101–6.

Gobetti, P. 1924. 'Illuminismo', *Il Baretti*, 1, 1, 23 December.

Goldberg, S.A. 1996. *Crossing the Jabbok. Illness and Death in Ashkenazi Judaism in Sixteenth- through Nineteenth-century Prague*, Berkeley–Los Angeles–London: University of California Press.

Goldman, E.A. 1983. *Visions, Images, and Dreams. Yiddish Film Past and Present*, Ann Arbor, Mich.: UMI Research Press.

Goll, I. 1937. 'Le *Dibbouk*', *L'Univers Israélite*, 93, 8, 22 October, p. 119.

Gonen, R. (ed.). 1994. *Back to the Shtetl. An-Sky and the Jewish Ethnographic Expedition, 1912–1914. From the Collections of the State Ethnographic Museum in St. Petersburg*, Jerusalem: The Israel Museum.

Gonsalez, L. 1991. Bibliographic note in P. Milano, *Note in Margine a una Vita Assente*, Milan: Adelphi.

Gotovitch, J. 1987. 'Franc-Maçonnerie, Guerre et Paix', in *Les Internationales et le Problème de la Guerre au XXe Siècle*, Conference Proceedings, 22–24 November 1984, Ecole Française de Rome, pp. 75–105.

Gravelli, A. 1929. 'L'Idea Storica Fascista', *Antieuropa*, 1, pp. 2–11.

Grossi, V. 1994. *Le Pacifisme Européen 1889–1914*, Brussels: Bruylant.

Gualino, R. 1966. *Frammenti di Vita e Pagine Inedite*, Rome: Famija Piemontèisa.

Guénon, R. 1935. 'L'Esotérisme Islamique', *Cahiers du Sud*, 175, August–September, pp. 37–45.

Guiberteau, P. 1935. 'Islam, Occident, Chrétienté', *Cahiers du Sud*, 175, August–September, pp. 84–94.

Guiraud, J.-M. 1993. 'Les Grands Moments des *Cahiers du Sud*: Jalons pour un Itinéraire', in *Jean Ballard et les* Cahiers du Sud, Catalogue de la Ville de Marseille, pp. 55–87.

Haedens, K. 1936. Review of '*Un Protestant* par Georges Portal', *Cahiers du Sud*, 188, November, pp. 856–58.

Haekal, M.H. 1935. 'Les Causes de l'Incompréhension entre l'Europe et les Musulmans et les Moyens d'y Remédier', *Cahiers du Sud*, 175, August–September, pp. 28–36.

Harrel-Courtes, H. 1936. Review of '*Théodoric Roi des Ostrogoths (454–526)* par Marcel Brion', *Cahiers du Sud*, 180, pp. 158–62.

Hasan-Rokem, G. 2001–2. 'L'Image du Juif Errant et la Construction de l'Identité Européenne', in *Le Juif Errant, un Témoin du Temps*, Catalogue of the exhibition held at the Musée d'Art et d'Histoire du Judaïsme, Paris, 26 October 2001–24 February 2002.

Hausmann, F.-R. 1995. 'Le Tappe dell'Esilio: Studiosi Tedeschi in Italia', in *Akademie*, op. cit., pp. 175–82.

Haykal, M.H. 1935. 'Les Causes de l'Incompréhension entre l'Europe et les Musulmans et les Moyens d'y Remédier', *Cahiers du Sud*, 175, August–September, pp. 28–36.

Hélisse, E. 1939. 'Du Mythe de Tristan et Iseult à l'Hitlerisme avec Denis de Rougemont', *Tribune de France*, 24, 14 July.

Hellman, J. 1999–2000. 'Alexandre Marc dans les Années 1930: Révolution de la Jeunesse, Idéologie et Religion', *L'Europe en Formation*: 'Fédéralisme Personnaliste, Idéologie et Religion', 315–16, Winter 1999–Spring 2000, pp. 139–50.

Hentsch, T. 1988a. 'L'Usage de l'Autre dans la Construction du Mythe de l'Europe', in *Du Personnalisme au Fédéralisme Européen. En Hommage à Denis de Rougemont*, Geneva: Editions du Centre Européen de la Culture, pp. 231–39.

————. 1998b. *L'Orient Imaginaire. La Vision Politique Occidentale de l'Est Méditerranéen*, Paris: Minuit (Eng. tr. 1992. *Imagining the Middle East*, tr. F. Reed, Montreal: Black Rose Books).

Hertz, H. 1937. Review of *Désespoirs*, *Europe*, 15 November, pp. 405–6.

Hertzberg, A. 1972. 'Jewish Identity', in *Encyclopaedia Judaica*, vol. 10, Jerusalem: Keter.

Hillman, J. 1983. *Healing Fiction*, New York: Station Hill Press, 1983.

Hirschmann, U. 1993. *Noi Senza Patria*, Bologna: il Mulino.

Hoberman, J. 1991. *Bridge of Light. Yiddish Film between Two Worlds*, New York: The Museum of Modern Art–Schocken Books.

Hollier, D. 1995. *Le Collège de Sociologie 1937–1939*, Paris: Gallimard (Eng. tr. 1987. *The College of Sociology*, Minneapolis: University of Minnesota Press).

Hourcade, P. 1938. 'Le Drame de l'Amour dans l'Œuvre de Thérèse Aubray', *Cahiers du Sud*, 204, April, p. 308.

Houssiau, B.J. 1994. *Marc Allégret Découvreur de Stars. Sous les Yeux d'André Gide*, La Léchère: Cabédita.

Hourcade, P. 1938. 'Le Drame de l'Amour dans l'Œuvre de Thérèse Aubray', *Cahiers du Sud*, 204, April, pp. 300–308.

Huchet, J.-C. 1985. 'Psychanalyse et Littérature Médiévale: Rencontre ou Méprise? A Propos de Deux Ouvrages Récents', *Cahiers de Civilisation Médiévale*, 2–3, April–September, pp. 223–33.

Ibn Al Fâridh, 1932. 'Poème', *Cahiers du Sud*, 139, April, pp. 180–83.

I Quartara – Nobili – Magnifici – Marchesi, 1931. Milan: Stabilimento lito-tipografico Macciachini.

I Sacchi di Mantova. Una Grande Famiglia Italiana. 1997. Bologna: Manduchi.

Idelsohn, A.Z. 1929. *Jewish Music in Its Historical Development*, New York: Holt,

Rinehart and Winston (It. tr. 1994. *Storia della Musica Ebraica*, Florence: Giuntina).

Incagliati, M. 1935. 'La Prima del "Dibuk" di Lodovico Rocca', *Il Messaggero*, 29 December.

Ingram, N. 1993. 'L'Envers de l'Entre-deux-guerres en France: ou à la Recherche d'un Passé Pacifiste', in M. Vaïsse (ed.). *Le Pacifisme en Europe des Années 1920 aux Années 1950*, Brussels: Bruylant.

International Biographical Dictionary of Central European Emigrés 1933–1945. 1980. Munich–New York–London–Paris: Saur.

International Women's News [IWN] 1928. *Jus Suffragii*, 23, 1 October, p. 8.

———. 1929. *Jus Suffragii*, 23, 6 March 1929, pp. 88–91.

———. 1930a. B. Sacchi and V. Benetti Brunelli, 'Memorandum', *Jus Suffragii*, 24, 4 January, pp. 45–46.

———. 1930b. 'An Italian Feminist. *Les Lois du Libre Amour*, by G. Quartara', *Jus Suffragii*, 24, 12 September, pp. 195–96.

———. 1930c. B. Sacchi, 'An Italian Feminist', in *Jus Suffragii*, 25, 1 October, pp. 6–7.

———. 1931a. 'Obituary for Dr. Beatrice Sacchi', *Jus Suffragii*, 25, 6 March, p. 87.

———. 1931b. Conference announcement, *Jus Suffragii*, 25, 6 March, pp. 83–86.

———. 1931c. Conference report, *Jus Suffragii*, 25, 8 May, pp. 116–17.

———. 1931d. Disarmament declaration, *Jus Suffragii*, 25, 11 August, p. 169.

———. 1933a. Conference programme, *Jus Suffragii*, 27, 5 February, pp. 34–37; 6 March, pp. 42–45; report, 7 April, pp. 51–56.

———. 1933b. Review of V. Benetti Brunelli, *La Donna nella Civiltà Moderna*, *Jus Suffragii*, 27, 6 March, pp. 46–47.

Ioanid, R. 2000. Introduction, in M. Sebastian, *Journal 1935–1944*, Chicago: Ivan R. Dee.

Irigaray, L. 1977. *Ce Sexe qui n'en est pas un*, Paris: Minuit.

Isastia, A.M. 1998a. 'La Questione Donna', *Massoneria Oggi. Rivista del Grande Oriente d'Italia*, 5, 3, June–July, pp. 36–39.

———. 1998b. 'La Massoneria e il Progetto di "Fare gli Italiani"', in F. Conti, A.M. Isastia and F. Tarozzi, *La Morte Laica. I. Storia della Cremazione in Italia (1880–1920)*, Turin: Paravia, pp. 179–271.

Ivanov, V. 2006. 'An-sky, Evgeny Vakhtangov, and The Dybbuk', in G. Safran and S.J. Zipperstein (2006), op. cit., pp. 252–65.

Izaly, Z. 2006. 'The Musical Strands of An-sky's Texts and Contexts', in G. Safran and S.J. Zipperstein (2006), op. cit., pp. 203–31.

Izard, P. 1988. 'Denis de Rougemont: du Personnalisme au Fédéralisme – 1930–1950', in *Du Personnalisme au Fédéralisme Européen. En Hommage à Denis de Rougemont*, Geneva, Editions du Centre Européen de la Culture.

'J.H.' 1949. Article on *Der Dibek* in Paris, *Cinématographie Française*, 1301, 5 March 1949, p. 14.

Jilek, L. 1992. 'Paneurope dans les Années Vingt: La Réception du Projet en Europe Centrale et Occidentale', *Relations Internationales*, 72, Winter.

J.M. 1938. 'Le Souvenir de Leo Ferrero', *L'Œuvre*, Paris: 13 April.

Jeanneret, P. 1933. 'Leo Ferrero (1903–33)', *Nouvelles Littéraires*, 9 September.

Johansen, B. 1967. *Muhammad Husain Haikal. Europa und der Orient im Weltbild eines Ägyptischen Liberalen*, Wiesbaden–Beirut: Franz Steiner.

Jona, D. and A. Foa. 1997. *Noi Due*, Introduction by A. Zargani, Bologna: il Mulino.

Kamitsuka, M.D. 2004. *Toward a Feminist Postmodern and Postcolonial Interpretation of Sin*, Chicago: University of Chicago Press.

Kampf, A. 1984. *Jewish Experience in the Art of the Twentieth Century*, South Hadley, Mass.: Bergin and Garvey.

Keller, T. 1998. 'Le Personnalisme de l'Entre-deux-guerres entre l'Allemagne et la 'France', in C. Roy (1998), *Alexandre Marc et la Jeune Europe (1904–1934): L'Ordre Nouveau aux Origines du Personnalisme*, Nice: Presses d'Europe, pp. 457–562.

———. 2001. *Deutsch-Französische Dritte-Weg-Diskurse*, Munich: Wilhelm Fink.

Kemp, R. 1928. 'Recensione della Messa in Scena del *Dibbouk* fatta da Baty', *La Liberté*, 2 February.

Kierkegaard, S. 1999. *La Malattia per la Morte*, Introduction by E. Rocca, Rome: Donzelli.

———. 2006. *Fear and Trembling*, C. Stephen Evans and S. Walsh (eds), tr. S. Walsh, Cambridge: Cambridge University Press.

Kimmel, D.M. 1990. Article on *Der Dibek* in *Cinefantastique*, 20, 3 January, pp. 44–45.

Konigsberg, I. 1997. 'The Only "I" in the World: Religion, Psychoanalysis, and "The Dybbuk"', *Cinema Journal*, 36, 4, pp. 22–42.

Kornfeld, A. 1993. *La Figura e l'Opera di Leo Ferrero*, Povegliano Veronese: Gutenberg.

———. 1994. 'Il Rapporto tra Guglielmo e Leo Ferrero', in L. Cedroni (ed.), *Guglielmo Ferrero. Itinerari del Pensiero*, Naples: Edizioni Scientifiche Italiane, p. 51.

Krupnik, I. 1992–94. 'Jewish Holdings of the Leningrad Ethnographic Museum', in M. Beukers and R. Waale (eds), *Tracing An-sky. Jewish Collections from the State Ethnographic Museum in St. Petersburg*, Zwolle: Waanders Uitgevers, pp. 16–23.

Kuperminc, J.-C. 1998. *La Presse Juive en France*, in J.-J. Becker and A. Wieviorka (1998), op. cit., pp. 140–42.

Labanyi, J. '(Un)requited Conquests: Love and Empire in the Work of Ernesto Giménez Caballero and Salvador de Madariaga', in L. Passerini, L. Ellena and A. Geppert (eds), *New Dangerous Liaisons: Discourses on Europe and Love in the Twentieth Century*, Oxford–New York: Berghahn, forthcoming.

Labriola, T. 1930. 'Problemi Morali del Femminismo', *La Donna Italiana*, 7, 6, June, pp. 331–36.

Lacan, J. 1999. *Le Séminaire. XX. Encore (1972–1973)*, Paris: Seuil (Eng. tr. 1998. *The Seminar of Jacques Lacan, Book 20, Encore*, New York–London: Norton.

Lafont, A, 1933. Review of '*L'Amour de Vivre* par Frédéric Lefèvre', *Cahiers du Sud*, 151, May, pp. 392–94.

Leimkugel, F. 1999. *Wege Jüdischer Apotheker*, Heidelberg: Eschborn.

Landini, G. 1986. 'La Vocalità nel Melodramma di Lodovico Rocca: Aspetti e Problemi', in *Ghedini e l'Attività Musicale a Torino fra le Due Guerre*, Turin: Proceedings of the Conference on the occasion of the European Year of Music, 14–15 January 1986, pp. 99–116.

Legris, P. 2000. 'Les Juifs Ashkénazes du XX Arrondissement durant les Années 1930'. Dissertation for MA in Modern History, supervisors M. Dreyfus and J.-L. Robert, Centre d'Histoire Sociale, Université Paris I Panthéon-Sorbonne.

Léon, C. and S. Walsh (eds). 1997. *Feminist Intepretations of Søren Kierkegaard*, University Park, Pa.: Pennsylvania State University Press.

Leuba, J.-L. 1939. Review, *In Extremis*, 2, pp. 59–61.

Levi Arian, G. et al. (eds). 1969. *I Lavoratori Studenti. Testimonianze Raccolte a Torino*, Turin: Einaudi.

Levi Arian, G. and E. Viterbo. 1999. *Simeone Levi. La Storia Sconosciuta di un Noto Egittologo*, Turin: Ananke.

Levi Arian, G. and G. Disegni. 1998. *Fuori dal Ghetto. Il 1848 degli Ebrei*, Rome: Editori Riuniti.

Levi, F. (ed.). 1991. *L'Ebreo in Oggetto. L'Applicazione della Normativa Antiebraica a Torino 1938–43*, Turin: Zamorani.

Levi, G. 1933. 'L'Evoluzione Sociale-politica degli Ebrei in Piemonte dalla Rivoluzione Francese all'Emancipazione. 1789–1848', degree dissertation, Turin University.

———. 1935. 'Gli Ebrei in Piemonte nell'Ultimo Decennio del Secolo XVIII', *Rassegna Mensile di Israel*, 9, 10–11–12, February–March–April.

———. 1937. 'Le Avventurose Vicende di un Rabbino Tunisino nel Regno di Sardegna', *Rassegna Mensile di Israel*, 12, 3–4, November–December, now in extended form in G. Arian Levi, D. Viterbo. 2006. *Un Rabbino Tunisino nei Ghetti del Regno di Sardegna 1818–1830*, Florence: Giuntina.

———. 1952a. 'Sulle Premesse Social-economiche dell'Emancipazione degli Ebrei nel Regno di Sardegna', *Rassegna Mensile di Israel*, 18, pp. 10–11.

———. 1952b. 'I Figli dei Minatori', *L'Unità*, 23 May.

———. 1979. 'L'Associazionismo Operaio a Torino e in Piemonte (1890–1926)', in A. Agosti and G.M. Bravo (eds), *Storia del Movimento Operaio, del Socialismo e delle Lotte Sociali in Piemonte*, vol. 2, Bari: De Donato, pp. 481–550.

———. 1985. *Cultura e Associazioni Operaie*, Turin: Franco Angeli.

———. 1995. *Isacco Levi. La religione del Cuore*, Turin: Zamorani.

———. 1999 [1971]. *Il Lingotto: Storia di un Quartiere Operaio (Torino 1922–1973)*, Turin: Trauben.

———. 2005. *Tutto un Secolo. Due Donne Ebree del '900 Si Raccontano*, Florence: Giuntina.

Levi, G. and M. Montagnana. 2000. *I Montagnana. Una Famiglia Ebraica Piemontese e il Movimento Operaio (1914–1948)*, Florence: Giuntina.

Levi, L. 2001. *L'Albergo della Magnolia*, Rome: Edizioni e/o.

Levi, M.A. 1994. *Colloqui con la Luce. Istantanee Piemontesi 1990–1940*, Savigliano: L'Artistica.

Levi, P. 1987. *Il Sistema Periodico*, in *Opere*, vol. 1, Turin: Einaudi (Eng. tr. 1985. *The Periodic Table*, tr. R. Rosenthal, London: Profile Books).

Levi, T. 1982. 'Il Dibbuk: dalla Tradizione Mistica al Teatro Nazionale Ebraico', *Rassegna Mensile di Israel*, January–June, pp. 210–14.

Lévinas, E. 1988–89. 'Le Judaïsme et le Féminisme', *Cadmos*, 11, 44, Winter, pp. 40–48.

Levy, E. 1979. *The Habima – Israel's National Theater 1917–1977. A Study of Cultural Nationalism*, New York: Columbia University Press.

Libro d'Oro della Nobiltà Italiana, 1977–80, edn 18 (ed. by Collegio Araldico di Roma).

Lewis, C.S. 1940. Review of *Passion and Society*, *Theology*, June, pp. 459–61.

Ligou, D. (ed.). 1998. *Dictionnaire de la Franc-Maçonnerie*, Paris: Presses Universitaires de France.

Lipgens, W. 1982. *A History of European Integration*, vol. 1: *1945–1947. The Formation of the European Unity Movement*, Oxford: Clarendon Press.

Lipson, D.S. 1965. *The Yiddish Theatre in America*, New York–London: Thomas Yoseloff.

Locatelli, S. 1965. 'L'Uomo e la Sua Opera', in *Denis de Rougemont. La Vita e il Pensiero*, Milan: Ferro.

Lo Gatto, E. 1952. *Storia del Teatro Russo*, vol. 2, Florence: Sansoni.

Lombroso, C. and G. Ferrero. 1894. *La Donna Delinquente, la Prostituta e la Donna Normale*, 2nd ed., Turin–Rome: L. Roux (Eng. tr. 2004. *Criminal Woman, the Prostitute, and the Normal Woman*, tr. N. Hahn Rafter and M. Gibson, Durham–London: Duke University Press).

Lombroso, G. 1921. *L'Anima della Donna. Riflessioni sulla Vita*, Bologna: Zanichelli.

———. 1926. *L'Anima della Donna: Intelligenza e Amore*, 3rd edn, Bologna: Zanichelli.

———. 1935. *Lo Sboccio di una Vita. Note su Leo Ferrero Lombroso dalla Nascita ai Venti Anni*, Turin: Frassinelli.

Lorenzer, A. 1970. *Sprachzerstörung und Rekostruktion*, Frankfurt am Main: Suhrkamp.

Lot-Borodine, M. 1939. Review of *L'Amour et l'Occident, Humanisme et Renaissance*, vol. 6, Paris: Librairie Droz, pp. 365–72.

Loubet del Bayle, J.-L. 1969. *Les Non-conformistes des Années 30. Une Tentative de Renouvellement de la Pensée Politique Française*, Paris: Seuil.

Luchaire, J. 1929. *Une Génération Réaliste*, Paris: Valois.

———. 1933. 'Leo Ferrero est mort', *Notre Temps*, 7 (third series), 10 September.

———. n.d. *Confession d'un Français Moyen*, 2 vols, 2 (1914–50), Florence: Olschki.

Lunel, A. 1936. 'Paul Valéry, la Méditerranée et l'Humanisme', *Cahiers du Sud*, 183, May, pp. 401–6.

Luti, G. 1995. *La Letteratura nel Ventennio Fascista*, Florence: La Nuova Italia.

Luzzatto, A. 1992. *Il Rinnovamento Culturale dell'Ebraismo Italiano tra le Due Guerre*, in D. Bidussa, A. Luzzatto and G. Luzzatto Voghera (1992), op. cit., Brescia: Morcelliana.

———. 1997. *Autocoscienza e Identità Ebraica*, in C. Vivanti (1997), op. cit., pp. 1831–900.

Luzzatto, G.L. 1996. *Scritti Politici. Ebraismo e Anti-Semitismo*, A. Cavaglion and E. Tedeschi (eds), Milan: Franco Angeli, pp. 83–91.

Lyons, M. 1999. 'Love Letters and Writing Practices. On Ecritures Intimes in the Nineteenth Century', *Journal of Family History*, 24, 2, 1999, pp. 232–39.

MacCarthy, D. 1927. 'The Dybbuk', *The New Statesman*, 9 April, pp. 797–98.

Macchia, G. 1965. *Il Mito di Parigi*, Turin: Einaudi.

Malan, R. 1996. *Amici, Fratelli, Compagni. Memorie di un Valdese del XX Secolo*, E. Lo Bue (ed.), Cuneo: L'Arciere.

Mambrini, L. 2003. 'La Godi-assenza nella Lettera di Marina Cvetaeva', *La Psicoanalisi*, 34, July–December, pp. 237–48.

Manacorda, G. (ed.). 1979. *Lettere a 'Solaria'*, Rome: Editori Riuniti.

Mancini, M. 1984. *La Gaia Scienza dei Trovatori*, Parma: Pratiche.

Mangiarotti, C. 2003. 'La Femminilità. Un Percorso Teorico da Freud a Lacan', *La Psicoanalisi*, 34, July–December, pp. 84–100.

Manzotti, F. 1965. *Il Socialismo Riformista in Italia*, Florence: Le Monnier.

Marcel, G. 1939. Review of *L'Amour et l'Occident*, *Le Jour*, 6 February.

Margolies, E. 2000. 'Ventriloquism: Kantor, Templeton and the Voices of the Dead', *The New Theatre Quarterly*, 16, 3 (63), August, pp. 203–10.

Marienstras, R. 1981. 'Un Réalisme Spirituel (*Le Dibbouk*)', *Positif*, 243, June, pp. 58–60.

Marrou, H. [under pseudonym of H. Davenson]. 1939a. Review of *L'Amour et l'Occident*, *Esprit*, 79, 1 April, pp. 70–76.

———. 1939b. 'Autour de *L'Amour et l'Occident*', *Esprit*, 84, 1 September.

———. 1947. 'Au Dossier de l'Amour Courtois', *Revue du Moyen Age Latin. Etudes Textes Chronique Bibliographie*, vol. 3, p. 81–89.

———. 1954. *De la Connaissance Historique*, Paris: Seuil (It. tr. 1988. *La Conoscenza Storica*, Bologna: il Mulino).

———. 1971. *Les Troubadours*, Paris: Seuil (It. tr. 1994. *I Trovatori*, Milan: Jaca Book).

Marzano, A. 2003. *Una Terra per Rinascere. Gli Ebrei Italiani e l'Emigrazione in Palestina prima della Guerra (1920–1940)*, Genoa–Milan: Marietti.

'Masques. Cahiers d'Art Dramatique', 9, n.d. *Le Théatre Yiddisch. Etudes et Documents*, Paris: n.p., 5, Notebooks sponsored by the Societé des Spectacles Gaston Baty.

Massignon, L. 1935. 'L'Arabe, Langue Liturgique de l'Islam', *Cahiers du Sud*, 175, August–September, pp. 71–77.

———. 1947. 'Situation Internationale de l'Islam', reissue of the special number of *Cahiers du Sud* on 'L'Islam et l'Occident', pp. 13–18.

Mastellone, S. 1994. *Il Progetto Politico di Mazzini (Italia-Europa)*, Florence: Olschki.

Matt, P. von. 1989. *Liebesverrat. Die Treulosen in der Literatur*, Munich: Hanser.

Mayer Modena, M. 'Le Parlate Giudeo-Italiane', in C. Vivanti (1997), op. cit., pp. 940–63.

Mazzini, G. 1976. *Scritti Politici*, 2 vols, Turin: Einaudi.

Memmi, A. 2003. *Portrait d'un Juif*, Paris: Gallimard (Eng. tr. 1962. *Portrait of a Jew*, New York: Orion Press).

Menocal, M.R. 1987. *The Arabic Role in Medieval Literary History: A Forgotten Heritage*, Philadelphia: University of Pennsylvania Press.

Michaelis, M. 1978. *Mussolini and the Jews. German–Italian Relations and the Jewish Question in Italy 1922–1945*, Institute of Jewish Affairs, Oxford–London: Clarendon Press.

Michman, D. 2004. 'A "Third Partner" of World Jewry?: The Role of the Memory of the Shoah in the Search for a New Present-day European Jewish

Identity', in K. Kwiet and J. Matthäus (eds), *Contemporary Responses to the Holocaust*, Westport, Conn.: Praeger, pp. 123–35.

Mila, M. 1934. 'Compositori Giovani: Lodovico Rocca', *Nuova Antologia*, 16 November, pp. 306–7.

———.1982. '*Dibuk*, il Fascino della Fiaba', *La Stampa*, 16 April.

Mille, P. 1930a. 'L'Italie Fasciste met à l'Index les Etats-Unis de l'Europe', *Le Quotidien*, 26 May.

———.1930b. 'L'Italie Fasciste et la Fédération Européenne', *Le Quotidien*, 4 June.

Milletti, N. 1994. 'Analoghe Sconcezze. Tribadi, Saffiste, Invertite e Omosessuali: Categorie e Sistemi Sesso/Genere nella Rivista di Antropologia Criminale Fondata da Cesare Lombroso (1880–1949)', *DWF*, 4 (24), pp. 50–122.

Minet, P. 1935a. Review of '*Les Cloches de Bâle* par Louis Aragon', *Cahiers du Sud*, 169, February, pp. 153–54.

———.1935b. 'Sur un Congrès de la Culture', *Cahiers du Sud*, 174, July, pp. 607–10.

Miniati, M. 2003. *Les 'Emancipées'. Les Femmes Juives Italiennes aux XIX⁰ et XX⁰ Siècles (1848–1924)*, Paris: Champion.

Minuz, F. 1989. 'Femmina o Donna', in V.P. Babini, F. Minuz and A. Tagliavini (eds), *La Donna nelle Scienze dell'Uomo*, Milan: Franco Angeli, pp. 11–160.

Missac, P. 1931. Review of '*Nous, à qui rien n'appartient* par Guy de Portalès', *Cahiers du Sud*, 133, August–September, pp. 461–62.

Mola, A. 1983. 'Dottrina e Pratica della Fratellanza nella Massoneria Italiana fra Otto e Novecento', in Centro per la Storia della Massoneria – Collegio Circoscrizionale dei Maestri Venerabili della Sicilia. *Il Contributo della Massoneria al Progresso della Fratellanza tra i Popoli nel corso della Storia*, Studies Conference, Palermo 5 May 1983, Rome: Editrice Erasmo, pp. 153–72.

———.1999. *Storia della Massoneria Italiana dalle Origini ai Giorni Nostri*, Milan: Bompiani.

Mola, A. (ed.). 1990. *La Liberazione d'Italia nell'Opera della Massoneria*, Proceedings of the Conference in Turin, 24–25 September 1988, Foggia: Bastogi.

———.1998. *L'Italia nella Crisi dei Sistemi Coloniali fra Otto e Novecento*, Proceedings of the Vicoforte Conference, Foggia: Bastogi.

Molinari, M. 1991. *Ebrei in Italia: Un Problema di Identità (1870–1938)*, Florence: Giuntina.

Möller, H. 1984. *Exodus der Kultur. Schriftsteller, Wissenschaftler und Künstler in der Emigration nach 1933*, Munich: Beck.

Monford, H. 1959–60, 'The Concept of Love in Sepher Hassidim', *The Jewish Quarterly Review*, ns, vol. 50, pp. 13–44.

Montagnana, M. 1944. *Ricordi di un Operaio Torinese (Sotto la Guida di Gramsci)*, New York: Prompt Press.

Montale, E. 1946. 'Diario di un Privilegiato Sospeso tra la Vita e il Sogno', *Corriere della Sera*, 30 July.

Morandi, C. 1952. 'L'Idea dell'Unità Politica d'Europa nel XIX e XX Secolo', in *Questioni di Storia Contemporanea*, 3 vols, Milan: Carlo Marzorati Editore.

Morteo, G.R. 'Il Teatro: Specchi e Miti di una Città', in *Torino tra le Due Guerre*, Catalogue of the exhibition sponsored by the Assessorato per la Cultura della Città di Torino between March and June 1978, Turin: Musei Civici, pp. 244–69.

Mosca, G. 1897. 'Il Fenomeno Ferrero', *La Riforma Sociale*, 4, vol. 7, issue 11, pp. 1017–31, and issue 12, pp. 1135–64.

Mounier, E. 2000. *Refaire la Renaissance*, Preface by G. Coq, Paris: Seuil.

Mühlen, P. von zur. 1989. *Politisches Engagement und Jüdische Identität in Lateinamerikanischen Exil*, in A. Schrader and K.H. Rengstorf (eds), *Europäische Juden in Lateinamerika*, St Ingbert, Röhrig, pp. 242–49.

Muncinelli, A. 1994. *Even. Pietruzze della Memoria. Ebrei 1938–1945*, Turin: Edizioni Gruppo Abele, 35n.

Munz, R. 2000. 'Aus Liebe zur Freiheit. "Charlotte von Kirschbaum liest Simone de Beauvoir"', *Dialektische Theologie*, 16, 2, pp. 202–26.

Nacci, M. 1989. *L'Antiamericanismo in Italia negli Anni Trenta*, Turin: Bollati Boringhieri.

———.1996. *La Barbarie del Comfort. Il Modello di Vita Americano nella Cultura Francese del '900*, Milan: Guerini.

Narbutt, S. 1993. 'Le 'Réseau Allemand' des *Cahiers du Sud*', in H.M. Bock, R. Meyer-Kalkus and M. Trebitsch (eds), *Entre Locarno et Vichy. Les Relations Culturelles Franco-allemandes dans les Années 1930*, 2 vols, Paris: CNRS, pp. 813–25.

Nathansen, H. 1931. *Jude oder Europaër. Porträt von Georg Brandes*, Frankfurt am Main: Rütten and Loening.

Nelli, R. 1933. 'Fragments d'une Erotologie', *Cahiers du Sud*, 151, May, pp. 326–37.

———.1935. 'L'Enfance et les Esprits', *Cahiers du Sud*, 174, July, pp. 530–35.

———.1942. 'De l'Amour Provençal', *Cahiers du Sud*, Le Génie d'Oc et l'Homme Méditerranéen, 249, August–September–October, pp. 44–68.

———.1963. *L'Erotique des Troubadours*, Toulouse: Privat.

———.1974. *L'Erotique des Troubadours*, 2 vols, Paris: Union Générale d'Editions, 10/18.

Neugroschel, J. (ed.). 2000. *The Dybbuk and the Yiddish Imagination. A Haunted Reader*, Syracuse: Syracuse University Press.

Nevin, T.R. 1991. *Simone Weil. Portrait of a Self-Exiled Jew*, Chapel Hill–London: University of North Carolina Press.

Nicault, C. 1998. 'Le Juifs de France et le Sionisme', in J.-J. Becker and A. Wieviorka (1998), op. cit., pp. 130–35.

Nicolodi, F. 1984. *Musica e Musicisti nel Ventennio Fascista*, Fiesole: Discanto.

Nolan, M. 1994. *Visions of Modernity: American Business and the Modernisation of Germany*, Oxford: Oxford University Press.

Normand, S. 1928. 'Entretien avec Simone Téry', *Nouvelles Litterairés*, August.

Noth, E.E. 1935. 'Portraits et Commentaire', *Cahiers du Sud*, 174, July, pp. 611–16.

Novarino, M. 1996. 'La Solidarietà al di là dei Confini: l'Impegno della Massoneria a favore della Pace e per la Libertà e l'Emancipazione dei Popoli', Proceedings of the II Regional Conference 'Tolleranza e solidarietà nella storia e nelle trasformazioni sociali', Montecatini Terme, 18 November 1995, *Il Laboratorio*, 23, pp. 23–32.

———.1999. 'Fra Associazionismo e Politica. La Massoneria a Torino e in Piemonte dal 1860 al 1925', *Memoria e Ricerca*, 4, July–December, pp. 63–83.

———.2003. *All'Oriente di Torino*. *La Rinascita della Massoneria Italiana tra Moderatismo Cavouriano e Rivoluzionarismo Garibaldino*, Florence: Firenze Libri.

Noy, D. 1994. 'An-Sky the Meshulah: Between the Verbal and the Visual in Jewish Folk Culture', in R. Gonen (1994), op. cit., p. xvii.

Nygren, A. 1982. *Agape and Eros*, London: SPCK.

Odic, J.C. 1936. 'Découverte de l'Amour', *Cahiers du Sud*, 179, October, pp. 24–29.

Oehlmann, C. 1995. 'Ah, Tremezzo, il Tempo Passerà e Io Ritornerò: Artur Schnabel 1933–1938', in *Akademie*, op. cit., pp. 227–79.

Oliva, G. 1993. 'Pacifisme et Antimilitarisme en Italie', in M. Vaïsse (ed.), *Le Pacifisme en Europe des Années 1920 aux Années 1950*, Brussels: Bruylant.

Operti, P. 1946. 'Ricordo di Leo Ferrero', *Solaria*, November–December, pp. 1–4.

d'Orsi, A. 1993. Introduction, in L. Ferrero (1993), *Diario di un Privilegiato*, op. cit., pp. vii–xxxi.

———.2000. *La Cultura a Torino tra le Due Guerre*, Turin: Einaudi.

Orsina, G. 1998. *Senza Chiesa né Classe*. *Il Partito Radicale nell'Età Giolittiana*, Roma: Carocci.

Otto, R. 1926. *West-Östliche Mystik*. *Vergleich und Unterscheidung zur Wesendeutung*, Klotz: Gotha (It. tr. 1985. *Mistica Orientale, Mistica Occidentale*, tr. M. Vannini, Casale: Marietti).

Oz, A. 2004. *A Tale of Love and Darkness*, tr. N. de Lange, London: Chatto and Windus.

Paire, A. 1993. *Chronique des Cahiers du Sud 1914–1966*, Paris: IMEC.

———.2002. 'Simone Weil à Marseille: "l'Écart et la Présence"', in *Cahiers Simone Weil*, 25, 2, pp. 105–19.

Panzini, P. 1999. 'Un Dramma Satirico contro il Fascismo? *"Angelica"* di Leo Ferrero', *Revue des Etudes Italiennes*, 45, pp. 35–57.

Paraf, P. 1928. 'Le Dibbouk', *L'Univers Israélite*, 83, 21, 10 February, pp. 649–51.

Passerini, L. 1991. *Mussolini Immaginario*, Rome–Bari: Laterza.

———.1992. 'Le Avventure del Soggetto Amoroso: da Tristano e Isotta a Don Giovanni', in Istituto di Psicoterapia Psicoanalitica, *Discorso Amoroso e Pratica del Transfert*, Turin: Rosenberg and Sellier, pp. 17–38.

———.1999. *Europe in Love, Love in Europe*. *Imagination and Politics between the Wars*, London–New York: Tauris–New York University Press (It. tr. 1999. *L'Europa e l'Amore*. *Immaginario e Politica tra le Due Guerre*, Milan: il Saggiatore).

———.2002. *Mito d'Europa*. *Radici Antiche per Nuovi Simboli*, Florence: Giunti.

———.2003. *Figures d'Europe: Images and Myths of Europe*, Berne–Oxford: Peter Lang.

———.2007a. *Memory and Utopia*. *The Primacy of Intersubjectivity*, London: Equinox.

———.2007b. 'Gender, Subjectivity, Europe: A Constellation for the Future', in *Women Migrants from East to West. Gender, Mobility and Belonging in Contemporary Europe*, L. Passerini, D. Lyon, E. Capussotti and I. Laliotou (eds), Oxford–New York: Berghahn, pp. 251–74.

Patai, R. 1959. *Sex and Family in the Bible*, New York: Doubleday.

Pavolini, A. 1926. 'Leo Ferrero – *La Chioma di Berenice*', *Solaria*, May, 5, pp. 54–56.

Paz, O. 1994. *La Flamme Double. Amour et Erotisme*, Paris: Gallimard (original version 2001 [1993]. *La Llama Doble. Amor y Erotismo*, Barcelona: Seix Barral).

Pearce, F. 2003. 'Introduction: The Collège de Sociologie and French Social Thought', *Economy and Society*, 32, 1, February, pp. 1–6.

Pegg, C.H. 1983. *Evolution of the European Idea 1914–1932*, Chapel Hill–London: University of North Carolina Press.

Pehau, C.-T. 1935. 'Songeries dans Cordoue', *L'Islam et l'Occident, Cahiers du Sud*, 175, pp. 55–70.

Pellegrini, E. 1982. 'Ebraismo ed Europeismo nella Toscana degli Anni Trenta', *Il Ponte*, 38, 10 (October), pp. 1017–51.

Pérès, H. 1947. 'La Poésie Arabe d'Andalousie et Ses Relations Possibles avec la Poésie des Troubadours', *L'Islam et l'Occident, Cahiers du Sud*, 175, pp. 107–30.

Persico, E. 1927. 'Lettera a Sir John Bickerstaff', *Il Baretti*, 4, 5–6, p. 6.

Petit, G. 1932. Review of '*Les Aveux Complets* par Jacques Chenevière', *Cahiers du Sud*, 144, October, pp. 645–47.

––––––. 1933. Review of '*Frieda ou le Voyage Allemand* par René Jouglet', *Cahiers du Sud*, 150, April, pp. 307–8.

––––––. 1934. Review of '*Victor et l'Etrangère* par René de Weck', *Cahiers du Sud*, 160, March, pp. 253–54.

Petitjean, A. 1939. 'L'Amour est-il une hérésie?', *Marianne*, 12 April.

Pétrement, S. 1973. *La Vie de Simone Weil*, Paris: Fayard [Eng. tr. *c*.1976 *Simone Weil: A Life*, tr. R. Rosenthal, New York: Pantheon Books].

Petrovsky-Shtern, Y. 2006. '"We Are Too Late": An-sky and the Paradigm of No Return', in G. Safran and S.J. Zipperstein (2006), op. cit., pp. 83–102.

Pézard, A. 1941. Reviews of five books by L. Ferrero, *Ausonia*, Notebooks of the section for Italian studies, Faculty of Letters, University of Grenoble, July–December.

Piasere, L. 2002. 'Au Cœur de l'Occident: l'Amour, la Mort, la Gitane', *Etudes Tziganes*, 4, p. 1.

Pick, D. 1989. *Faces of Degeneration. A European Disorder 1848–1918*, Cambridge University Press (It. tr. 1999. *Volti della Degenerazione. Una Sindrome Europea 1848–1918*, Florence: La Nuova Italia).

Picon-Vallin, B. 1973. *Le Théâtre Juif Soviétique pendant les Années Vingt*, Lausanne: La Cité – L'Age d'Homme.

Pieroni Bortolotti, F. 1963. *Alle Origini del Movimento Femminile in Italia 1848–1892*, Turin: Einaudi.

––––––. 1985. *La Donna, la Pace, l'Europa. L'Associazione Internazionale delle Donne dalle Origini alla Prima Guerra Mondiale*, Milan: Franco Angeli.

Pierre-Quint, L. 1933. 'Notes sur les Idées de Défense Nationale et de Patrie', *Cahiers du Sud*, 149, March, pp. 161–70.

Pillement, G. 1930. Review of '*L'Etrangère* par René Jouglet', *Cahiers du Sud*, 118, February, pp. 71–72.

Pingaud, B. 1950. *L'Amour Triste*, Paris: La Table Ronde.

Pinto, D. 2002. 'Il Terzo Polo? Verso un'Identità Ebraica Europea', *Rassegna Mensile di Israel*, 68, 1, January–April, pp. 3–36.

———. 2004. 'Can One Reconcile the Jewish World and Europe?', *Commentaire*, 107, Autumn.

Pistone, S. 1975. *Le Critiche di Einaudi e di Agnelli e Cabiati alla Società delle Nazioni nel 1918*, in idem (ed.), *L'Idea dell'Unificazione Europea dalla Prima alla Seconda Guerra Mondiale*, Turin: Fondazione Luigi Einaudi, pp. 25–37.

Poliakov, L. 1955–77. *Histoire de l'Antisémitisme*, Paris: Calmann-Lévy, 4 vols: 1: 1955. *Du Christ aux Juifs de Cour*; 2: 1961. *De Mahomet aux Marranes*; 3: 1968. *De Voltaire à Wagner*; 4: 1977. *L'Europe Suicidaire 1870–1933* (Eng. tr. 1974. *The History of Anti-Semitism*, London: Routledge and Kegan Paul).

Polito, P. 1993. 'Piero Gobetti e la "Rivoluzione Liberale"', in *Storia Illustrata di Torino*, Turin: Elio Sellino.

Poma, A. 1982. '*Il Dibbuk:* dalla Dualità all'Unità', *Rassegna Mensile Israel*, 48, January–June, pp. 215–18.

Poulain, R. 2000. *La Pornographie, come Faire-valoir Masculin*, in D. Welzer-Lang (ed.), *Nouvelles Approches des Hommes et du Masculin*, Toulouse: Presses Universitaries du Mirail, pp. 51–77.

Preti, L. 1968. *Impero Fascista, Africani ed Ebrei*, Milan: Mursia.

Probst-Biraben, J.H. 1935. 'Espagne et Islam', *Cahiers du Sud*, 175, August–September, pp. 46–54.

———. 1942a. 'Raymond Lull, Grand Méditerranéen', *Le Génie d'Oc et l'Homme Méditerranéen*, *Cahiers du Sud*, 249, August–September–October, pp. 161–72.

———. 1942b. 'Lull et Descartes', *Le Génie d'Oc et l'Homme Méditerranéen*, *Cahiers du Sud*, 249, August–September–October, pp. 215–23.

Puccini, S. 1981. 'Antropologia Positivistica e Femminismo (Teorie Scientifiche e Luoghi Comuni nella Cultura Italiana tra Ottocento e Novecento)', *Itinerari*, pp. 217–44, 187–238.

Pugliaro, G. 1978–79. 'La Figura di Ludovico Rocca nel Novecento Musicale Italiano', Dissertation for degree in History of Music, supervisor Prof. Paolo Gallarati, Faculty of Letters and Philosophy, University of Turin, academic year.

———. 1986. 'Lodovico Rocca', in *Ghedini e l'Attività Musicale a Torino fra le Due Guerre*, Proceedings of the Conference on the occasion of the European Year of Music, Turin, 14–15 January 1986, pp. 92–98.

Pugliese, S.G. 1998. 'Contesting Constraints: Amelia Pincherle Rosselli Jewish Writer in Pre-Fascist Italy', *Women in Judaism: A Multidisciplinary Journal*, 1, 2.

Raditsa, B. 1939. *Colloqui con Guglielmo Ferrero*, Lugano: Capolago.

———. 1982. 'Ferrero Uomo', in R. Baldi (ed.), *Guglielmo Ferrero tra Società e Politica*, Proceedings of the conference held in Genoa, 4–5 October 1982, pp. 21–30.

———. 1996. 'Guglielmo Ferrero et les Slaves du Sud', in *Guglielmo Ferrero. Histoire et Politique au XX Siècle*, Geneva: Droz, pp. 83–97.

Rageot, G. 1939. 'Que faisons-nous de l'amour?', *Le Temps*, 2 July.

Ragone, G. 1999. *Un Secolo di Libri. Storia dell'Editoria in Italia dall'Unità al Postmoderno*, Turin: Einaudi.

Ratel, S. 1934. 'Necrologio di Leo Ferrero', *Journal des Nations*, Geneva: 29 August, now in Ferrero (1936, pp. 38–39).

Raymond, J. 1993. 'Traversée des *Cahiers*', in *Jean Ballard et les* Cahiers du Sud, Catalogue de la Ville de Marseille, pp. 27–37.

Rechtman, A. 1992–94. 'The Jewish Ethnographic Expedition', in M. Beukers and R. Waale (eds), *Tracing An-sky. Jewish Collections from the State Ethnographic Museum in St. Petersburg*, Zwolle: Waanders Uitgevers, pp. 12–15.

Rey-Flaud, H. 1983. *La Névrose Courtoise*, Paris: Navarin.

Ricaldone, L. 2004. 'Il Salotto delle Sorelle Lombroso', in M.L. Betri and E. Brambilla (eds), *Salotti e Ruolo Femminile in Italia tra Fine Seicento e Primo Novecento*, Venice: Marsilio, pp. 509–23.

Richetti, G. 1962. *Il Teatro Habimah da Mosca a Tel-Aviv*, Bologna: Cappelli.

Richman, M.H. 1988. 'Introduction to the Collège de Sociologie: Poststructuralism Before its Time?', *Stanford French Review*, 12, 1, pp. 79–95.

———. 2003. 'Myth, Power and the Sacred: Antiutilitarianism in the Collège de Sociologie 1937–39', *Economy and Society*, 32, 1, February, pp. 29–47.

Rieger, A. 1991. *Trobairitz. Der Beitrag der Frau in der Altokzitanischen Höfischen Lyrik. Edition des Gesamtkorpus*, Tübingen: Niemeyer.

Rilke, R.M. 1991.*The Book of Images*, tr. E. Snow, San Francisco: North Point Press.

———. 1992. *Neue Gedichte/New Poems*, tr. S. Cohn, Manchester: Carcanet Press.

Riou, G. 1927. *La Naissance de l'Amour*, Paris: Baudinière.

———. 1928. *Europe, Ma Patrie*, Paris: Baudinière.

Riveline, C. 2000. *L'Amour dans la Tradition Juive*, Paris: Association Consistoriale Israélite de Paris, Centre Edmond Fleg.

Rivista di diritto processuale civile, 'Notizia de *Le leggi del Libero Amore* di Giorgio Quartara', 1928, p. 383.

Rocca, E. 1999. Introduction to S. Kierkegaard (1999), op. cit., pp. ix–x.

Roché, D. 1942. 'Les Cathares et l'Amour Spirituel', *Le Génie d'Oc et l'Homme Méditerranéen, Cahiers du Sud*, 249, pp. 112–40.

Roditi, E. 1942. 'Poétiques des Troubadours', *Cahiers du Sud*, 249, August–September–October, pp. 69–76.

Rodogno, D. 2003. *Il Nuovo Ordine Mediterraneo. Le Politiche di Occupazione dell'Italia Fascista in Europa (1940–1943)*, Turin: Bollati Boringhieri.

Roger, P. 2002. *L'Ennemi Américain. Généalogie de l'Antiaméricanisme Français*, Paris: Seuil, pp. 481–83 (Eng. tr. 2005, *The American Enemy. The History of French Anti-Americanism*, tr. S. Bowman, University of Chicago Press).

Rolland de Renéville, A. 1935. 'Les Poètes et la Société', *Cahiers du Sud*, 178, December, pp. 852–56.

Romano, R. 'Gavazzi', in *Dizionario Biografico degli Italiani*, Rome: Istituto della Enciclopedia Italiana, 1999.

Roskies, D.G. 1992a. Introduction, in *The Dybbuk and Other Writings. S. Ansky*, New York: Schocken, pp. xi–xxxvi.

———. 1992b. 'S. Ansky and the Paradigm of Return', in J. Wertheimer (ed.), *The Uses of Tradition. Jewish Continuity in the Modern Era*, Cambridge, Mass.–London: The Jewish Theological Seminary of America–Harvard University Press.

Rosselli, A. 2001. *Memorie*, M. Calloni (ed.), Bologna: il Mulino, pp. 120–21.

Rosselli, N. 1933. Obituary 'Una Giovinezza Stroncata: Leo Ferrero', *Nuova Rivista Storica*, pp. 546–54.

Rossi dell'Arno, G. de'. 1940. *L'Ebraismo contro l'Europa*, Rome: Maglione.

Rostagno, S. (ed.). 1984. *La Chiesa tra la Croce e la Svastica*, Turin: Claudiana.

———. 2003. *Karl Barth*, Brescia: Morcelliana.

Rota, E. 1952. *I Movimenti Pacifisti dell'800 e del '900 e le Organizzazioni Internazionali*, in *Questioni di Storia Contemporanea*, 3 vols, Milan: Carlo Marzorati Editore, pp. 1963–2018.

Roth, C. 1938. 'The Jew as a European', London, Presidential Address delivered before the Jewish Historical Society of England.

Rousseaux, A. 1939. Review of '*L'Amour et l'Occident*', *Le Figaro Littèraire*, 25 February.

Roy, C. 1998. *Alexandre Marc et la Jeune Europe (1904–1934): L'Ordre Nouveau aux Origines du Personnalisme*, Nice: Presses d'Europe.

Rupp, L.J. 1997. *Worlds of Women. The Making of an International Women's Movement*, Princeton NJ: Princeton University Press.

Ruppin, A. 1934. *The Jews in the Modern World*, London: Macmillan.

Rychner, M. 1930. 'Américanisation de l'Europe?', *Cahiers du Sud*, 120, April, pp. 174–85.

Sabbagh, A. (ed.). 2002. *Lettres de Drancy*, Paris: Tallandier.

Sachs, H. 1987. *Music in Fascist Italy*, New York–London: Norton (It. tr. 1987, *Musica e Regime. Compositori, Cantanti, Direttori d'Orchestra e la Politica Culturale Fascista*, Milan: il Saggiatore).

Safran, G. 2000. 'Dancing with Death and Salvaging Jewish Culture in *Austeria* and *The Dybbuk*', *Slavic Review*, 59, 4, Winter, pp. 761–81.

———. 2006. 'Timeline: Semyon Akimovich An-sky/Shloyme-Zanvl Rappoport', in G. Safran and S.J. Zipperstein (2006), op. cit., pp. xv–xxix.

Safran, G. and S.J. Zipperstein (eds). 2006. *The Worlds of S. An-sky. A Russian Jewish Intellectual at the Turn of the Century*, Stanford, Ca.: Stanford University Press.

Said, E. 1979. *Orientalism*, New York: Vintage Books.

Saint-Ouen, F. 1997. *Les Grandes Figures de la Construction Européenne*, Geneva: Georg.

———. 2000–2001b. 'Alexandre Marc et Denis de Rougemont', *L'Europe en Formation*: 'Hommage à Alexandre Marc', 319–20, Winter 2000–Spring 2001, pp. 155–62.

Sallefranque, C. 1947.'Périples de l'Amour en Orient et en Occident. Les Origines Arabes de l'Amour Courtois', *L'Islam et l'Occident, Cahiers du Sud*, 175, pp. 92–106.

Salomé, R. 1928. '*Le Dibbouk*', *Etudes*, 20 May, pp. 465–71.

Samuel, M. 1927. '*The Dybbuk* in Three Languages and Four Dimensions', *The Menorah Journal*, 13, 1, pp. 63–67.

Sandrow, N. 1977. *Vagabond Stars. A World History of Yiddish Theater*, New York: Limelight Editions.
———.2003. 'Romanticism and the Yiddish Theatre', in J. Berkowitz (ed.), *Yiddish Theatre. New Approaches*, Oxford–Portland, Or.: The Littman Library of Jewish Civilization.
Sansone, G.E. 1984. Introduction, *La Poesia dell'Antica Provenza. Testi e Storia dei Trovatori*, 2 vols, Milan: Guanda, vol. 1, 17.
Santillana, G. de. 1936. 'Y a-t-il un esprit méditerranéen', *Cahiers du Sud*, 187, October, pp. 754–60.
Sarfatti, M. 2000. *Gli Ebrei nell'Italia Fascista. Vicende, Identità, Persecuzione*, Turin: Einaudi.
Sartre, J.-P. 1939. Review of '*Amour et l'Occident*', *Europe*, 15 June, pp. 242–49, now in *Situations I*. 1947. Paris: Gallimard, pp. 62–69.
———.1975 [1948]. *Situations II. Qu'est-ce que la littérature?*, Paris: Gallimard.
Sauvage, M. 1953. *Le Cas Don Juan*, Paris: Seuil.
Savaldi, M. 'I Campeggi Ebraici (1931–1939)', *Storia Contemporanea*, 19, 6, December 1988, pp. 1121–52.
Scaraffia, L. and A.M. Isastia. 2002. *Donne Ottimiste. Femminismo e Associazioni Borghesi nell'Otto e Novecento*, Bologna: il Mulino.
Scheer, L. 1986. 'Un Chef-d'œuvre du Cinéma Yiddish: Le Dibbouk', *Cinéma et Judéité*, Dossier compiled by A. Goldmann and G. Hennebelle. Paris: CERF, pp. 70–75.
Schnéour, Z. 1937. 'L'Art de Habimah', *L'Univers Israélite*, 93, 7, 15 October.
Scholem, G. 1978. *Kabbalah*, New York: Meridian.
Schreiber, A. and M. Mathieson. 1955. *Journey towards Freedom. Written for the Golden Jubilee of the International Alliance of Women*, Copenhagen: IAW.
Scialoja, V. 1932. *Discorsi alla Società delle Nazioni*, with a preface by Dino Grandi, Minister of Foreign Affairs, Rome: A.R.E.
Scotti, M. 1984.'Oltre il Velo di Maya', and 'Notizia Biografica', in L. Ferrero (1984), *Il Muro Trasparente*, op. cit., pp. 19–26 and 27–29.
———.1993. Biographical notes and bibliography, in L. Ferrero (1993), *Diario di un Privilegiato*, op. cit., pp. 135–46.
Seelisch, W. 1989. 'Jüdische Emigration nach Bolivien Ende der 30er Jahre', in A. Schrader and K.H. Rengstorf (eds), *Europäische Juden in Lateinamerika*, St Ingbert: Röhrig, pp. 77–101.
Segre, R. 1995. *Gli Ebrei a Venezia 1938–1945. Una Comunità tra Persecuzione e Rinascita*, Venice: il Cardo.
Seillière, E. 1939. 'Une Interprétation du Mysticisme Passionnel', *Journal des Débats*, 18 February.
Selinger, S. 1998. *Charlotte von Kirschbaum and Karl Barth. A Study in Biography and the History of Theology*, University Park, Pa.: Pennsylvania State University Press.
Signoretti, A. 1940. 'La Nuova Europa senza Ebrei', *La Stampa*, 18 July.
Silberstein, L.J. and R.L. Cohn (eds). 1994. *The Other in Jewish Thought and History. Construction of Jewish Culture and Identity*, New York–London: New York University Press.
Simon, A. 1972. *Gaston Baty. Théoricien du Théatre*, Paris: Klincksieck.

References   357

Simoni, R. 1955. *Tutta l'Opera* (ed. L. Ridenti), *Trent'anni di Cronaca Drammatica*, 3 vols, 1927–32, Turin: ILTE.

Singer, C. 1998. 'Le Cinéma Yiddish: Entre Deux Mondes', *Les Cahiers du Judaïsme*, 2, pp. 49–58.

Singer, I. 1984. *The Nature of Love*, 2, *Courtly and Romantic*, Chicago–London: University of Chicago Press.

———. 1987. *The Nature of Love*, 3, *The Modern World*, Chicago–London: University of Chicago Press.

Singer, S. 1942. 'Influence du Génie d'Oc sur le Germanisme', *Le Génie d'Oc et l'Homme Méditerranéen*, *Cahiers du Sud*, 249, pp. 209–14.

Sipe, D. 2004. *Kierkegaard and Feminism: A Paradoxical Friendship*, http://www.publications.villanova.edu/Concept/2004/Kierkegaard.

Sire, P.-M. 1942. 'Bestiaire Provençal', *Le Génie d'Oc et l'Homme Méditerranéen*, *Cahiers du Sud*, 249, pp. 292–300.

Skorecki, L. 1981. Article on *Der Dibek* in New York, *Cahiers du Cinéma*, 320, February, pp. 50–51.

Smith, C.D. 1983. *Islam and the Search for Social Order in Modern Egypt: A Biography of Muhammad Husayn Haykal*, Albany: State University of New York Press.

Soldevila, F. 1942. 'L'Esprit d'Oc et la Catalogne', *Le Génie d'Oc et l'Homme Méditerranéen*, *Cahiers du Sud*, 249, pp. 173–81.

Sollers, P. 1989. 'Les Mésaventures de l'Amour', Preface to Denis de Rougemont. *L'Amour et l'Occident*, Paris: France Loisirs.

Spera, S. 2002. *Introduzione a Kierkegaard*, Roma–Bari: Laterza.

Spironelli, C. 1998. 'Pacifismo e Antimperialismo in Italia tra Otto e Novecento', in A.A. Mola (ed.), *L'Italia nella Crisi dei Sistemi Coloniali fra Otto e Novecento*, Proceedings of the Vicoforte Conference, Foggia: Bastogi.

Starobinski, J. 1986. 'Ecrire n'est pas un art d'agrément', *Cadmos*, 9, 33, Spring, pp. 87–93.

———. 1987. 'Remédier à la Défaillance', *Ecriture*, 29, Autumn, pp. 19–28.

———. 1988–89. 'Un Essai de Long Cours', *Cadmos*, 11, 44, Winter, pp. 27–33.

———. 1995. 'Paroles Prononcées lors de la Remise du Prix Quadriennal de la Ville de Genève à Denis de Rougemont', *Nouvelle Revue Neuchâteloise*, 12, 47, Autumn, pp. 61–63.

Stefani, P. 2004. *L'Antigiudaismo. Storia di un'Idea*, Roma–Bari: Laterza.

Steinlauf, M. 2006. '"Fardibekt!": Ansky's Polish Legacy', in G. Safran and S.J. Zipperstein (2006), op. cit., pp. 232–51.

Strowski, F. 1928. Review '*Le Dibbouk*', *Paris Midi*, 16 April.

Sweedler, M. 2001. 'Lieux Sacrés. Ou la Mise en Abyme du Collège de Sociologie', *Revue des Sciences Humaines*, 261, January–March, pp. 51–64.

'T'. 1927. '*The Dybbuk*', in *Punch, or the London Charivari*, 172, 13 April, 414.

Tamburini, L. 1966. *I Teatri di Torino*, Turin: Edizioni dell'Albero.

Taricone, F. 1992. *Una Tessera del Mosaico. Storia della Federazione Italiana Laureate e Diplomate di Istituti Superiori*, Pavia: Antares.

———. 1994. *Teresa Labriola. Biografia Politica di un'Intellettuale tra Ottocento e Novecento*, Milan: Franco Angeli.

_____. 1995. 'Sacchi Ada in Simonetta e Sacchi Beatrice in Ducceschi', in R. Farina (ed.), *Dizionario Biografico delle Donne Lombarde 568–1968*, Milan: Baldini and Castoldi.

_____. 1996. *L'Associazionismo Femminile Italiano dall'Unità al Fascismo*, Milan: Unicopli.

Temime, E. 1993. 'Mécénat et Publicité aux *Cahiers*', in *Jean Ballard et les* Cahiers du Sud, Catalogue de la Ville de Marseille, p. 102.

_____. 2002. *Un Rêve Méditerranéen. Des Saint-simoniens aux Intellectuels des Années Trente (1832–1962)*, Arles: Actes Sud.

Téry, S. 1928. *Fièvre Jaune: La Chine Convulsée*, Paris: Flammarion.

_____. 1930. *Passagère*, Paris: Valois.

_____. 1933. Obituary for Leo Ferrero, *Marianne*, December, now in *ATM*, pp. 41–42.

Tharaud, J. and J. Tharaud. 1927. *Petite Histoire des Juifs*, Paris: Plon.

Thibon, G. 1939. Review of '*L'Amour et l'Occident*', *Temps Prèsent*, 21 July.

Toaff, A. 1996. *La Vita Materiale*, in C. Vivanti (1996), op. cit., pp. 239–63.

Toscano, M. 1943. Review of 'Giorgio Quartara, *La Futura Pace*', *Rivista Internazionale di Studi Politici Internazionali*, 10, 1, pp. 266–68.

_____. 1988. 'L'Emigrazione Ebraica dall'Italia dopo il 1938', *Storia Contemporanea*, December, pp. 1287–314.

Touchard, J. 1960. 'L'Esprit des Années 1930: Une Tentative de Renouvellement de la Pensée Politique Française', in *Tendances Politiques dans la Vie Française depuis 1789, Colloques. Cahiers de Civilisation*, Paris: Hachette, pp. 89–118.

Trebitsch, M. 1998a. 'L'Image de l'Orient chez les Intellectuels Français et Allemands au Lendemain de la Première Guerre Mondiale', in E. François et al. in collaboration with Ph. Despoix (eds), *Marianne – Germania. Deutsch-französischer Kulturtransfer im Europäischen Kontext. Les Transfers Culturels France-Allemagne et Leur Contexte Européen 1789–1914*, vol. 2, Leipziger: Leipziger Universitätsverlag.

_____. 1998b. 'Les Ecrivains Juifs Français de l'Affaire Dreyfus à la Seconde Guerre Mondiale', in J.-J. Becker and A. Wieviorka (1998), op. cit., pp. 169–95.

Treves, P. 1981. 'Formiggini e il Problema dell'Ebreo in Italia', in L. Balsamo and R. Cremante (eds). *A.F. Formiggini un Editore del Novecento*, Bologna: il Mulino.

_____. 1982. 'Antifascisti Ebrei od Antifascismo Ebraico?', *Rassegna Mensile di Israel*, 48, January–June, pp. 234–61.

_____. 2002. Preface to Cavaglion and Romagnani (2002), op. cit.

Treves, R. 1985. 'Incontri di Culture nell'America Latina alla fine degli Anni Trenta', *Nuova Antologia*, 554, October–December, pp. 90–100.

Trolliet, G. 1933. Review of '*Le Paysan du Danube* par Denis de Rougemont', *Cahiers du Sud*, 156, November, pp. 722–30.

Turati, F. and A. Kuliscioff. 1977. *Carteggio. 1900–1909: Le Speranze dell'Età Giolittiana*, 2 vols, Turin: Einaudi.

Ungari, P. 2002. *Storia del Diritto di Famiglia*, Bologna: il Mulino.

Uritzkaya, L. 'The Ashkenazi Collections', in R. Gonen (1994), op. cit., p. xvi.

Vadet, J.-C. 1968. *L'Esprit Courtois en Orient dans les Cinq Premiers Siècles de l'Hégire*, Paris: Maisonneuve et Larose.

Vaïsse, M. (ed.). 1993. *Le Pacifisme en Europe des Années 1920 aux Années 1950*, Brussels: Bruylant.

Valentino, C. 1990. *Idee d'Europa nella Cultura Letteraria del Novecento*, Rome: Dimensione Europea/European Dimension.

Vannoni, G. 1979. *Massoneria, Fascismo e Chiesa Cattolica*, Rome–Bari: Laterza.

Vasteenberghe, E. 1936. Review, *Revue des Sciences Religieuses*.

Veil, S. 1984. 'Israël et l'Europe', in Colloque des Intellectuels Juifs de Langue Française, *Israël, le Judaïsme et l'Europe*, J. Halpérin and G. Levitte (eds), Paris: Gallimard, pp. 17–31.

Veltri, F. 2002. *La Città Perduta. Simone Weil e l'Universo di Linguadoca*, Soveria Mannelli: Rubbettino.

Vialatte, A. 1935. 'Le Concerto Européen', *Cahiers du Sud*, 176, October, pp. 626–40.

Vigni, F. 1990. 'La Massoneria e l'Emancipazione Femminile in Italia', in A.A. Mola (ed.), *La Liberazione d'Italia nell'Opera della Massoneria*, Proceedings of the Conference in Turin, 24–25 September 1988, Foggia: Bastogi, pp. 187–96.

Vigni, F. and P.D. Vigni. 1997. *Donna e Massoneria in Italia dalle Origini ad Oggi*, Foggia: Bastogi.

Vittorini, E. 1957. *Diario in Pubblico*, Milan: Bompiani.

Vivanti, C. (ed.). 1996. *Storia d'Italia*, Annali 11: *Gli Ebrei in Italia*, vol. 1: *Dall'Alto Medioevo all'Età dei Ghetti*, Turin: Einaudi.

———. 1997. *Gli Ebrei in Italia*, vol. 2. *Dall'Emancipazione a Oggi*, Turin: Einaudi.

Voigt, K. 1989. *Il Rifugio Precario. Gli Esuli in Italia dal 1933 al 1945*, Florence: La Nuova Italia.

———. 1995. 'L'Italia, Paese di Rifugio', in *Akademie* cit., pp. 25–32.

'v.t.' 1938. '*Il Dibuk* di Lodovico Rocca Accolto con Grande Successo al Verdi', in *Il Piccolo di Trieste*, 11 February.

Vuillermoz, R. 1999–2000. 'Le Fédéralisme et l'Idée d'Europe Unie: Quelques Réflexions à propos des Fondements Théoriques de la Construction Européenne', *L'Europe en Formation*: 'Fédéralisme Personnaliste, Idéologie et Religion', 315–16, Winter 1999–Spring, pp. 21–42.

Vulliaud, P. 1923. *La Kabbale Juive: Histoire et Doctrine*, Paris: Nourry.

Vuoli, R. 1918. Review of 'Giorgio Quartara, *Dalla Guerra Mondiale alla Civiltà Internazionale*', *Rivista Internazionale di Scienze Sociali e Discipline Ausiliarie*, 76, 301, pp. 356–59.

Waterhouse, J.C.G. 2001. *The New Grove Dictionary of Music and Musicians*, vol. 21, London: Macmillan, pp. 478–79.

Weil, P. 1998. 'De l'Affaire Dreyfus à l'Occupation', in J.-J. Becker and A. Wieviorka (1998), op. cit., pp. 103–68.

Weil, S. 1960. 'L'Agonie d'une Civilisation Vue à travers un Poème Epique', and 'En quoi consiste l'inspiration occitanienne?', in eadem, *Ecrits Historiques et Politiques*, Paris: Gallimard, pp. 66–84 (It. tr. 1997. *I Catari e la Civiltà Mediterranea*, Genoa: Marietti, pp. 17–37).

———. 2005. *L'Amicizia Pura. Un Itinerario Spirituale*, D. Canciani and M. Vito (eds), Troina: Città Aperta.

Welzer-Lang, D. (ed.). 2000. *Nouvelles Approches des Hommes et du Masculin*, Toulouse: Presses Universitaires du Mirail.

Werses, S. 1986. 'S. an-Ski's "Tsvishn Tsvey Veltn (Der Dybbuk)"/"Beyn Shney Olamot (Hadybbuk)"/"Between Two Worlds (The Dybbuk)": A Textual History', in *Studies in Yiddish Literature and Folklore*, Research Projects of the Institute of Jewish Studies, Monograph Series 7, Jerusalem: The Hebrew University of Jerusalem, pp. 99–185.

Wertheimer, J. (ed.). 1992. *The Uses of Tradition. Jewish Continuity in the Modern Era*, Cambridge, Mass.–London: The Jewish Theological Seminary of America–Harvard University Press.

Whittick, A. 1979. *Woman into Citizen*, London: Athenaeum with Frederick Muller.

Wohl, R. 1980. *The Generation of 1914*, London: Weidenfeld and Nicolson.

Wolfson, E.R. 'Woman – The Feminine as Other in Theosophic Kabbalah: Some Philosophical Observations on the Divine Androgyne', in L.J. Silberstein and R.L. Cohn (1994), op. cit., pp. 166–204.

Wolitz, S.L. 2006. 'Inscribing An-sky's *Dybbuk* in Russian and Jewish Letters', in G. Safran and S.J. Zipperstein (2006), op. cit., pp. 164–202.

Yehoshua, A.B. 2002. *La Sposa Liberata*, Turin: Einaudi (Eng. tr. 2003. *The Liberated Bride*, tr. H. Halkin, New York: Harvest Books).

Zambon, F. 1997. *La Cena Segreta. Trattati e Rituali Catari*, Milan: Adelphi.

⸺. 1999. Introduction, translation and notes, *I Trovatori e la Crociata contro gli Albigesi*, Milan–Trento: Luni.

Ze'evi-Weil, C. 1994. 'In Search of a Lost Innocence: A Biography', in R. Gonen (1994), op. cit., p. xiii.

Zemtsovsky, I. 2006a. 'The Musical Strands of An-sky's Texts and Contexts', in G. Safran and S.J. Zipperstein (2006), op. cit., pp. 203–31.

⸺. 2006b. 'Introduction: An-sky and the Guises of Modern Jewish Culture', in G. Safran and S.J. Zipperstein (2006), op. cit., pp. 1–30.

Zuccotti, S. 1995. *L'Olocausto in Italia*, Milan: Tea (Eng. tr. 1987. *The Italians and the Holocaust: Persecution, Rescue and Survival*, London: Halban).

Zumthor, P. 1952. *Miroirs de l'Amour. Tragédie et Préciosité*, Paris: Plon.

Zurlo, L. 1952. *Memorie Inutili. La Censura Teatrale nel Ventennio*, Roma: Ateneo.

Zweig, S. 1964. 'The Agony of Peace', in *World of Yesterday*, University of Nebraska Press.

⸺. 1966. *Silberne Saiten. Gedichte und Nachdichtungen*, R. Friedenthal (ed.), Frankfurt am Main: Fischer, pp. 88–89.

⸺. 1981 [1929]. *Vingt-quatre Heures dans la Vie d'une Femme*, Paris: Stock (Eng. tr. 2003. *Twenty-four Hours in the Life of a Woman*, tr. A. Bell, London: Pushkin Press).

Index